D1823580

$15

# A PORTRAIT OF THE ARTIST AS AUSTRALIAN

# A Portrait of the Artist as Australian

## L'Œuvre bizarre de Barry Humphries

PAUL MATTHEW ST PIERRE

McGill-Queen's University Press

Montreal & Kingston · London · Ithaca

© McGill-Queen's University Press 2004
ISBN 0-7735-2644-7

Legal deposit third quarter 2004
Bibliothèque nationale du Québec

Printed in Canada on acid-free paper that is 100% ancient forest free
(100% post-consumer recycled), processed chlorine free.

This book has been published with the help of grants from the Canadian
Federation for the Humanities and Social Sciences, using funds provided by
the Social Sciences and Humanities Research Council of Canada, and from
the University Publications Fund of Simon Fraser University.

McGill-Queen's University Press acknowledges the financial support of
the Government of Canada through the Book Publishing Industry
Development Program (BPIDP) for its activities. It also acknowledges the
support of the Canada Council for the Arts for its publishing program.

---

**National Library of Canada Cataloguing in Publication**

St. Pierre, Paul Matthew, 1953–
A portrait of the artist as Australian: l'oeuvre bizarre de Barry Humphries /
Paul Matthew St. Pierre.

Includes bibliographical references and index.
ISBN 0-7735-2644-7

1. Humphries, Barry – Criticism and interpretation. I. Title.

PN3018.H85S26 2004      792.7′028′092      C2004-901502-8

---

This book was typeset by Dynagram Inc. in 10/12 Sabon.

# Contents

# List of Tables

# Preface

> There is no more terrible fate for a comedian than to be taken seriously.
> – Barry Humphries, *My Life as Me: A Memoir*

In February 1977 I travelled from Vancouver to Sydney on a Commonwealth Doctoral Fellowship to begin studying with Professor (now Professor Emerita Dame) Leonie Kramer at the University of Sydney. As a Canadian, I stood out in Australia, partly because I insisted on wearing woollen sweaters in even the fiercest heat. "Aren't you hot with that jumper on, mate?" caring and sharing people would ask me, sensing my imminent sunstroke. Other people would inquire as to why I, a Canadian, had come all the way to Australia to attend university. "I am completing a doctorate in Australian literature," I would say, proudly. "Oh," they'd reply, "do we have one?" As a self-deprecating Canadian, I treated their irony with appropriate deference. Then I began to sense something beyond the rhetoric, a feeble plea to know. "Yes, you most certainly do have one," I would say. "Name a few of our writers," they'd implore, adding, "I have heard of Patrick White," who in 1973 had been awarded the Nobel Prize, the first Australian writer (and the first Commonwealth writer since Rabindrinath Tagore in 1913) to be so honoured (then, and since). Then I would recite my litany of great Australian writers: "Martin Boyd, Randolph Stow, Hal Porter, Christina Stead, Katharine Susannah Prichard, Catherine Helen Spence, Dal Stivens, David Ireland, Judith Wright, Christopher Brennan, Henry Handel Richardson, Joseph Furphy, Henry Lawson, James McAuley, A.D. Hope, Barry Humphries ..." "Barry Humphries? I didn't know he was a writer," they'd say, obviously having not recognized many of the other names on my list.

In 1999, in the months leading up to my year 2000 sabbatical, some of my colleagues and students in the Department of English at Simon Fraser University would ask me how I was planning to spend my leave. "I'm writing a book on Barry Humphries," I would announce, proudly. "Oh," they'd say, "I'm not sure I know who that is." "Barry Humphries is an Australian actor, comedian and writer," I would tell them. Then, seeing they still couldn't make an identification, I would add, "perhaps you've seen Dame Edna Everage on television. She's one of his characters." "Oh yes," they would concede, "now I know who you mean."

Identifying Barry Humphries with Dame Edna Everage is like linking Patrick White with the Nobel Prize: each writer is so much more than even his greatest creation or accomplishment. I had come to expect the "Barry Humphries? Who?" reaction from my colleagues. In 1998 I had proposed a graduate course entitled "The Many Faces of Barry Humphries: A Portrait of the Australian Artist as a Cross-Dressing Parodist" (see Appendix 1), but my proposal was turned down because, as the English graduate chair confided to me, with some embarrassment, "no one else on the graduate committee has even heard of Barry Humphries." It was then that I decided to write this book, partly to paper over the hole of ignorance in my department, partly as a gift to Humphries' "squillions" of fans, partly as a modest gesture of gratitude to Humphries himself for countless delights, and partly because spending a year with Humphries as a literary subject would be my very own quantifiable delight.

In Australia, as I was reminded on my most recent visit (2000), everyone knows who Barry Humphries is. In Melbourne people everywhere talk about him as "our Barry," a favourite son. Sydney-siders have the same reaction. Nicholas Pounder, the Double Bay bookseller, regaled me with Barry Humphries stories, as when Humphries, fully made up in the person of Les Patterson, once visited his book shop and proceeded to take it over, waiting on customers, in character, for the next several hours. I was reminded, once I stopped laughing at Nicholas's yarn, of Thomas A. Goldwasser, of Thomas A. Goldwasser Rare Books, San Franciso, who told me in 1998 how, during the premiere run of *The Royal Tour*, Humphries sauntered into his book shop, announcing regally, "Hello. I'm Mr Humphries and I'm going to have a look round your shop." Clearly, Barry Humphries is larger than life, and his reputation precedes him. But his reputation can also follow him for years, even after a simple visitation. So, who is Barry Humphries? In particular, who is Barry Humphries, the writer, the speech-actor, the performer, the music hall artiste, the Dada prankster, the visitant? Why is his *oeuvre* so bizarre? Where does it fit, if it fits anywhere at all, in Australian literary history? Does Humphries even write literature? I answer these questions in this book.

Barry Humphries, whose art is usually identified with his sixty-seven stage shows, twenty-four film and thirty-four video appearances, thirty-four television series among seventy-five television appearances, and seventy-two audio recordings, is also one of Australia's greatest writers. His output of twenty-nine books – comprising novels, biographies, autobiographies, editions, compilations, comic books, poetry, dramatic monologues and sketches, film scripts, and several unclassifiable works – identifies him as

a singularly important comic writer, a daring postmodern generic deconstructionist, a not-always-so-merry prankster in language, and a master of
*grotesqueries* and *bizarreries*. And his more than forty articles, introductions, and forewords, in contrast to his somewhat haughty theatrical image
and his reputation for being inaccessible, reveal him to be a generous and
humble servant of the artist communities of Australia and Britain, willing
to give young or neglected painters, writers, photographers, and other artists his endorsement.

I argue that Humphries' writing, along with his other theatrical art, is a
scream of the bizarre, *un sujet trouvé* ("a found subject"), to be sited/cited
in music hall, Dada, theatre and literary history, and (especially) in language – in words, in speech acts, and in books. Speech, whether spoken or
written, is Humphries' act of speaking up and speaking out.

As a Canadian Australianist I am not directly implicated in the national-
ist issue of whether Barry Humphries is an expatriate who has let down the
side, but I am concerned with it. As early as in his film *Barry McKenzie
Holds His Own* (1974), Humphries references the charges of cultural disloyalty levelled against him in a scene in which Barry McKenzie must suddenly fill in for his twin brother, the Reverend Kevin McKenzie, at a
religious service where Kevin is to preach on the theme of "Christ and the
Orgasm." Offering her encouragement, Edna Everage pleads, "You'll have
to do it, Barry. You can't let Australia down" (all transcriptions, unless otherwise noted, are my own). In *When London Calls: The Expatriation of
Australian Creative Artists to Britain* (1999), Stephen Alomes places
Humphries in the company of Germaine Greer, Clive James, Robert
Hughes, and many other so-called expatriates who have found greener
fields, or at least Green Park, in London. Ian Britain (1997) would seem to
take a less militant position than does Alomes. In his book *Once an Australian: Journeys with Barry Humphries, Clive James, Germaine Greer and
Robert Hughes*, he observes of Humphries, "Yet, as applied to himself, the
category 'expatriate' is as problematic as any other that we may be tempted
to file him under."[1] Humphries has attributed this debate to "tenth-rate academics with chips on their shoulders,"[2] which echoes, if echoes can have
bile, (1) the Critic's remark in Humphries' monologue "The Critic: Witchetty Grub Street," from his first one-man show, *A Nice Night's Entertainment* (1962), "They've sold their birthright for just a few plushy Chelsea
cocktail parties and a few art shows and first nights and plushy Mayfair
parties … You're a bunch of bloody traitors! Rats, Rats, RATS!!";[3] (2) Les
Patterson's allusion to "a long-haired Melbourne ex-pat called Brian
Humphry, who was already on our blacklist for tipping the bucket on his
superlative homeland for an easy quid";[4] and perhaps (3) Irish comedian
Dave Allen's famous quip that "Australians are the most well-balanced
people in the world: they have a chip on each shoulder." It also recalls

Richard Huelsenbeck's (1936) remark in "Dada Lives!": "Everywhere, throughout the world, where forces are at work to turn back the wheel of history, Dada will be hated."[5] I must be concerned with anyone who hates Barry Humphries as a Dada artist. But I need not concern myself with (what could be made into) the psychological or feminist issue of his four marriages, all of them to artists (an actor, a dancer, a painter, and a writer). My focus is only on Barry Humphries as an Australian artiste (an actor, a dancer, a painter, and a writer).

As such he is a credit to his birthplace (Melbourne), his homeland (Australia), his workplace (England), and his residence (London), and, evidently, to everyone who is not a xenophobe and who cherishes artistry and laughter, effrontery and talent. In 1977 Humphries confessed, "I'm still terribly nervous every night before a performance. In this kind of entertainment you can't afford to hesitate. You must have the courage to go on with it. Success is 80 per cent effrontery and 20 per cent talent."[6] From this I infer that, although he puts 100 percent of his considerable talent into his shows, including his literary shows, his effort constitutes only 20 percent of what has to pass through the (ef)front(ery) of the fourth wall of theatre.

Humphries is an embodiment of the excesses of success. He has said, with reference to Sandy Stone and the early Mrs Everage, "But it occurred to me that when I was going to start developing certain comic characters the thing was not to be grotesque, although I had a big background in the kind of full-frontal effrontery of Dadaism."[7] My purpose is to foreground Humphries' Dadaism, *grotesquerie,* and music hall artistry as they figure in his writing and configure his *oeuvre.* If I were a wizard,[8] I would like to translocate Humphries back to 1897 (his preferred decade) and into the quartet (with his participation the quintet) consisting of J.F. Wilfred, Walter Stanley, Charles Willoughby, and Harry Clifford, and featuring in this instance Master Barry Humphries, for a performance of the great music hall song "We're Australians but Still Britannia's Sons" (1897),[9] written and composed by Harry Leighton. The song reads as though Humphries himself contributed to the lyrics:

[verse 1 of 3 verses]
I represent my native land, a land that's dear to me,
Australia, a colony of England o'er the sea.
In spite of what the world may say Australians adore
The dear old mother country, yes, they're Britons to the core.

Long years ago when foreign trade broke many an English home,
And caused the true born Briton from his native land to roam;
Yet tho' our fathers had to seek fresh homes across the main,
Our love for proud Britannia we'll be glad to prove again,

[chorus: ]
Why should we turn our backs upon the land that gave us birth?
Why should we turn our backs upon the dearest spot on earth?
No pauper aliens can drive us from our guns,
Tho' we're Australians we're still Britannia's sons.[10]

Humphries might even add a coda line, singing: "And tho' I live in Britain, I'm still Australia's son." Every Australian should be proud of Master Barry, one of Australia's great writers, though few critics have noted it. As Clive James has observed, "The man who makes people laugh is rarely given quick credit, even in those fully developed countries which realise that serious writing can take a comic form."[11] As recently as 1991 Humphries seems to have concurred with this view in a 2BL (Sydney) radio interview with Andrew Olle, on the topic of his *Neglected Poems and Other Creatures* (1991):

OLLE: Barry, do you feel that the Barry Humphries who really does like to write this sort of stuff has been a little crushed and neglected himself over the years? You've brought it on yourself, I guess.
HUMPHRIES: It's a sort of sideline of mine. Another thing I like to do, of course, is to paint. I had an exhibition of my paintings a couple of years ago, which was fun. Some of them even sold. But I regard these things strictly as hobbies. If I am remembered at all, I'll be remembered as a comic and certainly not as a versifier.[12]

Is writing to Humphries simply a "sideline" or a "hobby," an amateur pastime, albeit an act of love? By 2001, after the publication of his greatest works – *More Please* (1992) and *Women in the Background* (1995) – Humphries seemed to have promoted himself from the amateur ranks, much as I promote him in this book, when he referred to writing as "my second career."[13] In *A Portrait of the Artist as Australian* I give credit where credit is overdue, formally acknowledging Barry Humphries as the great writer of an *oeuvre bizarre*.

In the end, as a Dada artist, I should perhaps observe, much as Marcel Duchamp once observed[14] of Arturo Schwarz's anticipated *Complete Works of Marcel Duchamp* (1969), "this book is not about Barry Humphries but by Paul Matthew St Pierre." But really it is all and only about Humphries, specifically *as an established writer* who emerged from Peter Cook's Establishment Club.

Barry McKenzie's Cartesian confession in *Bazza Comes into His Own* (1979), "I love Australia – I think,"[15] is also Barry Humphries'. Every one of Humphries' printed thoughts is an expression of his love for Australia. My portrait of Humphries as an Australian is that of a great artist for whom Melbourne is the centre of the universe; and for Humphries the universe is a proposition that he can squeeze into a ball and bounce about the halls in a novelty turn, in turns and twists of inventive syntax.

Music hall (1854–1936) perdures today in sign systems, in images and scripts, in the cinema, and in historical and critical records. As Humphries has donated his theatrical and literary properties – the signs of his music hall turns onstage and in language – to the Performing Arts Museum, Victorian Arts Centre, Melbourne (see my Addendum), so has he translated these signs into more durable forms, mediatizing them as film, video, recordings, discs, photographs, and texts, committing them, as it were, to the collective memory of Australia. Through writing, as through the other media, Humphries has made his music hall imprint indelible, the logotype of possibly the last Australian music hall performer. When he gave English comedian Tommy Trinder (1909–89), the veteran of fourteen feature films (mostly Ealing comedies), a role in his film *Barry McKenzie Holds His Own* (1974), he also gave him a place in Australian cinematic history. It proved to be Trinder's final film. By casting him, Humphries preserved Trinder in a permanent cinematic and cultural record. Similarly, in *My Life as Me: A Memoir* (2002), he commemorates "Tommy 'You Lucky People' Trinder – the first real comedian I had ever seen as a child, at Melbourne's Tivoli Theatre."[16]

Similarly, by donating his professional effects to the goddess PAM, and by publishing some of his scripts and monologues, and measuring out his life as a music hall artiste, not with Prufrockian coffee spoons but in a library of poetry, fiction, comics, biography, history, journalism, confession, memoir, and criticism, Humphries sets his record straight. His textual signature is not so much his autograph as his arrangement of signs, of signature tunes, whose signified is *music hall*. I have written this book as a signed portrait of Barry Humphries, music hall artiste, Dada performer, and writer of literature, and as a scholarly commentary on his texts. *A Portrait of the Artist as Australian* is his "print," as in a final cinematic take; his "imprint," as in a library copy's publication data; and my own modest contribution to keeping his books out of "out of print."

Is Barry Humphries really a writer of literature rather than simply the author and editor of twenty-nine books? Or is he a shameless self-promoter, a relentless publicist of his own career, the author of a series of inscribed publicity stunts – music hall turns that, as literature, are as silent and anachronistic as an abandoned theatre, or Dada pranks that amount only to so much Russian salad (which his audiences, now as in the 1950s, enjoy watching him eat off the sidewalk)? Is he, like Marcel Duchamp to "the post-Duchampians … no longer above criticism; nor was his work necessarily held to constitute a point of no return for Western art"?[17] In *A Portrait of the Artist as Australian* I make a case for

Humphries as a writer of literature, first by exploring his indebtedness to music hall and Dada; then by examining his work genre by genre and measuring his "bizarre" contributions to "the book" as artwork, commodity, and artifact; and finally by assessing his *oeuvre* and fixing his place in Australian literature and literary history, all in opposition to Australian tall-poppy cultural theorists who argue he has let down the side. And in gratitude to Humphries for having made the world laugh.

# Acknowledgments

I would like to offer my first thanks to Executive Director and Senior Editor Philip J. Cercone, Coordinating Editor Joan McGilvray, Editorial Assistant Brenda Price, Rights and Projects Officer Margaret Levey, and especially my personal editor Joanne Richardson of McGill-Queen's University Press for their invaluable advice and assistance in the preparation of my manuscript, and especially for supporting my project on a song-and-dance man. In addition, I must kindly thank Simon Fraser University and the Social Sciences and Humanities Research Council of Canada for generously providing me a travel grant that allowed me to complete my research at the Performing Arts Museum (PAM) in Melbourne. This book has been published with the help of a grant from the Canadian Federation for the Humanities and Social Sciences, through the Aid to Scholarly Publications Programme, using funds provided by the Social Sciences and Humanities Research Council of Canada. Dame Leonie Kramer inspired my career as a professor of Australian literature, for which I shall always be grateful. Anne Higgins, my department chair, supported my project throughout, even though other colleagues had never heard of Barry Humphries and still others would not hear of him: thank you, Annie, for believing in me. And Paul Delany made this book my reader's ticket to associate professor.

Without the help and support of these people, my book might not have happened. Roseanne Barr, for responding to my request for a video: Roseanne, you are hilarious and hysterical, a gynocentric goddess! Reverend Warren Debenham, for sharing information so willingly: God bless you! Mallory Catlett, for fetching me a program from New York; Kimberly Walker, my eyes and ears in Melbourne; and Brian Saunders, for his generosity and niceness, and for being *bijzonder*. Elizabeth Bernard, former research service coordinator, PAM, for providing me with your Barry Humphries Catalogue: you are kindness herself! Catherine O'Donoghue, former research service officer, and Joanna Leahy, current access-coordinator, PAM: thank you for your expert assistance and your friendly support during my visit to PAM. Nicholas Pounder, Sydney antiquarian book seller: your generosity and anecdotes reinvoked Barry Humphries in my imagination. David Martin Bruson, Megastar Productions, and Barry Humphries' personal assistant, for leading me into antiquarian book Web sites and especially his own site, <www.dame-edna.com>: may you know her joyous heart always. Eric Idle, for generously allowing me to quote from his composition "Penis Song (Not the Noël Coward Song" and for showing me what life is when you don't look at it. *The National Post*, for permission to quote a column by Shinan Govani and two of my own letters to the editor (see Appendices 3 and 4). I offer my deepest thanks to His Nibs, Barry Humphries, for his many kindnesses and for supporting me in my project, when he could have dismissed me as a tenth-rate academic with a chip on my shoulder, dispatched me as a Kenneth Grocock clone, or made a peremptory demand for royalties.

Barry Humphries has to be seen, as well as read, to be believed. By generously providing me with their photographs of him "as me," "as seen with" Dame Edna, and "as seen as" Dame Edna, Les Patterson, Sandy Stone, and Lance Boyle, photographers Lewis Morley, Polly Borland, and John Timbers have helped make him credible. Nicky Akehurst, Akehurst Creative Management, London, was instrumental in securing Morley's photograph of Humphries; Matthew Bailey, Picture Librarian, National Portrait Gallery, London, gave me free access to Morley's picture and Polly Borland's picture of Sir Leslie Colin Patterson, both of which are in the National Portrait Gallery's Photographic Collection. Without the support of John Timbers, in particular, this book could not have found its final form. Humphries' longtime iconographer, he indulged me as a kid in the candy shop of his intellectual property.

Especially, I thank my agent, Joanie Minott, for her indefatigable efforts not only to flog this book but also to flog me whenever my means of production waned. I also thank her for keeping me from drifting into the rogue koala academic states of the starstruck, the stalker, the collector, and the nonentity, yet tolerating my refugee state in fandom.

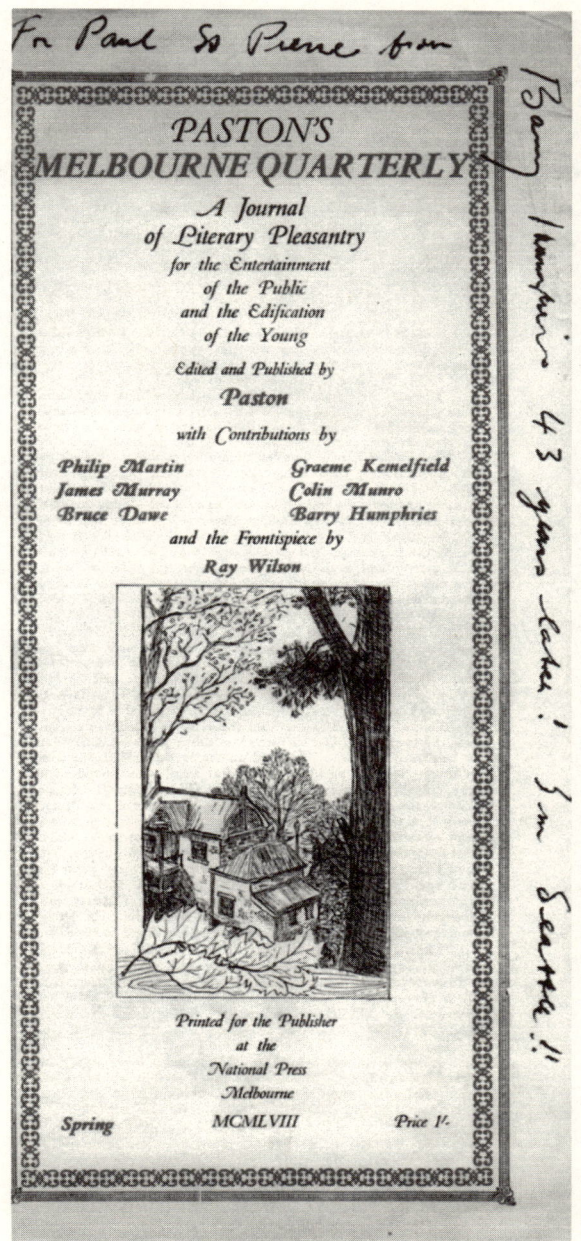

*For Paul So Pierre from*

*Barry Humphries 43 years later! I'm Seattle!!*

## PASTON'S MELBOURNE QUARTERLY

*A Journal of Literary Pleasantry for the Entertainment of the Public and the Edification of the Young*

*Edited and Published by*

**Paston**

*with Contributions by*

Philip Martin      Graeme Kemelfield
James Murray      Colin Munro
Bruce Dawe      Barry Humphries

*and the Frontispiece by*

Ray Wilson

*Printed for the Publisher
at the
National Press
Melbourne*

Spring      MCMLVIII      Price 1/-

*Paston's Melbourne Quarterly* (Spring 1958), my copy of which Barry Humphries signed on 9 March 2001 after his evening performance of *Dame Edna – The Royal Tour*, at the Moore Theatre, Seattle.

Barry Humphries (1960s), beginning the bizarre.  Photo © Lewis Morley/
The Lewis Morley Archive/Akehurst Creative Management; courtesy National
Portrait Gallery

Barry Humphries and Dame Edna Everage, smaller and larger than life, in *Harpers & Queen Magazine* (1973). Photo © John Timbers

Before I could barely toddle
I decided I would model
My brilliant career
On Queen Boadicea.
I dreamed I was a Queen in ancient Britain
And then I started to grow hair that I could sit on
And it's just amazing when you think I've come this far
Not just a wife and mother but - a Megastar.

Please don't think I'm just a hollow brittle shell
Because I'm a warm and deeply caring woman as well.

And thought I've travelled far and wide
It's lovely to be home like this
It's my big chance to confide
The spooky little London things I miss.

I miss funny little things
A prowl on Hampstead Heath
The hats of Mrs Schilling *Are Queen Mother.*
Esther Rantzen's teeth *Playa*
I miss Boots in Piccadilly for my daily pint of Nivea
I miss struggling to hear them on the stage of the Olivier
I miss the margarine commercials and the Tetley teabag jingle
I miss cruising with the Prince of Wales in the days when he was single
But even more than I miss the entire Britannia crew
I miss an evening's intercourse with you.

I've looked it up in the encyclopaedia it isn't such a yukky word
It means a cosy chat but if the media decide they want to miscontrue it
They can leave the theatre to do it.

What's missing from the book: page 1 of "What I Miss," from the typescript of *Neglected Poems and Other Creatures* (1991).

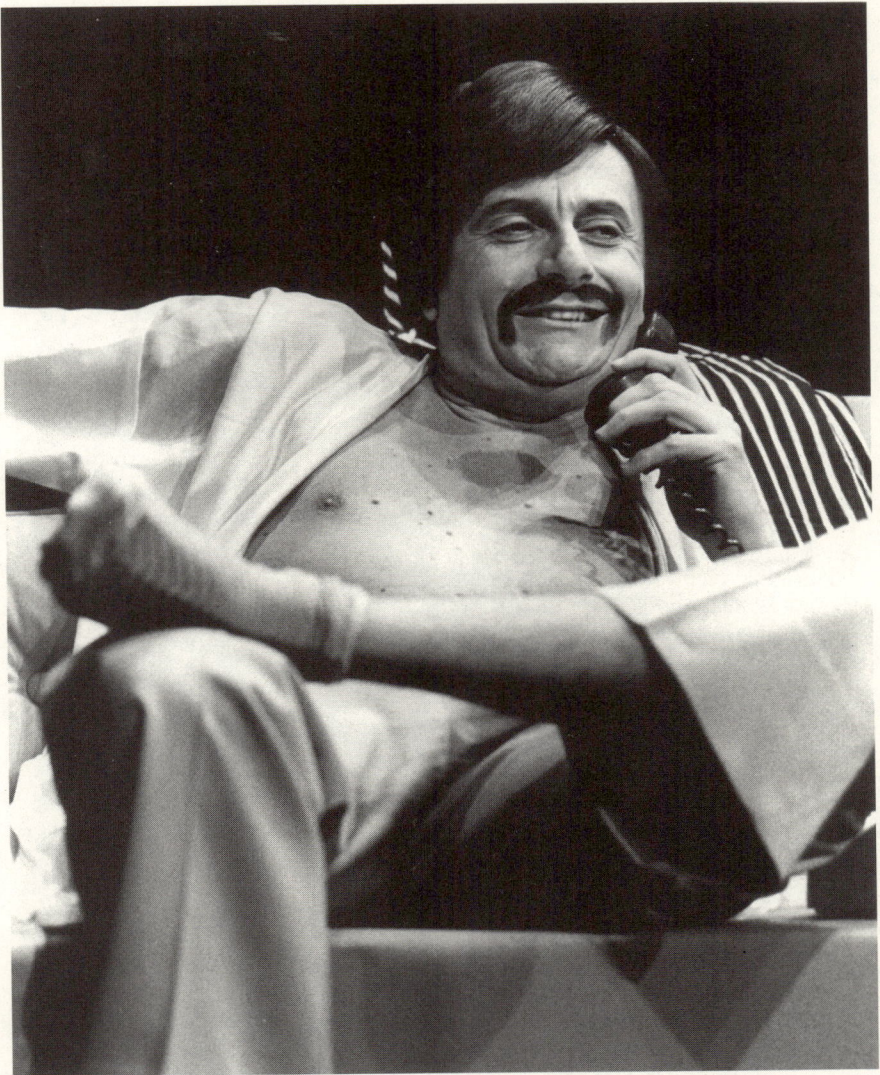

Barry Humphries as Lance Boyle, dress rehearsal for *"Isn't It Pathetic at His Age"* (December 1978). Photo © John Timbers; courtesy The Arts Centre's Performing Arts Museum Collection

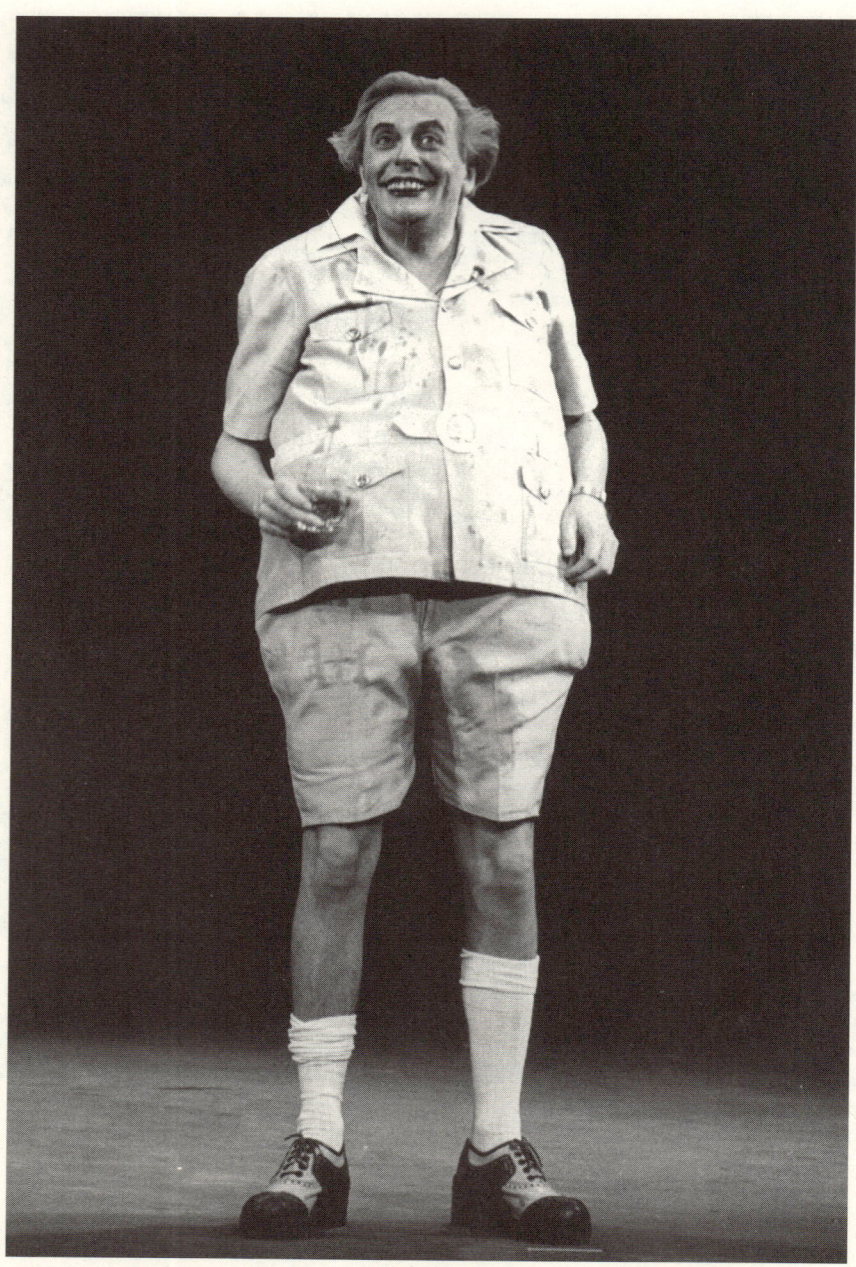

Barry Humphries as Leslie Colin Patterson, dress rehearsal for *An Evening's Intercourse with the Widely Liked Barry Humphries*, Theatre Royal, Drury Lane, London (January 1982). Photo © John Timbers

Barry Humphries as Sir Leslie Colin Patterson, tipping the bucket on Brian Humphry for Australia (1999). Photo © Polly Borland; courtesy National Portrait Gallery

Barry Humphries as Sandy Stone, location shoot (March 1976). Photo © John Timbers; courtesy The Arts Centre's Performing Arts Museum Collection

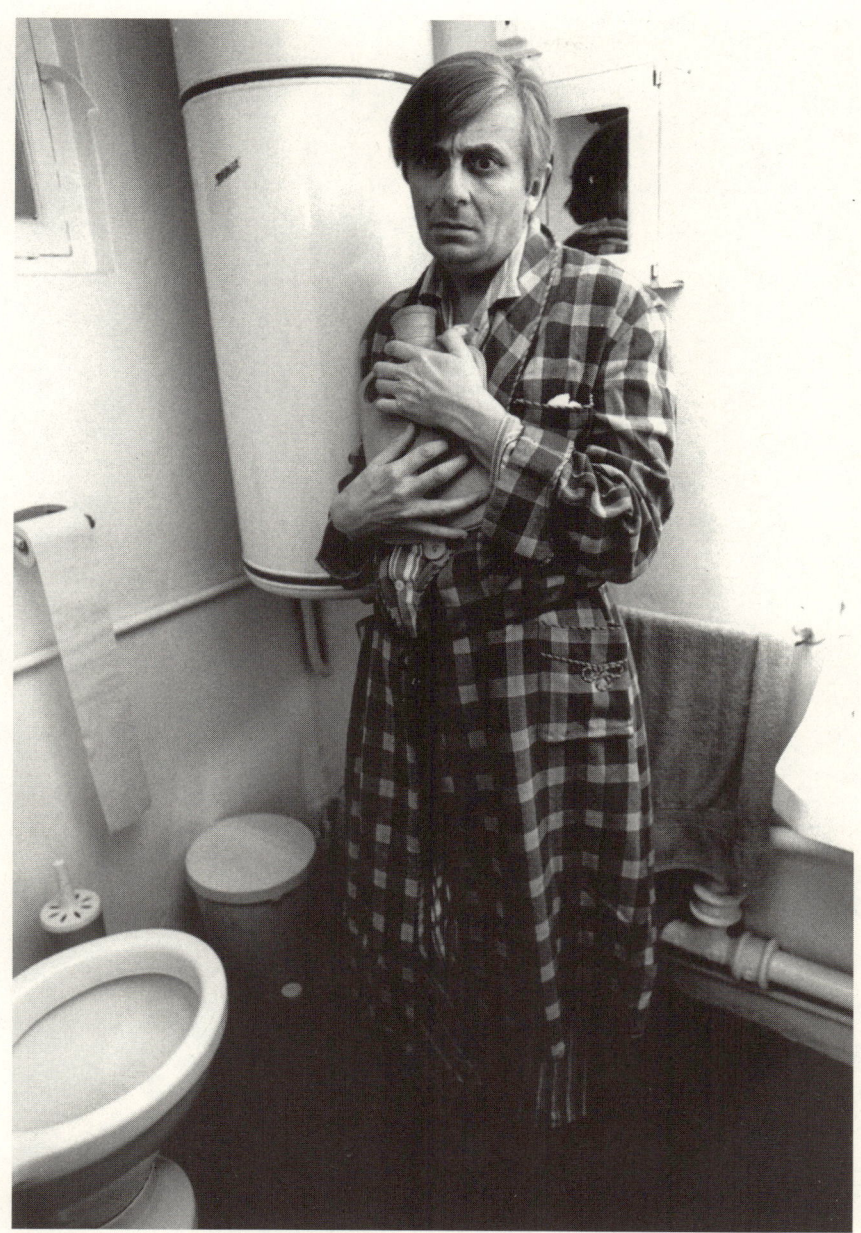

Barry Humphries as Sandy Stone, dress rehearsal for *An Evening's Intercourse with the Widely Liked Barry Humphries*, Theatre Royal, Drury Lane, London (January 1982). Photo © John Timbers

Barry Humphries as Dame Edna Everage, in her Sydney Opera House frock, studio shoot (January 1982). Photo © John Timbers

There are moments when the whole dada-surrealist performance world looks like some great data swindle perpetrated on the only too fallible researcher and critic. It is all too true, however. Tzara paraded around the stage in a top hat crowned with a lighted candle, Hugo Ball was carried of in a sweat after having recited "gadgi beri bimba." Mme Gaveau was splashed with rotten tomatoes. Eluard fell into the scenery of *Le Coeur à Gaz*. It remains only to believe it.
        – Annabelle Henkin Melzer, *Dada and Surrealist Performance*

MEN BEFORE THE MIRROR
Many a time the mirror imprisons them and holds them firmly. Fascinated they stand in front. They are absorbed, separated from reality and alone with their dearest vice, vanity. However readily they spread out all other vices for all, they keep this one secret and disown it even before their most intimate friends. (Rose Sélavy)
        – Man Ray, *Photographies, 1930–1934*

The activity of Dada was a permanent revolt of the individual against art, against morality, against society. The means were manifestoes, poems, writings of various kinds, paintings, sculptures, exhibitions, and a few public demonstrations of a clearly subversive character.
        – Georges Ribemont-Dessaignes, *The History of Dada*

One night, he showed us some of his travel snaps including some pictures taken in Canada of a river choked with bits of wood. "What do you make of that?" he asked me through his tobacco haze. Nobody else seemed to know. "A beaver dam?" I said. By coincidence, I had been reading a book about beavers the day before. Hicky took another suck on his pipe and looked up at my father. "You've got a very clever boy there, Eric," he said, "a very clever boy indeed."
        – Barry Humphries, *More Please*

# Kid on the Halls:
# Barry Humphries Speaks

Before the War he would have queued to hear Bea Lillie sing,
One imagined him in private dragging up like Douggie Byng.
                              – Barry Humphries, "Threnody for Patrick White"

Americans are not the only artists who invaded the English Halls: there were also
three famous Australians: Billy Williams, 1877–1915; Albert Whelan (born 1875
and died not long ago) who is said to have invented the "signature tune," for he
always came on stage whistling *Der Lüstige Brüder*; and Florrie Forde, born in
1876, who became, thanks to a famous song of World War I, a Music Hall
immortal. All three hailed from Melbourne, and knowing that grim city all
too well, it astonishes me that it should have had such illustrious sons and
daughters.
                    – Colin MacInnes, *Sweet Saturday Night: Pop Song 1840–1920*

Whatever the depressing aspects of this vaudeville life [at the Cabaret Voltaire,
Zurich, 1916], there is no doubt that it is in many of its aspects quintessential theatre. There are few better ways to learn to "work" an audience, to construct and reconstruct material for the stage, to be "up," to find sources of energy where there
are none, to mold an often banal activity into a theatre piece. Although the player is
rarely dealing with the work of actor-as-character, he is always working at the role
of actor as performer.
                         – Annabelle Henkin Melzer, *Dada and Surrealist Performance*

When cross-dressing ceases to be stylized, preserving a cool arena of illusion between performance and artist, only the grotesquerie remains.
                              – Peter Ackroyd, *Dressing Up, Tranvestism and Drag:*
                                                   *The History of an Obsession*

BARRY HUMPHRIES ARE ...

"Barry Humphries" are the most appropriate words with which to begin a book on Australian artist, showman, and (especially) writer Barry Humphries. Certainly, they are the most evocative words in my own lexicon, conjuring up the attractive figure of a man of the theatre, a player of men and women not only on stage but also in the audience. Given his versatility as a stage performer, and his elusive personality as a biographical subject (who may reveal himself but only when he is not looking),[1] one might posit various persons named Barry Humphries, a whole company of Barry Humphries. The most startling Barry of them all may well be Barry Humphries the writer.

In one sense, "Barry Humphries" *are* Dame Edna Everage, Sir Leslie Colin Patterson, Sandy Stone, Ern Deadpen, Barry McKenzie, Buster Thompson, Jeff Pritchard, Colin Cartwright, Morrie Tate, Morrie O'Connor, the Critic, the Snowy, the Surfie, Neil Singleton, Nipper Dixon, Lance Boyle, Rex Lear, Lionel Hunter, Big Sonia, Debbie Thwaite, Wendy Toole, Craig Foxtrot, Craig Steppenwolf, Neville Creamer, Daryl Dalkeith, Brian Graham, Brett Grantworthy, Martin Agrippa, Rosencrantz, Holofernes, Duke Orsino, Estragon, the Bunyip, Basil Clissold, Jonas Fogg, Mr Sowerberry, Fagin, Captain Jules Martin, Hoot, Dr Meyer de Lamphrey, Vicar Kevin Cock, Madame Barrie, Col Ball-Miller, Reverend Strachey, Bert, Clemens Metternich, Kangaroo, Humphrey Beal, Blind Wally, Kevin McMaxford, Rupert Murdoch, Richard Deane, Mrs Crummles, Bruce, and Dame Edna Everage's manager, Barry Humphries, and even Barry Humphries, the implied author.

In another sense, Barry Humphries "are" character actor, character comedian, composer, painter, dramatist, poet and writer, someone somewhere between "a droopy dilettante"[2] and a born-again Renaissance man, between a Victorian dandy and a dandy Dada merry prankster, between a traditional archivist and a postmodern deconstructionist, between a megastar and the most private of gentlemen. But in the end "Barry Humphries" are merely words. This is not because he has eluded all but the surface meaning of language but because, when given a screening – whether on stage (through the footlights and the fourth wall), on canvas, on disc, on the film screen, television, video monitor, or on the page – Barry Humphries, performance artiste, is always *on*. His medium is words, his means is the act of speech, and his message is a series of Dada truths underlying political correctness.

Why has this stage and television performer, who has achieved celebrity[3] and seems disposed to maintaining it through self-promotion, whose fame is so pronounced that he has even come to resemble "the megastar who won't go away," also distinguished himself as an author, co-author, and editor of twenty-nine books? Is Humphries a performer who has merely taken a turn at writing, maybe just another famous Humphries party turn? Or is he a legitimate writer whose writing is marked by performativity? If his writing is a turn, then it has lasted forty-five years, since the publication of his "A Novel Called Tid" (1958). Clearly, he has made a career of writing. Indeed, his writing is of sufficient originality and merit to be called literature, and his output is extensive and varied enough to form an *oeuvre*.

His *oeuvre*, whether spoken, sung, or written, is a Derridean speech-act, comprising a long run of speech-acts on which the curtain ought never to fall, whether to packed houses at the Booth Theatre on Broadway (1999–2000); loaded houses at the Granville Returned Servicemen's Club (1957) and the Australian National Press Club (1978); befuddled houses at the Establishment Club in 1962[4] and in the studio of the 1966 BBC television series *The Late Show*;[5] the waggish house at the ITV show *An Audience with Dame Edna* (1980), in which Ned Sherrin poses the disarming question, "Dame Edna, in the early sixties, when you played the Establishment with an audience of about seven and only one dress, were times very hard for you then?" (see Appendix 2); or even the full houses spilling out after Ginger Rogers' performances in *Mame* at the Theatre Royal, Drury Lane,[6] across the road from the Fortune Theatre, where Humphries was performing to modest audiences, making the outcry "I'm not full, I'm not full" seem more Humphries' comment on his own unfortunate London production of *Just a Show*[7] than Les Patterson's sobriquet for sobriety. As a speech-actor (speaker and actor) uttering the language of performativity, Humphries makes the indelible imprint of a great Australian artist: a voice-print in printer's ink.

In the notes that precede and in the books that follow these and Humphries' hundreds of other well received stage and studio performances – that is, in his prescripts and postscripts – "constative description is nothing other than the performative itself."[8] As an acting speaker, Barry Humphries has proven himself an Aristotelian actant, an imitator of actions that are comical, complete, and larger than life. As a performer in print as well as on stage, he might even be credited as the executant author of the (nonextant) comedy section of Aristotle's *Poetics*, and he might be teamed with another Aristotelian figure, Carlton, the humanoid character in Eric Idle's *The Road to Mars: A Post-Modem Novel* (1999), whose doctoral dissertation at the University of Southern Saturn, entitled *De Rerum Comoedia*, rounds out with "quantum comedy" the quantum physics of Stephen Hawking's *A Brief History of Time*.[9]

In this regard, Humphries is a pantomime Aristotelian, a successor to an implied Socrates in the arts of discourse and dialectic. But, tempting as it might be to cast Dame Edna Everage as a Socratic orator, or Sir Les Patterson as a Platonic or Xenophonic symposiast, I must concede that the professional antecedents of a twentieth-century artiste, even one as antiquarian as Humphries, are probably to be found this side of antiquity. His precursors, as he himself says in *More Please*, are to be found in Dada (1916–23) and Music Hall (1854–1936). Humphries contends (1) that his characters Barry McKenzie and Buster Thompson are exemplars[10] for the Winfield cigarettes, Foster's Lager, and (later) Subaru pitchman Paul Hogan's "Crocodile Dundee" character (popularized in the films *"Crocodile" Dundee* [1986] and *"Crocodile" Dundee II* [1988]); and (2) that the film *The Adventures of Barry McKenzie* (1972) and the Barry McKenzie comic strip itself (written by Barry Humphries and drawn by Nicholas Garland, which appeared in the satirical magazine *Private Eye* from July 1964 to March 1974), carry in their frames and panels formative ad copy for Foster's beer (then "the most obscure lager in the world").[11] Barry McKenzie's comic strip pitch for Foster's leads two "Sloane Yuppies," in a new panel that precedes *The Complete Barry McKenzie* (1988), to observe: "Old Barry Mac really put that product on the map. Reckon the Aussie brewery must have paid him a flippin' fortune." Of the now older Barry McKenzie, whom they happen to meet but do not recognize, they comment: "He looks like Crocodile Dundee's grandfather after a session on the sauce."[12] Compare Humphries' own reference, in the Prolegomenon to his *Neglected Poems and Other Creatures* (1991): "the loutish, albeit innocent Barry McKenzie, lantern-jawed progenitor of Crocodile Dundee, was a creature of the sixties when Fosters Lager was an obscure Melbourne beverage only obtainable at one disreputable pub in London."[13] That Humphries should imply that, in the Foster's ads, Hogan's ocker appropriated McKenzie's discourse (specifically the idiom "crack an ice-cold tube")[14] reinforces my contention that, to Humphries, although the speech-act is open to Aristotelian imitation, it should be subject to professional acknowledgment. Music hall patter may be re-pattered, but it may not be *patterned* (i.e., appropriated).

The currency of Humphries' media influence might be apparent even in EMI's merger with the American giant Time Warner (which was announced 24 January 2000). This amalgam, Warner EMI Music, could be seen to have been initiated by Humphries as long ago as 1954, when he was "a trainee executive" at the Melbourne offices of EMI. While there he was commissioned to smash discontinued 78 rpm recordings,[15] an act for which he has spent the rest of his life making restitution by collecting rare 78s. He alludes of this in his poem "The Turntable of Life" (1970) (in which the speaker recalls "how we kissed on that very first date / When the old needle hissed on a 78")[16] and in his double compact disc compilations *So Rare* (1999) and *So Rare 2* (2000), which feature songs that were popular between 1932 and 1943. Might Humphries, as an EMI junior executive icon-oclast, and an executant Dada collage and performance artiste, have secretly brokered and mediatized a megacorporation that came into being forty-six years later? It would seem that even the macroeconomics of globalization cannot rule out his pull in the arts and his push in the media. Humphries paces himself at 78 rpm.

Perhaps the greatest recipient of his putative comedic influence has been *Monty Python's Flying Circus*. Humphries has stated, for example, that Barry McKenzie is an exemplar for the Pythons' Australian character Bruce,[17] and he has even hinted that his BBC television show *The Barry Humphries Scandals* (1970), in which Michael Palin once appeared as a guest, had an influence on *Monty Python's Flying Circus*, the first series of which premiered on the BBC in October 1970. In the program of his 1998 show, *New Edna – The Spectacle* (Theatre Royal Haymarket, London), the biographical sketch on Humphries reads, with reference to *Just a Show* (Fortune Theatre, London, 1969): "this performance polarised the British critics as had an earlier performance at Peter Cook's Establishment Club but it led to a pioneering comedy series on the BBC, *The Barry Humphries Scandals*, a show which inspired Monty Python." Can this claim be true? Or is it just name-dropping, a "Dr Humphries" kind of "pictured with" self-promotion? How did Barry Humphries influence *Monty Python's Flying Circus*?

Almost no studies of the Monty Python show and the Python troupe ascribe either influence or inspiration to Humphries, not even Robert Ross's comprehensive *Monty Python Encyclopedia* (1997). Still, the biographical blurb from the *New Edna – The Spectacle* program would seem to be both perspicacious and sincere. In his book *Monty Python Speaks!* (1999), for example, David Morgan quotes Barry Took, who first pitched "Python" at BBC television:

I had seen Barry Humphries, the Australian, in a one-man show [*Just a Show*] and thought he would make good material for television, and I had this idea of putting this Cleese/Chapman/Palin/Jones together. So I arrive at the BBC and they said, "Well, Barry Humphries was a female impersonator." I said, "He's not, he's a very broad, interesting comedian, he does all kinds of things, and Edna Everage was just one of his jokes" – it came to overwhelm him in the end, but I mean in those days he had several characters. And they said, "Oh, this Palin and Jones, all that is much too expensive." I said, "You must do it, you've *got* to. Why the hell have you employed me? You said come in, bring us new ideas, I bring you new ideas, you say: *We can't do it. Too expensive.*"[18]

The (con)sequential appearances of *The Barry Humphries Scandals* and *Monty Python's Flying Circus* on BBC TV in 1970 confirm Barry Took's attribution of Humphries' influence.

Further acknowledgment of a Humphries/Python connection comes from Eric Idle, who, like Humphries, is a fine music hall performer. Idle is particularly gifted as a comic singer, as he proved in *Eric Idle Exploits Monty Python: A Rather Stupid Evening of Skits and Songs*,[19] his 27 and 28 June 2000 concert performances at Carnegie Hall (*the* Carnegie Hall, not the town hall in Carnegie, Australia, where, with Nigel Butterley, Humphries posed for the cover photograph of his 1972 album *Barry Humphries at Carnegie Hall*). In his composition "Penis Song (Not the Noël Coward Song)," from the film *Monty Python's The Meaning of Life* (1983), Idle offers a comic tribute and a scholarly attribution to Humphries in the line "Hooray for your one-eyed trouser snake." Humphries coined this euphemism in his own comic song about phallocentricity, "My Little One-Eyed Trouser Snake," which he recorded on *Private Eye's Blue Record* (1965), and which he has used in the Barry McKenzie comic strip and in the routines of Les Patterson.

Idle gives further credit to Humphries in *The Road to Mars: A Post-Modem Novel* (1999), where he places him in a select group of comedians who transcend the character Carlton's binary opposition of "white face" (neurotic and philosophical) and "red nose" (manic and exhibitionist) comedians. Patrick Beaver cites an alternative dichotomy of circus comedians, specifically Merry Andrew (or Mr Merryman) and Clown, the assistants to Harlequin in Victorian pantomime: "the white clown who is not particularly funny in appearance and who wears the traditional costume of sequined white satin with a conical hat, and the auguste (named after the first of his kind) who must be funny at first sight and who may wear any kind of clothes and make-up as long as they are grotesque."[20] In this regard, Barry Humphries is Clown and his act, on stage and in print, is literary *grotesquerie*.

Outside of his dichromatic list of ninety-two major twentieth-century comedians, Eric Idle places the "Double Controllers – White faces masquerading as Red Noses – a category of comedian, he says, who exhibit both elements in their personality." This short list consists of "Woody Allen's little nerdy Red Nose character ... inside which the White Face writer-director Allen is controlling everything. Other examples he cites are Rowan Atkinson as Mr Bean, Charlie Chaplin as the little tramp, Barry Humphries as Dame Edna Everage, and Eddie Izzard."[21] The term "red-nosed" comes from the music hall,[22] so, in applying it to Humphries, Idle would seem to be acknowledging his career on the halls. As host Dame Edna, Humphries has even performed on "Red Nose Day" on *Comic Relief* (BBC-1, 14 March 1997). As well as recognizing Humphries as one of the great comedians of the century, and as a complex *mise en abîme* performer, Idle confirms that he is one of his personal influences. Although he does not speak for all the Pythons, Idle does hint that *The Barry Humphries Scandals* may indeed have heraded *Monty Python's Flying Circus*.

Through the comedic ingenuity of Barry Took, Humphries almost became a founding member of Monty Python's Flying Circus. Similarly, in

1962, but for his contractual obligation in Lionel Bart's *Oliver!* Humphries would have become Peter Cook's replacement in *Beyond the Fringe*[23] when the original players moved the show to Broadway. He had beaten out David Frost[24] for Cook's role in the London production, in which Terence Brady (Peter Cook), Robin Ray (Dudley Moore), Bill Wallis (Alan Bennett), and Joe Melia (Jonathan Miller) eventually starred. Although Harry Thompson concedes that "the engagement, which lasted four years, did no favours for the careers of the victorious auditioners,"[25] one wonders how Barry Humphries' career might have been enhanced had he starred in *Beyond the Fringe* and in *Monty Python's Flying Circus*. Although *Fringe* and *Python* are arguably the most successful stage and television comedy shows in British history, Humphries' career has been well served by his not having become part of these companies. Humphries is not unlike most successful actors in that his career has been partly shaped by missing out. In *A Great Silly Grin*, Humphrey Carpenter both leaves Humphries out and acknowledges him as a left-out performer. He names only Richard Ingrams and John Wells as being among the performers who auditioned for the replacement roles in the West End *Beyond the Fringe*,[26] yet he quotes Humphries as saying "he 'always felt a little apart, a little excluded' from the Peter Cook circle" and "always had the feeling that [he] was only a guest in the group, and could easily be edged out, or [his] contribution dropped" from *Private Eye* recordings.[27]

For example, why, in the original Broadway cast recording (RCA Victor 4113-2-RG) of *Oliver!* (Imperial Theatre, New York, 1963), is Barry Humphries' performance of Mr Sowerberry's song, "That's Your Funeral," omitted? After all, his brilliant performance of this song was one of the highlights of the 1960 London production (Wimbledon and New [Albery] Theatres), and rightly made its way onto the London cast recording (Decca LK 4359). The Broadway cast recording was made precipitously in Los Angeles (on the show's pre-Broadway tour, which Humphries had joined in Toronto)[28] in an effort to market the disk before the premier and to compete with the best-selling Decca recording. Humphries somehow got lost in the shuffle of orphans' feet. But, with typical Australian pluck, he managed to find his footing when he next appeared in *Oliver!* (1967), finally, after his long apprenticeship as Ron Moody's understudy, in the starring role of Fagin.

Missing out on *Beyond the Fringe* and *Monty Python's Flying Circus* also provided Humphries with a precious opportunity to be true to himself as a solo performer, to try to perfect his one-man show, the kind of bizarre show that only he could do. And perhaps he *has* perfected it because Peter Coleman boldly calls him "the most popular one-man showman in the history of theatre."[29] With characteristic humility, Humphries is quick to point out (in his biographical sketches in the programs of *Tears before Bedtime* and

*Back with a Vengeance*) that his show *An Evening's Intercourse with the Widely Liked Barry Humphries* (Regent Theatre, Sydney, 1981; Her Majesty's Theatre, Melbourne, 1981; Theatre Royal, Drury Lane, London, 1982) was the first one-man show to be performed at the illustrious Theatre Royal, Drury Lane (the oldest theatre site in London). Curiously, in *The Arts and Entertainment in London* (1997), Francesca Collin notes the latter distinction but not the former. In citing his Drury Lane lineage, Humphries is also acknowledging his music hall performative. For example, in 1899, of 1,496 music hall acts in England, 35 (or 2.36 percent) were "grotesques/eccentrics."[30] One century later, it might be said that virtually all music hall acts are "grotesques/eccentrics" in that Humphries may well be the only true music hall artiste still on the boards.

Humphries is a double act only when Dame Edna Everage and Sir Les Patterson work on the same stage; when Madge Allsop appears as Edna's silent partner; and when Humphries, as a comic singer, collaborates with composers Nick Rowley, Stanley Myers, Diane Millstead, Nigel Butterley, Carl Davis, James McConnell, and Billy Philadelphia. He is an ensemble player only in that his one-man shows are either about one woman, Dame Edna, or about many characters; and because he has always kept close company with other music hall artistes as theatrical subjects. That in *Who's Who of Australian Writers* (1991) Humphries should identify himself as a "Music Hall Artiste"[31] is not just a Dada prank but also his most candid statement of his theatricality, his most carefully staged performative, an indication of "the *real* me"[32] who can never be mirrored.

John Lahr has stated that Humphries "is almost single-handedly bringing the vaudeville tradition into the twenty-first century,"[33] and Gilbert Adair has noted, "Though it is firmly anchored in a music-hall tradition, there is a terrorist dimension to the act which relates it to what used to be called the Theatre of Cruelty: Dame Edna is the sole offspring of Artaud and Max Miller."[34] In Murray Bramwell and David Matthews' *Wanted for Questioning: Interviews with Australian Comic Artists*, Humphries confesses, "I think I'm much closer to a music-hall performer," and he observes of Dame Edna, "She's also a music hall figure."[35] Similarly, his biographical notes in the program of *Just a Show* (Tivoli Theatre, Sydney; Australian tour, 1968; and Fortune Theatre, London, 1969), note that Humphries is "known abroad as ... 'The Dr Scholl of the Australian Music Hall" and "was once hailed as 'the Aubrey Beardsley of the Australian music hall.'"[36] In 1985 Max Bell called Humphries "a comic actor who survived the death knell of music hall" and observed that "Humphries has forged a series of characters perfectly suited to the post Music Hall TV generation."[37] In his foreword to Charles Osborne's *Max Oldaker: Last of the Matinee Idols* (1988), the biography of his old colleague, Humphries writes:

In 1956, soon after I had been fired by the Union Theatre Repertory Company, (now the Melbourne Theatre Company) I was invited to join the Phillip Street Revue Theatre in Sydney. News of this enterprising and energetic company had percolated to Melbourne, and I was already persuaded that my talents were better suited to the Music Hall than they were to the rigorous discipline of the conventional Repertory Theatre.[38]

The phrase "I was already persuaded" may seem an escape clause for professional failure, but I believe Humphries persuaded himself to go on the halls. John Lahr's reference to "the vaudeville tradition" recalls Anna Russell's patter in introducing her composition "I'm only a Faded Rose" on her LP *Anna Russell's Guide to Concert Audiences* (1954): "Everybody says that vaudeville is dead. Now it isn't dead at all. It just went to England. This is where you get the third English group, I would put, the music hall song." If the great Canadian comedians Mark McKinney, Bruce McCulloch, Kevin Macdonald, Scott Thompson, and Dave Foley can be known collectively as the Kids in the Hall, then perhaps Australian comedy and music hall great Barry Humphries deserves to be recognized, individually, as he continues his one-man show across three continents, as the "Kid on the Halls."

Humphries' assertion in *Who's Who* that he is a music hall artiste is verifiable, not only in a published text and critical sources but also in the tradition of music hall song, in his life experience, as documented in *More Please* (1992), and in the style and structure of his stage and recorded performances.

### BARRY HUMPHRIES' TRADITION OF MUSIC HALL SONG

The song "Niceness" (Humphries and Rowley 1978) is Humphries' signature tune – a concept originated by his countryman, music hall and variety performer Albert Whelan (Albert Waxman) (1875–1961). It is as much a part of his music hall act as "Thanks for the Memory" (Ralph Rainger and Leo Robin 1938) is of Bob Hope's act and "Love in Bloom" (Rainger and Robin 1934) of Jack Benny's. "Niceness" sets up Dame Edna's stage and television shows, but it also announces Humphries as a music hall artiste and sets up his *oeuvre* as a binary discourse of word-things that are "common" and "nice."

According to Humphries, niceness is as neat (orderly) as two columns, as neat (pure) as two fingers of Johnny Walker, as neat (adroit) as his uncommon insights into language, human nature, performativity, and music hall. Humphries' list of things common and nice shows that his poetic of niceness is fixed in language: in binaries of colloquial and standard English, in the discourse of domesticity, in columnar lexicons, and in the comic song.

Table 1.1
Isn't What Is Not Nice Just a *Little* Bit c-o-m-m-o-n?

| COMMON | NICE |
|---|---|
| WASHHOUSE | LAUNDRY |
| YARD | LAWN |
| RUNNERS | SANDSHOES |
| HAM + BEEF SHOP | DELICATESSEN |
| VERANDAH | PORCH |
| SWEATER | JUMPER (PULLOVER) |
| BLOODNOSE | NOSE-BLEED |
| ~~DINNER~~ *TEA* | LUNCH (*DINNER*) |
| PICTURES | THEATRE |
| SMOKES | CIGARETTES |
| RUBBISH | GARBAGE |
| PASSAGE | HALL |
| LOLLIES | SWEETS (CONFECTIONARY) |
| ICE-CHEST | FRIDGE |
| CARPET SWEEPER | HOOVER |
| TO PULL THE CHAIN | TO FLUSH THE TOILET |
| KETTLE | TEA-POT |
| TILL | CASH REGISTER |
| FLY PAPER | MORTENE |
| MEAT SAFE | COOL CUPBOARD |
| SHOES (BOOTS) | FOOTWEAR |
| WRITING PAD | COMPENDIUM |
| STRIDES | SLACKS |
| TOGS | |
| BATHERS (TRUNKS) | COSTUME (BATHERS?) |
| STOVE | OVEN? |
| GOODIES | EGGS |
| CHOOKS | FOWLS |
| QUILT | BEDSPREAD |
| PAPER SHOP | NEWS AGENT |
| HAIR CUT | TRIM |
| STOCKINGS | LINGERIE |
| IN-LAWS | RELATIONS |
| BOARDING HOUSE | GUEST HOUSE |
| HOSE | SPRINKERS (SIC) |
| SITTING ROOM | LOUNGE |
| SLEEPOUT | SPARE ROOM |
| BRIQUETTE | MALLEE ROOT |
| SIDEWAY (DOWN) | DRIVE (UP) |
| FACE-WASHER | FLANNEL |
| PILLOW CASE | PILLOW SLIP |
| RADIO | WIRELESS |
| SIDEBOARD | ? |
| HOUSE | HOME |
| BEER | ALE |
| PHOTO | PAINTING OR "ORIGINAL" |
| SHOPPING LIST | ORDER |
| PRETTY | ATTRACTIVE |
| NEXT DOOR | NEIGHBOUR |
| CARPETS + LINO | FLOOR COVERINGS |
| SOLDIER | SERVICEMAN |
| PUDDING | DESSERT |
| SERVIETTE | NAPKIN |

*Note*: Humphries, "List," MS, 1987.202.512, Barry Humphries Collection, Performing Arts Museum, Victorian Arts Centre, Melbourne, 1–3. (All transcriptions, unless otherwise noted, are St Pierre's.)

"Niceness" fits into a paradigm of nice and bright comic songs that run through music hall and variety, and that have identified their singers as stage greats. And niceness, whether voiced in sentiment or in irony, has been a condition on the halls and in working- and middle-class societies where entertainment has been a human right. Gracie Fields' "Looking on the Bright Side" (1932), Bud Flanagan and Chesney Allen's "Nice People" (1937), and George Formby's "It's Turned Out Nice Again" (1941) anticipate Humphries' "Niceness" and point to the spirit of his comedy and to the disposition of his leading lady, Dame Edna, who teeters between the binaries of kindness and cruelty. And this is very much in the spirit of the halls, where "the misfortunes of others were from the first infant flickerings a cue for hearty laughter, as absurdity was piled on top of absurdity."[39] One thinks, of course, of Edna's birthright, her ability "to laugh at the misfortunes of others." Eric Idle's composition "Always Look on the Bright Side of Life" (1983) also acknowledges this oxymoronic music hall tradition of kind cruelty/cruel kindness. Niceness, the *National Post* (Toronto) has argued, may even become the dominant political ideology of the twenty-first century![40] In this regard, Dame Edna may be recognized as an ideologue even before she is canonized as a saint.

These excerpts show the nice (i.e., neat or tidy, in the manner of Tid, Humphries' first published character in the 1958 narrative, "A Novel Called Tid") connection between late music hall and/or variety songs of the 1930s and 1940s and Humphries' signature tune. Humphries' connection with Gracie Fields is evident. Her remark to the audience, "remember where you are," at the Holborn Empire before she sang "There's a Cabin in the Pines" is echoed in Dame Edna's signature rebuke to her audiences: "remember you're out" (as in the shows *Remember You're Out: A New Barry Humphries Event* [1999], *Dame Edna: The Royal Tour (The Show That Listens)* [1999–2001], and *A Night with Dame Edna (The Show That Cares)* [2002–03]). Humphries also draws on the cheery sentiment and the hard-nosed ironies of Fields, Flanagan and Allen, and Formby to fashion a paradox within which Dame Edna is able to cloak herself and with which her audiences may be thematized into her niceties as she enters the stage, eventually to confess, as she does in *Dame Edna's Work Experience* (1996): "I'm going to let you into a little secret. I've been here before. I have. I lived in Wigan in another life. Isn't that spooky? Are you getting goose bumps? I am. Yes, I was George Formby's mother! I was. I was." In contrast, in *The Adventures of Barry McKenzie* (1972), Edna's nephew, Barry McKenzie, in his patter to the audience at the Arts Factory before he performs the song "Old Pacific Sea," concedes, "I'm no George Formby." Of course Bazza is "no George Formby" because, according to Edna's genealogy, he would have to be Formby's cousin.

Table 1.2
The Niceties of Song and the Niceness of Dame Edna Everage

| Gracie Fields, "Looking on the Bright Side" (1932) | Flanagan and Allen, "Nice People" (1937) | George Formby, "It's Turned Out Nice Again" (1941) | Dame Edna Everage, "Niceness" (1978) |
|---|---|---|---|
| I'm looking on the bright side, Though today's all care and strife. | Nice people, With nice manners, But got no money at all. | Last night I said, when I went to bed, "It's turned out nice again." | Many people ask me my secret of success. Is it in the way I speak or the lovely way I dress? Is it poise or personality – what elusive little facet Let me help you put your finger on my single greatest asset? It's my niceness. I pride myself on my niceness. It's such a gift without price – to be nice even when you feel blue – 'cos I really care and I've come here to share my wonderful wonderful niceness with you. |

Edna's quip draws on more than a topical allusion to George Formby's birthplace. Given that George Formby, Sr, "the later George Formby's father – who, at that time was one of the biggest draws in the country,"[41] was a legendary performer on the halls, Dame Edna might be making an oblique confession to her liaison with a music hall great and her role in engendering an enduring stage genre.[42] Her relationship with George Formby, Sr, might even be seen as the foreplay leading up to *An Evening's Intercourse with Barry Humphries* (Regent Theatre, Sydney, 1981; Her Majesty's Theatre, Melbourne 1981; Theatre Royal, Drury Lane, London, 1982), a two-act show consisting of "Foreplay" and "Interruption." Such is the duration of music hall that the mood of niceness can accommodate even the forthright cynicism of Eric Idle, who, in his song "Always Look on the Bright Side of Life"

(1983), tips his hat to Gracie Fields yet also plays a game of ontological and mimetic tipcat in the lines "Life's a piece of shit / When you look at it." Anyone moved to ponder what life is when you do *not* look at it will have taken on the mood of music hall, as Humphries reveals his moody music hall identity but only when he does not look at his image in the mirror.

As Patrick White makes an anti-war argument in his 1984 speech "Wigan to Wagga" (1989), Humphries makes a pro-music hall argument by taking Edna Everage from Wagga Wagga to Wigan. Humphries may have set *Dame Edna's Work Experience* in a Wigan baked bean factory partly to express his esteem for George Formby, father and son, and partly also to acknowledge his indebtedness to Lancashire music hall performers generally, who, according to Dagmar Kift, were "drawn from amongst the local working population. Some of them might even have been home-weavers. Their songs not only drew on traditional folksongs but also dealt with town and factory life."[43] Thus, when Dame Edna joined the ranks of Lancashire baked beanery workers, Humphries lined up with Lancashire artistes and honoured northern traditions of the halls. He may also have set his show at the factory because, according to music hall and variety artiste Clarkson Rose, during the Second World War "ENSA did a wonderful job of work, not only for the troops and the workers in the factories, but for a great number of artistes."[44] Perhaps in his performative Humphries was primarily referencing ENSA performers in Edna's show.

In *More Please*, he makes several telling references to music hall as a formative influence in his life, especially through radio broadcasts during the Second World War. Here, early in the autobiography, his writing comes alive (like music hall performers on the stage), as in his description of a recording session of a local radio program of choral music that he attended with family:

There was a vaudeville interlude when two comedians called Edgley and Dawe capered before the microphone and a strange woman called Nellie Colley [sic] [Kolle], dressed in top hat and tails and smoking a pipe, sang a comic song called "Burlington Bertie." It was my first enticing glimpse of the Music Hall.[45]

Could Humphries have imagined that, forty years later, in 1984, he would again respond to this enticement when he appeared in the Royal Variety Performance, where Flanagan and Allen (1932), Vesta Tilley (1912), and nearly every great music hall performer had put on a show for royalty? Similarly, in his biography *Rowan Atkinson* (1999), Bruce Dessau describes the Royal Variety Show cast as "a rainbow coalition of comics that extended from Barry Humphries to Ronnie Corbett."[46] He must have been able to imagine it, to make it happen. This "interlude" was the prelude to his own stage career, which he has summarized in verse, with reference to his indifferent tenure with the Melbourne Theatre Company in the 1950s: "I couldn't learn my lines, you see, which wouldn't do at all, / So I was driven to a sordid life in the sleazy music hall."[47] No doubt Stanislavski would have approved such a driven actor, who could effect a career and document it with a hard irony.

## HUMPHRIES' LIFE EXPERIENCE AND MUSIC HALL

Humphries' autobiographical reminiscences on music hall tend to link up with his nostalgia for mutable pop culture, anticipating Sandy Stone's fixation on *objets trouvés* and his own remembrance of things past (i.e., things past their sell-by dates), from kitsch to heritage architecture:

There were humorous interludes on the radio: mostly records of pre-war British vaudeville comics like George Tilly, Sid Field, Cyril Fletcher, Jack Hulbert and Cecily [sic] Courtneidge and my favourite, Horace Kenny [sic]. I would lie there in the darkened room through measles, mumps, whooping cough and scarlet fever, with my calamine lotion and Vicks Vaporub, laughing at those wonderful old-fashioned jesters.[48]

*Film Fun* and its companion comic *Radio Fun* were filled with the adventures of popular British entertainers we knew little or nothing about in Australia: Arthur "Hello Playmates" Askey, the Western Brothers with their top hats and monocles, and Will Hay and Tommy Handley.[49]

The music hall artiste who has given his greatest character, Edna Everage, the "formulated phrase" (Eliot) "call me old-fashioned" here identifies "old-fashioned" as a mark of the halls. Perhaps Sandy Stone, as a boring monologist, does owe something to Horace Kenney, whose comedy turned on slow delivery, repetitive buildup, and gentle sentiment. Similarly, the Western Brothers may have been the first to inspire Humphries to sport a monocle. Kenney's role in *The Face in the Window* – from his skit "Almost a Film Star," which demands that, four times, he show his face in the window ("And every time I showed my face, somebody committed a murder")[50] – anticipates Humphries' mirror trick in *More Please*, his conceit, but also his methodology of life-writing (as in Patrick White's *Flaws in the Glass: A Self-Portrait* [1981]). By naming these comedians, Humphries also commemorates them and, by casting himself as audience, adds his own show name, then a nondescript "I," to a roster of players "working the halls" (in Peter Honri's phrase). And he hints that "the darkened room" is not just an infirmary and a playroom but also a kind of music hall of the mind.

Perhaps there was a meeting of music hall minds, of the order of Voss and Laura Trevelyan in Patrick White's *Voss* (1957), when in 1939 George

Robey opened in Melbourne. Although Humphries has always attributed the maxim "remember you're out" to his mother, his earliest music hall source may have been George Robey, who, like Gracie Fields after him, would chide his audiences with "remember where you are!" As a boy, Humphries saw a performance of the English "blue" comedian Tommy Trinder,[51] and some thirty years later he was inspired to cast him in his film *Bazza McKenzie Holds His Own* (1974).

At the beginning of his acting career, after playing Estragon in *Waiting for Godot* (Arrow Theatre, Melbourne, 1957; Independent Theatre, Sydney, 1958), a play whose music hall themes[52] he must have found compelling, and after his brief run in Donald Cotton's musical *The Demon Barber* (Lyric Opera House, Hammersmith, London, 1959), Humphries worked on finding roles in the West End. In *More Please*, when he writes about securing "a theatrical agent in Regent Street called Myrette Morven, who had once understudied Cecily [sic] Courtneidge,"[53] his pride seems to arise less from the theatrical agent herself than from his own link with the theatre. A music hall great from his childhood list, Cicely Courtneidge was also a fellow Australian (albeit a Sydney-sider), and, like Edna Everage (in 1974), she was to be made a dame (in 1972). That after this allusion Humphries should describe "the first stage show I ever saw in London … at the Metropolitan Music Hall"[54] seems wholly appropriate: a performer about to go on the halls, in a stage career that is partly an anachronism (given that today music hall is more a historical study than a current theatrical practice), witnessed a "positively final appearance" (in Alec Guinness's phrase [1999]), of music hall. After pouring a libation for a cast that included the great artistes Hetty King, G.H. Elliot, and Randolph Sutton, Humphries gives the eulogy for an art:

Soon after this performance shamrocks were painted on the fire curtain and after a brief Hibernian interlude, the theatre was given over to bingo and within a year it had been demolished. Thereafter, except for the Palace of Varieties in Leeds and some small theatres in seaside resorts, the Music Hall died.[55]

The lament here is evident not in peroration but in syntax, in Humphries' subtle metonymic transition from the Metropolitan Music Hall to Music Hall, where he seems to acknowledge the semantics of the art, *music hall* having always been both place and process. Humphries was the right person to eulogize music hall: his speech-acts have kept the place/process on the halls and have shown that *Muntu*,[56] that which is, can die yet continue to exist. Humphries himself has died on stage a few times (although usually in character), but his existence in the theatre seems assured; like Dame Edna, he is "the megastar who won't go away." Although in 1964 Clarkson Rose, a seasoned music hall performer in a position to know, could write, "today there is not a single music-hall left in London,"[57] he may not have realized that, in May 1963, a young performer had launched a British music hall career. That was when Barry Humphries performed material from *A Nice Night's Entertainment*, his 1962 Australian show, at Peter Cook's Establishment Club.

In his subsequent career, Humphries, rather than positioning himself behind a stand-up mike, has concealed Dame Edna's microphone in her wig. Given that microphones are associated with the death of music hall,[58] Humphries' concealment – one never knows whether the volume of Dame Edna's voice is due to electronic amplification or to the perfect formation of her lungs and larynx – might be seen as his sign to the audience, like a wink from Edna herself, that music hall lives on in variety and beyond. If Edna gives audiences a wink, then Craig Steppenwolf delivers a fierce dig in Humphries and Fitzgerald's script "Craig Steppenwolf: A Monologue for the Music-Hall" (1975), from the show *At Least You Can Say You've Seen It* (1974). In this show Steppenwolf, the parodically progressive teacher at West Camberwell High School, delivers a performative lament on the state of education (and, indirectly, on the halls) when, in his monologue, the halls have become school corridors and the "turns" refer to predatory people turning on each other.

Peter Leslie cites four more reasons for the death of music hall: (1) the cost of lavish productions; (2) the movement from star turns to ensemble productions; (3) the emphasis on nudity, at the cost of traditional acts; and (4) the movies.[59] Compare James Harding, who, in *George Robey and the Music Hall* (1996), cites two causes: (1) the movies and (2) the "respectability" that the first Royal Variety Performance, in 1912, imposed on "the spirit of the street" and "the spontaneous expression of low life."[60] Aristotle was a music hall muse. Clarkson Rose recounts how, at Edwardian seaside pierrot and minstrel revues, artistes and attendants, known in this capacity as "bottlers," would take up a monetary collection from the audience by passing round a bottle. The practice went by the rhyming slang to "rattle the Aristotle."[61] As a kind of by-the-seaside neo-Aristotelian, Humphries has managed to cheat the death of music hall through (1) embracing Dame Edna's majestic costumes; (2) his willingness to work with his supporting casts of musicians, dancers, and actors, notably Emily Perry (who plays Madge Allsop), and to engage his participatory audiences as theatrical ensembles; (3) posing as the nude centerfold of the November 1982 number of *Cleo* magazine; (4) his admirable career as a film actor, chiefly in character parts; and (5) his undoubtedly disrespectful appearance at the 1984 Royal Variety Performance, both as himself (performing a warm-up with Eric Sykes and Spike Milligan "in Crazy Gang style") and as Dame Edna Everage (in a "ninety-second spot").[62] Leslie argues that, by 1978, music hall performers had become anachronisms: "With all these ingredients of the classic music hall available, the form as a whole has nevertheless failed to reappear."[63] But I believe that Barry Humphries is music hall's lingering "form."

Writing in 1962, the poet John Betjeman, who was one of the first Britons to recognize the brilliance of Sandy Stone, seems to concur with me: "Barry Humphries is one who, I have no hesitation in saying, will become internationally famous, because he is an artist with words, imagination and mimicry who belongs to the great tradition of music hall and theatre."[64] Hamlet might have said, it is the words of St Pierre and Betjeman, together with all forms, moods, shapes of mirth, that can denote the "me" of Barry Humphries, the "me" whom he acknowledges in his second volume of autobiography, *My Life as Me* (2002). With his avuncular monocle, his old boy fringe, his charming smile, his dapper dress, and his assured swagger, he looks the very model of a major music hall performer.

## MUSIC HALL STYLE AND STRUCTURE IN HUMPHRIES' STAGE SHOWS

In style and structure, Barry Humphries' one-man stage shows, from *The Olympic Hostess* (1956), *A Nice Night's Entertainment* (1962), and his premier at the Establishment Club (1962) to *New Edna – The Spectacle* (1998), *Remember You're Out: A New Barry Humphries Event* (1999), *Dame Edna – The Royal Tour* (1998, 1999–2001), *A Night with Dame Edna (The Show That Cares)* (2002–03), and *A Night with Dame Edna (The Family Show)* (2003–04), recall music hall. And, for anyone with a long memory and a good historical sense, they *are* music hall. Humphries' first stage performance as Edna Everage on 13 December 1955 in the revue *Return Fare* (Union Theatre, Melbourne), and his performance in the two-handed skit "Edna Everage: Olympic Hostess" with Noel Ferrier in the revue *Tram Stop Ten* (Union Theatre, 1956), launched his music hall career, as did his three revues at the Phillip Street Theatre, Sydney: *Tram Stop Ten* (1956), *Mr and Mrs* (1956), and *Around the Loop* (1956–57). His performance of "Edna Everage: Olympic Hostess" in Melbourne may even recall, to music hall aficionados, Léon Volterra and Jacques-Charles' 1924 revue at the Casino de Paris, *La Revue Olympique*,[65] in that each show was a kind of fringe Olympic event showing up the Olympics spectacle.

Writing in 1971 (and again in 1986), Michael Kilgarriff observed, "The revival of this very popular form of entertainment continues unabated, but I am only too aware that Music Hall production *per se* remains at a sadly low level."[66] I am sure Kilgarriff's "*per se*" would give Humphries a chuckle, as is evidenced in his poem "Edna's Prayer for Our Time," which concludes: "And though my input be minute / When Thou my shortfall dost compute, / Pray let my daily print-out say / Thy servant was relevant per se."[67] But Kilgarriff's point is well taken: revival of interest in an art form, especially as a historical curiosity or as the focus of a retro trend, does not ensure its survival, not even as a cultural legacy. Still, Humphries has consistently performed music hall, a new time variety, at a merrily high level; and in many ways his performances do seem to follow the patter-patterns in Kilgarriff's *It Gives Me Great Pleasure: Production Guide and Chairman's Handbook for Old Time Music Hall* (rev. ed. 1986). Consider, for example, Kilgarriff's index of remarks for the music hall chairman and their parallels with Sir Les Patterson's own on-stage patter.

Since the character's emergence in 1975, Les Patterson has often been the chairman of Dame's Edna's one-woman shows, sometimes the chairman of a variety show of characters, and other times the chairman of his own one-man show (i.e., of a variety show or one-woman show that never quite shows up). He might even be seen as a performer like Sid Field, another person from young Barry's list of music hall favourites who, in revues like *Piccadilly Hay-ride* and *The Convict's Return*, would play multiple characters.[68] In Patter-son's case, all the characters are Sir Les himself, and the quick-changes involve the audience's fluctuations between attraction and revulsion.

In that he created Patterson partly to take revenge on the Granville RSL's unappreciative club secretary,[69] Humphries recalls Harry Tate (Ronald Hutchinson), George Robey (George Wade), and Marie Lloyd (Matilda Wood), all of whom took their sobriquets from familiar business names, and especially Bud Flanagan (Reuben Weintrop), who, as an act of revenge, appropriated the name of the sergeant he had suffered under during the First World War.[70] However vengeful, Les Patterson has always acted (and acted up) as compère. He appeared for the first time in a Humphries show as chairman in *Isn't It Pathetic at His Age* (1978), whose program promises "some up-front input from Les Patterson, hopefully with a view to intro-ducing THE YARTZ."[71] Here, as chairman, he shows up the Humphries players Roger A. Nunn, Lance Boyle, and Sandy Stone (in the first act) and Dame Edna Everage (in the second).

Patterson has appeared as music hall chairman (a role also known as "compère" and "president") in Humphries' show *Tears Before Bedtime* (Australian tour, 1983), then as *Back with a Vengeance* (Strand Theatre and Theatre Royal, Drury Lane, London 1987–88; and UK tour, 1989), where, simply by opening the performance, he practically stops the show. In *Tears before Bedtime* he "presents his Broad-based Package"[72] which leads into a variety show featuring Lance Boyle and Sandy Stone in the first act, and, after the intermission, Dame Edna Everage, lecturing on "Aspects of Perception." *Back with a Vengeance* has the same music hall structure but omits the skit by Lance Boyle, as if, somewhere between Australia and England, along the expatriate middle passage,[73] Chairman Les Patterson chose to pull it from the program in order to give greater prominence to his own shtick and more mirth to the audience. Consider, for example, how he phrases his introduction of the variety cast of *Back with a Vengeance*:

Table 1.3
The Archetypal Chairman and the Patter of Sir Les Patterson

| Kilgarriff's Riffs | Kilgarriff's Chairman's Patter | Sir Les Patterson's Patter |
|---|---|---|
| Introduction of Chairman by Himself | My name is – don't bother to stand, just nod, and I have the pleasure to be your Chairman for the evening. I come from a very aristocratic family as you can probably tell. My grandfather was a peer ... and grandmother had kidney trouble as well. (51) | Good evening, ladies and gentlemen. Good evening, one and all. Good evening. As you were. Permit me to introduce myself to you good people, if I may. My name is Les Patterson, and I have the honour to be the Australian Cultural Attaché to the Court of St. James. I also have the distinction of being the first official failure of the Betty Ford Foundation. (*Another Audience with Dame Edna* [ITV, 1989]) |
| | | Good evening, ladies and gentlemen. Good evening, one and all. Permit me ... Permit me to introduce myself to you good people, if I may. My name ... My name is Les Patterson. And if I may say so on this lovely Saturday night in London town, you're all looking pretty good. And if you think I'm looking good, let's hear you say, "You're looking good, Les." How am I looking, ladies and gentlemen? (*Dame Edna, Back with a Vengeance: The Second Coming* [1989]) |
| Pianist | He's just had his instrument tuned so he's feeling rather highly strung. Never mind, Maestro – we're all on your side ... so far. (58) | I think I know what all you women are staring at. I know. You're all looking at my p'nis', aren't you? Well there it is, ladies and gentlemen. There it is. Laurie. Ah, Laurie Holloway. My fine upstanding pianist. God love him. (*Les Patterson Has a Stand Up: Live and Rampant* [1996]) |
| Lady Pianist | Here is our Madame Maestro – I don't like to call her Maestress, somehow. (58) | Pull yourself together, anyway, will you, girls. I think I know what all you ladies are staring at. I know. You're all looking at my p'nis', aren't you? And there she is, ladies and gentlemen. There she is. Yair. My beautiful ... my lovely little pink pianist, Vicki Silver. She's lovely. (*Dame Edna, Back with a Vengeance: The Second Coming* [1989]) |
| Latecomers | Good evening, how nice of you to come. We did wait for you, but we thought we'd have the show first and eat afterwards. (60) | Hello, hello. A couple of latecomers, creeping in here. Very very nice to see you. Lovely couple. Just shove past. Fart in their faces. Why not? Serve the bastards right for being on time, eh? Oh, you haven't missed anything, son. We've just been filling in till you arrived. (*Dame Edna, Back with a Vengeance: The Second Coming* [1989]) |

Table 1.3
The Archetypal Chairman and the Patter of Sir Les Patterson (*Continued*)

| Kilgarriff's Riffs | Kilgarriff's Chairman's Patter | Sir Les Patterson's Patter |
|---|---|---|
| Introductions for Ladies | that pleasing personification of pulchritude. (76)<br><br>I exhort, nay, I entreat, nay, I *expect* you to stamp, whistle, applaud and huzza for Miss N! (77)<br><br>Here's a young lady we haven't seen for some time, and personally I'm delighted to see her back ... her front's not too bad, either. (79) | I want to introduce you people to a little lady who has done a good deal more than Les Patterson to put Australia on the map ... ladies and gentlemen, without any further adieu and with the best yet to come I'd like you to put your hands together for the Melbourne mother, megastar, and millionairess, yes, it's the caring and sharing Dame Edna Everage! (*Another Audience with Dame Edna* [ITV, 1989]) |
| Introductions for Ladies | Now we come to the climax of our entertainment this evening with the welcome appearance (or reappearance) of Miss N, and I am reliably informed that Miss N is no slouch when it comes to climaxes. (79) | Hello, darling. You come up here. I want you up here on stage. Come on. Come on. Encourage her, ladies and gentlemen. Come on. My former research assistant. God love you. Don't be nervous. You're nervous. Ain't she beautiful? We go back a long way, ladies and gentlemen. She used to say to me, "Les, you go back a long way." Only, only, her eyes were usually watering when she said that. (*Les Patterson Has a Stand Up* [1996]) |
| Late Laughs | Are you being interfered with, madam? If not, why don't you move down here – I'm sure this gentleman would oblige. (97) | What's so fuckin' funny about that? (*Les Patterson Has a Stand Up* [1996]) |
| Heckle-Stoppers | The last time I saw a mouth like that there was a hook in it. (102) | She isn't in the bloom of youth, And I must stay she's started looking it. The last time you saw a head like hers It probably had a hook in it. ("My Old Lady," *Dada Days: Mooonee Ponds Muse, Vol. 2* [1993])<br><br>There's a stoney-faced old sheila sitting over there. She's got a head on her like a half-sucked mango, ladies and gentlemen. Last time I saw a head like that it had a hook in it, I kid you not. I reckon when she was a kiddie they had to hang a chop round her neck just to get the dog to play with her. Nothing personal, madam, I assure you. (*Les Patterson Has a Stand Up: Live and Rampant* [1996]) |

*Note:* Kilgarriff, *It Gives Me Great Pleasure: Production Guide and Chairman's Handbook for Old Time Music Hall.*

Well, we got a great line-up of talent. First cab off the rank is Barry Humphries in an artistic cameo. Barry isn't a poofter, but he gives a pretty good impression of one. He'll be followed by DAME EDNA EVERAGE, ladies and gentlemen! No worries! Yes, and when the beautiful megastar from Melbourne, Australia, steps aforth these boards, I want you all to give her the clap she so richly deserves. I want you to put your hands together very warmly on her opening, if you will.

In these and other stage shows Les Patterson is literally an archetypal music hall chairman: he is the son of patter.

As compère, he is literally like a father to his audiences, a father who will never have the bad manners to "pass away very quietly in his sleep between the bar and the gents," as, in *Les Patterson Has a Stand-up: Live and Rampant*, he says of his own father. He is, as Peter Bailey observes of the music hall proprietor, "the big man with the big heart doing things in a big way, representing himself as both larger than life and as humanity itself."[74] Hardly a light comedian, Les, with his innuendo and outright lewdness, might be better categorized as a dark and heavy comedian or, in his role as a piss-artist, a red-nosed comedian. As a dark front-cloth comedian, Les should always take care to use comedogenic makeup because he is a comedo, a lecherous blackhead that deserves to be crushed. As Bazza himself says in his song "Washed Down the Gutter" and his poem "If It Was Raining Virgins," "Where is the girl who'll beg and screech / To squeeze me blackheads on the beach?"[75] Dame Edna, who has acknowledged German coloratura and lyric soprano Elisabeth Schwarzkopf as "Scandinavian Elizabeth Blackhead (as she suffers in translation),"[76] might accompany this squeeze play by singing George Robey's music hall standard "The Simple Pimple," with Humphries' artwork "Tullulah Blackhead" (which was first shown in 1953 at the Second Pan-Australasian Dada Exhibition, University of Melbourne) displayed in the background. Even in his surface meaning, in his blemishes, whether cosmetic or moral, Sir Les Patterson presses the traditional comedics of music hall.

Les has even been known to perform his own music hall variety act, as in *Les Patterson Has a Stand-up: Live and Rampant* and other one-man shows. In *The Dame Edna Christmas Experience* (ITV, 1987), to cite a dazzling example from television, he sings and dances to the Sammy Cahn and James Van Heusen song "You've Either Got or You Haven't Got Style,"[77] with Roger Moore and Dennis Healey, suitably outfitted in tuxedoes, straw boaters, and canes. He proves himself a song-and-dance man, albeit a dishevelled and grotesque one, related to the *lion comique* archetype of the halls in France as well as England: "the hard-drinking Victorian equivalent of a modern playboy, complete with waxed moustaches, cane, and silk hat or boater, derived from [George] Leybourne himself."[78] In all his performances Patterson is a latter-day *lion comique*: the "waxed moustaches" of his Victorian antecedent may have been replaced with the real thing, "a large upholstered phallus"[79] that slides so insistently along his inseam that it stretches the spectator's imagination (although not his/her credulity).[80] For example, Alison Solomon observes, with reference to *Thesmophoriasuzae*:

The phallus is the "big thing" that prevents thoroughly convincing imitation, that gets in the way of total transformation and thus leaves a gap between what's staged and what's said; it's what makes theatrical mimesis possible. The phony phallus, in other words, is Aristophanes' ironic tool.[81]

In the case of Patterson, of course, it is "the traveller's [ironic] tool" and it is the eye (the "one-eyed trouser snake") through which the audience comes to recognize Humphries' irony by allowing us to see through Les, through his trousers to his phallus (which Marcel Duchamp might well have called his "*objet dard*")[82] as well as through his shtick. In fact, Humphries does acknowledge in Les "the persisting influence of Aristophanes' *Lysistrata*."[83]

Whenever Patterson appears on stage, whether as chairman or as performer, tilting a glass of Johnny Walker or Chardonnay, he is pouring a libation to the old music hall, whose audiences would drink and eat during performances, even as part of the performances. Peter Leslie notes, for example, that "contemporary prints of the Canterbury, the Oxford and other London music halls show flying-trapeze, high-wire and ladder acts performing without nets immediately above the unconcerned heads of diners seated in rows."[84] In his own tight way, Les teeters over the heads of his wondering audience, walking a tightrope between vulgarity and bad taste, with no netting to protect them should his spittle spray or his dribble drop. Even a poster for his only star turn in the cinema, *Les Patterson Saves the World* (1987), shows Patterson with an impossibly long (and seminal) gob of spit dangling from his lip, as though ready to drop onto the audience.

Like the music hall "performer who came on stage *threatening* to sing or play (Jack Benny, Jimmy Durante, Vic Oliver, Jimmy Wheeler, Arthur Haynes), only to interrupt himself continually with a flood of stories and anecdotes until he had time for nothing but one short number before his exit";[85] or like Ted Ray with his violin-playing; or George Robey as the German music professor who would fastidiously look over the many musical instruments strewn around the stage, threatening to play every one of them, until "finally he stopped in front of a humble triangle, gave it few timid taps ... and the act was over";[86] Les Patterson threatens to spit on his audience, to excrete other bodily substances on them, to rub up against them with his soiled clothing, even to come to climax over their heads, not to mention spill his drink on them, all before he bursts into comic song-and-dance.

He plays (and plays out) the music hall chairman, "a dignitary who, florid, heavily diamond-pinned, wearing an evening suit maculate with beer stains and cigar ash, sat at his own table and introduced the turns."[87] However distantly, Les is related also to the *chansonniers* of French music hall, performing balladeers who "typified ... smart and yet democratic, sophisticated yet iconoclastic chic ... replete with scabrous allusions, 'in' jokes and the latest argot."[88] He may recall also the British music hall comedian and juggler Griff (Henry Hadden Griffiths), who in the films *Pathetone 53* (1931) and *Pathetone 74* (1931) demonstrated his specialty as a "bubble blower."[89] In Les Patterson, Humphries also spits out his own Dada spirit, for "Dada art learned to spit in the eye; the new vision was to be clarified by violence."[90] From Les, expectoration is an essential part of Humphries' stagecraft; the violence of Patterson's *sexpectoration* conceives only ideas and, in them, new visions of cartoon character prophecy, all through an eye to dramatic irony.

Patterson is also *un diseur*, a monologist, and a singer who tends to speak his lines, as with recitative in opera. (Somebody, I think, should write an opera about Les and Gwen Patterson, entitled *Infidelio!*) Similarly, in *Barry Humphries' Treasury of Australian Kitsch* (1980), Humphries designates Edna as *diseuse* (and, in a sense, as Les Patterson's music hall counterpart) in his caption to Brack's painting of her: "the Melbourne-based Actress and *Diseuse* Dame Edna Everage executed in 1969 by John Brack (1920–   )."[91] But Les Patterson's speech is also song, patter: the tap of a cane, the tip of a top hat. His words have pitch and swagger. They are an opera that, as a music hall chairman, he speaks for other performers and that, as a writer (of "Mr Les Patterson's Historic Address to the British" [1977], *Les Patterson's Australia* [1978] and *The Traveller's Tool* [1985]), he records for posterity since, anticipating the THX slogan, he is always aware the audience is listening.

If Sir Les Patterson is music hall chairman, *lion comique*, and *diseur*, then Dame Edna Everage is the headliner of the show, the megastar of comediennes, and the *meneuse de revue*, who holds the show together with her patter and songs.[92] She is the show-leader, paradoxically the leader of, to all appearances, an anarchistic stage. From her earliest performances at the back of the bus in Ray Lawler's touring company of *Twelfth Night*[93] to her recent triumphant run on Broadway in *Dame Edna – The Royal Tour* (1999–2000), and the show's 2000–01 North American tour,[94] Edna Everage has distinguished herself as the headliner of Barry Humphries' bill of characters. She is his most serviceable, charismatic, memorable, and celebrated role; but she is also his most chilling creation, a creature whose life and whose fame sometimes seem to have taken over his own – "It was almost as though she were developing a life of her own, over which I had little, if any, control"[95] – to the point where she can even dismiss him, as an inept, even criminal, (mis)manager. This madness is part of Humphries' Stanislavskian method of not coming out of character (to which John Lahr attests [1992]), but it is also the folly of his estimable human comedy, in which Edna is *une meneuse* who marginalizes everyone else in a state of anarchy, of lawless rebellion against her authority.

With her songs and her patter she gives focus and unity to the show as performative, and she embraces the microcosm of her audience, her public, holding back the forces of anarchy, ridiculing class divisions, all with an air of superiority. Whether or not she has a microphone concealed in her wig, Dame Edna knows how to project her voice to the last row in the gallery, to the *poulailler*,[96] by giving her sincerest attention to all her "paupers," "in strict proportion to the amount that you have paid. Good bye!" as she says in *Back with a Vengeance*, and as she has said in her many stage shows since. Dame Edna, it might be said, is the only hen in the *poulailler*. When she laughs, for instance, she does have a tendency to cluck. In Episode 6 of *The Dame Edna Experience*, first series (1987), sporting tawny spectacles, wearing a lemon frock trimmed with saffron feathers, and with her beaky nose, she does look remarkably like a bird. In this ornithological guise, Humphries can be seen as anticipating Mark McKinney's Chicken Lady character in *Kids in the Hall* (CBC, HBO 1989–94).[97]

Michael Kilgarriff's *It Gives Me Great Pleasure: Production Guide and Chairman's Handbook for Old Time Music Hall* hints at Dame Edna's taking her chair as music hall *meneuse* by kicking it out from under Les.

In all her stage performances, Dame Edna Everage is *une meneuse de revue*, in the company of *les grandes verticales* on the halls such as Mistinguett, Damia, Bernhardt, Vesta Victoria, Fanny Fields, and Gracie Fields as well as early BBC radio revue artistes like Anona Winn (who had played musical comedy in Melbourne and was the first artiste to have broadcast on Australian radio), Janet Joye (the comedienne-mimic known as "the girl with a hundred personalities"), and Cecil Dixon (a pianist, singer, and radio pioneer known popularly as "Aunt Sophie," perhaps a [cor]relative of Aunt Edna, as the character was popularly known in her early days, and as Clive James still refers to her). And then there are music hall and variety performers such as Beryl Reid, who knew how to charm the crowd, and even "smart girls" like the singers Vera Lynn and Deanna Durbin (whose real name, Edna Mae Durbin, suggests a possible relationship with Edna May Beazley).[98] Indeed, Humphries acknowledges Lynn and Durbin in "War Savings Street Song" (1961), which he performed for his BBC show *The Barry Humphries Scandals* (1970) "as Edna impersonating Vera Lynn":[99] "Hardship, privation, we knew thy names / In kitchen and shop suburban, / But it freed us from care / When we heard on the air / Vera Lynn and Deanna Durbin."

In the tradition of these performers, Edna engenders the technique of the music hall chairman, notably her offsider Sir Leslie Colin Patterson, and walks over the chairman to speak as the chairwoman. She is what Peter Bailey terms an "independent music hall proprietor,"

Table 1.4
Dame Edna Everage Takes Her Chair as Meneuse

| Kilgarriff's Riffs | Kilgarriff's Chairman's Patter | Edna Takes the Chair as Meneuse |
|---|---|---|
| Latecomers | Good evening, how nice of you to come. We did wait for you, but we thought we'd have the show first and eat afterwards. (60) | You're gorgeous, Betty. Thank you for sharing. You're going to love Betty when she's on stage in a minute. You are. She's lovely. She's gone pink now. She's ... Not yet, Betty, but soo-oon. So soon that, if I were you, I'd start tensing up now, darling. But you wouldn't be alone, Betty. No. Phillip and Sarah will be on this stage, our latecomers writing their essays "Why We Were Late." (*Dame Edna, Back with a Vengeance: The Second Coming* [1989]) |
| Introductions for Ladies | Now we come to the climax of our entertainment this evening with the welcome appearance (or reappearance) of Miss N, and I am reliably informed that Miss N is no slouch when it comes to climaxes. (79) | I call it the E-spot. It is the Edna-spot. It's that little sensitive zone that responds to me, and to me alone. But amongst the avalanche of letters that came to me was one from a little old couple, who watch TV all the time. They said to me that they love TV comedy. But they said the problem is that the husband laughs at Norman Wisdom and the wife at Charlie Drake. They were insane, as a matter of fact. But they, bless their little hearts, but they said, when they saw my show for the first time in their married life, they achieved simultaneous paroxysms. They did. Though that's very thrilling and wonderfully gratifying for me ... but there's only one person on this planet who doesn't seem to have an E-spot, and that is Madge Allsop, my old friend and bridesmaid. (*The Dame Edna Experience*, series 2.2 [1989]) |
|  |  | Look at that smile on her [Madge Allsop's] face. Can you see it? Look at that smirk. I know why she's smiling. I can read this woman like a book. She must have had an intimate body search before she came in here, probably the most comprehensive body search since her honeymoon. (*Dame Edna's Work Experience* [1997]) |
| No Laughs | It may not be funny, but by the lord Harry – it's British! (98) | Why must you always be funny? Why can't you be like other Australian comedians? (*Dame Edna, Back with a Vengeance: The Second Coming* [1989]) |

Table 1.4
Dame Edna Everage Takes Her Chair as Meneuse (*Continued*)

| Kilgarriff's Riffs | Kilgarriff's Chairman's Patter | Edna Takes the Chair as Meneuse |
|---|---|---|
| Heckle-Stoppers | Now I remember you – ten years ago at the (local) Theatre ... I remember the dress. (104) | Have a look at Anne later. Have a peak at her. This woman has saved a fortune on clothes. I don't think I have seen a woman recently who has saved more on clothes than Anne. What is it, darling, a sleeping bag of some kind? It's a lovely blue, though. And it's warm, is it, Anne? I think you're wise to dress for warmth, rather than appearance. I think you are. (*Dame Edna, Back with a Vengeance: The Second Coming* [1989]) |

a liberal populist, believing in the natural merits of the open market and competitive self-advancement, yet claiming an unselfish dedication to [her] public through lavish personal service. It was an effective role, not only as a source of esteem, but as a means of control.[100]

Undoubtedly, Dame Edna holds her public in esteem, like a publican (the historical precursor of the musical hall proprietor),[101] but she also maintains severe control over her audiences, with her sharp tongue, her erratic body language, her admonitory stare, and her peremptory silence. She is always the first to speak, and hers is *vox populi*, the voice of a populist performer who can represent the people because she commands the stage and because, like Les Patterson, she is humanity.

The most immediate antecedents of the theatrical music hall are to be found in nineteenth-century English public houses when they began to provide musical entertainment for paid admission and when, in the role of "president" or "chairman," the publican began to preside over the acts and to interact with the pub patrons. The legends of music hall outline two stages of development from public house to theatre. One legend cites the publican William Rhodes, who, by the 1820s,

had taken over the disreputable Cyder Cellars in nearby Maiden Lane and developed the role of "president" or "chairman" during the entertainment. In both places he acted as master of ceremonies to introduce the performers, heckled and was heckled by the noisier customers, and added, to the succession of singers he offered, sketches, conjuring acts, and a seemly precursor of striptease entitled "plastic poses."[102]

The other legend concerns Charles Morton and Canterbury Hall:

In 1852, he re-opened it, much rebuilt and improved, and presented a higher quality of entertainment; it was the first true music hall in the style that was to become widespread. He provided a high quality of refreshment and entertainment – he also ran a book on races until this practice was made illegal in 1853 – and he gradually introduced the idea that ladies might come to a music hall. This of course meant a toning-down of the bawdier aspects of the entertainment.[103]

But the current music hall legend is Dame Edna Everage herself, whose stage act is indebted to Rhodes's strategy of implicating the audience in the act and, of course, to Morton's decision to admit women to the stage.

Dame Edna is also in debt to Patterson, who, when he took the stage of *Housewife-Superstar!!* (1976), his first major show, by making his entrance through the audience,[104] was following the example she had set with her own stage entrances in *Just a Show* (1968, 1969): she "would enter shrilly from the back of the stalls, an ordinary member of the audience wishing to address publicly several popular misconceptions about the Australian way of life."[105] Dame Edna's give-and-take with her audiences (even though it is mostly take) is the singular feature of her music hall performative, especially as it ends with some members of the audience coming up on stage and with Edna going into the audience, sometimes bodily, and always in the body of her gladioli. Her "gladdie song" has changed over the years, but her sung-to-the-tune-of versions have referenced both "Daisy Bell, or A Bicycle Built for Two" (1892) (composed by Harry Dacre and figuring on Peter Leslie's top-100 list of music hall songs) and "I've Got a Loverly Bunch of Cocoanuts" (1944) (composed by Fred Heatherton and which American entertainer Merv Griffin popularized as a single and recorded with Arthur Treacher[106] on their LP *'Alf & 'Alf: Songs of the British Music Hall* [1966]).

Another important feature of Humphries' music hall performative is his use of cinema: slides in *A Nice Night's Entertainment* (1962); a home movie in *Excuse I: Another Nice Night's Entertainment* (1965); Bruce Beresford's art-house film parodies in *Just a Show* (1968, 1969) and *At Least You Can Say You've Seen It* (1974); and, most recently, documentary film in *Dame Edna – The Royal Tour (An Appropriate Show)* (1998), *Dame Edna – The Royal Tour (The Show That Listens)* (1999–2001), and *A Night with Dame Edna (The Show That Cares)* (2002–03). In *More Please* Humphries acknowledges the functional aspect of the cinematic: "I had always wanted to include short films in my solo shows, both to give me a rest and a chance to transform myself into Edna or some other character who required an elaborate makeup or costume change."[107] The film montage that opened *The Royal Tour* and *A Night with Dame Edna* served an additional function, that of introducing the somewhat uninitiated American audience to Barry Humphries' forty-five-year career (not to mention Madge Allsop's signing skills). The cinema in Humphries' shows recalls the "shadow theatre" that accompanied and acted out Jules Jouy's song performances at the Chat Noir, a late nineteenth-century Paris music hall theatre that was modelled on Coal Hole, another of William Rhodes' chairmanned pubs in London. The tableaux of the Paris music hall, which were directed at women in the audience, included "Fashion through the Ages": [108] this screen complement to the stage act calls to mind Humphries' exhibitions at the Performing Arts Museum at the Victorian Arts Centre in Melbourne: *The Fashion Diary of a Victorian Housewife* (1983), *A Peep in Dame Edna's Closet* (1986), and *Dame Edna's Frock-a-Thon* (1999),[109] fashion shows that Humphries seems to have anticipated in his retort to Ned Sherrin in the 1980 *Audience with Dame Edna* (see Appendix 2). In their 2000 North American tour, the Kids in the Hall preceded their performance with a video show on multiple screens, summarizing the troupe's lives and careers; then the Kids entered the stage from behind the screens, appearing first as shadow puppets, as at the Chat Noir. Like Barry Humphries, the Kids in the Hall are legitimate new generation music hall stars. And, like him, and many others on the halls, they are known to have crossed the gender line.

In introducing her composition "I'm Only a Faded Rose," comedienne Anna Russell jokes about music hall songs: "Now these songs are either frantically jolly, or extremely dismal. Tonight we're going to hear a dismal one. And these songs are frequently sung by female impersonators, and vice versa. But of course in England this is considered extremely traditional."[110] Barry Humphries is part of this noble tradition of cross-dressing in music hall song and comedy, which extends from Aristophanes, who in *Thesmophoriasuzae* "presents femininity as a set of effects; suggesting that femininity does not require a woman's body,"[111] through Shakespeare's *As You Like It* and Sarah Bernhardt's *Hamlet*, right up to, but not quite touching (for categorical, not homophobic, reasons) the drag queen tradition of cross-dressing[112] (although it too is marked by performativity). Humphries lines up, on the male-femaling side, with such music hall greats as Douglas Byng, Barbette, George Robey, G.S. Melvin, Tom Wootwell, Dan Leno, Will Evans, and Clarkson Rose; on the female-maling side he lines up with Ella Shields, Vesta Tilley, Bessie Bonehill, Gertie Gitana, Sarah Bernhardt, Fanny Robina, Millie Hylton, and Hetty King. During the 1950s and 1960s, Barry Humphries, as Edna Everage, did a good imitation of a pantomime dame in search of a pantomime, in contradistinction to English comedian Eddie Izzard ("I'm a male transvestite, and I fancy women")[113] and to Douglas Coupland's character Dagmar in *Generation X* ("Dag says he's a lesbian trapped inside a man's body. Figure *that* out").[114] But since the 1960s, and particularly since Edna's elevation to damehood in the film *Barry McKenzie Holds His Own* (1974), Humphries has refined his vocal skills (from falsetto, "a high-pitched squeak,"[115] to distinctive voice-print) and upscaled his makeup and costuming to turn Dame Edna Everage into an autonomous character, as much a person as Humphries is a character, showing up in *Back with a Vengeance* and Edna's life-telling *My Gorgeous Life: An Adventure* (1989).

Working within the traditions of the pantomime dame and of cross-dressing, Humphries engages Dame Edna Everage in a saturnalia of performance, gendericity, and merriment; a carnivalesque of classlessness, clothing, and comestibles in which Les Patterson, Barry McKenzie, and others also partake, turning the "establishment" quite upside down.

The mythology of the celebration contains the inversion of daily life in its development: feast, binge, drunkenness, dissolute ingestion of food, and regurgitation all demonstrate that it is not simply a matter of getting unusual pleasures but of pushing them to their very limit. Exchanges, undersides: partners cross-breeding, borrowing the forbidden other's clothes – transvestites, masks, and music at a different tempo signifying the break with the tempo of work.[116]

As a music hall artiste, speech actor, and writer, Barry Humphries breaks with his audiences: he distances himself from them through *mise en scène* but he also joins in with them, in the asylum of theatre, as though breaking bread with them. He surrounds them with his orality, and its shadow, textuality. As Marie Maclean observes, "The carnivalesque text, such as *Ulysses* or *Ubu Roi*, permits the ordering of disorder, the inclusion of the excluded, the eruption of the repressed."[117] Similarly, Humphries orders a disordered crowd into an audience, assigning them seats in rows (even relying on particular seat numbers to target Dame Edna's victims); he includes marginalized people ("paupers") in his audience; and he provokes eruptive applause and laughter. He takes his audiences out of the constructs "time," "place," and "work" and introduces them to the principles of play (which falls either side of the interval), the stage (which is a fluid space and a kind of utopia), and entertainment (for audiences of ladies and gentlemen, people who do not need to work for a living, at least for the duration of the entertainment).

In these regards, Humphries creates his own "mythology," or mythic system, his own storytelling, complete with supernatural and suprahuman beings: a goddess (Dame Edna), a demon (Sir Les), a sage (Sandy Stone), a *naïf* (Barry McKenzie), a fool (Laugh), an agent (managerial Barry Humphries), and a healer (authorial Barry Humphries), all in a supernatural setting (Australia), like Eden or Olympus, from which the mythic players can be cast out (exile and death) and into which they can be granted (re)admittance (home and life). The Humphries *muthos* comprises everything he has uttered by mouth (*omnis*, by mouth), whether as a music hall artiste on the stage or as a writer of monologues, songs, poems, articles, and books. Humphries uses his *muthos* (1) to explain the principles of human nature, from Sandy Stone's cheery resignation, to Edna Everage's sharp tongue, to Les Patterson's lurid leer, to the audience's shock and joy; and (2) to tell a memorable story of Australia (including his own love story of Melbourne) and to bring an efficacious healing laughter to audiences, old-fashioned laughter that still peals in the cultural memory of the halls and whose imprint can be found in Humphries' books.

As a music hall impresario books acts to delight audiences, so Barry Humphries writes books, all of them facsimiles of his life on the halls, to bring healing delight to his readers but also to document music hall and to turn music hall into documents. Documentary music hall is a place for Humphries to continue performing his stage shows after his run has come to an end, should the unthinkable (retirement or death) ever happen, and a fluid theatrical space that might be filled again should singers, actors, dancers, musicians, comedians, jugglers, ventriloquists, acrobats, clowns, impersonators, magicians, hypnotists, filmmakers, or mimics, including pantomime dames, ever wish to work the halls and charm the crowd.

Dame Edna Everage, Sir Leslie Colin Patterson, and Sandy Stone are durable and enduring characters. But Barry Humphries is an inimitable and timeless music hall artiste, a performer never to be repeated, whose name deserves to be uttered reverently not only with those of Beatrice Lillie, Douglas Byng, and Patrick White (as in Humphries' poem "Threnody for Patrick White") but also with those of Max Miller, Charlie Chaplin, Gracie Fields, Beryl Reid, George Formby (Sr and Jr), Bud Flanagan, Chesney Allen, Elsie Waters, Doris Waters, Michael Flanders, Donald Swann, and Eric Idle. Peter Nichols has acknowledged Humphries as "the heir to Max Miller's territory, but his eavesdropping androgyny gives him the edge,"[118] and Clive James has observed how he tilts his hat "at an angle reminiscent of Aristide Bruant."[119] John Lahr has gone so far as to say that "Humphries has even talked of the feeling of 'allegiance to the fellowship of music-hall artistes,' but his articulacy separates him from the old-timers whose glorious tradition he is carrying almost single-handed into the twenty-first century."[120] Finally, Humphries has equated himself with "stage performers, stage artistes and vaudeville personages."[121] Whenever he utters his *muthos*, whether on stage, on disc, in print, or off the cuff, music hall seems to answer him. In his bizarre stage, recording, and literary career of kidding around, he has distinguished himself as Kid on the Halls.

But the most telling (i.e., diegetic) signifier that Humphries has paid his music hall dues is his having sung, in the unmistakable cackle of Sandy Stone and in the style of an 1890s showman (the *fin de siècle* is, after all, his preferred artistic period), the Allie Wrubel and Ray Gilbert Disney classic "Zip-A-Dee-Doo-Dah" (from the film *Song of the South* [1946]) on his LP *Barry Humphries at Carnegie Hall in First Day Covers: A Philharmonic Philateria* (1972). The most showing (i.e., mimetic) signifier of his music hall status is to be found in some of Dame Edna's costumes. To publicize a 1917 performance of his ballet *Parade* (1919), Jean Cocteau arranged for music hall artistes and chairmen to perform on the sidewalk outside, enticing patrons into the theatre. In the show itself, to which Erik Satie, Sergei Diaghilev, and Pablo Picasso also contributed, Picasso had designed a fusing of costumes and sets: "Moving towards a totally plastique conception of the stage, he gave the set a new active role by building it into the characters."[122] Similarly, in the 1917 productions of Guillaume Apollinaire's play *Les Mamelles de Tirésias* (1924), "Sets and costumes often merged, with the actor carrying both as one on his back."[123] Barry Humphries may well have drawn on the *mise en scènes* of Cocteau and Picasso in *Parade* and Apollinaire in *Les Mamelles* for his costumes for Dame Edna Everage.

Consider the glorious bonnet (designed by Lorraine McKee) in the form of the Sydney Opera House, which Dame Edna wore to Royal Ascot, an event documented in *Dame Edna's Coffee Table Book* (1976), and her frock (designed by Stephen Adnitt) in the form of a stone house in the Georgian style, complete with a roof, a chimney, windows, and (at Edna's "opening") a door, which she wore in the television show *Dame Edna's Neighbourhood Watch* (1992). Dame Edna is a Picasso model, Barry Humphries a successor to Cocteau and Apollinaire. As music hall artistes, Everage and Humphries form an enduring double act within the arch(itectural) tradition of Dada theatre. But even though his theatrical career began in 1955 at the back of the bus with Edna Mae Beazley, who has never since left his side, his literary career began a little later, in 1958, with the story "A Novel Called Tid." Then Humphries learned to be alone with paper and ink, and then he found that his music hall imagination could be put to good use in print.

# 2

# It All Begins with Bizarre:
# Barry Humphries Makes Print

La pensée se fait dans la bouche.

> – Tristan Tzara, *La Vie des lettres*

You know what thought did? He thought he did!

> – Salopean proverb

"What am I going to do, Poll? It's bizarre."
> – Kenneth Grocock in Barry Humphries, *Women in the Background*

If you want people to listen, entertain them.
> – Ben Wicks, *Master of None: The Story of Me Life*

## WHEN YOU BEGIN THE BIZARRE

When Barry Humphries published his "youthful folly"[1] *Bizarre* (1965), a heterodox compilation of stories and pictures about eccentrics, freaks, aberrations, and monstrosities – Clive James called it "a freak show that you had to be a pathologist to find funny"[2] – he gave notice, to anyone willing to take notice, that he was a Dada prankster and a bookmaker, less like Charles Morton at Canterbury Hall than like William Burroughs, Gertrude Stein, bill bissett, Marcel Duchamp, Salvador Dali, and others for whom the propositions *écrire des livres* and *faire des farces* ("to write books" and "to play tricks") are often synonymous. But *Bizarre* was also a more sober absurdity, a first venture in free speech and academic freedom that Humphries would almost lose: (1) when the book was banned from an Australian public library;[3] (2) when the magazine *Private Eye* was banned throughout Australia because the two Barrys' language in *Barry McKenzie* was deemed obscene[4] (or, as Les Patterson puts it in his preface to *The Complete Barry McKenzie*, "for gratuitous smut and uncalled-for lingo");[5]

and (3) when Bruce Beresford's film *The Adventures of Barry McKenzie* (1972) was banned in New Zealand.[6] That in the new edition (2000) of his first book, *Obscenity, Blasphemy, Sedition: The Rise and Fall of Literary Censorship in Australia* (1962), Peter Coleman should not update his study to recount Humphries' struggles against Australian censorship seems a slight against friendship.

*Bizarre* sets a pattern for Humphries' published work over the next thirty-eight years. His books are extensions of his stage acts: they are speech-acts that stage readers as slow-moving audiences whose physical responses (such as watching, listening, moving, thinking, speaking, singing, laughing, and applauding) are acted out in their imaginations. In the act of reading *Bizarre*, which consists of words and graphics (consisting of photographs, paintings, and drawings [consisting of illustrations and cartoons {consisting of caricatures and parodies}]), all in an inventive Dadaist *mise en abîme*, the audience, in shocked amazement, realizes it is watching a sign show, it is doing semiotics, it is ([{}])ing. ([{}]) is a Saussurean sign that signifies that the members of the audience are in the midst of a farce, the absurd situation of holding and reading a book.

Even the book's packaging, depicting "Lionel, the 'Dog-man,'"[7] a hypertrichotic circus turn, and Humphries' first encounter with the *lion comique* archetype (positioned under the word BIZARRE, printed frontward on the front book jacket and backward on the back jacket) is a Dada turn, one that Francis M. Naumann also picks up on in the design (by studio blue, Chicago) of the dust jacket of his *Marcel Duchamp: The Art of Making Art in the Age of Mechanical Reproduction* (1999). For Humphries' *trompe l'oeil* to work, the reader must turn the book not temporally (i.e., clockwise, left-to-right, or counterclockwise, right-to-left, which would appear to be the usual ways of handling a book front-to-back) but spatially, top-to-bottom (towards the reader) or bottom-to-top (away from the reader). This Dada turn, and also early show turn, exposes the reader to the shock of the obverse (or verso), calling into question the nature of the book as cultural artifact and calling out of question the bizarre issue of otherness. The effect is continued on the title page, which depicts two homosocial young men (like the "two chatty Australian androgynes"[8] in his Dada sketch "Jim and Jim"), whose eyes are focused elsewhere (like Bazza McKenzie, who, in the poem and the song "Washed Down the Gutter," confesses "it isn't that I'm all that many inches / Short of Casanovas I've seen underneath the showers"),[9] reading a book that features the word BIZARRE written backwards, as if in a mirror (like the mirror Humphries looks into in "Alzheimer Remembers" and, recently, "as in the hall of mirrors at the fairground").[10]

In his introduction to *Bizarre*, which he playfully calls "A Note of Exclamation," Humphries, with an irony that anticipates Dame Edna's having to remind snickering guests and audiences "this is a family show," prepares his readers for "a family book, and one which we confidently expect will stand on every shelf between *Pears Encyclopedia* and *Mrs Beeton.*"[11] As a show turn, *Bizarre* stands less on the bookshelf than on the boards of music hall, setting up an interrelation of systems: at once a music hall performance and a literary and picture show of *bizarrerie*.

[Yury] Tynyanov sees the various systems, at a given moment of history, as standing at relatively fixed distances from each other. Relationships between the most distant ones are therefore mediated by the intervening systems, particularly by those standing closest to the literary system itself, namely the system of "everyday life," and its own sub-systems of verbal expression. Thus, for instance, a society in which letter-writing is a particularly absorbing and intrinsically interesting activity offers a unique type of verbal raw material which under given circumstances was absorbed into the literary system in the form of the letter-novel.[12]

In *Bizarre*, Humphries sets up his very own "prison-house" of voices and images, positing the book as a system that intervenes between two *grotesqueries*: the curious entertainments of the halls and the lurid entertainments of the freak show, the circus, and the carnival side show but also, and more emphatically, contemporary culture's show of voyeuristic fascination with everything from genocide and mass and serial murder to hand transplants, breast and penile implants, and the separation of conjoined twins.

Canadian director David Cronenberg has made graphic this voyeuristic fascination with misfortune – compare Dame Edna's confessions to her congenital gift, "the ability to laugh at the misfortunes of others" – in his film *Crash* (1996), based on J.G. Ballard's novel (1973). Thus, a culture that regards freak shows as "a particularly absorbing and intrinsically interesting activity" produces a discourse and taxonomy of the grotesque, "a unique type of verbal raw material which under given circumstances was absorbed into the literary system" that Humphries elected to call *Bizarre*. Charges that the book was obscene have proven to be self-accusatory, exposing culture itself as bizarre because of its obsession with *grotesquerie*. Subverting the construct "book," Humphries created circumstances that allowed Australians to break out of "the prison-house of language" – a prison house consisting not only of discourses of the grotesque but also of colonial and standard English. His other early publications are similarly circumstantial, provocative, and liberatory.

At the turn of the nineteenth century, at the height of the art form, *grotesquerie* was quite characteristic of music hall. Lois Rutherford records that, in 1899, thirty-five of 1,496 music hall acts in England were "grotesques/eccentrics."[13] If the category of music hall *grotesquerie* is expanded to include specialty and acrobatic acts and male and female impersonators,[14] then, again according to Rutherford, 553 of 1,486 acts, or 37 percent, could be classed as grotesques of the type found in Humphries' *Bizarre*. By constructing his book as an installation, Humphries acted as a mediator between *fin de siècle* music hall entertainment and twentieth-century *grotesquerie*; the fascination with circus freak shows, notably the genocidal atrocities of the Second World War; and the amorphous brutality of the deformed imagination, as evidenced in the movement to censor and to ban *Bizarre*.

Ignoring his detractors, in his "Note of Exclamation" Humphries alludes to a cross-cultural "delight in folly and a profound pleasure in the presence of the marvellous and the gruesome" and calls for a "return to the dandia-cal and bizarre conjectures of long whiles agone."[15] As well as spirited de-scriptions of Humphries' compilation of data in *Bizarre*, these statements hint at some of the principles of his stagecraft and his poetic: the "delight" he gives his audiences; the "folly" he exposes in them; his own sartorial and aesthetic status as a dandy (a dandy fellow, a dandy in the elegant fop-pish tradition of Oscar Wilde, and a dandelion whose *dentes de lion comique* smile reeks from Sir Les Patterson and beams from Dame Edna Everage); and his preoccupation with "long whiles agone" in his many in-dices of culture's *objets trouvés*, as in *Barry Humphries' Treasury of Aus-tralian Kitsch* (1980) and in Sandy Stone's many remembrances of things past (notably "Sandy Agonistes" [1960], the finest Australian song of the twentieth century).

*Bizarre* is a gathering wound, a gathering of society's wounded, people marginalized not only from society but even from the fashionable margins of postmodernity. Yet these freaks, these circus folk in search of a circus that will take them, are people of considerable distinction, in the manner of some of Patrick White's most memorable outsider characters, such as Theodora Goodman in *The Aunt's Story* (1948), Alf Dubbo in *Riders in the Chariot* (1968), and the title character in the short story "Clay" (1964), whose dedication reads: "For Barry Humphries and Zoe Caldwell." Still, Humphries' freaks are not literary characters but legendary and historical figures (the categories are not always clear) who distinguish themselves by drinking urine, mutilating the *Mona Lisa*, and being conjoined identical ("Siamese") twins; whose distinctive conditions are sadism, witchcraft, circumcision, transvestism, monstrosity, genetic mutation, physical and mental retardation, hypertrichosis, albinism, giantism, dwarfism, obesity, and ichthyosis; and who are distinctively heteradelphians, pygomelians, half-men, half-women, and lesbians.

But when one considers that Indian Prime Minister Murarji Desai (1977–79) drank his own urine, that French Dada artist Marcel Duchamp mutilated a 19.7-by-12.4-centimtre postcard of the *Mona Lisa* by adding a moustache and goatee in his print *L.H.O.O.Q.* (1919), that Dame Edna Everage is monstrous[16] and Wiccan,[17] and that her daughter, Valmai, is a lesbian,[18] one realizes that "abnormality," while it may seem shocking, is quite normal. What is abnormal is that "familiarity has blinded us to the beauty of the Mona Lisa's pose."[19] Humphries and Duchamp have a conjoined contempt for familiarity. They are dedicated to making the familiar seem bizarre and to inviting readers and spectators into *bizarrerie* so that they might say to everyone who is Other (i.e., to everyone) *je vous pardonne votre bizarreries* ("I forgive your oddities"). Like Marcel Duchamp defacing the *Mona Lisa*, Humphries created in *Bizarre* "a non-linguistic sign system" in which "the priority of the language model is maintained,"[20] in which a company of deformed and disenfranchised people maintain a language model for their dumbfounded onlookers – readers shocked by the challenge they face, particularly whether or not to interpret *Bizarre* as literature. Humphries' endeavour to subvert the constructs of literature, the book, and print culture was daring in 1965, and it still swings with the spirit of the sixties and with the "youthful folly" of the ever-avant-garde.

In 1963, while appearing in the first American run of *Oliver!* Humphries actually had the honour to meet Marcel Duchamp.[21] Duchamp was seventy-six, Humphries twenty-nine, and his audience with the hobby-horse riding champion of the twentieth century, by then a chess master, undoubtedly inspired him in his construction of *Bizarre*, particularly in his "household hints for the mutilation of the Mona Lisa," a series of twenty-six defaced prints in the style of *L.H.O.O.Q.* (which Duchamp painted in New York, where he had moved in 1915). However, in *Bizarre* Leonardo's subject is everything but mustachioed and goateed. The painting is: stepped on, erased with "a soft rubber," erased with "a hard rubber," brushed, stained, dipped in urine, rubbed with sand, dissolved in spirits, dunked in spirits, quilted, sandblasted, obversed ("by scraping off the back and mounting in reverse"), doused in oil, cut and pasted, twisted, sawn, drilled, mishandled, rent, folded, punctured, crumpled, grated, rubbed with sugar, scraped, and burned, with the enigma of La Gioconda's smile arising through each defacement, even out of the ashes.[22] That no moustache or beard masks her smile or hides her mouth in *Bizarre* suggests Duchamp's influence as well as Humphries' respect for Duchamp and his reverence for *L.H.O.O.Q.* He reiterates his esteem in *Dame Edna's Coffee Table Book* (1976) in a parody of old masters' portraits, including Leonardo da Vinci's *Mona Lisa*, in which the female subjects have been *ednafied* with "face furniture."[23] This photo montage hints that Edna Everage is in every woman's visage. Humphries' continued association with Leonardo and Duchamp's iconography is evident in his posing as the *Mona Lisa* (along with Van Gogh's self-portrait and Hals's *Laughing Cavalier*) in a cover article in Australian *GQ.*[24]

Duchamp's *L.H.O.O.Q.* and Humphries' *Bizarre* were harbingers of another kind of *La Gioconda* parody: replication for profit. For example, Robert A. Baron's Web page, *Mona Lisa Images for the Modern World*, or a

*Giocondophiliac's Delight: Resources and Web Links to Monalisiana and re-*
*lated subjects*, <http: //www.studiolo.org/Mona/MONALSIT.htm>, lists sites
on Mona Lisa in artistic production, popular culture, and mercantile capitalism, including *Monalisiana Kitsch, Commercial Products & Advertisements*,
which catalogues, inter alia, Mona Lisa jigsaw puzzles; Mona Lisa cross-
stitch patterns; a Mona Lisa mouse pad; a race horse named Mona Lisa; an
inflatable Mona Lisa; advertising Mona Lisas designed to sell everything
from spaghetti sauce to cigars; and Mona Lisa images in art (such as Fernand
Léger's *Mona Lisa with Keys* and Andy Warhol's *Two Golden Mona Lisas*),
journalism, and literature. Despite all these imitations and mutilations, Leonardo's original painting is still protected, immutable, behind glass at the
Louvre, whereas Duchamp and Humphries' *mi(me)ses en abîme* hide "me":
the transition <Mona Lisa del Giocondo → Mrs Norman Everage of Moonee
Ponds>, a bizarre alliance of women who are willing to sit (pose) for men.

Humphries' citation in *Bizarre* from Arthur Machen's novel *The Hill of
Dreams* (1907)[25] marked the beginning of his long fascination with this
master of the macabre, which he formalized in the introduction he wrote to
the 1997 edition of Machen's story collection *Ornaments in Jade* (1924)
(for which, in his capacity as president of the Arthur Machen Society, he
provided the revised typescript).[26] When Humphries observes that "the
reputation of Arthur Machen has suffered many vicissitudes, amongst them
shameful neglect and disproportionate praise,"[27] he seems to be speaking
as much about himself as about Machen. As the compiler of *Bizarre*, he
was decidedly inexperienced as a writer. For much of his content he relied
directly on material from the journal *Bizarre*, published in the 1950s and
1960s (Paris: Jean-Jacques Pauvert), a situation that continues the *mise en
abîme* of the jacket and title page. But *Bizarre* (1965) is wholly Humphries'
arrangement in black and white, his *objet trouvé*, his work of art, an installation of *bizarrerie* that declared his aesthetic less by his authorship than by
his subjectivity. It is a celebration of abnormalcy, of odds, sods, gods, mods,
and, most of all, bod(ie)s in all their permutations.

*Bizarre* is a disengaging exercise in Derridean Dadaist play, which plays itself out throughout Humphries' writing career. It is a daring experiment in
the architectonics of the book as consumer/consumed object, and, three years
before Roland Barthes published his influential essay "The Death of the Author" (1968), which charted the postmodern shift from authors towards
readers as meaning-makers, it makes an intriguing proposal to readers to
take on a tentative authority by disputing the construct *compiler-as/is-author*.
Humphries may have drawn his aesthetic from Marcel Duchamp, who, in
April 1957, delivered a talk entitled "The Creative Act" to the American
Federation of Arts Convention in Houston. In this talk he proposed that the
spectators of art complete the artist's process, filling in spaces in creativity.[28]
In *Bizarre*, Humphries takes a seat (a *poseur*'s pose) beside his readers as

together they view the spectacles of *bizarrerie* and of a book that seems to have defied the construct "authorship."

In the end, Humphries' dismissal of *Bizarre* as "a youthful folly" proves an accurate assessment. It is the final work of his juvenilia, and it is part of his foolish output as a Dada artist – recall the image of Humphries in a fool's cap on the jacket of his second recording, *Wild Life in Suburbia, Volume Two* (1959) – and one of his first turns as a music hall artiste. It is also an act of folly (cf. the French idea of *folie*, meaning "folly" but also "madness," as in the Folies Bergère). In his irrationalities and extravagances, on stage and off, it must be said, *il fait des folies* (he acts irrationally; he acts wildly).

### TID-BITS

If it all began with *Bizarre*, if folly, parody, our Edna, our Barry, and even our cultural monstrosity entered the pattern of his early speech-act career, when did Humphries first single himself out, when did he first "me" himself as a writer of remarkable merit fashioning "my life as me"? In his introduction to Humphries' first script collection, *A Nice Night's Entertainment: Sketches and Monologues, 1956–1981* (1981), R.F. Brissenden recounts how

in December 1951 as a very junior member of the English Department at the University of Melbourne I found myself for the first time marking matriculation examination papers. In the midst of a long dull stretch of semi-literate mediocrity I remember coming upon one paper that (if I may borrow a phrase from Raymond Chandler) stood out like a tarantula on a slice of angel food. It was written in a large flowing hand in purple ink. The answers in it were short and bore little direct relation to the set questions – but they were dazzlingly sharp and intelligent and revealed a bizarre knowledge of some of the more obscure areas of English literature.[29]

"This eminently successful candidate was Barry Humphries," Brissenden adds, as if his readers did not already know that, by the age of seventeen, Humphries had begun to distinguish himself as a writer. Brissenden does not note, however, that young Humphries' preference for "purple ink" anticipates Edna Everage's "natural wisteria hair colour" and that his own adjective, "bizarre," implies an aesthetic link between a matriculating student and a book he would compile about maculated people. In fact, this examination essay opens up a file of Barry Humphries' juvenilia. The New Zealand novelist Janet Frame (1924–2004) similarly distinguished herself as a young writer, at the Dunedin Teachers' Training College, in a bizarre essay of her own entitled "The Growth of Cities," which "was passed around among staff; again, opinion was divided as to its merit."[30]

Humphries' next important contribution to this file of formative writings was "A Novel Called Tid," which appeared in *Paston's Melbourne Quarterly: A Journal of Literary Pleasantry for the Entertainment of the Public and the Edification of the Young* (Spring 1958). Humphries was inspired to write this narrative by his participation in the Melbourne University Dada group and "the Wubbo Movement," which led to his creation of the minimal character Tid, *un enfant terrible*, whom Humphries has called "a cretin."[31] The performance piece "Introduction to the Wubbo Movement," which the Melbourne University Dada group recorded on acetate in the early 1950s (partly as a joke), and which Humphries reissued in the nine-part sequence "The Dada Tapes" on his compact disc *Dada Days: Moonee Ponds Muse, Vol. 2 (1951–1983)* (1993), recounts the movement's origin:

In the evening, when the sun had set, Tid found his way to the back gate to welcome the man who comes every week to collect the rubbish, called by Tid, Mr Rubbo. When the rubbish collector drew near in his cart Tid shouted out, "Hello, Mr Rubbo." And as he trumbled past, Tid shouted "Wow, Wubbo. Wow, wow, wow, wow, wee, abo."[32]

Phonetically, this nominal transformation from *rubbish* to *Wubbo* recalls that from *Hébert* to *Ubu*[33] in Alfred Jarry's adolescent composition – Jarry was fourteen when, with his schoolmate Charles Morin, he wrote *Les Polonais* – of his play *Ubu Roi* (1896), which Annabelle Henkin Melzer calls "a fitting antecedent to the theatre of dada which would be born 20 years later [in Zurich, 1916]."[34] John Lahr parallels my idea on wubbo, stating that Les Patterson, with his phallic prop, makes "Humphries look for all the world like an Aussie Ubu."[35] Jarry's use of masks throughout *Ubu Roi* might suggest Tid's mask-like, expressionistic face (recto) and the man (Humphries) acting behind it (verso). In his preface to *Ubu Roi*, which he addressed to the audience at the play's premiere on 10 December 1896 at the Théâtre de l'Oeuvre, Paris, Jarry noted that "our actors have been willing to depersonalize themselves for two evenings, and to act behind masks, in order to express more perfectly the inner man, the soul of these overgrown puppets you are about to see."[36] In this sense, Humphries' Tid could be called an undergrown puppet.

The most famous Wubbo sketch is "Tid and the Psychiatrist," also dating from the early 1950s, a four-minute double act about a therapy session in which a psychiatrist, Dr Scott (played by Barry Humphries), and Tid (played by John Perry) end up exchanging personality disorders. Humphries went on to perform the sketch professionally in 1956 in the revue *Mr and Mrs* and in 1957 at the Granville Returned Servicemen's Club.[37] All these performances inspired Humphries to write "A Novel Called Tid," a spare, clever,

Beckett-like and Jarry-like narrative, which presents six ephemeral chapters and promises "to be continued," although it never was.

The story involves Tid's endeavours not to be seen: "Tid's main snag was trying not to be seen" (Chapter 1);[38] "Tid has found a trick for not being noticed" (Chapter 5); "Tid always knew when people knew he was somewhere" (Chapter 6). The narrative is a remarkable document not only because it is "exceedingly rare"[39] but also because (1) it imprints for the first time "Norm and Edna, Bruce and Valmai, and even little kenny ... at grannie's party" (Chapter 3) and "Norm and Edna and Bruce and Valmai, and even little kenny, clapping and laughing" (Chapter 4); (2) it features Humphries' stylistic flourish and encrypted meaning, as when Tid overcomes Mister Neale Hunter, who is threatening to shoot him: "Tid was probably too big to see; but Tid wasn't too big to see. He saw Mr Hunter alright and ate him" (Chapter 5); and (3) it records Humphries' first published cartoon enterprise and anticipates the Barry McKenzie comic strip. Humphries draws Tid minimally, as a wholly flat, spare figure, with a huge monolithic head, stern facial features reduced to point, line, and plane; a square nondescript body; stubby, robotic arms; and skinny L-shaped obverse and reverse, or verso and recto, legs.

"A Novel Called Tid" is at once "wubbo," an important juvenile work, and a fabula "to be continued" throughout Humphries' art, most immediately in his early Dada street and gallery performatives, and then in the *Barry McKenzie* comic strip, which he wrote with Nicholas Garland for *Private Eye*. Eventually, even before wearing the creations of Kenny Everage, Humphries would go on to wear "la mode pratique, création Rrose Sélavy: / La robe oblongue, dessinée exclusivement pour dames affligées du hoquet [For practical wear, a Rrose Sélavy creation: / The oblong dress, exclusively designed for ladies afflicted with the hiccups],"[40] the ready-made frock invented and worn by Marcel Duchamp as his cross-gender pseudonym and character Rrose Sélavy (whom Man Ray photographed in 1916), whose name puns on, among other things, "eros c'est la vie" [eros, that's life] and "arroser la vie" [raise a glass, to life] (see Chapter 3), and so might be associated with Les Patterson and Edna Everage's respective philosophies.

For Humphries, clothing – Les Patterson's leisure suits, Dame Edna's frocks, and Sandy Stone's dressing gowns but also his own Savile Row suits, and even the paupers' tatters of his audience – is the skin of writing, as character is of the body. Through writing, he enfleshes and clothes his performances; and through performance, he humanizes his writing. Humphries' writing forms the exteriority of all his personae, in particular their speech and speech-acts.

Writing, sensible matter and artificial exteriority: a "clothing." It has sometimes been contested that speech clothed thought. Husserl, Saussure, Lavelle have all questioned it. But has it ever been doubted that writing was the clothing of speech? For Saussure it is even a garment of perversion and debauchery, a dress of corruption and disguise, a festive mask that must be exorcised, that is to say warded off by the good word.[41]

In paraphrasing Saussure, Jacques Derrida could almost be describing the costumes of the lecherous Sir Les Patterson (soiled powder-blue suit), the duplicitous Dame Edna Everage (designer frock and *diamanté* spectacles), and the laudatory Sandy Stone (robe and hottie), respectively. All Humphries' stage shows, recordings, and, of course, books begin in writing and, before that, in speech and imagination, just as his career as a writer begins with "A Novel Called Tid." His readers clothe themselves with the Derridean/Saussurean "clothing of speech," wearing these costumes as confidently as Les, Edna, and Sandy wear theirs, along the runway of *haute couture* and across the proscenium of performativity. As a costume designer, Humphries changes audience's rags into costumes that might have come from the vaults of the Barry Humphries Collection at the Performing Arts Museum, Melbourne. He works this sartorial make-over for everyone who keeps his storytelling contract with them (as I describe below); that is, every audience member who has to come up onto Dame Edna's stage. To invoke changes of dress, form, mood, pose, heart, and ideas – as when "Tid was probably too big to see; but Tid wasn't too big to see. He saw Mr Hunter alright and ate him" – has been Humphries' Dada prank from the beginning.

Humphries has documented his Dada pranks and shows fondly and frankly in nine tracks on *Dada Days*, in the chapters "Shithouse Spaghetti" and "Russian Salad Days" in *More Please*, and in the chapter entitled "Aaron Azimuth" in *My Life as Me*. A 1985 exhibition entitled "Irreverent Sculpture" at the Monash University Gallery, which featured works by Humphries and seven other artists (Colin Lanceley, Mike Brown, Ross Crothall, Ti Parks, Clive Murray-White, Les Kossatz, and Aleksander Danko), satisfied what had become the public's nostalgia (their return to the construct "home" that Humphries has always favoured) for art that shocks not just the spectator but art itself. In the catalogue of this show (1985), Margaret Plant observes, somewhat as R.F. Brissenden does with regard to his writing, that "Barry Humphries at the age of 18 was in confident possession of the sense (and nonsense) of European Dada unparalleled in Australia."[42] She also cites five exhibitions, between 1952 and 1968, at which Humphries showed eighteen works of art, all of them as shocking as the shock of hair he lets fall over his forehead. These works include: *Eye and Spoon Race* (1952), perhaps inspired by Luis Buñuel and Salvador Dali's 1928 film, *Un Chien andalou*;[43] *Big Brown Scape* (1966), one of many Humphries canvases that figure and disfigure the word *BIG*; and

*Forkscape* (1958), an installment in which Humphries salvages deformed cutlery (in anticipation, it might be said, of *Bizarre*). These Dada works, including Humphries' adolescent street performatives, as art-for-deconstructing-art's-sake, resemble the circus acts of music hall, specifically a juggling act – of forks, shoes, hats, gloves, rocks, pieces of string, bottles, school ties, custard, bicycle wheels, and, especially, printed and written words. This kind of Dadact[44] recalls music hall performers such as Bagessen, whose spinning plates, after first seeming to defy gravity, ultimately obeyed it with a crash; Gaston Palmer, who nervously flipped twelve spoons out of and, all at once, back into twelve glasses; and the juggler Rob Murray (an Australian), who apparently resented the eight balls he had to keep in the air,[45] and for whom failure or near-failure was the mark of success. For Humphries the Dada artist, the only credo to pass on to spectators through his art, a belief system that his "Manifesto" and "Dadalogue[s]"[46] seem to support, is *"n'en croyez rien"*[47] ("don't believe it" or "believe in nothing"). And this is not surprising, given that nothingness is Dada's first principle. Hence, Humphries is a member of "Duchamp & Co." who, in his ready-made drama, art, and literature, has exploited "the morphological units of a new artistic language."[48]

In literature, credibility is often the measure of character; whether we find characters believable is how, in a Homeric sense, we measure their length upon the earth. But like shadows, whose length is set less by the Leonardo dimensions of the people who cast them than by the Galileo pitch of the sun, literary characters are fraught with subjectivity. Thus, Humphries' first literary character, Tid, could be a cartoon character figured in a minim of point, line, and plane, or a human being enacted on acetate or on stage; Tid could start out as *un enfant terrible*, then transform into the examining psychiatrist. Are these shape-shifts believable? Do they make Tid, *as character*, more believable than if he were not to have shape-shifted?

According to Humphries' non-credo, Tid's characterization is neither credible nor incredible: it is part of whatever performative he happens to be in, whether a cartoon, a speech on the stage, or "a novel" that is clearly not a novel – that is, if the categories "a novel" and "not-a-novel" can apply to a character who may not even be the kind of character in whom readers believe. Yet, as a speaker and a speech-actor, even the linear Tid engages in a performative, at least according Marie Maclean's outline in her *Narrative as Performance* (1988):

Indeed, it is in everyday vernacular narration that the effect of fiction, one of enhancement rather than radical change in the status of narrative, may first be observed. We see the difference when we say not "I will tell you *the* story," but cast off even the restrictions of the available choices from the referentiality of this world, and create another *possible* world. We allow ourselves the full freedom of the narrative contract when we say "I will tell you *a* story." This illocutionary act is, as I have said, a sort of performative, since it not only sets up a two-way contract between addresser and addressee, as all true speech acts do, but it also promises a performance and constitutes the hearers as audience. Implicit in every narrative performative is the double contract, "*Listen*, and I will tell you *a story*."[49]

Tid's "double contract" with his audience is designed to counteract any opposition to his acting up as a child and a monster. Thus, the psychiatrist, because he will not listen to Tid's story, preferring to try to cure him of his childishness and monstrosity, is forced to become his subject: the psychiatrist is tidied up. This is the pattern for most of Humphries' characters, especially on the stage: the audience will either honour their music hall contract by listening to Tid (or Edna, or Les, or Sandy, or Bazza, or even Humphries) tell a story or they will be forced to become them. There may be a little bit of Dame Edna or Sir Les in everyone, but how many people would be prepared to *be* her or him; that is, how many people other than Barry Humphries? And who among us would be ready to be *him*?

To be a member of Humphries' audience one must be willing to understudy all his characters, to be ready not so much to take over *for* them as to be taken over *by* them. This is what happens in *Back with a Vengeance* (1989) and in *Dame Edna's Work Experience* (1996), when a member of the audience (Ann from Johannesburg in *Back with a Vengeance*, Sandra the factory worker in *Dame Edna's Work Experience*), someone from the stalls who has foolishly broken her performative contract, is brought on stage and made over into Dame Edna. Everyone who is not brought up on stage (such as Peter Conrad, who confesses to having "kept my distance from Barry Humphries for twenty-five years," preferring "a seat in the middle of a row in the back of theatre"),[50] has managed to keep safe by keeping their end of the performative contract. Instead of being dressed as Edna, the faithful are given another kind of costume change, their decorous silence and wild laughter clothed in Humphries' gestures, thoughts, and language. At the performance I attended of *Dame Edna – The Royal Tour (The Show That Listens)* at the Booth Theatre, New York, 11 March 2000, I sat in seat H1, on the aisle. Although I was exposed, in Dame Edna's direct line of vision, I was perhaps beyond her six-row range. But, in performativity, I know Edna spared me because I had honoured her contract.

### BAZZA, AS A BIZARRE

Humphries' second literary character is Barry McKenzie, who made his entrance, at Peter Cook's invitation and with some of his creative input,[51] in 1963 in Nicholas Garland's preliminary drawing of the character, and on

Friday, 10 July 1964, in Cook's fortnightly satirical magazine *Private Eye*. The opening credits of the film *The Adventures of Barry McKenzie* (1972) also acknowledge Peter Cook: "Based on the 'Barry McKenzie' comic strip written by Barry Humphries with drawings by Nicholas Garland, as published in 'Private Eye' from an idea by Peter Cook." Cook had a "guest artist" role in the film, as the Granada Television executive Dominic, Gaylene/Lesley Allsop's ex-husband. In the first strip, Barry McKenzie is called (both in the title and in his speech balloon) "Barry McKensie," a typographic signifier that was to shift shape in his second strip (24 July 1964), which has no title and in which he calls himself "Barry McKenzie," the name that would stick, and that would stick in the consciousnesses of *Private Eye*'s British and Australian readers.

But the credibility of Barry McKenzie as a cartoon character seems to have to do less with semiotic signs than with his cultural design: his Australianness. The first strip, the full title of which is "Barry McKensie, Australian at large," emphasizes the issue of Australianness played out in England, much as in his BBC television series *Dave Allen at Large* (BBC-1, 1971–73, BBC-2, 1975–76) the Irish comedian offers his audience the largess of his satire of the British. Even Barry "McKensie' "s first words, "Excuse I what's gone flaming wrong?"[52] instantly signify him as Australian, whether or not actual, non-literary Australians would use these idioms. In this regard, Bazza's language, like *Bizarre*'s images, might be considered a Jamesonian "non-linguistic sign-system" in which "the language model is maintained."[53] For some readers and critics of the comic strip, however, the equivocal actualities of Barry McKenzie and his language have been the issue within the issue of his Australianness.[54] But as Humphries has eloquently observed in reference to reactionary takes on his film *The Adventures of Barry McKenzie* (1972), "only a real dumdum believes that the bigotries of a fictitious character are shared by his inventor."[55] That in the first comic book of *Barry McKenzie* strips, *The Wonderful World of Barry McKenzie* (1968), and the collected edition, *The Complete Barry McKenzie* (1988), the spelling of the protagonist's name and the wording of the title in the first episode have been regularized to just "Barry McKenzie" (along with many other verbal and graphic revisions from the original magazine strips) underscores the character's protean nature (as well as that fact that the original has been revised, proof-read, and tidied up), his ability not only to shift his own shape (doing that trick with his jaw or taking on or being mistaken for his brother, the Reverend Kevin McKenzie) but also to take on, in the spirit of Dadaist Expressionism, the shapes of all the readers and critics who gather around his speech balloons, dinky-di Aussies, Pommy bastards, and cartoon characters alike.

As a literary character, Barry McKenzie has his most immediate source in Humphries' vinyl and stage character Buster Thompson, who first appeared on the LP *Sandy Agonistes* (1960), whence he came to the attention of Peter Cook, who had heard the recording in 1962 in New York, where he was performing in *Beyond the Fringe*. Peter Coleman also likens McKenzie to Humphries' character Nipper Dixon,[56] but in his booklet notes to *Dada Days* and in *More Please* Humphries makes only the Buster Thompson-Barry McKenzie connection.[57] In his introduction to the monologue "Les Patterson: Introducing the Yartz," Humphries recognizes in Les Patterson "the baroque scatology of Barry McKenzie's discourse."[58] Coleman also calls McKenzie "a colonial Candide in an Akubra hat,"[59] which could suggest Voltaire's short story (1759?), of course, but also Leonard Bernstein's comic operetta (1956). By terming him "the innocent abroad,"[60] Stephen Alomes casts Bazza as an expatriate Australian and, thus, leaves him open to charges that he is a cultural stereotype and, therefore, a false character, a Platonic imitation of an imitation.

But the British public's first reaction to Bazza McKenzie was merely one of "stunned indifference," severe enough to remind Humphries of his own cold reception at the Establishment in 1962.[61] The Australian public, on the other hand, took Humphries to task for Barry McKenzie's *différence*: Bazza, apparently, was a dodgy Aussie. Perhaps the fairest assessment of McKenzie has come from Roger Wilmut, who, albeit within a brief discussion of *Private Eye*, calls him simply "an Australian character" and cites Humphries' assessment of McKenzie as simply "a very vulgar working-class character."[62] McKenzie identifies himself similarly in the first number of the strip, when he confesses to a London cabbie, "I'm just an ordinary-honest-working bloke like yourself,"[63] and the narrator, in his synopsis frame in the *Private Eye* strip of 21 August 1964, calls him simply "a strapping young specimen of Australian manhood,"[64] as if his manhood and nationality were inseparable. In the dramatis personae of the published script, or "photoplay," of the film *Barry McKenzie Holds His Own* (1974), Humphries, in collaboration with Bruce Beresford, describes Barry McKenzie as "a typical young Australian."[65] When Bazza first utters the words "Excuse I," which have become Dame Edna's, Les Patterson's, and all Melbourne's catch-phrase, he is begging pardon not for his nationality but for his personality, for the "me" in his Aristotelian (i.e., post-Platonic) mimesis. Bazza must be an Aristotelian, after all, because "he has never read the Symposium of Plato."[66] His dubious grammar in the clause "Excuse I" actually signifies the emergence of the first person of Barry Humphries' comedy.

Like much of his shtick, this character has antecedents in British music hall and Australian comic literature (e.g., the "Dad and Dave" narratives of Steele Rudd, Henry Lawson's yarns and poems, the narratives of Joseph Furphy, Banjo Patterson's poems, and Dal Stivens' stories), and he has a descendant in the later performance oratives of Gary Macdonald as his character Norman Gunstan.

Barry McKenzie is an "innocent abroad" but not in Alomes' expatriate sense; rather, McKenzie is "one of the most enduring of the stock characters to appear on the halls: the greenhorn provincial taken for a ride by city slickers (but who often proves smarter in the end than his tormentors)."[67] That Bazza is a music hall innocent, Humphries attests to in his article "Why Bazza Is a Virgin" (1973), which he wrote as a commentary on the release of *The Adventures of Barry McKenzie* (1972). As well as enumerating the reasons an evening's intercourse with the widely liked Barry McKenzie is not on, why the character's devoutly-to-be-wished coitus is inevitably interruptus, Humphries situates Bazza in the curious company of virgins, whether professional, frustrated, or born again "in the pantheon which includes Boadicea and Beardsley, Romeo and Juliet, St Paul, Rumpelstiltskin, Alice B. Toklas, Hitler, Savonarola, Lewis Carroll, Dr Watson, Jesus, and (naturally) His mother."[68] Is this "pantheon" not, etymologically, the place of all the gods but, mythologically, the place of Pan, the goat-man-god of forests and flocks (in this instance of the eucalyptus groves and sheep droves of McKenzie's Australia)?

In having the horns (as well as the ears and legs) of a goat, is not Bazza, as Pan, in a "pantheon" of virgins, a man who is cuckolded by every other Australian not-so-innocent male abroad who succeeds in bringing his sexual adventure to climax? When Humphries observes of Bazza that "the Desire and Pursuit of the Whole drives him from one sexual disappointment to the next,"[69] he seems to be acknowledging the mythological connection between Pan and the Whole, especially in the symbol of skins or clothes.[70]

Whereas, according to Sir Les Patterson, Barry Humphries is an imitation poofter, Barry McKenzie is a Pan(sy). In *When London Calls*, Stephen Alomes cites "an era [1940s and 1950s Australia] when colourful shirts and longish hair were associated with 'pansies' and 'poofs.'"[71] In *More Please*, Humphries also documents how, since his first days at Melbourne Grammar School in the 1940s, when "the headmaster ... fulminated against long hair," and his last days, when "the small theatre [of the New Music Society] was thronged with long-haired youths in suede shoes and corduroy trousers smoking Turkish cigarettes with the wrong fingers,"[72] he has proudly worn his hair long, even now, when he is approaching seventy. In contradistinction to Les Patterson, who has conceded in *Dame Edna, Back with a Vengeance: The Second Coming* (1989) that "Barry isn't a poofdah, but he gives a pretty good impression of one,"[73] and to Garryl Kurdish, who, in *Women in the Background* (1995), asks Derek Pettyfer, "Gay? Aren't you just a little bit gay?"[74] many of Dame Edna Everage's fans (as at the 1998 San Francisco run of *Dame Edna – The Royal Tour [An Appropriate Show]*), simplistically mistake Humphries for a homosexual transvestite. And this, of course, totally misses the point of his life and art (given his four marriages and his music hall heritage, the raison d'être of his career). Rather than a poofter, I call Humphries a *spoofter*, which is my neologism for a person who sends up, or spoofs, social constructs such as gender. Humphries is a parodist. Still, a case could be made that Humphries is gay. According to Les Patterson in *The Traveller's Tool*, "Any bloke ... who uses the adjectives 'bizarre' and 'stunning' in the same sentence munches the mattress."[75] If it could be proven that Barry Humphries wrote this sentence, then it follows that he must be a poofter!

As a goat-man-god, a Pan(sy) who is known, within the microcosm of his comic strip (which, of course, consists of a series of "panels," from the Latin *pannus*, meaning "cloth"), (1) to "have a skinful" now and again and (2) never to have been out of his clothes (even though he has dropped his trousers several times and, in an addendum to *The Complete Barry McKenzie* entitled "Holt! Who Swims There?" he does dress down to his swimming costume [singlet and shorts]), Bazza is, philosophically, but also sexually, the part in search of the whole. Consider how Humphries rhetoricizes McKenzie's sexual prospects:

Will it be ever thus? If Miss Right materializes and McKenzie marries, will it be a *mariage blanc*? Will the Son of Bazza be an immaculate conception? Does Barry merely pretend to sexual ambition in the same way as he drinks, namely to be one of the boys?[76]

Despite his theological error – the "Son of Bazza" would be a virgin birth not an immaculate conception – Humphries offers a compelling rhetorical assessment of the other Barry as a sexual pretender and a homosocial piss artist, or, as he characterizes the reluctant celibate in the chorus of his poem "If It Was Raining Virgins," which Bazza performs: "If it was raining virgins / I'd be washed down the gutter with a poof. / When I feel me heartthrobs surgin,' / The sheilas just tell me to bugger off!"[77] Compare the song "Washed Down the Gutter," from the LP *Bazza McKenzie's Party Songs*, the chorus of which features the variation "If it was raining virgins, / I'd be locked down the dunny with a poof." In *Bazza Pulls It Off* (1971), when Dr Melanie Joberg instructs Bazza, "Furthermore, our questionnaires reveal that a startling proportion of males under twenty-five find themselves virgins!" he offers the drollest of replies, "Lucky bastards!"[78] (This exchange is repeated in the film *Barry McKenzie Holds His Own* [1974].) Barry McKenzie's conditional clause about virgins, "If it was raining virgins / I'd be washed down the gutter with a poof," which is not gender specific, could suggest Bazza might actually be showered with other male virgins. In this queer theoretical sense, the women's dismissive remark "bugger off" and the song's allusion to being "locked down the dunny with a poof" hint at Barry McKenzie's homophobia – not his fear of homosexuals as much as his fear (Woody Allen has called it "homosexual panic") that his sexuality might be confused with his sexual orientation, that his virginity might out him as homosexual (in his words, as "one of the boys").

As the stock figure of a "greenhorn provincial," Barry McKenzie, even though he does not sing and dance (with the exception of doing what Les Patterson, in the song "My Old Lady," calls "the trouser dance"), is in the tradition of music hall performers such as May Moore Duprez; Fanny Fields; George Formby, Sr; Tom Foy; Jack Pleasants; Reg Dixon; Dave Morris; many northern comedians; and, especially, cross-dressing performers who ventured from the provinces to prevail in the city, or from their own gender to prevail in a kind of cross-gender city, a club scene of the mind.

In the first *Private Eye* strip, Barry McKenzie, upon arriving in England, mistakes Southampton for Dover, has a confrontation with a class snob, is "fleeced" at customs, has his transistor radio nicked on the train, is overcharged by a taxi driver, is clipped for a dingy hotel room, and is "poisoned" by his first unsuspecting swill of tepid English beer. Here Humphries cues up his hero for the whole series of comic misadventures in which a wild colonial boy who is too easily taken into other people's confidences comes to prevail as a confidence trickster, like Anancy in West African and Caribbean traditions, and Nanabush in North American First Nations traditions.

Bazza's tricks are tests of English resolve, of the truisms of British spunk and of his own commitment to virginity. Like Les Patterson, as *un lion comique*, a front-cloth comedian and a music hall chairman or president, Barry McKenzie hovers over his audience (in his case a leering audience just outside the frames of his strip), threatening to vomit ("chunder," "chuck," "hurl," "play the whale," "park a tiger," "cry Ruth," "technicolour yawn," etc.) over them. This may be spontaneous or a deliberate act of vengeance, as when, in *The Wonderful World of Barry McKenzie*, he throws up on his psychiatrist (cf. Tid), Dr Meyer de Lamphrey, whom Nicholas Garland has drawn to resemble Barry Humphries, a likeness confirmed by Humphries' portrayal of the character of Dr de Lamphrey in the films *The Adventures of Barry McKenzie* (1972) and *Barry McKenzie Holds His Own* (1974). Thus in vomiting over his psychiatrist he is, by extension, vomiting over his scriptor (Humphries), even managing to spew out a well placed punitive phrase: "Cop that, you pommy bastard!"[79]

Bazza gives notice to his audience to listen to his story, and honour his performative contract with them, or else suffer the consequence of becoming him by wearing the contents of his stomach, which may be seen as like the clothing or animal skin (the "skinful") of Pan. Bazza also acts as a kind of front-cloth man for Les Patterson in his role as an interruptive comedian. As Humphries soliloquizes him:

Our hero had started soliloquizing rather in the manner of one of my long-winded stage characters, yet whereas in the theatre I tried to get the dialect and vocabulary of a class or profession exactly right, "Bazza" spoke in an invented idiom; a synthetic Australian compounded of schoolboy, Service, old-fashioned proletarian and even made-up slang.[80]

Humphries' syntax here suggests both that Bazza *speaks* in "a synthetic Australian compounded of" and that Bazza *is* "a synthetic Australian compounded of" various speech acts. As "a synthetic Australian" he is a post-Platonic fake or mock Aussie and, therefore, no real threat to such home-grown constructs of the male Australian as ocker, larrikin, bushman, swagman, bushranger, yobbo, anti-intellectual, traveller, ratbag, drunk, churl, knocker, wild colonial boy, egalitarian, expatriate, or one of the "wild men from the colonial bush," "wild men of the frontier," or "untutored wild men"[81]; that is, every Australian cultural stereotype short of music hall artiste and, of course, wowser. As a "synthetic" Aussie, he is also a cunning unilinguist standing on the peak of the linguistic Tower of Babel,[82] "compounding" all the discourses and dialects of Australia into a single Australian man who speaks a kind of protolanguage. Finally, "synthetic" Bazza is the synthesis of Humphries' relentless Aristotelian analysis of Australian attitudes, posturings, pretensions, and humours, of the nature of language and the turn of the comic book.

Humphries' reference to "schoolboy … slang" recalls G. Legman's claim that "Jarry's French is straightforward. It has been said that his language is strange, archaic, invented. Nothing of the sort. He speaks with the language of a child. His scatology – like his punning and nonsense – is that of the nursery, where 'little children laugh at what will often frighten grown-ups.' "[83] Barry McKenzie's language is puerile in the spirit of Dada, and it is as uninhibited, unself-conscious, and amoral as discourse overheard on children's playgrounds. It is surely designed to shock "grown-ups," the Establishment. Of the four volumes of collected *Private Eye* strips:

1 *The Wonderful World of Barry McKenzie* (1968) has no annotations.
2 *Bazza Pulls It Off! More Adventures of Barry McKenzie* (1971) features a three-page "Glossary of McKenzieisms" (comprising 179 words and idioms).
3 *Bazza Comes into His Own: The Final Fescennine Farrago of Barry McKenzie, Australia's First Working-Class Hero* (1979) features an introduction by Bruce Beresford, a four-page glossary (comprising 245 words and idioms), and, as addenda: ten reprints of newspaper articles and reviews on Humphries and *The Adventures of Barry McKenzie*; three newspaper and journal articles and one letter by Humphries; an excerpt

from an Australian National University lecture by Geoffrey Dutton; letters to Barry [Humphries] from Manning [Clark] at ANU; and, from *Private Eye*, an invitation from Sun Books to a "Chunder Party" and a picture of Kevin McKenzie.

4 *The Complete Barry McKenzie* (1988) features a seven-page glossary (comprising 260 words and idioms) and, as "Learned and Scholarly Appendices," Beresford's introduction and four of the addenda, reprinted from *Bazza Comes into His Own*.

Readers of *The Wonderful World of Barry McKenzie* are free to wander through Bazza's vocabulary, as Bazza wanders through London, without a map (and, as most people negotiate their way through life, without a dictionary in their pocket). Like Peter Cook, to whom Humphries dedicated the book (as he did *The Complete Barry McKenzie*), readers can encounter oaths such as "stone the crows," "whacko the diddle oh," and "shit a brick"; idioms such as "splash the boots," "strain the potatoes," and "come the raw prawn"; and words such as "drongo," "tubes," and "feature" and infer their meanings from syntax, context, or comic strip cell. Or they can just be content to be confused, like the English characters who meet Bazza's *parole* with consternation, as if it is an assault on standard English, on *langage*.

Humphries' invention of Australian English here, and throughout his comic strips of the 1960s and 1970s, is as innovative within the context of Commonwealth literature as is V.S. Naipaul's invention of Port-of-Spain street vernacular in *Miguel Street* (1959); Ken Saro-Wiwa's invention of Lagos street vernacular in *Sozaboy: A Novel in Rotten English* (1985); and Ray Lawler's promotion of Australian dialects in the 1957 London staging of *Summer of the Seventeenth Doll* (1957): all three works have no glossaries and offer no apologies for neologisms. Writer and actor Mike Myers, in his films *Austin Powers: International Man of Mystery* (1997), *Austin Powers: The Spy Who Shagged Me* (1999), and *Austin Powers in Goldmember* (2002), also invents a language, the re-imagined or historicized argot of the "swinging sixties" in London, for comic purposes. Some of his phrases (e.g., "shagadelic" and "groovy, baby") like Barry McKenzie's idioms (e.g., "chunder" and "go for a feature") have even entered into received usage.

Barry Humphries, the former Melbourne University law student, contracts Bazza to tell a story and readers to listen. Even in the liberally glossed *Bazza Pulls It Off!*, *Bazza Comes into His Own*, and *The Complete Barry McKenzie*, he invites readers simply to listen, allowing them to consult the glossaries yet daring them to disregard them. The glossaries themselves are cross-referenced, often absurdly, as in "bonzer (see under whacko-the-diddle-oh)" and "whacko-the-diddle-oh (see under bonzer),"[84] suggesting that they are less explanation than obfuscation, a metafictional part of the cartoon's frame-story content. Even the idiom "drilling for Vegemite," which Sir Les Patterson uses in his preface to *The Complete Barry McKenzie*, is Dada-glossed as "an obscure Australian usage unknown to us. (The Publisher)."[85] Examining the glossaries, one may find oneself forced to deal with a kind of untranslated foreign language, much as in her novels *Potiki* (1986), *Cousins* (1992), and *Baby No-Eyes* (2000), for example, New Zealand writer Patricia Grace confronts her Pakeha readers with many unglossed and untranslated Maori words and passages. Except that Bazza's language is "foreign," whether to Australian or to non-Australian readers, only because it is invented, "a non-linguistic sign-system." One might *voltairize* his special brand of "strine" by saying, *Humphries had to invent it because it did not exist*. It is Humphries' greatest linguistic accomplishment, and it is the most generous of his many contributions to Australian cultural discourse.

Like the patter from a music hall dummy's ventriloquist, everything McKenzie says comes from Humphries' mouth. Bazza's love of language and his exploitation of its seductive and efficacious powers, its powers to disrobe and to disarm, come directly from Humphries' sesquipedalian,[86] neological,[87] enumerative,[88] and lexicographical[89] tendencies. These are evident throughout his writing, as in the word *noctambulations*[90] (which Humphries could undoubtedly utter walking in his sleep), from his bibliophilia,[91] and from what could be called, after Ian Britain, his "word childhood." As Humphries has admitted: "Bazza talked dirty with lyricism; he revived a dialect that had been vitiated by respectability, he was the Voice of Vulgarity." His "crime against Niceness"[92] would be protected from recidivism when, in 1978, and after the characters' encounters in the two Barry McKenzie films, Edna Everage, Bazza's aunt, adopted "Niceness" as her signature tune (on the LP *The Sound of Edna*), and in 1988, when, after he is cured of blindness, Bazza observes, "I can see! Whacko-the-diddle-oh, isn't the world a nice place from a visual point of view."[93] Bazza's nice language may not often be very agreeable to classist English society, or even to egalitarian Australian society, but it is always subtle, and it is always taken neat, like Johnny Walker in a shot glass.

If *Barrington* were to be cut again, in a tasteful ceremony of circumcision, from the diminutive *Bazza* to *Baz*, he could be seen to scan the alphabet from A to Z and Z to A, thus performing his function as Humphries' proto-speech-actor, working from what Janet Frame, in 1962, termed "the edge of the alphabet" and drawing his readers into the heart (not the dead heart) of Australian discourse. Like Frame, McKenzie seems to say, "If you object to my language, put your better language where your mouth is." Humphries is not demanding that comic strip readers speak what Bazza speaks – an invented language; he is only inviting them to recognize the beauty, dynamism, and humour of their own Australian *parole* and *langage*. Even Bazza's vulgarity is merely a sign of the vulgate, the colloquial speech common to all Australians, not at all, as Edna says, c-o-m-m-o-n.

The linear-cellular comic strip Barry McKenzie is marked by orality: his speech is alive, ballooning; his writing is dead, and he is rarely shown to write. His speech balloons, while in writing (i.e., handwritten print), are the outlines of what he is saying more than the outlines of what Humphries has written or the outlines of what Garland has printed or drawn. His dialogue bubbles suggest Bazza's breathing, even his spittle, anticipating what I have called Les Patterson's *sexpectorations* (see Chapter 1). Bazza's inscribed speech also has sexual overtones, as when, in *The Wonderful World of Barry McKenzie* (1968), he describes an aphrodisiac: "it puts lead in your pencil, if you see what I mean."[94] His preference for orality is evident in oaths such as "Shit a brick you wouldn't read about it,"[95] an utterance that resurfaces in Humphries and Stanley Myers' Rolf Harris parody, "Wendy the One-Eyed Wombat," from *Barry Humphries' Savoury Dip* (1971): "Gosh, you wouldn't read about it! It was just like a zoo!" And this utterance, in a new panel at the end of *The Complete Barry McKenzie*, is the first from Bazza's mouth "A Quarter of a Century Later" and, in what could be called a sight gag, his last before going into the surgery that will cure his blindness: "You wouldn't read about it."[96] Ironically, throughout the Barry McKenzie comic strips, and throughout all Humphries' other writings, people do read about it, of course, the ideas of the It Kid.

In *The Wonderful World of Barry McKenzie* Bazza is commissioned to write his autobiography for the underground magazine *Fuzz* thanks to the publicity arising from his chance appearance on television. His two attempts to write his life, which begin "I was born in Sydney in Australia of parents" and "Once upon a time I got the brainwave of going to the Old Country to get a dekko at the Poms and a few swift slides of the Queen and Phil the Greek also to cop a few ruined castles and a bit of the old pompageantry,"[97] fizzle into a party of discourse and intercourse at *Fuzz* editor Crispin Walthamstowe's home and environs, where nothing is written down and nothing downed but Foster's. In a festive mood, Bazza abandons the generic discipline of autobiography for the undisciplined life, the spontaneity, of spoken words. He speech acts out his autobiography in the halls and the streets of London. Why does he need to write his life down, an adventurous life – compare Dame Edna's *My Gorgeous Life: An Adventure* (1989) – that is difficult enough for him just to live down, when nice people like Barry Humphries and Nicholas Garland are willing to write, draw, and print it, and even wrap it up in a bubble, just as he likes it?

Humphries and Bruce Beresford acknowledged the literary basis of the Barry McKenzie comic strips in two fleeting visual puns in the film *The Adventures of Barry McKenzie* (1972). When Barry saunters into the Gorts' den, where Mr Gort, a pedophile masochist who fancies him, lies in wait, he glances round the room at the keepsakes of the former public schoolboy. When he peruses a children's book entitled *William Holds His Own*, then returns it to the shelf, next to a book entitled *Bentley Pulls It Off*, Humphries and Beresford reference the film sequel, *Barry McKenzie Holds His Own*, which would appear in 1974, and the cartoon collection *Barry McKenzie Pulls It Off*, which had appeared in 1971. Barry McKenzie is a worded character. His referentiality is linguistic, and he is cross-referenced in comic strips, cartoon anthologies, films, film scripts, videos, micro-grooves, and sound stage props.

If it all begins with *Bizarre*, Barry McKenzie is the "It Boy," a speech-act performer, arguably inanimate, yet without equal. With the exception, of course, of Roaring Twenties actress and flapper Clara Bow (1905–65), who became known as the "It Girl" after her starring role in the film *It* (1927) (based on Elinor Glyn's collection *"It," and Other Stories* [1927]). Bow undoubtedly had "it" (i.e., vitality, allure, pluck, spunk, *zeitgeist*, modernity, and madness); and she certainly got "it" (i.e., popularity, fame, notoriety, wealth, love, caring, and sharing). These are the qualities that inform Barry McKenzie, as a character and, like so many of Humphries' characters, as an ersatz human being who seems to exist independently of its author. In *Narratology: Introduction to the Theory of Narrative* (1985), narratologist Mieke Bal refers to the narrator with the pronoun "it," as distinguished from the conventional personal pronouns for narrators ("he," "she," and "they"), arguing that narrators are literary constructs and are not to be mistaken for human beings. But Bazza, as the "It" boy, is more than a construct, more even than a character; and "It" can be easily mistaken for a human being, even though, for some people, taking him for a fellow Australian does remain problematic. As a human being, Bazza is an individual subject, vulnerable to mutability and mortality; as a cartoon character, from the pens, not the leaded pencils, of Humphries and Garland, Bazza lives forever in the adventure of the alphabet, moving at c-speed, from A to Z, Z to A, A to Z, Z to A – imprinting all his readers with the words "BAZ" and "bizarre," and even "Beazley."

Although Barry McKenzie may prefer not to express himself in writing, Barry Humphries, in the unlikely generic spaces of a cheeky comic strip, a freak show anthology, and a somewhat derivative short story (for which he is indebted, as is often noted, to Samuel Beckett but also and especially to Alfred Jarry), began to distinguish himself as a writer of literature. "Barry Humphries writing Australian literature" may seem a bizarre proposition, but only until one remembers that *bizarrerie* is the heart of his very heterodox *oeuvre*. His doxology takes in all that is weird, as Dame Edna's favourite adjective, "spooky," has intimated for decades. In his pantheon of weirdness, the gods Tid, Bazza, and all the weirdos and widos[98] in *Bizarre* assemble to ponder the fate – the word "weird" derives from the Old

English "wyrd," meaning "destiny" – of the career of Barry Humphries. They foresee for him a distinguished and celebrated career on the stage as a music hall artiste: comedian, singer, dancer, raconteur, chat show host, actor, and "It Boy." They also prophesy for him a prolific, eclectic, ingenious, dazzling (but quite unappreciated) career as a writer of literature. However, in the end they divine the critical recognition he deserves for an *oeuvre* that has taken audiences to "It": the sage ideas of *bizarrerie* and a wido known as It Boy. As Derrida says, "And when a name comes, it immediately says more than the name: the other of the name and quite simply the other, whose irruption the name announces."[99] If the name is "Barry Humphries," it speaks volumes. While most people would identify "the other of the name" Barry Humphries as Dame Edna Everage, in fact his other is not his alter ego but his literary *oeuvre*. His writing is "quite simply the other, whose irruption" Humphries merely announces, like a chairman on a music hall stage. Beginning with "A Novel Called Tid," *Bizarre*, and *Barry McKenzie*, Humphries, by putting "It" in writing, irrupts into the collective consciousness of Australians (and honorary Aussies), breaking it down the middle; provoking anger, confusion, and indignation; but in the end evoking adulation, respect, laughter, and delight.

# Humphries as Poet, Poet Taster, Lyricist, and Comic Singer

lush of summer, yes, but what use the green river, the gold place, if time and death pinned human in the pocket of my land not rest from taking underground the green all-willowed and white rose and bean flower and morning-mist picnic of song in pepper-pot breast of thrush?

– Janet Frame, Owls Do Cry

### A POCKET FULL OF POESY

Barry Humphries is an occasional poet. He deserves the designation "occasional" not because he writes poetry infrequently (which he does not), or even because he writes exceptional verse (which he does), but because he has the expertise to write poems for just about every occasion and because he has the facility to do it well and make it look easy. In his acknowledgments he refers to *Neglected Poems and Other Creatures* (1991) as "these occasional verses," as if his poetry were merely a hit and miss amateur pastime. But it seems it has always been a hit with his audiences, both spectators and readers, and only critics have missed out on his achievement in poetry and poetics.

He has written, and sometimes read and performed, poems on and for the following occasions: a dinner party with friends ("The Ballad of Charles Blackman"); an art exhibition opening ("Ode to the New Nine-by-Five"); a theatre colleague's retirement ("Ode to the Melbourne Theatre Company"); a stage show ("A Prologue to the Fifties," for *The Life and Death of Sandy Stone* [1990]); a protest against mining ("Ode to Conservation"); Dame Edna Everage's installation in Madame Tussaud's Wax Museum ("Madame Tosshard's Waxworks"); Les Patterson's reception of an honorary doctorate ("Cambridge Couplets") and his debut at Drury Lane ("Les Patterson's Historic Address to the Press"); his own appearances on a popular chat show ("Ode to Parky") and at the Australian Press Club

("Dr Sir Les Patterson's Press Club Epic"); Dame Edna's first Australian audience ("Salute to Edna"); a hotel opening ("Ode to the Merlin Complex"); the openings of an international airport ("Ode to Cairns") and a flower show ("Ode to the Weston and Louis Weedon Flower Show"); book launches ("Ode to the SMH Good Food Guide," "Ode to 'The Big Cook Book,'" and "Lament for Maid Melbourne"); audiences with Queen Elizabeth ("Silver Song") and Princess Diana ("Dame Edna's Historic Ode to Barnardo's"); Olivia Newton John's shop opening ("Ode to Koala Blue"); the death of Norm Everage ("I Can't Let My Public Down"); a Harrod's sale ("Ode to Harrods"); a student fundraiser ("The Cranbrook Steinway"); the birthdays of his father-in-law, Stephen Spender ("After the Event") and of a fellow Australian poet, Peter Porter ("Collecting Porter"); and even a poetry reading ("Terribly Well").

In all these appearances, one might say, although not quite in concert with Stephen Alomes, that he is "the ubiquitous Barry Humphries."[1] However, in this case, he is ubiquitous not because he is overexposed or because, like horse muck, he is all about but, rather, because he is a little god present in eternal laughter. As an occasional poet, Humphries is not an ocker but a rocker: he rocks the foundations of free verse. As T.S. Eliot observes in "Reflections on *vers libre*" (1917), "the division between Conservative Verse and *vers libre* does not exist, for there is only good verse, bad verse, and chaos."[2] That Humphries writes verse well, even ordering the chaos of language, like a lower-case god or goddess, would seem to be irrefutable.

Still, critics continue to be slow to sacrifice at Humphries' little altar of verse. "Threnody for Patrick White," which he wrote in 1991, is his most anthologized poem, appearing in three recent collections,[3] but it is very nearly his only anthologized poem. Although it is undoubtedly one of Humphries' finest poems, the fact of its one-and-onliness suggests that some of its appeal to the compilers of poetry anthologies (such as Australian Chamber Orchestra violinist Richard Tognetti, who made the selection of "Threnody for Patrick White" for *A Return to Poetry 2000*) comes from its association with Patrick White (1912–90), the great Australian writer and Humphries' friend.

When I was studying for my doctorate at the University of Sydney in the late 1970s, people outside the uni (that is, C-O-M-M-O-N people) often expressed surprise that someone, especially a Canadian, would be doing a doctorate on Australian literature (see Preface). After confessing they didn't know many Australian writers, they would say, "Of course, I have heard of Patrick White." But, like White, Humphries is also a great writer (as well as poet). He deserves a more prominent place in Australian poetry anthologies, especially anthologies of international comic verse. Still, in "Threnody for Patrick White," playing cantor at White's funeral rite, Humphries fulfills the ancient role of the poet as singer and as chronicler, a role he also plays in all his non-elegiac comic verse.

If, in the tradition of the psalmists and troubadours, poetry is meant to be sung, then Humphries is also a cantor in a synagogue where Dame Edna Everage, a "Red Sea Pedestrian,"[4] worships, and a bard at court, the Court of St James, where Sir Leslie Colin Patterson practises the art of courtly love. Even without its periodic meter and lyrical cadences, his verse would be meant to be sung (so much of it has ended up on vinyl, on disc, on screen, and on stage) in performance. Metrically, his poetry might have a sing-song quality. I mean this in a "kind and caring way" because reading his verse or hearing it performed leaves one singing the praises of his witty, funny, arch, parodic lyrics and often humming the snappy melodies of his collaborators (notably the composers Stanley Myers and Nick Rowley).

One of his earliest ventures into published poetry was in the role of "poet taster." He was not a "poetaster," a hack or trash-talker, a writer of verse not of merit but of meretriciousness, as according to the *Oxford English Dictionary*, in Ben Jonson's coinage of the word in his play *Cynthia's Revenge* (II.i.): "Madame Moria ... is like one of your ignorant poetasters of the time."[5] On the contrary, Humphries is a poet taster: (1) a collector and an anthologist who shows good taste in poetry selection; (2) a person who eats poets for breakfast, specifically out-of-humour postmodern poets; and (3) a poet of good taste.

Even as an adolescent Humphries was interested not just in writing poetry but also in collecting it. While he was gathering the miscellanea for *Bizarre* (1965), he was also collecting some of the little known poetry of Australia (i.e., Australian poetry, which, in the 1950s and 1960s, was little known) and, especially, obscure verse that had fallen out of favour and out of print. In his "Proem" to his compilation *The Barry Humphries Book of Innocent Austral Verse* (1968), he notes:

The verses reprinted here are taken from a comparatively few volumes which it has been my good fortune to acquire over the last fifteen years. There must, I know, be many more; buried in forgotten journals, or published "at the author's expense," in slim, faded, paper-bound editions. I wish that I had read them all, for the backwaters and billabongs of Austral verse are rich in such trove, and I can only hope that this personal selection will encourage the reader to do his own prospecting.[6]

Wittily, Humphries characterizes himself as a verse antiquarian and conservator, and a champion of unknown, marginal, and vain (i.e., vanity-published) poets. His editorial work here is efficacious and salvific: it achieves Humphries' desired effect of imprinting the moribund and it saves the souls of poets who otherwise might have been damned to an out-of-print hell (e.g., Jack Moses, Elizabeth Hardwicke, Joan Torrance, Tilly Aston, May Middleton, F.C. Meyer, and Elsie Carew).

The book's tripartite structure, consisting of "Songs of Innocence," "Songs of Experience," and "Songs of People and Places," suggests, with its Blakean overtones, Humphries' belief that, at least in verse from the 1890s to the 1920s, Australians and Australia are in a state of innocent joy. And it anticipates his professional development as a lyricist and a comic singer (particularly his performances with Carl Davis at the Albert Hall, *The Last Night of the Poms* [1981]; and at the Regent Theatre, Sydney, and the Melbourne Concert Hall, *Song of Australia* [1983]). His bizarre selections for his *Book of Innocent Austral Verse* compose his original loyal song of Australia, which should quell all but the nastiest rumours of his having let down the side. This verse book is a celebration of niceness and naïveté, and of Australia. As Humphries asserts:

I have deliberately called this an anthology of "innocent" verse because it includes the work of many "professional" poets as well as verse by naïve and "primitive" writers, and the quality of innocence seems to me to be the disarming and delightful virtue which all share in common.[7]

One might contend that such an egalitarian compilation implies a deconstruction of the binary opposition of class in poetry. However, even more tellingly, in his uneasy arrangement of minor poets Humphries is exercising his prerogative of taste and is playing a Dada prank, as he seems to hint at in his proem, in the manner of the Ern Malley hoax or in the spirit of Canadian Paul Hiebert's mock autobiography of a poetess, the "sweet songstress of Saskatchewan," in his novel *Sarah Binks* (1947). Like Hiebert, Humphries is mocking not his poetic subjects but the establishment of academic judgment, the canon of acceptance that relegates amateurs to the loveless margins. His mockery of minor poets is partly defensive, indirectly making a case for his own traditional verse.

In his complementary recording, *The Barry Humphries Record of Innocent Austral Verse* (1972), Humphries leaves out many poems from the book (which is to be expected when the book contains 102 poems and the single LP has room for only twenty-seven). But he also includes nine poems that are not in the book, notably two of Dame Edna Everage's poems, "Turntable of Life" (1970) and "Lament for Maid Melbourne" (1971), which would not be published in book form until 1991 (in his *Neglected Poems and Other Creatures* [1991]). The record jacket notes: "Many of the verses in this album were included in 'The Barry Humphries Book of Innocent Austral Verse' published by Sun Books, 1968 to whom Mr Humphries extends his profound gratitude." There are three cases for arguing that *The Barry Humphries Book of Innocent Austral Verse* is a Dada prank, all issuing from the recording and from the book.

First, as Humphries reads the poems, he seems to make them his own compositions (as much as "Turntable of Life" and "Lament for Maid Melbourne" are his own). He enacts them superbly, in the voices of Edna Everage, Sandy Stone, Nipper Dixon, Buster Thompson, pre–1976 Les Patterson, and several ad hoc voices, creating engaging characters in speakers who seem quite innocuous on the page and finding some exciting tonal nuances in apparently flat language and unadventurous prosody. As speech and as characterization, the anthologized poems and the two poems by Humphries seem quite indistinguishable. In compiling the anthology, Humphries was clearly inspired to write his own "innocent Austral verse" in the style of the poets of the period between the 1890s and the 1920s.

Second, some of the compiled verse bears a remarkable resemblance to Humphries' own sentiments. Consider, for example, these lines from G.A. Froment's "Australia," which Humphries positions last on the LP, allowing it to scoop A.D. Hope's "Australia" (1943): "She cares not if you live in the mansion or shack, / If your father's a Duke or a drunk. / Come and seduce her with kindness and might, / Show her that you have some spunk."[8] Compare these lines with Humphries' "True British Spunk" (1969): "Spunk, spunk, spunk, / You're so full of British spunk; / You're never in a panic; / You're never in a funk. / So in this time of crisis / There's nothing quite so nice as / Singing / Spunk spunk spunk spunk spunk spunk spunk."[9] That Humphries recorded the song just one year after the publication of the anthology suggests that Froment's "Australia" might have influenced him. But the stylistic and sentimental coincidence might also suggest a kind of co-authorship.

Third, in the proem to *The Barry Humphries Book of Innocent Austral Verse*, Humphries alludes to the fact that "my friend Mr Geoffrey Dutton tells me that he and Mr Max Harris once made a selection of Australian primitive verse for the quarterly *Australian Letters* called 'The Stuffed Galah.'"[10] Max Harris, editor of the journal *Angry Penguins*, was the publisher of *The Darkening Ecliptic* (Autumn 1944) and the first of many people to be taken in by James McAuley and Harold Stewart's Ern Malley hoax. But Harris also extended the hoax when, with John Reed and Barrie Reed, he edited *Ern Malley's Journal* (1952–55). Perhaps, by citing Harris in his proem, Humphries was also invoking the spirit of Australia's greatest literary hoax and of a person who played along with it like a card-carrying Derridean while, at the same time, reminding his readers that Australian poetry could play a penguin prank at any time.

Clearly, Humphries has a reputation for Dada pranks, stemming from his now quite legendary adolescent street theatre in early 1950s Melbourne, which he recounts in the chapters "Shithouse Spaghetti" and "Russian Salad Days" in *More Please*, and "Aaron Azimuth" in *My Life as Me*

(2002). Like Humphries, Canadian comedian and actor Tom Green (b. 1971) got his start in Dada pranks and street theatre, which he performed in his native Ottawa and on his own television show, *The Tom Green Show*, on Rogers TV, an Ottawa cable station, 1992–96.[11] Like all confidence tricksters, pranksters are sometimes credited with and/or accused of deceptions for which they are not responsible, simply because such deceptions are the kind of things they might have done. For example, when American comedian and prankster Andy Kaufman announced that he been diagnosed with lung cancer, some of his fans thought his illness was just another of his ruses. Some even believed (and a few persist in the belief to this day) that he faked his death (1984) and will one day reappear: such was his reputation for notorious pranks.[12]

Humphries was also recently implicated in a prank by association when his name came up in the story of a painting that Sotheby's had attributed to Sidney Nolan and placed in their London catalogue only to withdraw it "after it turned out to be a prop from a show put on by the comedian Barry Humphries 30 years ago."[13] The *Independent* article names Humphries only in association with the original commission of artist Max Robinson for his London production of *Just a Show* (at the Fortune Theatre, 1969) and does not name the current vendor. Nor does it suggest whether the attribution of the painting to Nolan is due to misappraisal or fraud (or, for that matter, trickery). Yet the newspaper headline, "Dame Edna's Prop Tricks Sotheby's," implies that Dame Edna (and, by association, Humphries, whom Rosanna de Lisle identifies with the appositive "best known today as Dame Edna Everage") has played a thirty-year-long confidence trick. His only prank of this long standing is to have convinced people like de Lisle that, even today, he is still not best known as Barry Humphries, as "me."

Any attempt to classify *The Barry Humphries Book of Innocent Austral Verse* as a Dada prank, whether because his name appears in the title or because the compiled verse resembles his own, would succeed only as a Dada prank in its own right. Otherwise, it would be exposed as fake, like the prop-Nolan on Sotheby's auction block. In fact, the poets in *The Barry Humphries Book of Innocent Austral Verse* are, in the word of Les Patterson's song "genuine" (1981), as legitimate as publication has made them.[14]

In its title *The Barry Humphries Book of Innocent Austral Verse* also identifies "Barry Humphries" as a qualifying rather than a possessive influence on book production, emphasizing (1) that every book to come from this writer will be a "Barry Humphries Book," (2) that this book does not belong to Humphries but, rather, is his gift to the people of Australia; and (3) that Humphries is not the author of the book but, rather, the gatherer of its contents, which is consistent with his personal role as an assiduous collector (of Charles Conder, of antiquarian books, and of many other *objets d'art*). His non-authorial role here is consistent with his role as the compiler of *Bizarre*.

But his post-authorial role is even more telling due to the coincidental publication of *The Barry Humphries Book of Innocent Austral Verse* and Roland Barthes' essay "The Death of the Author" (1968). Perhaps, if only in a synchronous Dada moment, Humphries is acknowledging the distanci-ation of the traditional author and the emergence of readers as the negotia-tors of meaning. He seems to entrust his readers with finding new ways of reading "Barry Humphries"-modified works, which might be recognizable as books but that are also non-books, or anti-books, or post-books shaped by his heterodox and Dada-historicized aesthetic (as in Susan Rubin Suleiman's observation, "If I had quoted the Futurist Marinetti or the Dada Duchamp, or the Surrealists of the Pop artists, then we could speak of the antiaesthetic [even though those artists and movements are no longer recent but have become historical]).["][15] The anti-aesthetic modifier "Innocent," which in his proem Humphries likens to "the disarming and delightful virtue which all share in common," is an essentializing predilection shared by all his theatrical characters. It is also obviously very important to Humphries' anti-aesthetic and his anti-poetic, and is significant in antici-pating the virginal Barry McKenzie in the company of the *innoscenti*.

In reading the poems, one cannot help wondering about the poets and, in particular, about the company they keep with Humphries. They seem to re-semble him so strongly as speech-actors – playful, witty, arch(itectonic), ironic, amusing, naive, delightful, keen, and outspoken – that, despite the counter evidence of a publication list, readers might still suspect that the entire compilation (including the publications, no doubt planted in univer-sity libraries) is Humphries' elaborate Dada prank. One can easily imagine that Humphries wrote all the poems himself, just as Paul Hiebert wrote all Sarah Binks's poems, as James McAuley and Harold Stewart wrote all Ern Malley's poems, and as Doris Lessing wrote all Jane Somers' narratives: as a word-hoax and a literary-critical send-up.

Although Stephen Alomes is willing to concede some "affectionate mo-ments"[16] in the book, which he mistakenly calls *A Book of Innocent Austral Verse*, the anthology's good-heartedness is anything but intermittent, pre-cisely because it is *The Barry Humphries Book* and, as a modifier, "Barry Humphries" is exceedingly good-hearted, generous with the precious com-modity of laughter as well as with his fellow Australians. He is not at all the Aussie-basher whom the Humphries-basher Stephen Alomes has made him out to be.[17] Like the few remaining colonial-mentality, inferiority-complex Australians, Alomes would seem to be suffering from the social disease I like to call ho-Humphobia (and that Dame Edna calls "Hmmph").[18]

But Humphries is actually a performer who challenges Australians to like themselves as themselves and not as mere likenesses of Britons, Americans, and others. Alomes defies anyone who happens to admire Humphries, notably John Lahr and Peter Coleman, whom he dismisses as "sympathetic."[19] His dislike of John Lahr, Humphries' most "sympathetic" supporter, is so great that Alomes seems to have found it necessary to exclude him from both the index and the bibliography of *When London Calls*. Humphries is similarly conspicuous in his absence from Trevor Leighton's collection of his own photographs, *The Jokers* (1999), a who's who of British comedians. Humphries might be absent because *The Jokers* is a "whose who" (i.e., peculiarly Leighton's "who's who") and he has simply not made the A-list. In contrast, in *Comedy Greats: A Celebration of Comic Genius Past and Present* (1989), Barry Took places Humphries at the end of his own A-list of distinguished comedians, including Dudley Moore, Buster Keaton, W.C. Fields, Laurel and Hardy, Woody Allen, John Clease, Tony Hancock, Peter Sellers, Jack Benny, and Charlie Chaplin. Yet, it might be argued, Humphries is missing from *The Jokers* because he is a prankster, maybe a jokester, but not a joker, a joke-teller. Les Patterson tells jokes and often has a stand up, but Humphries does not tell stand-up jokes. His comedy is from music hall knockabout traditions of patter and storytelling not from American stand-up traditions of gags, wisecracks, and one-liners. In an interview for the program *Artist of the Week* on the BRAVO! cable television network (on the subject of his reception, at the Banff Television Festival [1997], of the Sir Peter Ustinov Endowment in honour of his life's work as an entertainer), Humphries outlines his approach to his comic art:

I love studying audiences, and that's something, of course, I can't do on television. So I have to imagine the television audience, even when we're doing a funny little interview in a corner of a hotel, here in Banff. I'm thinking of people at home, perhaps watching this, thinking, "who's this strange person with laryngitis, in a suit, talking about humour?" Because if I tried to be a comedian, as I am [indicating his attire], like a stand-up comic in a suit, I don't think I'd be very successful. I'm much more successful if I'm very *very* heavily in disguise!"[20]

Humphries' approach to comedic performance may be attributable in part to his difficult experience as a young performer at the Granville Returned Serviceman's Club, Sydney, in 1957. According to Took: "It's interesting to note that in his early days Barry had the unfortunate experience (common to anyone who has embarked on a career as a stand-up comedian) of playing to an audience at one of these clubs, which greeted him briefly with stony silence before returning to the fruit machines."[21] As a music hall storyteller, whether on stage or in print, Humphries prefers to tell non-narrated narrative (i.e., "narrative with an absent narrator").[22] Humphries absents himself from his narratives by giving his voice over, like his voice-overs in the animated films *Napoleon* (1994) and *Finding Nemo* (2003), to his characters, notably Dame Edna and Sir Les, with their bents for breaking into songs and stories. In the Broadway run and North American tour of *Dame Edna – The Royal Tour (The Show That Listens)* and the North American tour of *A Night with Dame Edna (The Show That Cares)* Humphries acknowledged his "non-narrated narratives" when Dame Edna explained to a "senior" whom she had set upon in the audience that "this is a good show to take a senior to, because there's nothing to follow: there's no story."[23]

*The Barry Humphries Book of Innocent Austral Verse* is Humphries' gift to the Australian people: he gives them back their neglected poets, and he offers himself to Australia, as an editorial poet-*manqué* for now, and a poet proper to come in *Neglected Poems and Other Creatures* (1991), in which he formally aligns himself with the "neglected" poets of his earlier anthology. A comparison of the two works reveals a twinned poetic of innocence and kindness, not Alomes' "sympathy" but an ASPCA (Australian Society for the Prevention of Cruelty to Animals) compassion for his "possums" and for *la sale brute* ("the filthy animal"), Les.[24]

For example, Humphries' poem "Edna's Plea" reads and sounds like a burlesque (i.e., a parody of the form) of A.G. Major's "O God I Pray Thee Lash Me No More." What in Major is heartfelt sentiment and middling verse –

O God I pray Thee lash me no more
    With the whip of affliction,
Hast Thou not taken to the eternal shore
    All my dear children?
    O leave my wife behind;
    The sunshine of my mind
      She is to me
      Now so unhappy.[25]

– is in Dame Edna shocking sentiment and chock-full verse:

ASSUME KNEELING MODE
Lord
As I face the daily storm
Let me not forget my Norm,
Spoilt and wrapped up nice and warm
Prostrate in his hozzie dorm.
Quiescent, like a gladdie corm.
But, if your wonders you perform –
Restoring Norm to shipshape form –
Pray first, Thy Servant, You inform
(for Heaven's sake).
YOU MAY STAND[26]

Whereas Major humbles himself before the Lord, Edna aggrandizes her servitude, even typographically: as God answers Edna in her bidding, Humphries parodies Major.

That God should answer her prayer is appropriate not just because Edna is the personification of importunity but also because her name derives from the Hebrew word *ednah*, which means "delight" and "pleasure" (by coincidence, the passions she stirs in her audiences), and which may be linked etymologically with the Garden of Eden.[27] Perhaps in one of her previous incarnations Edna was the goddess in a Garden of Eden where gladiolas waved in the breeze and the only snake was a one-eyed Sir Les performing a trouser-dance. The opening words of her autobiography, *My Gorgeous Life: An Adventure* (1989), "I am probably Jewish"; her announcement near the start of her 1999–2000 Broadway show, *Dame Edna: The Royal Tour*, that she *is* Jewish; and Humphries' hinting at his own Jewish heritage – "My mother had dark hair and olive skin, and it was by no means certain that if her ancestry were ever traced it would necessarily reveal a purely Anglo-Saxon heritage"[28] – all hint at Edna's possible Edenic origin. Perhaps in a "spooky" way she is the mother of us all, and Humphries, or Barry H (as Edna calls him) is, in the end, the only difference between *Ednah* and Edna, who has always seen Barry H as an aspirant, taking credit for her art and yearning for her megastardom.

In *My Gorgeous Life*, when Dame Edna takes over the show after Humphries has flopped at The Establishment, she observes, "Barry H took it rather well considering. After all he wasn't being cut from the entire show and the presence in the cast of a comparatively famous person who had been on the cover of the *Woman's Weekly* would only put money in his pocket at the end of the day."[29] This pocketed sum is transmuted into a poesy "of time and death pinned human in the pocket of my land,"[30] in which, as a comedian who has cast himself in a human comedy of Australia, Humphries has used laughter to mediate between the philosophical construct of time and the ontological construct of death, giving his readers the courage, or the face, to laugh off any threat, even when the threat comes from motherhood.

Motherhood is a poetic as well as an autobiographical issue with Humphries. His preoccupation with motherhood in his autobiography and stage performances might account for his choice of Tilly Aston's poem "She is your Mother" in *The Barry Humphries Book of Innocent Austral Verse*:

If sometimes her temper's a little short,
And hard words are uttered ere stayed by thought,
And rising anger must oft be fought,
Still, girls, she is your mother.

Have you quite forgotten the day when you
Determined your own sweet will to do
And who it was that restrained you, too?
Why, girls, it was your mother.[31]

In *Neglected Poems*, Dame Edna's monologue "Licking the Beaters" makes a telling companion to Tilly Aston's poem, revealing (1) her (and Humphries') harshness towards maternal authority, which in his stage and TV shows he has. institutionalized as Mrs Beazley's "maximum security twilight home," and (2) his "fantasies for vengeance,"[32] giving his mother a verbal and scribal "licking" for having "beaten" him with her conformity:

When I was a wee girlie,
And brought tea to Mummy early,
Or went shopping on my scooter
For the family veg and meat,
My good deeds were not rewarded
With a coin or something sordid,
But my Mother always saved for me
A truly wondrous treat.[33]

Compare Aston's figure of a mother who denies her daughter her free will with Edna's figure of a "Mummy" who fails to reward "good deeds" (i.e., Edna Mae's willful acts). Free will is perhaps the only true freedom people have. To rob somebody of their will is to take them back to the postlapsarian Garden of Eden and forward to Milton's philosophic puzzle in *Paradise Lost* (of Adam and Eve's free will qualified by God's foreknowledge). But in the Garden of Edna(h), which has never been known to lapse, everybody's will is unfettered, like the will of spectators, free to laugh and to applaud at any time.

As another parallel between Humphries' poetic selections and his own verse, consider his preference for "food, glorious food," Lionel Bart's melody having figured even in the Broadway run of his recent stage show, *Dame Edna: The Royal Tour (The Show That Listens)*, when pianist Phil Reno played a few familiar notes of the chorus to accompany a couple from the audience who, at Dame Edna's insistent invitation, have come up on stage to eat dinner. When Stephen Alomes states in *When London Calls*, "Humphries entitled his autobiography *More Please* not in recognition of his role in *Oliver!*, but of his desires: 'I ALWAYS WANTED MORE,'"[34] he could not be more wrong. Sowerberry and Fagin are among Humphries' finest characters, and *Oliver!* is his greatest musical and his big break. Food figures in all his shows, Dame Edna includes recipes in all her books, and Humphries even prepares "Passionfruit Pavlova" for Peter Coleman's

compilation *The Old Boys' Cookbook* (1996). In his poetry also, the proof
of the utterance is in the presentation of a bill of fare, in a manner reminiscent of Henry Fielding's narrator in *Tom Jones* (1749).

Humphries' fare consists of his very genial metrics, poetics, and imagery.
As a music hall artiste with food on his mind, Humphries is most reminiscent
of Harry Champion (1865–1942), who, in his performances on the halls,
"specialized in songs about homely comforts, such as 'Hot Meat Pies,'
'Savaloys and Trotters,' 'Hot Tripe' and 'Boiled Beef and Carrots.' "[35] It
would appear that, as musical composers, music hall artistes Humphries and
Champion may have exchanged recipes.

One might also consider, in the culinary mode, Elsie Carew's little recipe
recitative "Instant Potato," from *The Barry Humphries Book of Innocent
Austral Verse*, as the starchy ingredient in Dame Edna's patisserie performance "Piece in the Form of a Meat Pie," from *Neglected Poems*:

> Followed faithfully I, the directions as told:
> Put ½ cup of water in saucepan and bring to boil.
> Remove from stove: then add ½ cup of cold milk or
> cold water, add flakes, etc. Everything went swimmingly.
> The next time I thought
> The water I'll get hot
> Straight from the tap
> And not bother with the pot
> But work it would not.
> Now, what I want to know
> How does the potato know
> Whether the water has been boiled or not.[36]

Edna Everage could have written these lines of Elsie Carew, especially if she
had been Elsie in an earlier incarnation. She might have penned them for
the cookery section of one of her books: *Dame Edna's Coffee Table Book:
A Guide to Gracious Living and the Finer Things of Life by One of the
First Ladies of World Theatre* (1976), *Dame Edna's Bedside Companion*
(1982), or *My Gorgeous Life: An Adventure* (1989), all of which feature
Dada recipes for food glorious food that would make the Two Fat Ladies
(Clarissa Dickson Wright and the late Jennifer Paterson), Keith Floyd, and
Jamie Oliver go off food altogether. But for Dame Edna Everage food is
also a main ingredient of her poetics:

> I think that I could never spy
> A poem lovely as a pie.
> A banquet in a single course
> Blushing with rich tomato sauce.

A pie whose crust is oven kissed,
Whose gravy scalds the eater's wrist.
The pastie and the sausage roll
Have not [thy] brown mysterious soul;
The dark-hued Aborigine
Is less indigenous than thee.
Like Phillip Adams rich and chubby,
Tasteful as Patrick White,
With an ice-cold Carlton stubbie,
You're the Great Australian Bite.[37]

This poem is as piebald as Gerard Manley Hopkins' aesthetic (as in his poem "Pied Beauty" [1877]): its colourations are those of divine praise and of the camp desert striations of Australian consumer culture.

Through his speaker, Humphries opposes the postmodern proclivity for reification, "the 'effacement of the traces of production' from the object itself, from the commodity thereby produced."[38] A recipe, because it always balances its product and its means of production (perfectly, if the chef is proficient) is generically anti-reificational. But "Piece in the Form of a Meat Pie" opposes reification in another of its connotations, when

it suggests the kind of guilt people are freed from if they are able not to remember the work that went into their toys and furnishings. Indeed, the point of having your own object world and walls and muffled distance or relative silence all around you, is to forget about all those innumerable others for a while; you don't want to have to think about Third World women every time you pull yourself up to your word processor, or all the other lower-class people with their lower-class lives when you decide to use or consume your other luxury products: it would be like having voices inside your head; indeed, it "violates" the intimate space of your privacy and your extended body.[39]

Humphries uses the occasion of his poem and its Aussie rhyming slang of "meat pie"/"I" to reiterate his position on Australian issues of heritage, preservation, and kitsch – that is, on acknowledging and commemorating some of the means of production of Australian culture: Aborigines (Dreamtime culture), Philip Adams (mediatized culture), Patrick White (artistic culture), Carlton beer (recreational culture), and the Great Australian Bite (cultural geography). Humphries is the custodian of the Australian subject-world, the shared subjectivity of non-exclusive culture, extending from Dreamtime to tomorrow and tomorrow and tomorrow, and even into the worm hole of out-of-print editions (including, unfortunately, most of his own books) and into the quark of pulped publication.

When CollinsAngus and Robertson published *Neglected Poems and Other Creatures* in an Angus and Robertson imprint in 1991, all but five copies of the first edition of 5,000 copies, as printed and delivered to the publisher, were then deliberately destroyed because of "poor paper quality." A note, handwritten in ballpoint ink on the title page of one of the five copies from the original run of *Neglected Poems and Other Creatures* (in my possession) reads:

> Actual first edition
> This edition of 5000
> was pulped because of
> poor paper quality, and is
> one of 5 held by the
> publisher for file use only.
> Tom Thompson
> A & R
> 1991

One month later the book was printed again, in an edition identical to the first in every way – dust jacket, covers, title page, copyright page, dedication page, acknowledgments page, table of contents, and the poems themselves – except that, in the second run the paper is slightly thicker and stiffer than it was in the first run. That publisher Tom Thompson should designate the five remaining copies (and, one presumes, the 4,995 scrapped copies) as "*The actual first edition*" could suggest that the subsequent edition, which was successfully published (printed and released), might be designated "*The virtual first edition*," given that as many as five earlier copies ("neglected" copies, in a sense), and definitely the copy in my possession, may still survive: all predating the putative first edition.

In this regard, all Humphries' poems in *Neglected Poems and Other Creatures* might be considered virtual poems, like the poems in *The Barry Humphries Book of Innocent Austral Verse*, conjuring up virtual realities: the Aristotelian realities of poetic imagination (not banished from the Platonic republic) and of obscure poets lost in the causalities of the past. Whereas in his *Summa Theologica* Thomas Aquinas cannot attribute even to an omnipotent God the power "to make the past not to have been,"[40] Humphries, as editor, found the power to retrieve "neglected" poets and poems from Australian literary history, and, as poet, he preserved his own verse from the "not to have been," the habitual "threnody," of periodical publication. Through Tom Thompson's divine intervention, he was able to spare it the status of pulp poetry and the reputation of urban legend: the ghost of Humphries. Humphries, with his power to make "the past not to have been," may have anticipated Thompson's editorial disposal work on *Neglected Poems* when the jacket of his LP *The Sound of Edna* (1978) had to be modified from a "*Sound of Music*" motif to an "Edvard Munch, *The Scream*" motif.

In his "Prolegomenon" he explains that the selections in *Neglected Poems* "have been reprieved here in the hope that they will amuse, and cast a fitful light on contemporary prejudices, fashionable jargon, and withal, on the Author's more cherished and persistent bugbears."[41] In transposing the possessive "my" with "the Author's," he hints that Roland Barthes' "death of the Author" is greatly exaggerated and seems to align himself, rather, with the great tradition. In my view, Humphries is an author who will never die within the construct "Australian literary history" and whose *oeuvre*, preserved in public libraries, private collections (including Tom Thompson's file cabinet), and, especially, the Humphries collection at the Performing Arts Museum in Melbourne, will never suffer the fate "not to have been." But if the goddess PAM is the most permanent custodian of Humphries' *oeuvre*, then the most enduring repository must be the collective consciousness and non-reificational culture of Australia, which honours both his means of production and his product itself: *bizarrerie*.

Although in the "Prolegomenon" he concedes that "my own contribution to this book is a comparatively modest one" and that "I have been persuaded by my Editor [Louise Thurtell] to publish pasquinades from the sixties and assorted doggerel and facetiae from the seventies and eighties,"[42] in fact his editorial role in arranging the poems was more hands-on than these self-deprecating remarks might imply.

The typescript of *Neglected Poems*,[43] which is inscribed "BH's working copy," reveals how Humphries did indeed work his words, right up until the end, doing standard copyediting but also making more substantive changes: to the contents of the collection and to the diction, imagery, design, dating, typography, placement, and annotation of the individual poems. The typescript consists of seventy-nine numbered white A4 sheets, paginated by hand, in red ballpoint ink, the page numbers circled (with the exception of 77, which is in blue ballpoint ink and not circled); plus three white A4 unnumbered sheets, placed between pages 46 and 47, on which are printed two versions of "My Little Philatelist" and one version of "The Gladiolus Stamp"; and two mauve (or, more likely, wisteria) A4 unnumbered sheets, on which are printed "What I Miss." All the poems are typewritten and are printed on the recto sides only, with all alterations and annotations made by hand in fine-point black felt pen. Corrections and revisions tend to be printed by hand, and the annotations tend to be handwritten.

The typescript features, for example, the poem "The Ballad of Camberwell Jail," crossed through with a diagonal line, and with the handwritten instruction "(Replace with Ode to City of C'well)," a change effected in the published edition. Similarly, "Ode to Melbourne" is emended by hand to "Ode to the Melbourne Grammar School"; "Song for the Swinging Seventies" in the typescript becomes "Untitled Song for the Sixties" in the book; "Thespian Les" becomes "Les at Leisure"; "Nature is Red in Tooth and

Claw" becomes "My Drawer"; "~~Dame Edna's Song~~" is retitled as "I Can't Let My Public Down"; "Cranbrook" is extended into "The Cranbrook Steinway"; "Les the Work-a-holic" becomes "The Workaholic"; "Les Sings Brecht" is metonymized as "The Ballad of Les the Knife"; "Health and Fitness" becomes simply "Fitness"; "Introducing Edna" becomes "Saluting Edna"; "Ode to John Laws" is genderized from a "Barry Humphries" to a "Dame Edna Everage" poem; "Washed Down the Gutter" is hypothesized as "If It Was Raining Virgins"; and "Edna's Song" is anathematized into "I Can't Let My Public Down." Other poems in the typescript simply do not appear in the book, possibly because of their personal bitterness and their satirical bite, although I believe they would have given the collection even greater distinction: "My Pontiac," "Meditations on a Mysterious Decorative Motif in the 'Great Space' at the Wentworth Hotel, Melbourne," "Ode to the New Nine by Five," "Top Filmic Nation," "Abo Smoker's Stand," "A Reasonable Parent's Plea," "The Diplomatic Corps," "Lines for a Child's Autograph Book," "Encore," and, most notably, "What I Miss." If *Neglected Poems and Other Creatures* were to be published in a revised edition, these distinguished poems should undoubtedly be included in it.

In his Prolegomenon, a form that, generically, promises a long and complex work, Humphries actually categorizes his poetry as rather winsome, its meaning linked not with print but with the original occasions of their recitation: "It was never intended that they should be divorced from the authorial voice or outlive their ephemeral purpose and appear on the printed page."[44] Elsewhere, Humphries does refer to his poems as "recitations," as in this example from his *Bulletin* article "The Confessions of Barry Humphries" (1965): "I also devised a recitation called 'Maroon' in which Edna examined an aspect of the colour question."[45] Always meticulous with his diction, Humphries delivers in his Prolegomenon a careful and guarded message to the reader. He does this not to distance himself from the "youthful folly" (see Note 1, Chapter 2) of his insistent pentameter or his lilting prosody but, rather, to emphasize the essential orality and performativity of his verse (which, at least for readers who are not thoroughly familiar with Humphries' voice and image as an actor and a stage performer, tend to flatten out on paper), and of his keynote speakers in *Neglected Poems*: Barry Humphries (i.e., the implied poet), Barry McKenzie, Sir Les Patterson, and Dame Edna Everage. But for readers who know these voices and images – and in performance they are quite unforgettable – the words of his poems, even on paper, are *Nommo* (the word alive on the tongue and in the ear, and animating its hearers) not *Kintu* (the word as merely "thing," dead).[46]

In *Orality and Literacy* (1982), Walter J. Ong summarizes a poetics that points to Humphries' distinction between verse that rises to the occasion of performance and verse that flattens out on the occasion of publication: "Communication is intersubjective. The media model is not."[47] As a poet,

Humphries is about his audience: he must get around them, like surround sound. In *Neglected Poems*, he does manage to encircle his readers because his, and his characters', voices ring out intersubjectively in monologues that demand to be read aloud but that also defer to readers who must admit they could not possibly "do" Humphries, McKenzie, Patterson, or Everage. The poems resound in the voices of the speakers and the ears of their hearers, rising so far above the page as to dissolve it before it can be pulped. The poems' intersubjective orality takes precedence over the "media model" of the book, which, to Humphries, is a convenient presentation package, like a CD jewel case or the shrink-wrap around it.

"What I Miss" is a draft of a Dame Edna monologue in the *ubi sunt* convention, reflecting Humphries' interests in kitsch, conservation, chronicles, lists, nostalgia, and (be)longing. The fifty-line, nine-stanza poem is typed on two A4 wisteria-coloured sheets at the end of the manuscript. (The entire *Neglected Poems*, "BH's working copy" typescript is on A4 paper, white, excepting "What I Miss.") The poem reads like a song lyric, with a lilting introduction, three verses, two choruses, and a coda. The verses, most of whose lines begin "I miss," enumerate Dame Edna's longings and belongings, consisting mostly of British people (especially royalty and performers) and London sites (especially shops not left standing). For instance: "I miss Lilly I miss Skinner / I miss Lyons Corner House for that modest little dinner." His handwritten and hand-printed marginalia hint at directions the unfinished poem might have taken and, perhaps, offer an insight into his process of composition.

For example, for the line "I miss looking for a telephone box that someone hasn't wee'd in" Humphries notes in the margin the alternative endings "a read in" and "playing the lead in"; for the couplet "I miss little Bernard Levin the discoverer of Mahler / More than I miss my furry family, the wombat and koalas," he cites the alternative rhymes "galas," "goannas," and "massage parlours"; and the closing lines of the third verse, "I miss little Meg from Crossroads and Whiteley's for my bedding / I miss the old Cortina and I missed Di and Charles's wedding / That's why I wasn't sitting in the Royal pew / But most of all I've missed my little chats with folk like you" seems especially tentative as Humphries tests the rhyming-dictionary rhymes "brew," "loo," "askew," "flu," "queue," "drew," "shoe," "view," "clue," "brew" (again), and "for the funny things they do."

At the end of the second page, Humphries has jotted down an idea for his list of misses: "I miss my loyal British public / I miss my ~~darling~~ little gyno." All these annotations are quite probationary, suggesting that the poem is a work in progress that Humphries may have had to abandon in his haste to ready the manuscript for publication. Still, "What I Miss" is what I miss most from the published *Neglected Poems*. It is the kernel (in the narratological sense) of a fine poem, and the kitsch-sketch of a libretto

Table 3.1
Missing Contents of *Neglected Poems*: Typescript and Book

| Section Title and Speaker | Titles of Poems in Typescript but not Book | Titles of Poems in Book but not Typescript |
|---|---|---|
| Barry Humphries | My Pontiac | After the Event |
| Barry Humphries | Meditations on a Mysterious Decorative Motif | Journo |
| Barry Humphries | | Threnody for Patrick White |
| Barry Humphries | | Tycoons |
| Barry McKenzie | | Australian Repartee |
| Sir Les Patterson | Top Filmic Nation | Les at Leisure |
| Sir Les Patterson | Thespian Les | My Gong |
| Sir Les Patterson | Abo Smoker's Stand | Up the Republic |
| Dame Edna Everage | The Diplomatic Corps | Edna's Accolade |
| Dame Edna Everage | Polyester Bearded Santa | My Drawer |
| Dame Edna Everage | Nature Is Red in Tooth and Claw | Nostalgie de la Jeunesse |
| Dame Edna Everage | Why Do They Do It? | Dame Edna's Mega Plate |

that would make one of Humphries' best music hall songs, especially if Dame Edna would get round to raising Humphries' collaborator composer Stanley Myers (who died in 1993) from white noise or if Sir Les Patterson could beguile Myers away from the bruitism that is death.

And there are further disparities between "BH's working copy" and "virtual" *Neglected Poems and Other Creatures*. These changes in the contents of *Neglected Poems* reflect Humphries' efforts (1) to characterize Sir Les Patterson and Dame Edna Everage as aesthetic, not just comic, poets by replacing four rather winsome poems in the typescript with four more serious poems in the published text; (2) to underscore Barry McKenzie's role as a comic singer by leaving his score as it is; and (3) to declare himself as a true poet (who would never leave the taste of poetaster in the mouths of his readers) by working into the book four poems that are not in the typescript (somewhat as he included on the LP *The Barry Humphries Record of Innocent Austral Verse* nine poems that are not in *The Barry Humphries Book of Innocent Austral Verse*).

Of the poems missing from the published edition of *Neglected Poems*, "Pontiac" is positioned in the typescript to lead off the entire sequence. Its figure is a car ride – "Slide in beside me in my Pontiac / ... while I drive you back / Down Melbourne byways" – and a double-look (1) at the "riders in the chariot," at "your Ensign tie, your Bedgegood shoes"; and (2) "through my magic windscreen at some views / Of Melbourne ere the Triumph of the Goth." The speaker of the poem sets Humphries' speaker-readers apart from conventional readers of poetry by setting them off on a journey through the imagination, as if Australia, and other postmodern nation-constructs, had not already suffered the deaths both "of the Author" and (according to Mordecai Himmelfarb in Patrick White's *Riders in the Chariot* [198]) of the Intellect. In the published text, Humphries sets off on this voice and image journey with his speaker-readers in his "Prolegomenon," with its curriculum vitae motif, and in the first poem, "The Ballad of Charles Blackman," with its rite of passage motif, moving speaker-readers through the boroughs of Charles Blackman's London, "under the bed clothes" of his detailed paintings, and back to the symposium table to celebrate Blackman: "Three cheers for Charles / His name is Black / He is the sweep of Art!" Like Blackman, Humphries sweeps through his typescript, leaving editorial traces like black printer's ink left on the slugs of an old linotype, before printing became naughty, making last-minute changes, for "In a minute there is time / For decisions and revisions which a minute will reverse,"[48] excepting that publication is irreversible.

Humphries' changes to the typescript are descriptive, telling editorial tales, if not about his composition process, then at least about his method of touching up. Some of the changes are indeed cosmetic. For example, in "Washed Down the Gutter" Humphries has corrected a typographical error, changing by hand the word "proof" to "poof" in the lines "If it was raining virgins, / I'd be washed down the gutter with a poof," as they appear in the poem's concluding couplet and in "If It Was Raining Virgins." Yet his alteration of the word "brick" to "prick" in the line "At the knock shop wedding, I'm the spare prick" is typological rather than typographical: it turns a metaphor of reliability (Bazza is a good bloke, a brick) into a metaphor of danger (Bazza is proudly phallocentric, with his prick up your ears, in Joe Orton fashion, capable of surprising you in a convincing E.M. Forster way).

In "Madame Tosshard's Waxworks," a poem that Humphries performed on the occasion of Dame Edna's installation in Madame Tussaud's Wax Museum, the first Australian to be so honoured, the typescript version features a concluding couplet that is not in the published version: "~~And so here she is for all to view / Eat your heart out, Danny La Rue~~." These lines would serve only to perpetuate the misidentification of Humphries with female impersonators. John Lahr straightens the seams in Humphries' stockings and sets the record straight when he reminds us, in his *Age* (Melbourne) article "Edna Takes Manhattan," that "Dame Edna ... is not a drag act but a character actor in a dress who makes points about life."[49] Syntactically, Lahr, like Groucho Marx's Captain Spaulding, famous for having shot an elephant in his pyjamas, suggests that it is Dame Edna's "dress who makes points about life." Yet, even outside the rule of syntax,

Lahr is correct: frocks are Humphries' *haute mode* of address. As Humphries observes, "Acting the part of Edna is the perfect Method acting exercise, for the Method actor, when contemplating a new role, must fabricate his character's history,"[50] which, in Edna's case, is partly a history of frocks, to which Humphries' exhibition *Dame Edna's Frock-a-Thon: A Journey from Cardigan to Couture* (George Adams Gallery, Victorian Arts Centre, Melbourne, 3 April – 30 May 1999) attests.

Thus, by omitting the line referring to Danny La Rue, Humphries ensures that the focus stays on Dame Edna. The poem ends: "For now it's with pleasure that I unveil yer / Woman of Wax – Queen of Australia. / From the tip of your glad to the jewels on yer glasses, / You've proved Australians have culture right up to our arses." No poet says it – the word "arses" – more eloquently than Humphries, with the possible exception of Marcel Duchamp, whose painting of a mustachioed *Mona Lisa* bears the inscription *L.H.O.O.Q.*, which is homonymous for " 'elle a chaud au cul' or 'she has a hot ass,' "[51] and, alternatively, "she is hot-arsed" (St Pierre's translation), a body-marking with which Les Patterson would undoubtedly concur.

Her installation in Madame Tussaud's emphasizes Dame Edna Everage's Aristotelian actuality, from which the waxwork sculpture is once-removed and the poem "Madame Tosshard's Waxworks" is twice-removed. For example, in his interview on the BRAVO! television program *Artist of the Week* (see Note 20, this chapter), Humphries refers to Dame Edna as an installation: "In a sense Edna is a sort of artistic creation. You might almost call her a living installation."

Similarly, "Ode to the Melbourne Theatre Company," which Humphries first performed on the occasion of MTC director John Sumner's retirement, concludes with the speaker's bittersweet effort to smooth over some of the philosophical differences between appearance and reality:

> When told how old this company was, I scarcely could believe it.
> For it only seems like yesterday that I was asked to leave it.
> I couldn't learn my lines, you see, which wouldn't do at all,
> So I was driven to a sordid life in the sleazy music hall.
> Since those far days the wound has healed, I've learned to weigh all factors;
> Although I but a comic be, I don't envy real actors.
> Of bitter dregs I've drunk enough; of fame I've sipped the cup,
> They still have lines to learn by heart, I have to make them up.[52]

These lines must have pealed in Humphries' performance of them because, even in print, the speaker's variously ironic, biting, accusatory, self-deprecating, comic, and sarcastic tones are insistent, giving form and shape to the speaker, a prophet come home to Nazareth, a mariner returned to Ithaca, a poet and musician making his way back from Hades, catching everyone up in the moment – a moment that is as poignant in the telling of this odious ode as is Humphries' account, in a chapter appropriately entitled "Licking the Beaters," of catching up (if only in imagination) with his former school teacher Miss Jensen.[53] The well-learned line running through the Melbourne Theatre Company, and through Mrs J.A.E. Humphries and Miss Jensen, reiterates not only the moral teaching that "Licking the beaters was one of the great privileges of an Australian childhood"[54] but also one of the priceless prerogatives of a Messianic candidate, an Odyssean estranged spouse, an Orphic seer and teller, and, ultimately, Humphries the poet taster.

The brilliant final punch line of "Ode to the Melbourne Theatre Company" would have been just a pulled punch had Humphries not deleted the five additional lines at the end of the typescript version of the poem. They read:

The object of this SOCIETY is to close the yawning gap
Between audience and performer and keep our theatre on the map.
So let's drink to this enterprise, and welcome a New Age,
When you aren't stuck with your chocs all alone in a box,
But can rustle them loudly on a stage.

Cutting the clever internal rhyme "stuck with your chocs all alone in a box," which is positively augustan and archly Dada (cf. Tristan Tzara's "each chocolate / wash your brain / dada / dada / drink water" in his poem "dada song"[55] and Marcel Duchamp's artworks *The Box of 1914* [1913–14], *The Green Box* [1934], *Boîte Alert* [1959–60], and *Chocolate Grinder* [1913, 1914]), must have been difficult for Humphries. However, if he had not done so, the conclusion would have been bathetic for it neither scans nor scandalizes. But the published poem makes a scandal nevertheless, in calculated words, each one of which Humphries would seem to have licked personally.

Dame Edna's signature poem (and recitative song) "Lament for Maid Melbourne," which Humphries has performed on the LP *The Barry Humphries Record of Innocent Austral Verse* (1972) and on the CD *Moonee Ponds Muse, Vol. 1* (1991),[56] is an *ubi sunt* peroration on Melbourne's past glories and an imperious polemic on urban conservation, which concludes with a couplet that is distinguished by its trapeze-catch rhyme as much as it is by Dame Edna's closing paroxysm of indignation:

Let us unite in this great fight against Pollution's menace,
Or Melbourne will be filthier than Paris, Rome – or Venice.[57]

As she pounces upon the word "Venice," Dame Edna ensures that her audience and she come to "simultaneous paroxysms,"[58] and she turns her conservational message into a Munchian scream. In the typescript, Humphries has wisely crossed out two subsequent lines, which, had they been printed, would have squandered his melodious conceit of the Venetian navy for the lumbering zoetrope of a ride on the buses:

> Leap up on my bus and see with me how large this menace looms,
> But stand clear pray, as we drive away, to avoid our diesel fumes.

Clearly, this bus is not as important to Humphries as are the double-deckers that passed by 2a Pembridge Gardens in the winter of 1960. In reviewing his closing lines for "Lament for Maid Melbourne," he must have realized that he already had an excellent poem to this point and that adding another couplet would choke it in "diesel fumes."

Without the final couplet, the poem is an exemplar of Humphries' own kind of sprung rhythm, seemingly dependent on nothing more than the verbal whimsy of the speaker. Here Dame Edna Everage, like Humphries in his performances on the LP *The Barry Humphries Record of Innocent Austral Verse*, is an expert character actor who speaks the part trippingly. As recitative, "Lament for Maid Melbourne" is typical of Humphries' mixture of speech and song both in poems whose cadences recommend them for singing and in songs that his characters often recite to musical accompaniment.

On stage, his performers often feel a song coming on and sometimes interrupt their singing to recount an anecdote, tell a joke, or chide spectators (e.g., for their rudeness in reading the theatre program during the song). In this regard, Dame Edna is Humphries' most remarkable performer, with her ease for breaking out into song and into speech merely on a whim rather than at the audience's request. Even the inimitable Sarah Bernhardt, like Dame Edna, a great music hall artiste, had to admit:

In the evening our last performance was to be *Là Dame aux camélias*. I had fourteen curtain calls. For a moment I was confused because, amongst the tempest of cries and bravos, I could hear a strident cry coming from hundreds of mouths that I did not understand. I kept asking in the wings after each curtain call what this word meant that reached my ears over and over like a terrible fit of sneezing.

Jarret arrived and helped me out. "They are asking for a speech." As I looked at him in astonishment he said, "Yes, they want you to make a little speech."

"Ah, no!" I cried as I went back for another curtain call, "No!" As I curtseyed to the audience I murmured in English, "I can't speak, but I can tell you 'thank you, thank you, with all my heart!'" I left the theater admidst thunderous applause with cries of, "Hip, hip, hooray! Long live France!"[59]

Upstaging Bernhardt, Dame Edna Everage, who could be known as *la dame aux glaïeuls* (not in Alexandre Dumas' play but in her own flower shows on stage), is always ready to give a speech to her audience. Their applause, and their outcries (e.g., "Splish splash wrinkle sink hurrah three hips," "Hoo-roo!"[60] and "Long live Australia!") are the sounds of approval, of shock, of kindness, of niceness.

As Dame Edna knew "diesel fumes" would smother the end of "Lament for Maid Melbourne," so Humphries seems to have realized that, by appending a recipe for lamington cakes to his poem "The Lamington" (entitled "The Lamington Stamp" in the published version), he would clog in patter his stirring tale of Lord Carrington's inheritance of what would become an Australian national recipe.

Humphries performed this poem, as "Histoire du Lamington," along with other poems ("The Shark," "The Blowfly," "The Funnel Web-Spider," "Morceau en forme de 'meat pie,'" and "The Pavlova") collected in 1991 under the rubric "First Day Covers," with composer Nigel Butterley and conductor John Hopkins and the Sydney Symphony Orchestra, in the LP *Barry Humphries at Carnegie Hall in First Day Covers: A Philharmonic Philatelia* (1972). His performance suggests how important moving words have always been to him: emotive words but also words in motion, unfixed by the arbitrary rules of grammar and usage. In performance and on disc Humphries goes on to deliver the recipe, prefacing it with the stage directive "Excuse I. Now I'd like, if I may, in praise, to pass on to you ladies my own special little lamington recipe." As Dame Edna delivers each step in the recipe, Butterley and Hopkins orchestrate the line with outbursts of minor chords and threats of atonality. The contrast between the domestic and the theatrical is magnificent:

Take a nice stale sponge cake,
Cut into cubes.
Mix some delicious chocolate icing.
Take your sponge cubes and roll about in icing.
Sprinkle the lamingtons with desiccated coconut
And serve on a paper doily on a tupperware plate.

A cookery segment at the end of a poem may seem solely comic (notably the directive to "roll about in icing"), but in a stage show, and with the proper orchestration, these lines work theatrically as they could never work on the page.

The orchestrated lamington recipe, in its discordant pairing of words and music, anticipates, for example, Gavin Bryars' series of compositions *A Man in a Room, Gambling* (1992), in which sculptor Juan Muñoz' narratives on cheating at cards at first seem unconnected with their poignant orchestral accompaniment and detached from the audience. These sound poems of Humphries-Butterley and Muñoz-Bryars work not because, having heard them, people can set out to bake a lamington or to cheat at cards but, rather, because they now have the knowledge to do something that they may never have to do. And, in an Aristotelian sense, this is what free will is mainly about. I need to hear Edna's recipe because I may never need to make it; I need to hear Muñoz' instructions because I may never need to cheat at cards. Each sound poem is a recipe of the human will, as in the Garden of Edna(h), a place I may never need to visit, and of the human condition that has been sold the postlapsarian bill of "may"/"may not." Humphries' recipes are not *petits madeleines*, important as they are in a Proustian milieu; rather, they are, under the aspect of *haute cuisine*, philosophical meditations on free will and critical dialectics on the fictionality of telling.

Humphries' poems are textual as well as oratorical, musical, philosophical, and critical, and they have to do with what Michel Sanouillet and Elmer Peterson call "textiles"[61] (in reference to Duchamp's *petite oeuvre* of notations on postcards and scraps of paper [which, coincidentally, he started making in 1934, the year Humphries was born]). Humphries is also a note-taker. His "Notes on the Poems,"[62] which he began writing in the typescript, are like Duchamp's notes, or indeed Aristotle's notes (specifically, his students' notes, which formed the basis for the reconstruction of the *Poetics*).

As "textiles" *Neglected Poems and Other Creatures* might inspire the reader to say, echoing Humphries' retort to guest Magnus Magnusson in an episode of the TV show *The Dame Edna Experience*, 2nd series (1989), "Barry, stop playing with your texticles!" In this episode of *The Dame Edna* Experience, series 2.2, guest Magnus Magnusson, who is host of the BBC-1 quiz show *Mastermind* (1972–   ), talked about what he used to eat as a child growing up in Iceland:

MAGNUS: And finally, the *pièce de résistance*, that we give to really special guests. They are a mixture of rams' scrota and lambs' testicles.
DAME EDNA: This is a family show, Magus! May I assume that as a very special treat, on a special occasion, your mother would serve up something like that, would she?
MAGNUS: Oh yes, indeed she would.
DAME EDNA: And she'd be probably pretty disappointed if you little kiddies didn't eat it when you got home from school.
MAGNUS: Yes, she would.
DAME EDNA: I mean, I think I'd probably just push it around my plate a bit, I'm afraid.
MAGNUS: No, they're very good for the hormones.
DAME EDNA: Oh, are they?
MAGNUS: Yes, they are.
DAME EDNA: So your mother never said, "Eat up! Stop playing with your testicles!"

If one were to dip into Les Patterson's trouser pockets, what would one find? If his pockets were deep enough – given the prêt-à-porter or bespoke cut of his leisure suits (as distinguished from Humphries' made-to-measure Savile Row lines), one suspects they would be quite shallow – one might happen upon a "one-eyed trouser snake." But if one were to poke into one of Humphries' trouser pockets, then one might be surprised to find his poesy, in the words of Janet Frame, "pinned human in the pocket of [his] land,"[63] Australia. I imagine Humphries to have inscribed his entire poetic output on texticular notepapers (think of a pack of cigarette papers), including his poetics of composition, while the goddess Australia, who is his land and muse, is watching on, like Hal Porter's "watcher on a cast-iron balcony" (1963).

## PUTTING SPEECH-ACTS TO MUSIC: HUMPHRIES AS LYR(IC)IST

Music brings Humphries' poems to life, reminding his readers that his words-on-the-page ring with the cadences of his narrators' speech acts, that their condition, and the reader's condition of reading, is tonality, with a hint of dissonance: as poems, they are monologues but never monotonous; as lyrics, they are songs coming on, as in a world (Dame Edna's stage-struck world) where, when anyone feels a song coming on, they simply set about singing it.

As a music hall artiste, Humphries is a comic singer. His lyrical compositions, and his collaborations with music composers Stanley Myers and Nick Rowley, in particular; and with Nigel Butterley, Carl Davis, Peter Best, Diane Millstead, James McConnell, Kit Hesketh-Harvey, and Billy Philadelphia; and his performances in Lionel Bart's musicals *Oliver* (1960, 1963, 1967, 1997) and *Maggie May* (1964); and of course many other shows, including Geoffrey Dutton's virtual production of *The Magic Flute*[64] (in which Humphries was cast as Papageno), all characterize him as a great musician: lyricist, singer, and composer. His career as a song-writer refutes his friend Dutton's shocking fib – "Barry cannot read music"[65] – and even his own admission that his "compositions are either picked out with one finger on the keyboard or hummed or warbled to an amanuensis, after which they often sound very impressive."[66] The fact is, his "read" on the comic song is among the most perspicacious and productive in music hall, variety, tin pan alley, and comic and popular traditions.

As a reader of scores, he is a music hall bicycle act, like Eddie Gordon and Nancy; Lotto, Lilo, and Otto; the Elliotts; Henri French; Ad Robbins;[67] and even Les Patterson, who, in his curse "may your balls turn into bicycle wheels and backpedal up your arse," has proven himself a kind of trick cyclist. Yet, more than any of these pedallers, Humphries resembles the cyclist in Marcel Duchamp's drawing *To Have the Apprentice in the*

*Sun* (1914), who appears to be riding across a sheet of music paper. Humphries' reading of song is as true as is a well tuned bicycle wheel. His reliance on composers to orchestrate his lyrics is not unusual for a music hall artiste. As Clarkson Rose has noted, "Song-writing is a heterogeneous job, and collaboration is not always easy, but I found it smooth-going with Conrad Leonard. He married his tunes to my lyrics in a splendid way, and, like myself, was a quick worker."[68] Humphries' marriages with Rowley and Myers have issued some of the greatest Australian comic songs on the halls.

His animal songs are fabulous not only generically but also qualitatively, as witty and elegant as *The Bestiary* compositions of Michael Flanders and Donald Swann. Humphries' animal songs include: "Wendy the One-Eyed Wombat" (1969) and "Great Big Fish" (1970), both from the LP *Barry Humphries' Savoury Dip* (1971); his recitative songs "The Shark," "The Blowfly," "The Funnel Web-Spider," and "Koangankâla Symphony," all from *Barry Humphries at Carnegie Hall* (1972); "Canto Two" of his *Song of Australia* (1981);[69] and, to stretch a point, "My Little One-Eyed Trouser Snake," from Humphries' collaboration with Peter Cook, Dudley Moore, and others (the LP *Private Eye's Blue Record* [1965]). Even his performances of other people's animal songs are bestial, for example Lionel Bart's "Ballad of the Liver Bird," from the stage musical *Maggie May* (1964); and the songs of the wolf, the duck, the cat, and the bird in Dame Edna Everage's narration of Sergei Prokofiev's *Peter and the Wolf* (1997); and of Babar in Humphries' narration of Francis Poulenc's *The Story of Babar, the Little Elephant* (1997). Finally, almost any composition sung by Les Patterson could be considered an animal song because most of his songs are autobiographical, and Patterson is, after all, a beast. In "Fanfare for a Dame," her introduction to "Song of Australia" (on the LP *The Last Night of the Poms* [1981]), Dame Edna Everage dismisses Sir Les Patterson, who has performed the first half of the concert, "Fanfare for a Cultural Attaché" and "Sir Les Introduces Peter and Shark," as "an animal act" (although in "Canto Eight" she seems to take Patterson back into her favour, when she confesses, "I miss my bushland pals / You see they're all marsupials"). Other marginal animal songs include the sketch "The Migrant Hostess" and the monologue "Sandy Stone" on the EP *Wild Life in Suburbia* (1958), and the song "Highett Fidelity" and the monologue "Dear Beryl" on the EP *Wild Life in Suburbia, Volume Two* (1959), in that Humphries tends to view suburbanites as beastly creatures, like Mrs Flack and Mrs Jolly in Patrick White's *Riders in the Chariot* (1961).

Sometimes the company of animals is preferable to the company of people. Similarly, silence can be preferable to speech, but sometimes breaking out into song, breaking away from "excessive" speech and even "intolerable" silence, is what the theatrical moment calls for. Hélène Cixous teaches,

"It is not necessary to speak to let the other be. There is no need for silence or speech. But human beings do not tolerate silence and tend to speak excessively."[70] Humphries seems to have responded to this teaching by making Edna Everage and Les Patterson break into song whenever their speech becomes excessive (or when "there is no need for silence or speech") and by letting animals sing (or at least letting people sing about animals) whenever silence, such as the silence of an unresponsive audience or of a dark music hall theatre, has become intolerable.

"Wendy the One-Eyed Wombat" and "Great Big Fish" are the most telling of his animal songs. They tell on him as a lyricist of conscience, a meistersinger on the halls, and also as a lyr(ic)ist – a lyre-player who tells the truth:

Wendy the One-Eyed Wombat

Wendy the one-eyed wombat
Went walking down Wogga-Wogga way,
Saw a witchetty grub hiding in the scrub,
So he raised his wombat hat and said "Bonzer Day!"

*Phew!* Graham the grey-faced witchetty grub
Was sliding over Sydney Harbour Bridge,
When a funnel-web spider sidled up beside her,
Said, "Come and share a tube of Foster's from my fridge."

Phyllis the funnel-web spider
Was fumbling with his fuzzy furry feelers,
When an old kangaroo, an Aborigine too,
Said, "Lead us to the bonzer sheilas!"

Ady the aimless Abo
Was riding on a yellow kangaroo,
When the 'roo said, "Ouch! There's a spider in me pouch!
"Let's all go up the road and have a few."

So the one-eyed wombat and the grey-faced grub,
The furry old spider went along to the pub,
With the blacka blackam Abo and the old kangaroo –
Gosh, you wouldn't read about it! It was just like a zoo!
Wombat, witchetty, funnel-web, Abo-Abo – Hoo-roo![71]

This song is a bestiary of Australian fauna and of Australian social conduct: a comic ditty but also a song in the classical and medieval traditions of the fable, and of the fabula or the narratological kernel, in which animals teach moral lessons because human beings cannot.

Note the alliteration throughout, which establishes a mellifluous euphony to complement the simple *abab* rhyme scheme. Note also the speaker's manifold structure, folding one stanza into the next, like beaten egg whites into a soufflé (as from the book *French Provincial Soufflés*, a copy of which Dame Edna sent to her Uncle Victor,[72] or in her recipe for "Australian Frozen Christmas Pudding" in *Dame Edna's Coffee Table Book*: "In another basin beat the egg whites stiffly, add remaining sugar. Blend both together by folding gently").[73] In "Wendy the One-Eyed Wombat" Wendy meets "a witchetty-grub" in Stanza 1, which folds "gently" into Stanza 2, where the witchetty grub rises into Graham, who meets "a funnel-web spider." Then Stanza 2 folds "gently" into Stanza 3, where the funnel-web spider rises into Phyllis, who meets "an old kangaroo" and "an Aborigine," who rise into Ady and "a yellow kangaroo" in Stanza 4, where they meet Phyllis and head to the pub with Wendy and Graham. Humphries exploits the manifold technique further in "Wendy the One-Eyed Wombat" in a series of nominal-to-pronominal gender changes: Wendy → "he," Graham → "her," Phyllis → "his"; in addition, Ady is of unspecified gender, to which the cross-gender "pet" name "Abo-Abo" attests; and the kangaroo, who is noted as having a pouch, is female, so, in the poem's gender openness, could be pronominalized "her" or "his."

In the film *Napoleon* (1994), Barry Humphries plays the voice-part of a yellow kangaroo that is instrumental in restoring unity among animals and human beings. Compare John Lahr, who in his book on his father, *Notes on a Cowardly Lion: The Biography of Bert Lahr* (1969), recounts a conversation between Frank Morgan, who played the Wizard, and Bert Lahr, who played the Cowardly Lion, in the 1939 film *The Wizard of Oz*: " 'Bert,' said Morgan, 'you're going to be a great hit in this picture. But it's not going to do you a damn bit of good – you're playing an animal.' 'If I'd made a hit as a *human being*,' Lahr muses, 'then perhaps I'd be sailing in films now.' "[74] (In Chapter 7 Humphries hits the big-time as a human being.)

Humphries, when in character as Les Patterson or Edna Everage, often jokes about the simplicity of Aboriginal languages or about things that pre-date Aborigines, as in "Piece in the Form of the Meat Pie," where the speaker apostrophizes, "The dark-hued Aborigine / Is less indigenous than thee."[75] In "Wendy the One-Eyed Wombat" the singer characterizes Ady as "aimless" and places him/her in the company (a "public" house) of animals and insects, in a pub that is "like a zoo." Yet closer inspection reveals Ady as a person who, like Humphries as a stage performer, transcends gender, and whom the singer of the song has chosen so as to represent humanity – not a white Euro-Australian but a Black subject – and whom the singer has placed with a distinctively Australian coat-of-arms culture of wombat, witchetty grub, funnel-web spider, and kangaroo. Even the classification "aimless" (i.e., without free will, outside the Garden of Edna[h]) comments only on a Eurocentric stereotype of the Nyoongah and other First Nations peoples of Australia.

The other characters are similarly disabled, at least to appearances: Wendy is "one-eyed," Graham is "grey-faced," Phyllis "fumbles" with "his feelers," and the kangaroo is in pain. But in fact Ady and the others have a common purpose: to go to the pub. Theirs is a peculiarly Australian journey not just to the public house but through some public perceptions of the house of Australia, about which one rarely reads. Poems by other poets, sublunary poems, unfold their meanings, but Humphries' poems – lunatic songs such as "Wendy the One-Eyed Wombat" – fold in their meanings, folding in readers-hearers like beaten eggs that, having responded to Edna's invitation to lick the beaters, they have on their tongues and lips.

"Great Big Fish" is another of Humphries' fine fabular songs, enfolding hearers into its subtle structure of verses and chorus, and making their lips smack of fish:

Great Big Fish

Why do I keep swimming round and round my pond,
When there's a great big ocean lying just beyond?
I can hear those breakers crashing on the shore.
They can have their ocean, but I don't ask for more.

Cause I'm a great big fish in a tiny little pool,
I'm the big headmaster of a tiny little school.
I love the things that fishes do; I'm always in the swim.
I'm really that much fishier than it or her or him.

Cause I'm a great big fish in a tiny little lake.
When all the fish are half asleep, I'm always twice awake.
I hear the tales about those whales who've made it overseas,
But my little fishy world is good enough for me.

Splish splash wrinkle sink hurrah three hips,
I'll end up in the papers, and I'll end up in the chips.

I'm a great big fish in a little billabong.
If there's any competition, it doesn't last for long,
Cause as a rule they leave the pool in search of bigger baits,
And talk to all those foreign fish and not their Aussie mates.

Not like this great big fish in me teeny little creek,
I only have to make a splash and I'm famous for a week.
A mate of mine swam overseas intending there to linger,
And then he came back home again stuck up like a fish finger.

Splish splash wrinkle sink hurrah three hips,
I'll end up in the papers and I'll end up in the chips.
I'm a great big fish in a small aquarium.
What's the point of swimming so far away from mum?
The water here's so nice and warm; the plankton's fresh and green,
And all those little tiddlers think I'm the biggest fish they've seen.

I'm such I'm a big fat fish in a teensy weensy pool.
I blow the biggest bubbles of any in the school,
And when I swim to heaven, I've only got one wish,
That the golden fish pond in the sky ... is just as small as this.

Singing splish splash wrinkle sink hurrah three hips,
I'll end up in the papers and I'll end up in the chips.

In this song, the speaker, a singing fish, ponders the verities – the truths, but also the unities, of space, action, and time, which in the *Poetics* Aristotle applies (appropriately) to the fable – of its life in water, the element through which fish swim and that flows through the human body, a remnant of when people swam the oceans.

This song might be interpreted as a correlative of Barry Humphries' desire to jump from the "pond," "pool," "lake," "billabong," "creek," and "aquarium" – that is, the Moonee Ponds – of Australia into the "ocean" and "overseas" to unlimited success. But "Great Big Fish" is actually about the folly of Australians who still believe that success is to be found not in their homeland but elsewhere, apparent in the "mate of mine" who "came back home again stuck up like a fish finger" and in the speaker, who, because of his hamartia, will "end up in the papers and ... in the chips." That Humphries views Australia as a site for success is evident in his imagery. Ponds, pools, lakes, aquariums, and oceans are self-contained, circumferential bodies of water, and a creek forms a ring of its own by flowing into the ocean from which it came.

But the billabong is a peculiarly Australian body of water (even though backwaters – oxbow lakes, for example – exist in all geographies with mature meandering rivers and streams and/or arid climates subject to heavy rain storms). Billabongs break the circle of perfection, at least as it is sought overseas. "Billabong," a Wiradhuri word that may be some 40,000 years old, figures also in the most famous of Australian songs (and the poem by

Banjo Patterson), "Waltzing Matilda" (and in Dame Edna's 7-inch EP single of 1979, *Disco Matilda*). Humphries has become well placed in fame not because "when London calls" (in Alomes' phrase) he answers, but because in his songs and his other writing he has "camped by a billabong, / Under the shade of a coolibah tree." The billabong in "Great Big Fish" is a lyrical site where entities and "non-entities" alike can camp while they are working on their fame or just being Australian.

In *More Please*, Humphries recounts how, when he was nine, his family and he, motoring to their vacation home at Healesville, investigated a swagman's camp beside a billabong of the Yarra River "in the hope that we might glimpse one of these legendary vagabonds boiling his billy, or stuffing a jumpback in his tucker bag like the hero of that incomprehensible song 'Waltzing Matilda'"; he tells also about "a real swagman called Smithy ... like a peasant in a story by Turgenev."[76] Despite his slight against Australia's other national anthem, in "Disco Matilda" Dame Edna Everage makes "Waltzing Matilda" comprehensible again.

"Great Big Fish" itself is an Aristotelian discourse on effect and cause. Effect: "Why do I keep swimming round and round my pond"? Cause: "Cause I'm a great big fish in a tiny little pool ... lake ... [billabong ...] creek ... aquarium." Effect: "If there's any competition, it doesn't last for long." Cause: "Cause as a rule they leave the pool in search of bigger baits / And talk to all those foreign fish and not their Aussie mates." Effect: "What's the point of swimming so far away from mum?" Cause: "all those little tiddlers think I'm the biggest fish they've seen." The singer's marks of causality are the unities of space (the billabong and its replicas: pool, lake, creek, aquarium), action (disloyalty and loyalty occur "as a rule" because of rules of conduct, specifically, because of precedent), and time (the ontological continuum from tiddler to "great big fish").

Hearers are enfolded into the song's undulating cadence and metre, like waves, not just breaking on the shore – "I can hear those breakers crashing on the shore" – but churning overhead, into its bubbling Dada chorus of "Splish splash wrinkle sink hurrah three hips, / I'll end up in the papers, and I'll end up in the chips"; and into the unities of billabong, patriotism, and life, the Aristotelian poetics of comedy that Humphries has had to enact simply because rumour has it (see Chapter 1) that he wrote the (non-extant) second part of the *Poetics*.

As a lyricist and a comic singer, Humphries walks a long line of music hall, variety, and popular composers and performers, most notably George Formby, Jr; Gracie Fields; Max Miller; Whispering Jack Smith; Elsie and Doris Waters; Bud Flanagan and Chesney Allen; Michael Flanders and Donald Swann; and Noël Coward and Charles Aznavour. Consider the "nice" parallels (see Table 1.1) among Gracie Fields's "Looking on the Bright Side" (1932), Bud Flanagan and Chesney Allen's "Nice People"

(1937), George Formby's "It's Turned Out Nice Again" (1941), and Barry Humphries' "Niceness" (1978). With Dame Edna, of course, niceness is an ambivalent condition and proposition, like the wooden spoon, which mother can use to prepare a bread pudding for tea, then use again to deliver a licking to anyone (excepting father) who misbehaves at tea. In this regard, Humphries' signature tune and Dame Edna's hallmark song "Niceness" (Humphries and Rowley 1978) has a source in cruelty as well as in the niceties of Fields, Flanagan and Allen, and Formby, specifically in George Arthurs and Bennett Scott's composition "I Had to Be Cruel to Be Kind" (1903), which was in George Robey's repertoire. The song title, and the chorus, which begins "Now, you may think that was cruel, but I did it for the best,"[77] evoke Dame Edna, who has said of Madge Allsop,

Every time I see her, she looks more and more like something that's been excavated from a peat bog, don't you, Madge? I have to be a little bit cruel. I have to be cruel to be kind. And if I want to be very kind to Madge, I have to be very cruel. I'm sorry but I do. In fact, I love her so much I'm willing to be utterly monstrous to her, possums.[78]

Edna may be playing on a cliché, but more likely she is alluding to Arthurs, Scott, Robey, and turn-of-the-century music hall. Her referentiality is usually of the halls.

Consider also Elsie Waters and Doris Waters' ingenious patter and their propensity to break into song, and Dame Edna's disingenuous patter and her willingness to sing whenever she feels a song coming on (which is usually once on a television show, four times in a stage show, or whenever "there is no need for silence or speech"). Other parallels might be found between Noël Coward's "Any Little Fish" (1931) and Humphries' "Great Big Fish" (1970); between Humphries' "True British Spunk" (1969) and Flanders and Swann's "Commonwealth Fair" (1973); between Flanagan and Allen's "The Washing on the Siegfried Line" (1939) and "On the Outside Looking In" (1930s) and Humphries' "War Savings Street Song" (1961) and "Highett Waltz" (1958); between George A. Stevens and Charles Ridgwell's "I'm Shy, Mary Ellen, I'm Shy" (1910s)[79] and Humphries' "I'm Shy" (Dame Edna's duet with Charles Aznavour on the TV show *Another Audience with Dame Edna* [1984]); between B.W. Rogers' "Following in Father's Footsteps" (1900s)[80] and Humphries' "Never Trust a Man Who Doesn't Drink" (which Les Patterson sings in the stage show *Sir Les Patterson Has a Stand-up: Live and Rampant* [1996]); and between G.W. Hunt's "Dear Old Pals" (1877)[81] and Humphries' "My Bridesmaid and I" (1978) (which Dame Edna performs on the LP *The Sound of Edna* and on *The Dame Edna Experience*, 2nd series [1989])

Some of Les Patterson's more bawdy songs, such as "Genuine" (1981) (from *An Evening's Intercourse with the Widely Liked Barry Humphries*

[1981–82]); and "My Old Lady" (1983) (from *12 Inches of Les, The Album* [1985]); and Barry McKenzie's ejaculatory "Earls Court Blues" (1965) and "My Little One-Eyed Trouser Snake" (1967) (from the *Private Eye* flexi-disc *The Abominable Radio Gnome*) are in the spirit of nineteenth-century music hall ribald songs such as "The Way to Come over a Maid," "There's No Shove Like the First Shove," "Come Sleep with Me," and "Man's Yard of Stuff."[82] Through his bawdy songs, Humphries has contributed to a noble ballad tradition in Britain, Ireland, Australia, and Canada,

a tradition that goes back, through the lighter moments of Burns, Purcell, D'Urfey and Shakespeare to Chaucer and the Middle Ages, and that goes forward behind the veil of Victorian respectability to the songs we sang on route marches in the Army or that rugby players sing in their baths today. They are unashamedly vulgar and licentious, but they surely reflect a fundamentally healthy approach to life.[83]

Although Barry McKenzie and Les Patterson would seem to be "unashamedly vulgar and licentious," their songs, it must be said, hardly "reflect a fundamentally healthy approach to life." Still, the laughter their songs inspire is undoubtedly salubrious. They recall Rudy Vallee, who is reputed to have said "I sing with dick in my voice."[84] In addition, their songs might prompt listeners to question their own vulgarity and licence as well as the sexualizing gazes that they bestow upon those whom they approach.

Dame Edna Everage's success as a *chanteuse*, albeit of songs composed by Humphries (her manager), Nick Rowley, and Stanley Myers, has been so extensive as to warrant the publication of her own songster, *The Sound of Edna: Dame Edna's Family Songbook* (1979), along with companion recordings *The Sound of Edna* on LP (1978) and audiocassette (1993). John Lahr has even been so bold as to suggest that Dame Edna "fancies herself the Cole Porter of the Antipodes."[85] Given that, in 1969, Lahr called Cole Porter "the Alexander Pope of American musical comedy,"[86] it follows, according to a wonky syllogism, that Dame Edna Everage is the Alexander Pope of Antipodean musical comedy. (But this is already universally known.)

In her annotations to her songbook, she does acknowledge some of her music hall predecessors. She says of "My Bridesmaid and I," "This is a soft-shoe style number, to be rendered in an attractive husky whisper, like old Flanagan and Allen – though I suppose young fans don't know what the dickins I'm going on about."[87] She notes that "I Miss My Norm" "was inspired by some of the lovely old Franz Lehar operas."[88] Of "I'm Sorry," she points out: "This is my big French-style cabaret number, possums, and it isn't surprising that I'm known in some circles as Edna Piaf, or Melbourne's answer to Charlene Trenet"; and: "I suppose if Piaf was the 'Little

Sparrow,' I'm the 'Big Kookaburra.' "[89] In her reference to "an attractive husky whisper" she may also be acknowledging her indebtedness to the American crooner Whispering Jack Smith as well as to Bud Flanagan and other "whispering" singers (although, as a singer, she could hardly be accused of whispering her lines).

Humphries' greatest songs are Dame Edna's, just as his greatest dramatic monologues are Sandy Stone's. Among her most enduring numbers are "The Highett Waltz," from the EP *Wild Life in Suburbia, Volume Two* (1959); "War Savings Street Song"(1962), from the LP *Barry Humphries* (1970); "True British Spunk," from Humphries and Ian Davidson's BBC TV series *The Barry Humphries Scandals* (1970); and on the EP *A Track Winding Back* (1972) and the CD *Moonee Ponds Muse, Vol. 1* (1991), the 45 rpm single *Disco Matilda* (1979); and the nicest song of all, "Niceness," from the LP *The Sound of Edna* (1978). Dame Edna, it could be argued, must be nice because she comes from "Melbourne, Australia's nicest city."[90] Even though he is a Sydney-sider, Les Patterson is also known for his niceties as a singer (if only because he prefers to sip Johnny Walker, neat, as he sings), as in "My Old Lady" and "Genuine." Sandy Stone is at his very nicest when he intones "Zip-A-Dee-Doo-Dah" and atonalizes "The Lord's Prayer" on the LP *Barry Humphries at Carnegie Hall* (1972).

My professorial advice to Humphries would be to consider going on tour, performing all his music hall songs, as himself, "in a suit" (as Eric Idle did in 1999–2000, to great critical acclaim, in Los Angeles and Vancouver, and then at Carnegie Hall). Peter Gammond has noted that music hall songs

are specifically "music hall" songs simply because music hall happened to be the most popular form of entertainment at the time they were written in the late 1800s and early 1900s, some time before the gramophone, radio and TV came along to keep people at home and close down hundreds of theatres dedicated to keeping the working classes (and others of lowbrow inclination) happy.[91]

Given that the music halls have closed, and that he has performed his songs on the gramophone, radio, and television (the media that have replaced the halls), should not Humphries, arguably the last music hall performer, revive the halls in contemporary theatres not only in the characters of Edna Everage and Les Patterson but also in his own character, that of one of the twentieth century's greatest composers of comic songs? Although "The spirit of Music Hall will never die; it lives on in the entertainers of today,"[92] without a body (i.e., a house and an *oeuvre* as well as a performer) "the spirit of Music Hall" is just an abstraction, as ethereal as a dying fall or a trill of nostalgia. But with a body to back it, music hall can continue to perform its double takes and pratfalls. In a one-man show in the form of a song recital, performing as himself in a Savile Row suit, Humphries would be working in the tradition of not only Eric Idle but also Noël Coward, Marlene Dietrich, and other great artistes.

## KICKING SANDY, IN HIS EYES AND YOUR EARS

Humphries recorded his monologue and aria "Sandy Agonistes" in early 1960, in his Notting Hill basement flat. As he explains the logistics of the engineering:

I borrowed a tape recorder which had an unusual device – perhaps even a design fault – which made it possible to superimpose one's voice over a layer of pre-recorded sound, producing an evocative, three-dimensional echo effect. Making much use of this facility, and guided by a sheaf of notes, I improvised into the machine a litany of city streets, railway stations, brand names and obsolescent advertising slogans, interspersed with snatches of popular song.[93]

The kinetic interplay of human being and machine – "I improvised into the machine" is a telling construction – recalls Dada (even more than Futurism, even more than the cyborg of cyberpunk), particularly Marcel Duchamp's *Sad Young Man in a Train* (1911), *The King and Queen Surrounded by Swift Nudes* (1912), *Nude Descending a Staircase (No. 2)* (1912), *Coffee Grinder No. 2* (1914), *The Bride Stripped Bare by Her Bachelors, Even* (1915–23), and many other of his works.

Had Duchamp ever occupied 2a Pembridge Gardens, Notting Hill, he might have been prompted to make an utterance like "Sandy Agonistes"; however, in contradistinction to Humphries, he would have engineered it as "if a straight horizontal thread one meter long falls from a height of one meter onto a horizontal plane distorting itself *as it pleases* and creates a new shape of the measure of length."[94] Had Tristan Tzara ever lived there, he would have written his text automatically, as in his instructions "Pour Faire un poème dadaiste": "Découpez ensuite avec soin chacun des mots qui forment cet article et mettez-les dans un sac. / Agitez doucement. / Sortez ensuite chaque coupure l'une après l'autre. / Copiez consciencieusement / dans l'ordre où elles ont quitté le sac."[95] Humphries' staging of chance in "Sandy Agonistes," by his own admission "guided by a sheaf of notes," may have been more deliberate than pure improvisation, depending on the writing and design that went into his annotations, yet it seems to have been as extemporé as Dada-inspired automatic speaking.

While not all speech and speech-acts are Dada-inspired, speaking is by nature automatic. Throughout her fiction and poetry Janet Frame argues that ready-made phrases such as clichés, euphemisms, and slogans are the dead signs of the dead cultures that use them and that the only sign that people are still alive is their own original speech – speech acts that are not an act (at least not somebody else's act). Humphries has spent much of his career ridiculing the empty discourse that people tend to pick up and pass on like a virus: "hopefully" and "in terms of" are two expressions that rightly make him cringe because they suggest the absence of thought and will, as in the postlapsarian Garden of Edna(h). Dame Edna can always be quick with her tongue because she is always thinking, always willful, like Duchamp playing chess with/against a naked woman,[96] always several steps ahead of the audience. Above all, Humphries credits Edna with the quality of orality: "Able to talk fluently on any subject whatsoever without drawing a breath, Edna became the living, glittering incarnation of Tristan Tzara's famous Dadaist dictum, 'Thought is born in the mouth' "[97] (see epigraph to Chapter 3: "La pensée se fait dans la bouche.").

In Sandy Stone, Humphries has put together another composing Dada figure. Even though "Sandy Agonistes" is, in its surface structure, an amalgam of ready-made nominal phrases (product names, place-names, advertising copy), Sandy's speech-act is transformative, turning words from objects of consumer culture into signs of art and turning ready-made words into a Dadaist readymade, a found object whose status as art derives from the artist's discovery and declaration of the object as always already art. In a talk he gave at the Museum of Modern Art in 1961, Marcel Duchamp identified sententiousness as a figure of his *objets trouvés*: "One important characteristic was the short sentence which I occasionally inscribed on the 'readymade.' That sentence instead of describing the object like a title was meant to carry the mind of the spectator towards other regions more verbal."[98] Similarly, Sandy Stone's readymade of ready-made words and phrases, especially in his sedate monotone "like gold to airy thinness beat" over a performance time of 20:50 and a complete side of the 1960 LP *Sandy Agonistes* (which features monologues by Buster Thompson, Debbie Thwaite, and Colin Cartwright on Side One), transports listeners "towards other regions more verbal," more verbal than the words on the page, both Humphries' note paper and Collin O'Brien's transcription in his edition *The Life and Death of Sandy Stone* (1990). Sandy engages the members of his audience in a performative act, commissioning them to complete his telling through their own act of listening.

Humphries seems to allude to the Bakhtinian bivocalism of Sandy's audience when, in his annotations to the CD *Moonee Ponds Muse, Vol. 1*, (1991), he advises, "one does not have to listen too carefully to hear the rumble of the big red double-deckers outside my Notting Hill basement window." By telling listeners they do "not have to listen too carefully," of course, Humphries actually instructs them, through his subtly equivocal syntax, to listen carefully not just for double-deckers but also for every nuance in Sandy's voice and, in a sense, to round out his vowels and his entire performance. Listener bivocalism in "Sandy Agonistes" (and Sandy's other monologues) is analogous to Humphries' own bivocalism as a performer, specifically his linguistic hybridization in the character of Edna Everage, in whose performances "we are presented with a female voice in which two genders vie for supremacy and constantly overlay each other."[99] "Sandy Agonistes" is bivocal in another sense: like the Dada readymade that functions as both a consumer product and an art object, "Sandy Agonistes" takes domestic and cultural products and gives them second voice as art, especially the art of utterance, as in Dame Edna's reference to having to be "*utterly* monstrous" in her speech towards her bridesmaid, Madge Allsop.

Humphries' experience with duchampioning readymades started with his Dada art exhibitions of the 1950s and 1960s, most notably in his BIG-scapes. It barked up the right tree in 1955, when Humphries had a small role in John Steinbeck's *Of Mice and Men* "which required the offstage noise of a barking dog. I did the barking,"[100] and in the process may even have referenced Kurt Schwitters' performance with Theo van Doesburg at a 1923 Dada congress in Den Hague, at which Schwitters, sitting incognito in the audience, "suddenly began to bark furiously" whenever Van Doesburg, who was delivering a lecture on Dada, prompted him by drinking from a glass of water.[101] Eric Idle used a similar Dada strategy in his North American stage show *Eric Idle Exploits Monty Python*, as at the performance I attended at the Orpheum Theatre in Vancouver, 12 May 2000. A backdrop video montage of dogs barking out the tune of "Always Look on the Bright Side of Life" (1979) introduces Idle's on-stage performance of his song.

Since *Of Mice and Men* his Dada performative has extended through sightings of Humphries with street signs that he has turned into readymades, documented in photographs of Mrs Edna Everage standing before "HUMORESQUE ST." and "THIS IS A WAR SAVINGS STREET" signs nailed to a pole,[102] and of Humphries carrying a "MOONEE PONDS" sign.[103] And it has reached an apogee in the 1999 exhibition *Dame Edna's Frock-a-Thon* and in the permanent collection of Humphries' costumes, programs, posters, manuscripts, and papers at the Performing Arts Museum, which Dame Edna calls "the Dame Edna Museum in Melbourne."[104] By donating almost fifty years of his personal memorabilia to PAM, Humphries has transformed them from artifacts and collectibles into art and anti-artworks.

He has duchampioned readymades most recently by devoting 29:21 of the 70:06 duration of his CD *Dada Days: Moonee Ponds Muse, Vol. 2 (1951–1983)* (1993) to early – Humphries was a seventeen-year-old Melbourne University undergraduate in 1951 – and rare audiotape and acetate recordings, mostly with very fragile sound quality, of his and his friends' (John Perry, Robert Nathan, Robert Maclellan, and John Levi) Dada experiments, sketches, pranks, and performances. And, of course, by making

"Sandy Agonistes" literally the centrepiece of the CD *Moonee Ponds Muse, Vol. 1* (1991), positioning it as the sixth of eleven tracks and allotting it 20:50 out of the 77:24 total playing time (nearly twice the track spacetime, or *Hantu*,[105] of the next longest work, a monologue by Colin Cartwright [10:39]). By bringing out these lingering sounds, Humphries turns what could be called the alreadymades – following the Derridean principle of "the time before first"[106] – of the Dada-year 1916. This also holds for the years 1951–53 and 1960, when Humphries recorded the Dada works and "Sandy Agonistes" into *readymades nouveaux*, with new meanings (or the absence of new meanings) within the contexts and constructs of his career; of art, music, and literary history; of the timeframes "nostalgia" and "post-modernism"; of the concepts "Moonee Ponds Muse" and "performance"; and the utterances "Dada" and "no worries."

Mary Ann Caws has rightly emphasized "the whole constellation of issues surrounding the reading of what we know as the ready-made, in Duchamp's terms" and noted how "the whole Dada cycle of presentation and reaction must be related to the notion of objective chance as the surrealists state it, in which the encounter with the 'real' or exterior object enables us to find, outside of us, an answer to the interior question we are not aware of having."[107] So, how is "Sandy Agonistes" a readymade?

First, whether taken as a poem or as a recitative song, "Sandy Agonistes" is not read but heard, according to my Dada formula "read + h(umphries) = heard." To hear it while playing *Sandy Agonistes* (1960) or *Moonee Ponds Muse, Vol. 1* (1991), or even to hear it in one's mind's ear while reading it in *The Life and Death of Sandy Stone* (1990), is to return to 2a Pembridge Gardens, Notting Hill Gate, in the winter of 1960 and to improvise into a tape recorder. As Derrida describes this kind of return: "The memory of a promise initiates the circle of appropriation, with all the risks of technical repetition, of automated archives, of gramophony, of simulacrum, of wandering deprived of an address and destination."[108] By listening to a recording or imagining the sound of "Sandy Agonistes," the hearer induces Humphries' original state of "gramophony" and finds the "location of culture,"[109] the "address and destination" of his original moments of creation, of the "time before first," or before "the past not to have been." Humphries evokes this temporal recovery in his "perfunctory sleeve notes" to *Sandy Agonistes* and *Moonee Ponds Muse, Vol. 1*, conceding that "Sandy Agonistes" is "by far the best recording I have ever made."[110] In the spirit of Homi Bhabha, he locates postcolonial Australian culture in Sandy Stone.

As a poem and song, in the gramophonic groove of Lee Harwood's collection of Tristan Tzara's verse *Chanson Dada* (1987), "Sandy Stone" is neither stream of consciousness nor interior monologue but, rather a readymade and a speech-act. The work in its entirety is a readymade, but each of its *objets trouvés* also is a readymade, which the speaker, Sandy Stone, re-

claims from Australian popular culture. Humphries initiates Sandy's recla-
mation, as if from a stone quarry, and the performative listeners help enact
it bivocally by reading it to themselves or aloud:

Weeties ... Crispies ... Kornies ... Malties ... Granose ... Weet Bix ... Vita-Brits ...
Kelloggs Corn Flakes ... Kelloggs All-Bran ... Kelloggs ... Rice Bubbles ... snap,
crackle, pop ... Semo-lina ... John Bull Oats ... Phosphatine ... Heinz Tomato
Sauce ... Rosella Tomato Soup ... Kia ora Tomato Sauce ... White Crow Tomato
Sauce ... AJC Tomato Sauce ... PK Spearmint ... Wrigley's Juicy Fruit Chewing Gum ...
Allen's Irish Moss Gum ... Jubes ... Allens Cure-em Quick ... Allen's Butter Menthols
– the menthol clears the head and the butter soothes the throat ... Throaties. ✦ TIME
FOR A CAPSTAN – THEY'RE BLENDED BETTER! ✦ Three threes always please ...
Minties ... BVDs. ✦ WE, TOO, SMOKE TURF! ✦ Craven A's ... Columbine Caramels
... Hoadley's Violet Crumble Bars ... Ford Pills ... Fan Tales ... Jaffas ... Sun Buds ...
Sun News Pictorial ... Monty Blandford ... Mont Albert. East Camberwell. Camber-
well. Auburn. Hawthorn. Glenferrie. Burnley. Richmond. East Richmond. Flinders
Street Station. Swanston Street. Flinders Lane.[111]

As these words and the subsequent words of "Sandy Agonistes" fly out of
Humphries' pocket as note paper cuttings, or texticles; as Humphries "im-
provises them into the machine," as Sandy Stone enunciates them in a
staged space; and as readers read them on the page and hear them in their
(minds') ears, a great Dada utterance takes shape, and the greatest Australian poem of the twentieth century takes form. Sandy is no Samson, and
"Sandy Agonistes" is more a Dada pun than a parody of Milton's epic
"Samson Agonistes," but his stock taking is at once minimalist and encyclopedic, absurd and significant, nostalgic and contemporary, incoherent
and comprehensive, flat and round, dead and quick, stone and mouth,
Sandy Stone and Barry Humphries.

The text of "Sandy Agonistes," which is fewer than five and one-half
pages (17–22) in *The Life and Death of Sandy Stone*, yet, in Sandy's ponderous delivery, is stretched out to nearly twenty-three minutes on disk, is a facsimile of Sandy's speech and Humphries' performance, a typographical
semblance of a character's and a character actor's speech-acts. But it is also a
kind of linotypical transmission, as far removed from the original sounds as a
signature on a source document, for example, is from the same signature on a
faxed document. The text of "Sandy Agonistes" looks authentic. Its typography of ellipses and shifting font sizes gives some indication of how it might be
read, spoken, sung, even enacted or performed, much as Dame Edna's
notations in the scores of *The Sound of Edna: Dame Edna's Family Songbook* – conventional notes such as "*colla voce*" for "Niceness" and more
heterodox notes such as "Rauncho masochismo"[112] for "S & M Lady" –
give direction on the key, pitch, tempo, tone-colour, and parts of each song.

But the text "Sandy Agonistes" is more than a facsimile of performance, more even than the lyrics of a song: it is the libretto of a sound poem or tone poem, an aria, in a single scene, in the *opéra bouffe* (as in Offenbach's music hall operettas) of the seemingly endless monologues of the seemingly endless Sandy Stone: "Sandy Stone's Big Week," "Days of the Week," "Dear Beryl," "Sandy Agonistes," "Can You Keep a Secret?" "Sandy Claus," "Sandy's Stone," "The Land of the Living," "Sandy and the Sandman," "Sandy Soldiers On," "Shades of Sandy," "Sandy Comes Home," "A Letter from Limbo," and "Anzac Sandy."[113] Despite his string of words in "Sandy Agonistes" and his sequence of monologues, Sandy Stone never attains the authority of an author. Even Humphries seems willing to surrender some of his authority, not to defer to Sandy in a Barthesian move of de-authorialization but just to let him speak, unfettered, without the restraints of characterization, dramaturgy, and received pronunciation.

In this way, understanding culture as a discourse may lead us to understand that authority is never real, no matter how binding it may appear in an interpretive situation. It is always the effect of an identification with an imaginary community: with an imaginary totality of relations.[114]

As the speaker of "Sandy Agonistes," Sandy Stone is less an archivist or enumerator of nostalgia, kitsch, or ephemera than a schoolmaster (albeit a bit of stodgy pedant) delivering a lecture on understanding Australian culture (albeit as "an imaginary community"). His pedagogy is decidedly extemporaneous; his lecture notes are mere scraps of paper he draws at random from his pocket. But, in his lecture, Sandy Stone succeeds in promoting cultural understanding and in establishing "an imaginary totality of relations" (not a relationship between people, as between Sandy and his listeners or between Humphries and his readers, but a relation between things, Dada *objets*, the imaginary constructs of "character," "author," "listener," and "reader," yet a totality all the same). When we hear or read the poem "Sandy Agonistes," it seems, we are whole.

As a musical recording "Sandy Agonistes" is an example of bruitism, the noise-music experiments of Dadaists and Futurists. In 1959–60 Humphries started to explore second-hand book shops in London. Among his purchases was "in orange wrappers a rare copy of *Zang Tuum Tuum*, Marinetti's Futurist manifesto on 1913."[115] In "En Avant Dada: A History of Dadaism" (1920), Richard Huelsenbeck ascribes bruitism to Tristan Tzara, Filippo T. Marinetti, and the Cabaret Voltaire:

Tzara for the first time had poems recited simultaneously on the stage, and these performances were a great success, although the *poème simultané* had already been introduced in France by Derème and others. From Marinetti we also borrowed "bruitism," or noise music, *le concerte bruitiste*, which, of blessed memory, had created such a stir at the first appearance of the futurists in Milan, where they had regaled the audience with *le reveil de la capitale.*[116]

Whenever Les Patterson sings, he, like Sandy, invokes the spirit of bruitism, although less because he is a dada than because he is *une sale brute* ("a filthy beast"). In French, the word *bruit* means "noise." Les Patterson is also a noise! The French word *noise* is used in only one expression: *chercher noise à quelqu'un* ("to try to pick a quarrel with someone"). *Je cherche noise à Les Patterson* ("I'm trying to pick a quarrel with Les Patterson"). *Les Patterson est un sale brute et un sale bruit* ("Les Patterson is a filthy beast and a nasty [that is, not a nice] noise").

One of Patterson's linguistic peculiarities is liaison, as in his signature watchword "The Yartz" (see Note 71, Chapter 1). Liaison is also a feature of stage continuity, as in *"un bruit,"* a noise that serves as a linking device by drawing a character onstage in search of its source. As *un bruit*, Les links his audiences with Australia. Together, Humphries' poems and songs stage *une concerte bruitiste* ("a bruitist concert") because, given that noise resounds forever, they call up the noises of the past, of Melbourne, Sydney, and London, as if, according to the Bantu concept of *Hantu*, Humphries were to answer the question "when did you first hear the noise?" by saying: "in my home at 2a Pembridge Gardens, Notting Hill Gate."

The noise in "Sandy Agonistes" is not the rumbling engine of a double-decker bus, a background noise, but the gramophony of foreground noises, grinding to a halt, then starting up again, the "snap, crackle, pop" of boxes, tins, jars, packets and cartons, of radio programs, train station calls, advertising slogans, litanies of movie stars, lists of demolished music halls and variety houses ("The Smile-Away Club. The Myer Musicale. The Lux Radio Theatre."), and snatches of popular songs, including Jaan Kenbrovin and John William Kellette's music hall waltz "I'm Forever Blowing Bubbles" (1919) and Hoagy Carmichael and Stanley Adams' quickstep waltz "Little Old Lady" (1936), which music hall star Gracie Fields performed with distinction, and which may have inspired Humphries to write Les Patterson's anti-feminist ballad "My Old Lady."

All these items seem marked by the randomness of free association, yet they balance an equation of *chanson et choses* ("song and things") and, in their contiguity, *ils font du bruit* ("they make a noise"): the sound of Sandy Stone and an early rumour of Humphries' greatness. In "Sandy Agonistes" Humphries made a noise that had not been heard in 200 years of Australian history, or in 40,000 years of Nyoongah dreaming, and that had never been imagined by previous residents in Notting Hill Gate.

As a readymade poem and song "Sandy Agonistes" is a truly profound utterance, a Dada masterpiece, and even an important work of literature.

That poetry anthologies and songbooks prefer to leave it out is a cultural shame. To omit this great work is to kick sand in Sandy Stone's eyes. But, given that Sandy has already "kicked it," readers and hearers can still kick back, however feebly, against this sin of omission, and "Sandy Agonistes" can continue to survive as noise. But how is Humphries, as occasional poet, music hall lyricist and composer, and comic singer, to endure the agon of Sandy's critical neglect? The ghosts of Tristan Tzara and Marcel Duchamp will undoubtedly help, and I hope that, on this side of the Barthesian death of the author, this chapter will help secure "Sandy Agonistes" as the greatest Australian poem and song of the twentieth century. Once you hear Sandy's "cackle crackle," you never forget it.

His utterance of brand-name Australian culture, of a totality of Australian subjects, real and imaginary, and of speech as an evocation of an Australian discourse community is also Humphries' distinctive mode of literary production, marking 1960 as a height of land between modernism and postmodernism, and a postgeneric artwork, at once speech, poem, readymade, story, advert, and utterance. His product-poem "Sandy Agonistes" is consistent with Jameson's vision of possibility in modes of production.

I am here, however, essentially concerned with the conditions of possibility of the concept of a "mode of production," that is to say, the characteristics of the historical and social situation which make it possible to articulate and formulate the concept of "totality" in the first place.[117]

By enacting two modes of production in "Sandy Agonistes" and through Sandy, the mode of producing a poem or utterance and the mode of producing Australian consumer or mutable culture, Humphries produced for Australian literature "the historical and social situation" of modernism as it leaned into postmodernism and of the imaginary totality (whether essentialist, egalitarian, or multicultural) of Australia.

Like "A Novel Called Tid," "Sandy Agonistes" ends with a promise "to be continued," but its promise is less in words, or even in ellipses, than in its spirit of possibility: (1) the possibility that words can always fill silence, and silence complete words, because speech need not be excessive nor silence necessarily intolerable; (2) the possibility that the poem may be continued indefinitely, that, even despite its many pauses, it may be continuous; (3) the possibility that Sandy Stone may live to tell again, despite the vicissitudes of life and death and despite narratological conventions; and (4) the possibility of rendering "the past not to have been" not only in "innocent Austral verse" but also in superseded things, including the products of memory, brought closer to permanence as readymades. Through Sandy's deliberate verbosity and his bizarre ontology, Humphries defies mutability, the seemingly ineluctable force that has closed the music halls, halted old modes of production, razed Melbourne architecture, and killed off good friends like John Betjeman, Peter Cook, Dudley Moore, Spike Milligan, and Stephen Spender just because they happened to be literary figures and not literary characters. But Sandy, because he is a literary character, can defy constructs such as closure and death, and act as the antiquarian for dead arts, superseded products, demolished buildings, and departed friends.

Humphries has inspired other comedians to mask themselves in characters. For example, Bruce Dessau has noted how Rowan "Atkinson compared himself to Barry Humphries in the way he would hide behind characters."[118] But by masking himself in characters "in the hall of mirrors at a fairground, and with whiffs of scent, incoherent voices, shards of music,"[119] Humphries has found his own roundabout way to immortality and totality.

# 4

# Dressing Up Discourse, Dressing Down the Audience: Humphries' Stage Scripts

VLADIMIR: Charming evening we're having.
ESTRAGON: Unforgettable.
VLADIMIR: And it's not over.
ESTRAGON: Apparently not.
VLADIMIR: It's only beginning.
ESTRAGON: It's awful.
VLADIMIR: Worse than the pantomime.
ESTRAGON: The circus.
VLADIMIR: The music-hall.
ESTRAGON: The circus.

– Samuel Beckett, *Waiting for Godot*

Now I'm just an ordinary bloke
The same as you out there.
Not made for women, I'm not a soak,
I never really care.
I'm what you call a moderate,
I weigh all the pros, and the cons.
I don't push and shove
At the thing they call love,
I never go in for goings on.
Thank God I'm normal, normal, normal.
Thank God I'm normal.
I'm just like the rest of you chaps.

– Archie Rice, in John Osborne, *The Entertainer*

"Witchdoctors like Derrida dismiss themselves by the way they speak," Chance went on. "It's the language of sophistry and nothing sensible can be said in it even by accident. But you can go further. An apparently more lucid pundit like Barthes is usually talking flapdoodle too."

– Chance Jenolan, in Clive James, *The Remake*

Barry Humphries' stage scripts have appeared in five books: *A Nice Night's Entertainment: Sketches and Monologues 1956–1981* (1981); *The Humour of Barry Humphries*, compiled by John Allen; *Shades of Sandy Stone: The Reveries of a Returned Man* (1989), comprising "Shades of Sandy" and "Sandy Comes Home"; *The Life and Death of Sandy Stone*, edited by Collin O'Brien (1990); and *Single Voices* (1990), based on the BBC TV series, which features dramatic monologues by Roy Clarke, Sheila Hancock, Carla Lane, Bob Larbey, and John Sessions as well as Humphries (i.e., "Sandy Comes Home," a monologue that Humphries adjudges "has been filmed by the BBC, a little too cheerfully for the author's taste.")[1] That all these books showcase speeches and meditations by Sandy Stone – only *The Humour of Barry Humphries* and *A Nice Night's Entertainment* contain scripts by other Humphries characters – suggests his enduring importance in Humphries' career and in Australian literature and performance studies. In "A Letter from Limbo," for example, Sandy even transcends death: he is a "returned man," having come back both from the war[2] and from the dead. In an annotation to the dramatic monologue "Sandy's Stone," Humphries states:

Although there were frequent references to the Repat, I could never be quite sure which war if any Sandy had served in … Like many Anzac Day revellers of today, his military status is nebulous. He seemed then [1968] too old to have taken part in the Second World War and somehow too much a creature of the thirties and forties to be an Anzac, so I didn't trouble to be too specific on this. No one ever asked awkward questions, although his life and "mythology" were by this time becoming more and more detailed and intricate.[3]

Despite his hazy military and even ontological conditions, his thick script portfolio suggests his pre-eminence among Humphries' *dramatis personae* as well as his charming and touching popularity with theatre audiences.

Unlike Dame Edna and, for hygienic reasons, Les Patterson, Sandy never needs to invite audiences to come backstage to touch him after the show because he knows he has touched them during the show. His words are deliberate, words to be deliberated upon, possibly for generations. He rolls them round his mouth like a pebble on a hot afternoon or like a monk at plainsong. Sandy is credible because he is a character, not an automaton but an autonomous man, capable even of carrying off a mixed metaphor, as in my preceding sentence. In acknowledging his "predilection for the extended monologue intoned in a range of Melbourne dialects,"[4] Humphries makes a place at choir for Sandy to extend his voice in a plain plainsong.

As Sandy, Humphries can carry a trope, and sometimes even a tune, so in his monologues he carries Sandy, from old age to older age, to death, and back. Sandy is "an adaptable man," in Janet Frame's phrase (1965), but he is also a portable man: he can be transported, as in Malcolm Lowry's phrase "a corpse will be transported by express";[5] he can be carried off in five books, even pinned in one's pocket; and he can use his importance to carry off spectators, hearers, and readers through the ebbs of his consciousness and the flows of his discourse.

Sandy Stone started out his life as a character in several short stories that, in 1956, Humphries, then working as an actor in Sydney, submitted for publication. The only one of these stories to have survived, "Sandy Stone's Big Week," was published, under the pseudonym H. Grahame, in the student magazine *Prometheus* (1958) and reprinted in an appendix of *The Life and Death of Sandy Stone*. "Sandy Stone's Big Week" was the first run of a run of firsts.

"Days of the Week" is Sandy's first dramatic monologue, and Humphries' first script, which appeared on his first record, *Wild Life in Suburbia* (1958), and it features a first-class emulation of Estragon, a character that Humphries portrayed in *Waiting for Godot* (1954) in the first-ever staging of a Samuel Beckett play in Australia (Melbourne, 1957, and Sydney, 1958). Humphries' role as Estragon may have inspired both Sandy Stone's minim personality and his la(o)co(o)nic delivery. Humphries has acknowledged the influence of Beckett's novel and eponymous character *Watt* (1953) on Sandy's formation in the 1950s.[6] Australians paid notice both to Sandy Stone as actant and to Barry Humphries as an actor. Patrick White, for example, acknowledged "a brilliant record of Barry Humphries doing his characters Mrs Norm Everage and Sandy Stone. He has crammed all the horrors of Australian suburbia into a very short space – really quite uncanny."[7] Geoffrey Dutton's comment on first hearing *Wild Life in Suburbia* was similarly laudatory: "Not only was it one of the funniest things I had ever heard in Australia, but it was entirely new and yet unmistakably old; this was Australia, but a region now visited for the first time by a comic genius."[8] Humphries opened up this wholly new Australian character space through his talents as a writer, an actor, and, especially, a speaker, as if, in the spirit of "a mad Dada artist,"[9] he had stepped into the "very short space" and "region" of Australia and, in a distinctive twang, declared it art.

When listeners to *Wild Life in Suburbia* (1958) and *Barry Humphries* (1970) first heard Sandy Stone pronounce his a-arousing dramatic monologue "Days of the Week," they would have encountered his peculiar contrapuntal idiom:

I went to the R.S.L. [Returned Servicemen's League] the other night and had a very nice night's entertainment. Beryl, that's the wife, came along too. Beryl's not a drinker but she had a shandy. She put in quite a reasonable quantity of time yarning with Norm Purvis's good lady and I had a beer with old Norm and some of the other chappies there. I don't say no to the occasional odd glass and Ian Preston, an old friend of mine, got up and sang a few humorous numbers – not too blue, on account of the womenfolk – so that altogether it was a really nice type of night's entertainment for us both. We called it a day round about ten-ish; didn't want to make it too late a night as Beryl had a big wash on her hands on the Monday morning and I had to be in town pretty early, stocktaking and one thing and another.[10]

Hearing him for the first time, listeners might notice the peculiarity of Sandy's character more than the singularity of his vernacular. But hearing him on and on and on, they would come to take notice of his lilting cadences and tilting idioms: "a very nice night's entertainment," "quite a reasonable quantity of time," "I don't say no to the occasional odd glass," "a really nice type of night's entertainment," "Beryl had a big wash on her hands on the Monday morning." These unformulated phrases are disposed directly from Sandy's disposition, what in postmodern terminology would be called his "subject position," and what in his own terminology Sandy would call his "possie."[11]

But they also take their place within Australian dialects and discourses, and what Sidney J. Baker (1966, 1978) has called the Australian language. Even Barry McKenzie picks up one of Sandy's 1958 idioms, "I don't say no to the occasional odd glass," in his song "Earl's Court Blues," on Humphries' LP with Peter Cook, Dudley Moore, William Rushton, John Glashan, John Wells, and Richard Ingrams, *Private Eye's Blue Record* (1965):

Oh I wouldn't say no to an ice-cold beer
And I wouldn't say no to a naughty.
I've lived in English half a year
In a bed-sitter in Earl Courty.
The beer over here isn't fit to drink
And the sheilas are cold and haughty.
So I wouldn't say no to an ice-cold beer
And I wouldn't say no to a naughty.

Sandy did not, in turn, adopt Barry McKenzie's variation idiom, "I wouldn't say no to a naughty." His references to sex are more euphemisms than argot. In "Can You Keep a Secret?" he concludes, after his and Beryl's disastrous experience looking after Clive and Glenda Nettleton's children (Wayne and Marilyn) over the Easter weekend:

Beryl isn't a terribly well type of person. There's nothing organically wrong with her – she's never ill – she just isn't a hundred per cent. It strikes me if you're going to embark on a family you have to take all the particular factors appertaining to it into a certain amount of consideration. Look what happens when they grow up. They either wipe their boots on you, or they marry the first one that comes along and pack you off to a twilight home.[12]

If asked what a "naughty" was, Sandy Stone would likely say "Wayne or Marilyn Nettleton at the Easter weekend," just as his definition of being "stiff" is having bad luck, and of being "stiff as a board" is, as he confides in "Sandy and the Sandman," having dried Milo on his pyjamas.[13] If asked to define a "possie" (as it features in Sandy's statement: "Anyway, we found a possie in the long run just when we were beginning to think we might miss the blessed newsreel")[14] Bazza McKenzie might hazard a guess that it is a typographical error for the word "pussie," which bell hooks would perhaps confirm.[15] In their discourse idioms, as in their sexual practices, Sandy and Bazza are as unlike as the phonemes "sa" and "az."

In "Days of the Week" Sandy Stone counts out his and Beryl's weekly activities as if they made up a serialized story, and with the existential patience of Estragon (and Vladimir) counting out the time (not time, *the* time) until Godot comes, or until they realize (Estragon, Vladimir, and Sandy) that time does not exist (except as a construct allowing people like J. Alfred Prufrock [a character who is as much rock as Sandy is sand and stone, and who even, at least in his closet of dresses, resembles Edna Everage] to measure out his life with coffee spoons).

Sandy measures out his life (1) as "Beryl and I went to bed" on Sunday, "Beryl and I went to bed" on Tuesday, "Beryl and I went to bed" on Wednesday, "I went straight to bed" on Thursday, and "round about ten I filled a hottie and Beryl and I went to bed" on Friday;[16] (2) as he and Beryl enjoy "a really nice type of night's entertainment" on Sunday, "a really lovely night's entertainment" on Monday, "a really lovely night's entertainment" on Tuesday, "a pretty nice night's entertainment" on Wednesday, "a very nice night's ... rest" on Thursday, "a nice night's home entertainment" on Friday, "a very nice afternoon's entertainment" on Saturday, and an anticipated "very nice night's entertainment" on Sunday;[17] and (3) as Sandy "had a bit of strife parking the vehicle" at the pictures on Tuesday, "had a bit of strife parking the vehicle" for grocery shopping on Saturday morning, "had the usual trouble parking the vehicle" before the football match on Saturday afternoon and "a bit of trouble shifting the vehicle" after it, and would "always clean the car of a Sunday morning."[18] These remarks fix Sandy (who, as childless, is already "fixed") in but also provide the rhythm of his life, the cadences of his speech, and the good humour of his disposition (his subject "possie" as well as his parking "possie").

Strategically placed in the narrative, these three phrase motifs also measure out Humphries' exact timing as a stage monologist, a sketch comedian, an actor, and a music hall artiste. Compare William Matthews' list of "catch-lines from music-hall ditties," most notably "Gus Elen's ironic 'A nice quiet day,'" which Sandy Stone's equally ironic catch phrase "a nice night's entertainment" seems to echo.[19] In his essay "Approximately in the

Vicinity of Barry Humphries," Clive James recalls how Sandy Stone manages to tell time on stage, with gestures (body language) as well as with
words:

On the page, it is impossible to savour Sandy's eloquent silence. "So, Beryl and I
went to bed." On stage, his eyeballs slowly pop and then roll slightly upwards after
that line, telling you all you need to know about the hectic love-life of Sandy and
Beryl. (Not that a torrid romance is any longer on the cards, what with Beryl rarely
feeling 100 per cent, although, as Sandy is always as quick as he can be to point out,
there is nothing *organically* wrong.) But there is plenty to cherish in just reading the
words, even if you have to fill in the timing and the facial movements as best
you can.[20]

But neither Sandy nor Barry is just marking time. Sandy is dressing up discourse in addressing an audience and inviting them to review his weeklies,
as a director on a film set will invite the actors to review the dailies.[21] Barry
is dressing down his audiences (listening, viewing, and reading audiences),
challenging them to look into the semantics of their own *semaines* and say
whether they have ever had a week as productive as Sandy's (and Beryl's),
and, if not, whether they are not more laughable than he. People who think
Sandy Stone is a stock comic character – he is not – prove themselves laughing stocks. By laughing at Sandy, and laughing at themselves, the audience
members reveal meaning in the empty ritual of waiting for the day, and the
week, to end, as comically and as caustically as do Vladimir, Estragon, and
Beckett, in *Waiting for Godot*.

Sandy's second dramatic monologue, which Humphries wrote aboard
the *Toscana* en route to Venice, and which appeared first on the EP *Wild
Life in Suburbia, Volume Two* (1959) and "has never been performed on
stage,"[22] is, as the title "Dear Beryl" promises, epistolary. Sandy's letter to
Beryl in the "Old Country," in response to her "post card from Aden,"[23] is
in its surface structure like an international number of *News of the World*
as Sandy keeps Beryl up to date on events in the middycosm – the suburban
middle ground between the macrocosm and the microcosm of Glen Iris (see
Appendix 7). One might imagine Beryl wearing a middy blouse on her voyage through the Gulf of Aden. In its deep structure, however, "Dear Beryl"
is a metaletter, a letter about letters: his own letter, other people's letters,
and the letters of the alphabet, as they might fall in a Dada chance-encounter
with free association.

Sandy begins, albeit colloquially, by referring to his letter as a letter: "By
the time this letter reaches you you'll be in the Old Country." Next he acknowledges having received Beryl's letter: "I was thrilled to get your post
card from Aden," thus creating a letter about a postcard. Next he brings a
neighbour into the diegesis: "Yesterday I had a tingle from Nora Manly to

see if I'd heard from you yet. I gave her your last news and she asks to be remembered." Then he cites the alphabet in the form of *Woman's Day* and the fiction of Georgette Heyers, both of which Nora wishes to borrow, and he raises the possibility of ending the alphabet: "It's not worth stopping *Woman's Day* is it?" Then he invokes the dead, "old Mrs MacLeod Senior," who in "a card from the MacLeods" he has learned "fell asleep last Tuesday."[24] Like Janet Frame's character Mattina Brecon in *The Carpathians* (1988), who "died in February, surrendering at last her point of view,"[25] Mrs MacLeod is discarded (postcarded) in the alphabet after she has had the bad ontological manners to fall asleep, undoubtedly while reading.

In contrast to the communicative MacLeods, the Rusts "have never been what you'd call neighbourly have they? Always kept themselves to themselves – see them in the street and they wouldn't say boo." Still, Sandy, as a speech-actor, and of course a good neighbour, has invited Mr Rust into his field of discourse: "who should come across the street for a bit of a yarn but Mr Rust." He also tells of having some meals at the home of the Longmires, where he "always like[s] a yarn with old Jim." Finally, after noting that he has reported "just about all the news at present," Sandy informs Beryl "I'm enclosing tonight's 'Wally and the Major'" and invites her to "send me the odd snap."[26] Alphabetic signifiers (male discourse) yield to imagistic signifiers (female discourse) as the letter leaves the hands of the writer for the consciousness of a goddess, as Sandy petitions Beryl to remember their friends (as if he were "implicating the written word as the agent responsible for the decline of the Goddess").[27]

Beryl's goddesshood is evident in that, in the middycosm of Sandy's letter, she is insubstantial (bodiless) and silent (inscrutable). That Beryl is a goddess (the goddess $Be_3Al_2Si_6O_{18}$) is further evidenced in her nominal nature: like the mineral beryl, she has the properties to be transparent or translucent. "Dear Beryl" allows listeners and readers to imagine her in a diaphanous frock and to see their likenesses in her glassy eyes, knowing that, unlike Mrs MacLeod, she will never fall asleep reading something as "ordinary"[28] as a letter.

In "Sandy Agonistes" Beryl is conspicuous by her absence, or at least by Sandy's failure to mention her and think her name. Like Dada, which is about the absence of meaning, Beryl (as a word-construct in Sandy's monologues) is about the absence of Beryl (i.e., about Beryl who is not about). Yet, perhaps, in "Sandy Agonistes" Sandy invokes her presence when he misquotes (or, more likely, quotes from memory) Hoagy Carmichael and Stanley Adams' song "Little Old Lady" (1936): " 'Little old lady passing by, there's a tear in her eye ... eye' "[29] Read correctly, the lines are: "Little old lady passing by, / Catching everyone's eye." The Carmichael and Adams composition is about the singer's affection for his or her grandmother (or possibly about a woman who calls her to mind). In calling up the line Sandy might be calling up Beryl, who, for whatever reason, brings a tear to his eye (possibly because he and she have had a quarrel or because she is ill, as the surrounding references to "Carter's Little Liver Pilll-l-s" and "Aye, it's me, doctor Mac … kenzie's Methoids"[30] might suggest). Sandy's distress for Beryl might account for his disoriented state and his clutter of aposiopeses, or line fragments, which, in linotypography, are called "widows." Perhaps Sandy knows that, in his preoccupation with language and the speech-act, he has widowed Beryl, leaving her weeping.

To bring her back, to herself and into the speech-act, and to open up the monologue at least to the possibility of dialogue, he makes catalogues of things with which Beryl might be associated: grocery and other household items that she has fetched from the shops and that she has used; television and film stars whom they have seen at home and at the pictures; train routes they have travelled; pharmaceuticals they have taken; words they have read in newspapers and magazines; and phrases they have seen and heard in advertisements (like the newspaper clippings that showed up in Dada and Cubist paintings); and, especially, song lyrics that they have sung together. Had Beryl accompanied Sandy here, she undoubtedly would have corrected " 'there's a tear in her eye … eye …' " and he seems to know as much.

Being without Beryl is his agon, in two senses of conflict: (1) as the speaker-protagonist he is engaged in a word-conflict with the absent Beryl, or the absence of Beryl, the silent-antagonist; and (2) within the comedy of his monologue, Sandy agonizes over one side of their verbal conflict. He is a hero for taking on language before it has been ordered, edited, revised, and censored. Peter Coleman's statement that, in " 'Sandy Agonistes' there is no narrative or action at all, only the quavering recital of ante-bellum advertising slogans, headlines, public figures, snatches of song and especially brand names,"[31] is not quite accurate: "Sandy Agonistes" is actually, in the narratological sense, a "nonnarrated narrative,"[32] one in or from which the narrator is absent. "Sandy Agonistes" is non-narrated (1) because Sandy is "in" the narrative as a speaker but detached from it, as can be discerned in his very thin voice; and (2) because Beryl is detached "from" the narrative but is in it in Sandy's catalogue of things that seem to be narrating themselves. Thus, "Sandy Agonistes" is the non-narrated narrative of Beryl Stone in the form of a series of readymades that Sandy declares art.

Humphries' first stage performance as Sandy Stone was in *A Nice Night's Entertainment* at the Assembly Hall, Melbourne, in 1962. This was his first one-man stage show, and it formed the basis of his performances at Peter Cook's Establishment Club in London. "Can You Keep a Secret?" is a storytelling monologue that snares the listener in the convoluted genealogy of acquaintance. It all starts, narratologically, with the words "It all started," but it quickly turns illogical in the stops and starts of Sandy Stone's bizarre idioms of telling:

When I first heard the new people were a Clive and Glenda Nettleton it didn't ring a bell but Beryl said to me, Nettleton ... Nettleton ... Nettleton. Then she remembered; that Valda Clissold's younger sister Wanda had married a Brian Hiscock, one of *the* Hiscock boys who worked in exactly the same office – so it eventuated – as a Clive Nettleton who had married an old school friend of Wanda's by the name of Glenda Hibbotson and who now had a couple of kiddies – boy six, girl eight. Put it another way. When Beryl was in Bethesda having her veins done she met Valda Clissold who was in the next bed. They got on like a house on fire and later on, through young Valda, we met her sister Wanda. Now the amazing part about it was that Wanda Hiscock, who was a Wanda Clissold, had been to school with Glenda Hibbotson, who later married a Clive Nettleton, who worked in exactly the same office as her husband.

It sounds a bit on the complicated side, I know, but it's not if you think that Valda Clissold who was in Bethesda with Beryl has a brother-in-law, Brian Hiscock – one of *the* Hiscock boys – who worked in exactly the same office as the husband of sister Wanda's old school friend, Glenda Hibbotson.

Isn't it a small world?[33]

The middycosm of suburban society seems threatened as Sandy's explanation of a quite simple relationship – Clive Nettleton works with Brian Hiscock, whose wife, Wanda, is Beryl's friend Valda Clissold's sister and an old friend of Glenda Nettleton, Clive's wife – swells up (Les, disputing the pronunciation of the name, would say, "like Hiscock")[34] in the first paragraph; then returns to the safety of Sandy's pyjamas, dressing gown, hottie, armchair, and a genealogical lucidity in the second paragraph; and to kindness itself in the third. This adventure in telling sets up Sandy and Beryl's misadventure in child-minding and upsets the secret of their childlessness. Perhaps Sandy and Beryl Stone would agree with Georges Ribemont-Dessaignes, who, in his "History of Dada" (1931), observes:

There are undertakings of the human mind which, at the moment of bursting, make such a noise that no one can tell whether it is God's thunder or a string of firecrackers set off by village children. Then time passes, everybody goes off shrugging his shoulders, and the undertaking in question loses interest. God's most authentic thunder has ceased to be anything more than a child's firecracker.[35]

Sandy and Beryl's anticipatory excitement over having (playing host to) little Wayne and Marilyn Nettleton over the Easter weekend seems at first as great as is the participatory excitement of actually having (giving birth to) children of their own. But, by the end of a weekend of struggle and frustration, "God's thunder" has become "a child's firecracker": the promise of a DNA bundle of joy turns into the impossibility of giving birth to other people's children – as Sandy says, "What can you say to other people's kiddies?" – and the reality of two nettling brats, "like a wagonload of monkeys."[36] Sandy's statements "*A man doesn't want kiddies* carting half the beach through his vehicle and scratching a brand new pair of tartan seat protectors" (my emphasis); "I really think you've got to be cut out to cope with children"; "goodness only knows how we'd have managed if we'd ever embarked on a family"; "Look what happens when they grow up. They either wipe their boots on you, or they marry the first one that comes along and pack you off to a twilight home"; and "those few days took a lot out of Beryl and, well she got quite weepy when they went. You don't mind doing the neighbourly thing once in a while, but it's nice to get back to your interests"[37] reveal the Stones as what I would call (with apologies to Clive James) dull creatures but also as people who are quite comfortable with their childlessness. And they reveal Sandy to be a Socratic monologist who, under the guise of weakness and pathos, is actually a man of ideas.

Despite plying the children with sweets, tea, baths, bedtime stories, homemade sandwiches – "Egg and lettuce. Peanut butter. Marmite and walnut. Cheese and apricot jam. And lots of bread and butter and hundreds and thousands"[38] – at the zoo, taking them to Easter service, offering them leg of lamb for dinner and the run of the house (as when Wayne was "clopping around in a pair of Beryl's high-heeled shoes, lipstick all over his chops, bangles and earrings and goodness knows what"),[39] they are rewarded only with "a child's firecracker" when the Nettletons come to pick up their children: "the chimes went and they shot to the door like greased lightning."[40] While child-minding has not rewarded them with parenthood, Sandy's subtle account has revealed them both as Dada. If Sandy's summation, "There's no doubt about it – Beryl's marvellous with kiddies,"[41] sounds as hollow as Sandy's crackly voice (as crackly as crackling and as hollow as Wayne and Marilyn's chocolate Easter bunnies), in the end Sandy and Beryl are as solid as stone, as Dada stone.

The cause of Humphries' lingering preoccupation with Dada in his Sandy Stone monologues is most evident in this observation concerning his last year in school:

I devoted most of my energy to the Art Club and to my new passion for the Dadaists and Surrealists of the early 1920s. Everything I read about their antics and outrages excited me, and the work of Duchamp and Picabia and Schwitters seemed so much more amusing than the landscapes I had been painting in plodding imitation of Cézanne.[42]

In making this retrospective interpretation, Humphries, himself a painter, a collector of the works of Charles Conder,[43] and a connoisseur of painting, would know that the Fauves, Cubists, and Dadas all began "in plodding imitation of Cézanne," only to make a sharp break from him as they shattered the painting surface geometrically. Duchamp, when questioned about his own indebtedness to Cézanne, protested "if I had to say what my initial starting point was, I'd have to say it was the art of Odilon Redon."[44] To end relations with Cézanne is commensurate with entering the company of Dada; to state that one has ceased relations with Cézanne is tantamount to calling oneself a card-carrying Dadaist, except that, of course, true Dadas do not carry cards.

In one of his Dada art exhibitions of the early 1950s Humphries ceased his relations with Cézanne in the work "Yes! We Have No Cézannas!"[45] His remark in "The Confessions of Barry Humphries" (1965) – "Dadaism, that thrilling poetic movement which split with such fortuitous bad taste into the visual arts, had always enthralled me"[46] – explains how he got involved with Dada and also hints at how Dada "spilled" into Sandy's speech, possibly intravenously.

Marcel Duchamp has been credited with creating Dada even before 1916 at the Cabaret Voltaire, when Richard Huelsenbeck and Hugo Ball opened at random a French-German dictionary,[47] when "a paper-knife slipped at random between the pages of the dictionary acted as the necessary intermediary."[48] With reference to Duchamp's painting *The Passage from Virgin to Bride* (1912), for example, New York's Museum of Modern Art notes that he "began in this picture a reversal of Cubist propositions that would eventually lead him to create Dada (years before that movement got a name)."[49] One presumes that the period between "eventually" after 1912 and "years before" 1916 is a wormhole just big enough – as big, perhaps, as Humphries' BIGscapes – to admit the word "Dada." Perhaps in his BIGscapes, monologues, and other art Humphries has wormholed his way back into Dada, like a bookworm in his *oeuvre*.

Humphries first performed the dramatic monologue "Sandy Claus" in his show *Excuse I: Another Nice Night's Entertainment* (1965). The occasion, Sandy and Beryl's Christmas celebration, seems dramatic enough, given that Wayne and Marilyn Nettleton, along with their parents, are among the dinner party and because all Sandy and Beryl's careful preparations, especially in his wry telling of them, go terribly awry. To begin with, Sandy "tried on my Father Christmas costume again but I still had a certain amount of strife with the beard"; then the guests arrive early, and "Alan and Elaine Hotchkiss popped in unexpectedly for a few minutes with some presents and Beryl slipped into the bedroom and wrapped up some bath salts and after-shave lotion so they would never have known"; then Sandy "turned on the fairy lights" to create a proper ambience for dinner "and fused everything in the place."[50] The "turkey was as tough as Old Nick. On top of that I couldn't get the pudding to light and when it finally did the plastic holly melted giving it a rather funny taste."

But only when, dinner now at an end, Sandy concedes that "the crackers were a bit of a disappointment"[51] does the *trompe l'oeil* of Christmas cheer become clear, as, again, "God's thunder" becomes "a child's firecracker" and reality turns Dada. So, later, when Clive Clissold accidentally backs his Packard over a food package that the Nettletons were to have taken to "the Louisa Hutchinson Home for Handicapped Kiddies,"[52] he seems to have done the only thing possible, a charitable act in a Dada universe. As the monologue draws to a close, Sandy comes to bed and observes Beryl talking in her sleep. But in the morning, "When I told Beryl she said she'd slept like a log and not to talk a lot of twaddle," the state of Dada absurdity is invoked again, as Beryl's kindly speech is reduced to "rambling"[53] and Sandy's orderly speech-act is soundly deconstructed as "twaddle," both dissonant discourses recalling the "Wubbo" speech of Humphries' Dada stickman, Tid.

"Sandy Claus" also contains Sandy's clause on Aussie anti-Semitism in the anecdote that pops up when "Alan and Elaine Hotchkiss popped in unexpectedly."[54] In his story of how Alan avoids helping Dave Cohey – whose proper name, David Cohen (like the name of G-d in Jewish tradition), Sandy never utters – to get a membership at the Yarradale Golf Club. As the Yarradale golf pro, Alan is also a proponent of the lingering White Australia Policy, which at the time of this monologue (1965) was no longer on the books but still found systemic expression in public discourse. Sandy voices his own racism not only in othering and racializing epithets but also (1) by not telling why David Cohen might wish to belong to a golf club that excludes Jews, (2) by not explaining how Alan Hotchkiss managed to kiss Cohen off, and (3) by failing to realize that even Jesus (Sandy's God and a Jew) would be excluded from Yarradale. In "Sandy Claus," as in "Sandy Comes Home," Humphries politicizes Sandy's speech-act, using it to expose Australian xenophobia, active racism, systemic racism, and bigotry not in any sanctimonious way but with humour. Dame Edna's confession in the Broadway and touring productions of *The Royal Tour* (1999–2001), a confession that was absent in the San Francisco production (1998), that she is Jewish is Humphries' most public declaration of his own Jewishness, as, in the guise of performativity, Edna "outs" him and sheds his foreskin.

A conspicuous Dada ploy is to make characterization dependent on killing the character off. Only a few monologues into the series, in "Sandy's Stone" (which dates from 1968, and first appeared on Humphries and Nigel Butterley's 1972 LP *Barry Humphries at Carnegie Hall in First Day Covers: A Philharmonic Philatelia*), Humphries began to deconstruct Sandy Stone, making his name an eponym for his "little op,"[55] for a kidney or gall stone.

Humphries suggests in an annotation that the "internal evidence points to a prostatectomy,"[56] thereby engaging Sandy to make a bed for Norman Everage.

Yet, even as an invalid, Sandy has validity: in his speech-act he validates our being by outing the absurdity of mutability and suffering. He pushes his "stone" on the audience, reminding them they are Sisyphus, even if they can say with Sandy, "I have never enjoyed a day's illness in my life apart from a few funny turns Beryl couldn't put her finger on."[57] Is Sandy saying (1) he has never before been ill in his life, outside of "a few funny turns"; (2) the only illnesses that he has ever "enjoyed" have been his "few funny turns"; (3) he has never in his life been ill for an entire day, except when he has had "a few [daylong] funny turns"; or (4) statements 1, 2, or 3, conditional upon Beryl's being able (or unable) to "put her finger on" the "few funny turns"?

As the possibilities of mutability and suffering fan out from Sandy's seemingly innocent remark, listeners come to imagine themselves in the "hossie" with him, which, because it is a Repatriation, or military veterans, hospital is the blueprint, like old veins pulsing under thin skin, of Mrs Beazley's "maximum security twilight home," the asylum that awaits everyone foolish enough to grow old (or foolish enough, like Sandy, to remember the time when he was vigorous). As in some languages, the verb "to remember" is reflexive (e.g., the French *se souvenir* and the Dutch *zich herinneren*), so in this monologue Sandy can be seen remembering himself as well as remembering past events. Humphries is familiar with the reflexive verb. He concludes "Alzheimer Remembers," in *More Please*, with the German translation *"Alzheimer! Erinnern Sie!"*[58]

His reclaimed selves and events tend to be "funny" to Sandy, like a "funny turn," of course, but also with some of the absurdist colourations of the word "funny," as Peter Cook and Dudley Moore were also using it in their sketches of the 1960s. Sandy turns from the warm, and quite beautifully poetic, memory "but somehow it always seems afternoon when you're playing mixed doubles," to a, for him, sharp complaint about the noisy players at the tennis club next to the hospital: "I can hear them playing right up until the light goes and the couples laughing when there's nothing particularly funny."[59] From this point on, the word "funny" invokes the disjuncture of the present and the past, like two jarring faults in a cubist canvas: "A funny thing happened when Beryl and I were courting."[60] Funny things, funny turns, tennis courts, and courting rituals combine in Sandy's poignant play of discourse to form not only *le cubisme* but also *le cubitus* – the ulna, or "funny" bone.

The ulna bone extends from the elbow to the wrist, on the side of the arm opposite the thumb. Where the ulnar nerve draws close to the skin near the elbow, it forms the funny bone. In delineating a series of cubist planes, Sandy, despite his anxiety, is touching our funny bones. Sandy's closing lines, the philosophical "I only hope and pray that when the time eventually does come – and it will – Beryl's the first to go," and the senti-mental "It was different in the old days of mixed doubles and the crazy whist and the couples. But you can't win the Lucky Spot all your life,"[61] make another break in existential and narratological time, fracturing the ineluctable future and the irrecoverable past, and spotting Sandy in a "Lucky Spot" (whether it is his site of narrativity or a shadow showing up on the X-Ray screen). His progressive deterioration, or decomposition, and brief final illness, from his treatment in hospital in "Sandy's Stone" (1968) to his death in "The Land of the Living" (1971), suggest cancer (cancer of the prostate, to cite an obvious example, based on Humphries' marginal notation) as the most likely "spotted" cause of death. In the course of his illness, Sandy would likely have lost body mass, to which, in "The Land of the Living," his repeated assurances to Beryl about his eating habits seem to attest. In this regard, one might imagine Sandy losing stone after stone – until, in the end, there was simply no Stone left.

Sandy returns to the epistolary mode from what can only be described as his death-bed, the luckiest of spots, in "The Land of the Living." Humphries wrote the monologue, in what he calls his "first attempt to kill Sandy Stone off,"[62] for his Australian miscellany show *A Load of Olde Stuffe: A Divertissement in Two Acts, for Those Too Drunk to Dance* (1971).[63] In a series of letters to Beryl (who is again absent because she is Dada, because of the restrictions of the monologue form, and because she is in England, where, according to the postcard, the "smell was so bad"),[64] Sandy fills her in on the economy of Kia Ora, 36 Gallipoli Crescent, Glen Iris: "Things at Gallipoli Crescent are just the same and I'm pottering round on my own very nicely thanks to your list."[65] This time Sandy's idi-omatic motif is "just a note to let you know I'm still in the land of the liv-ing,"[66] with a chilling variation in the final letter, from Gweneth Longmire: "Jack and myself were shocked to hear of Alexander's sudden passing last week."[67]

The motif reminds the audience that Sandy has always been nominally close to the earth, but the death-knell variation, especially with Humphries' gloss on the name "Alexander," "the first reference to the name given Sandy at the font,"[68] hints that Sandy's "Lucky Spot" has been called and that his death is not the "middycosm" of Glen Iris; or the screened realities of *General Hospital, The Young and the Restless, Peyton Place,* and *Coro-nation Street* (the soap operas whose storylines Sandy summarizes for Beryl);[69] or even the euphemism of passing away but, rather, the Aristote-lian causality that extends from the baptismal font into typographical fonts, from the speech-act into silence.

The character's full name, Alexander Horace Stone, a heroic, and Hom-eric, name, suggests that, in death, he measures his length upon the earth, like the fallen warriors in *The Iliad*. Sandy's da-da-death is, as Gabrielle Buffet-Picabia has described Dada, "a kind of auto-inoculation of the absurd by the absurd, assuming the unforeseen dimensions of an immanent, inexorable force, born of circumstances."[70] In fact, within a Dada milieu, Beryl Stone is to Sandy Stone as Gabrielle Buffet-Picabia was to Francis Picabia – a goddess who spoke for a dead man.

The import of Sandy's *demise-en-scène* is meaninglessness: it simply is not important. If it is curtains for Sandy, the curtain can always rise again for another "positively final appearance,"[71] as in "Sandy and the Sandman" (1971), "Sandy Soldiers On" (1978), "Shades of Sandy" (1981), "Sandy Comes Home" (1985), and "A Letter from Limbo" (1990). In fact, Sandy has delivered as many monologues after death as he did before his fatal illness. Of the twelve full-length published Sandy Stone monologues, five precede "Sandy's Stone" and five follow "The Land of the Living." But Sandy can also rise again in his continued existence after death. He continues to exist just like spectators and readers because, in a "spooky" old sense, they are also dead: they are "the absurd by the absurd." In this sense, Sandy Stone's five postmortem monologues draw audiences out of their own absurdity and into his absurdity. The curtain may fall on Sandy, leaving him homeless, yet he remains so only until the next house arrives and his next ontologizing monologue.

In this inability to deliver his last words in time, Sandy may be a distant relative of Melpomenus Jones, who appears in Stephen Leacock's short story "The Awful Fate of Melpomenus Jones" (1910). This story is about a curate on a pastoral visit, who, when his hosts importune him not to leave just yet, to stay for another cup of tea, then for dinner, then overnight, ends up staying for months, eventually becoming immovable, until

when the last moment came, he sat up in bed with a beautiful smile of confidence playing upon his face, and said, "Well – the angels are calling me; I'm afraid I really must go now. Good afternoon." And the rushing of his spirit from its prison-house was as rapid as a hunted cat passing over a garden fence.[72]

Perhaps Sandy is to be distinguished from Melpomenus only in that, in all likelihood, he "dropped off the twig," as Gweneth Longmire puts it, "as lively as a cricket."[73]

"Sandy and the Sandman," which Humphries performed in his show *At Least You Can Say You've Seen It: A Tragi-Farce in Two Acts, for Those Too Drunk to Dance* (1974), is a study in the self-consciousness of human being. Sandy begins the monologue by explaining how he came to realize he is dead. He knows that he knows that he knows that he is dead or, as he puts it: "I just had a horrible dream. I dreamed I dropped off the twig."[74] He ends the monologue by committing the ultimate speech-act, attributing to himself his last living words: "My last words would have been: 'Only half a pint today please Milko. Money under brick. P.S. Nothing tomorrow.' "[75] Given that probably no one other than Hamlet has ever been able to utter the last words "the rest is silence," and that few people manage to get out any kind of theatrical, poetic, philosophical, or otherwise profound speech immediately before dying, Sandy's conditional last words (lactic, yet somehow lacking) seem appropriate to the human condition.

Sandy himself alludes to the "famous last words like for instance when Doctor Livingstone said Kiss me Hardy, I presume. All of the historical celebrities and oldendays personalities made some little philosophical quip before they jumped the twig."[76] For Sandy, as existent, or, as Humphries prefers to call him, "revenant" ("the character was always something of a revenant"),[77] the rest is not silence but more speaking parts, more monologues in the land of the living, where monotony, or the speech-flatline, goes by the name "Death."

In between his out-of-body experience and his "not-to-have-been" last words,[78] Sandy meditates on the last things of letterboxes: "This morning I toddled down to our front gate to look in the letterbox to see if there was anything there rather than snails to ascertain if Beryl had managed to scribble me a little line from gay Paree."[79] Sandy's fix is eschatological (not scatological, like Les's fixation). Sandy believes that cosmology, the universe beyond the "middycosm," can be reduced to anything that will fit in a letter box, from snails to letters (which may allude to the real meaning of "snail mail").

His walk to the letterbox and his dialectic there with the postie are accompanied by a referential chorus of "Returned men," or war veterans: Les Bullock, the postman himself, Pat Hennessy, and even the "vestryman at Holy Trinity – he wasn't a Returned man, but he was one of the nicest people you could ever wish to meet."[80] Sandy is also a Returned man. As a vet, a vetted man (subject to the scrutiny of Humphries and the spectators), he is both an old soldier and an old-timer, outside the theatres of war and time. His seemingly naïve observation, "I'm a firm believer that we're all given a little warning we're going to cash in our chips just to give us a chance to rustle up a little speech for posterity,"[81] may not be true of life, but it is certainly true of the theatre, where, in "Sandy and the Sandman," Sandy might rise from the dead Tuesday through Sunday at 8:00 PM, with matinee performances on Wednesday and Sunday at 3:00 PM.

Few actors can boast they have never died on stage, but how many can say they have staged a resurrection? Most actors have played understudies at the start of their careers, but how many can say they have ghosted for a character? Humphries, who is a brilliant comic, character, cameo (too often), and serious (not often enough) actor (see Appendix 8), and, contrary to some critics' beliefs, not above dying on stage, is perhaps the only actor who can say he has risen from the dead while getting a rise out of the audience (not to mention having ghosted for Les Patterson, who thinks resurrection a double-feature with a Girl Friday). Given that, since the Renaissance, death has been a pun and a euphemism for sexual climax, one might hint that the rumours of Sandy Stone's death have been greatly exaggerated, diverted into a series of great death masques.

Sandy's opening words in "Sandy Soldiers On," from *"Isn't It Pathetic at His Age"* (1978), "I AM DECEASED,"[82] could be interpreted to mean (1) I am dead or (2) my cessation has reversed: I am de-ceased. Thus, his death masque is a Dada paradox: "I am dead, I am not dead." Sandy's masque takes the form of the monologue not because of generic demands but because he has a monologic imagination: his mind follows the singular logic of memory images and expresses itself in a series of uninterrupted dramatic speeches, unlike a talk show (which, according to Dame Edna's preferred definition, is "a monologue, interrupted by total strangers"). But even in the context of uninterrupted speech, Sandy's imagination is also dialogic in that he always directs his singular logic of memory images to Beryl, who is his primary theatrical addressee and narratological narratee, and only through her to listeners, spectators, or readers. Bakhtin defines "dia" in "The Problem of Speech Genres":

The utterance is filled with *dialogic overtones*, and they must be taken into account in order to understand fully the style of the utterance. After all, our thought itself – philosophical, scientific, and artistic – is born and shaped in the process of interaction and struggle with others' thought, and this cannot but be reflected in the forms that verbally express our thought as well.[83]

In his dialogic monologues Sandy may well "express our thought as well," not our idiosyncratic thoughts but our collective thought. Perhaps the only thought that people still have in common (with Sandy, and with one another) is the thought "death," the thought "I AM DECEASED" (which is the antithesis of *ego sum* ["I am"]), the thought that prompts our dying fall and, most tellingly, the thought "*I thought I might have known, which is the thought before the stealth of fate.*"[84] Yet, to the extent that his monologues are didactic as well as amusing, Sandy allows us to exchange our epistemological dilemma "I might have known" with his ontological and narratological dilemma "My last words would have been." In other words, he allows us to trade up from John Locke to René Descartes.

Sandy's reference to the death of Cliff Jennings, of a "massive coronary occlusion in the middle of the Changing of the Colour. Poor old beggar keeled over. Brand new Nikon hit the deck – zoom lens, in-camera sound system, the works – they were both a total write-off,"[85] hints at Humphries' position on the breakdown of imagination and language not just in death (Sandy's, Cliff's, our own) but also in contemporary postpictorial, postliterate society. This society might be "a total write-off," but Sandy resocializes it by trading script for speech and imagination.

As Roland Barthes says in *La Chambre claire: Note sur la photographie* (1980), "Toute photographie est un certificat de présence"[86] ("All photography is a certificate of presence" [my translation]). "Sandy Soldiers On" and the other postmortem monologues are certificates of Sandy's presence, of his having been present, as if Cliff's Nikon were revealed to contain a photograph of the "poor old beggar keel[ing] over," an image of his imagination, or what it "would have been." In a sense, by re-entering the middy-cosm from death, Sandy reaches into a Barthesian well to retrieve a child's ball (that of the child whom Beryl and he never had), which bears the inscription "The word and the image are one."[87] In that the written word is male and the image is female (see Shlain), Sandy might be seen as reconciling male and female genders through his death.

Yet, on the contrary, the news of his death seems to widen the division between man and woman, husband and wife, as Sandy himself observes:

Beryl was on her Scandinavian leg when she received Gweneth Longmire's tragic news of my decease. I wrecked Helsinki for Beryl – if ever a man ruined Scandinavia for a loved one it was me. And she could have caught her death rushing out of that sauna as quick as she did.[88]

On the surface, Sandy is saying, most decorously, that, by dying, he "ruined" Beryl's holiday. Yet the "loved one" is not just Beryl, his beloved wife, but also Sandy himself, who has become, referentially, the euphemism of a living man, as in Evelyn Waugh's satire on the funeral business, *The Loved-One* (1948). Thus, observing proper decorum, his obituary notice refers to him as "beloved brother" and "much-loved husband."[89] Similarly, Beryl, who is "quick" when she emerges from the sauna, would seem to be the antithesis of Sandy, who is here a dead letter.

Yet Beryl's "could have" conditionality actually unites her with Sandy through the "would have" conditionality of his last words, which are not made up of dead letters. Even the name "Sandy" seems to contain a phonemical death clause, the "Sandy Claus(e)" "sand + die," when in fact it proposes another clause, like a codicil in a will, "sans + die" ("without dying") or possibly *sans dieu* ("without God") or *sans dire*, as in *cela va sans dire* ("that goes without saying"). Sandy, the speech-actor, who has always gone *with* saying, now must go without saying, *sans dire*. Whether he is with or without God, only he knows. Apparently, whether or not he has had a theophany also goes without saying.

Yet if one part of the afterlife has to do with separation from or association with God, another part has to do with separation from or association with people. If to Sartre (i.e., to the character Garcin in his play *Huis Clos* [1947]) "l'enfer, c'est les Autres" ("hell is other people"),[90] then to Sandy *la vie, c'est les autres* ("life is other people"), or as Inès expresses this Stoney sentiment in *Huis Clos*: "Tu n'es rien d'autre que ta vie" ("You are nothing else than your life") (my translations). At the end of the monologue, Sandy summarizes his views on otherness:[91] "Beryl's moving up to Noosa soon. Noosa. She's selling up. This place is a bit small for them. I'll miss her too. We do miss people. But Beryl needs a holiday after the terrible shock I gave her."[92] One "we" (Beryl and Sandy: people) seems to have been replaced by another (the dead: *les autres*), yet the subsequent monologues suggest otherwise, that Beryl and Sandy (the "we" berylandsandy) are inseparable in death, like the lovers in the sonnets of Shakespeare and Donne.

Despite the impediment of death "Sandy soldiers on," not like a sexually undeveloped ant but like a Returned man who is making a show of continuing in death (i.e., of showing death up). Like Lazarus and Jesus, he has returned *from* the dead; like Orpheus and Dante, he has returned *to* the dead. He is a soldier not because he happened to die for a *sous* but because he is still not willing to die, to go under (*sous*), to go irretrievably into the underworld, where he is eternally *autre*. In this regard, Sandy "soldiers on": he is *sur* ("on", not *sous* ("under"). *Il persévère* ("he perseveres"); *il ne succombe pas* ("he does not go under"). He will not even underwrite his monologues: (1) by bringing them to an end; (2) by writing them poorly, (3) by writing them at all, as distinguished from speaking them off the top of his head, from what is, for him, the "Lucky Spot" of orality; or (4) by ensuring their success, their outcome in closure or resolution, or in applause or awards.

The monologue "Shades of Sandy," from *An Evening's Intercourse with the Widely Liked Barry Humphries* (Sydney and Melbourne, 1981, and London, 1982), begins, like "Sandy Soldiers On," with a declaration that seems the antithesis of the *ego sum* of human being: "I'M NOT LIVING at home any more."[93] For this sketch, Sandy has relocated himself – bilocation is one recognized condition of sainthood – to an opportunity shop:

*Racks of cast-off frocks and overcoats, superseded television sets,* Readers Digest *Special Offers, early microgroove albums, toast racks, prosthetic devices, tea cosies, gimcrack fifties furniture, gewgaws, kickshaws, and a clutter of heterogeneous bygones reeking of moth repellent and another sourer odour.*[94]

This catalogue of things is a Dada artist's workshop, a source of *objets trouvés* and readymades, as in "Sandy Agonistes." Although formally a stage direction, it is a kind of found poem, finding its syntax in the cadences of speech and breathing, and in the metres of nonexistent *vers libre*.

Humphries' use of the term "superseded" as a watchword of mutability anticipates V.S. Naipaul's use of the term in *The Enigma of Arrival: A Novel in Five Sections* (1987), which takes its title from a 1912 painting by Dada, Surrealist, and Metaphysical artist Giorgio de Chirico.

Jack lived among ruins, among superseded things.[95]

The old man first, then. And, after him, the garden, the garden in the midst of superseded things.[96]

It seemed that in that patch of ground, amid the derelict buildings of a superseded kind of farming (fewer and less efficient machines, many more human hands available in this county of Wiltshire, known in the last century for the poverty of its farm labourers), Jack had found fulfilment.[97]

In the word "superseded" Naipaul might be alluding to how people of colour and colonials have been set aside inside "Thatcher's Kingdom" (see Jones). Similarly, Humphries might be using the word to cite how, in Margaret Thatcher's regime (1979–90), working-class people, like the audiences of music hall, have been set aside, "pauperized," Edna might say, too indigent even to afford a ticket to the theatre. But both Naipaul and Humphries, I believe, are commenting less on people marginalized in an English Thatch(er)ed Cottage than on the paradigm of mutability, in which men and women die, and even literary characters can hardly resist dying.

Like Beryl, "rushing out of that sauna as quick as she did"[98] in reaction to the news of Sandy's death, Naipaul's narrator confesses at the end of the novel, "faced with a real death, and with this new wonder about men, I laid aside my drafts and hesitations and began to write very fast about Jack and his garden."[99] (Cf. "I wrote very simply and fast of the simplest things in my memory.")[100] People must be "very fast" indeed to outstep death, yet Sandy (in his languorous speech) and Naipaul's narrator (in his ponderous prose) seem able at least to take death on a quickstep, in the rhythm of human nature. People might be subject to mutability, but at least they can linger in the company of things, even become things. Sandy takes the opportunity of being in the Holy Trinity Voluntary Helpers Opportunity Shop to reflect on the nature of things, particularly things that have died and so can never be found, just as "a lot here in the Opportunity Shop, they never get a message from the other side at all. *Nobody's got their finger on the glass for them.*"[101] Perhaps the most conspicuous of Sandy's things is Beryl's Aspaxadrine Inhaler.[102]

It might call to mind Tristan Tzara's play *La Première Aventure céleste de M. Antipyrine*, which, in the edition *avec des bois gravés et coloriés par M. Janco* (1916), was the first Dada publication. Stone and Tzara connect in the Aspaxadrine-Antipyrine play on words and in a respiratory antilogy: whereas an Aspaxadrine inhaler increases the supply of oxygen to the lungs, M. Antipyrine ("fire-extinguisher") cuts off the supply of oxygen to the fire. As Sandy concludes this story, "Anyway, we had to fit this Aspaxadrine Inhaler together. It said 'even a child could do it,' but we could never find a kiddie to show us how[f]."[103] If Sandy's allusion to Aspaxadrine reveals his Dada first causalities, then his witticism "but we could never find a kiddie to show us how" shows his music hall last effects. Humphries' note on "f" is perhaps no more coherent than what should be attributed to a speaker who is at once composing and decomposing: "Then there was a snap of my brother Victor who fell at the Battle of the Somme. I never knew Vic, never set eyes on him."[104] Such a non sequitur is worthy of variety stars Elsie and Doris Waters.

Compare Gert and Daisy's exchange in the Waters sisters' wartime BBC radio sketch "Gert, Daisy, a Piano and How!" in which Daisy Barlow reluctantly takes delivery of a piano that the delivery man insists is for her. However, he later realizes his mistake, returns, and takes it back, admitting that it was tagged for "Harlow." Daisy and Gert probe their lorry-drop before Daisy tentatively fingers the keyboard:

GERT: Can you play it?
DAISY: I used to when I was a kid.

But the kiddie does not arrive to show her how, so Daisy and Gert engage in some impertinent off-key capriccios. Just as they prefer to play their tunes out of tune, so Sandy fancies leaving things dismantled, whether Beryl's Aspaxadrine Inhaler or anything else in the opportunity-knocks shop of things. Childlessness is nothingness to him:

But I wouldn't want to be a misery to myself and a burden to others. That's why I'm very glad and grateful Beryl and I never had any kiddie … any close relations. You hear terrible stories about kids, bundling their old folks off to homes. Some of them dragged off the bowling green. I've heard that.[105]

A kiddie will never come to put the deconstructed Sandy back together or to restore any of the things in the Opportunity Shop to their former places in the middycosm. Nor will a kiddie ever put Sandy into a "maximum security twilight home," even if it passes for an opportunists' shop, the place where ontological snobs hide from death.

Sandy may be a shade who no longer casts a shadow, but his "shades" are the mnemonics that figure in his postmortem monologues exactly as they figure in his premortem monologues: they simultaneously prefigure and postfigure. When Humphries, who is as much Sandy's amanuensis (or linotype óperator) as he is Dame Edna Everage's manager with signing authority, transcribes Sandy's monologues: he sets the type in the font *Sandy's Cast Shadows* or *Shades of Sandy*.

Yet in the end typeface only masks the photographic image of Sandy's true face, which survives in "an old snapshot album" that Clarrie Lockwood retrieves from under the house after Sandy's death. It had "a couple of snaps in it that could have upset her. Pictures of me and a lass from the Sunday School that I used to court before I met Beryl. Little Phil Tremlow. She was a goer."[106] Although Clarrie destroys the evidence – "Clarrie had to carry it to the incinerator on his shovel. It was a beggar to burn; a tin of kero didn't do it"[107] – he also provides a kind of photographic image of Beryl for Sandy to take with him into eternity in that he imagines himself moving in on Beryl:

He took the erica, the shrimp plant, the malaluka, the paligonia and he's had his eye on Beryl's cumquat for years. But I mustn't speak ill of the living. I just hope and pray that Beryl won't do anything too hasty. And I don't think she will – she wouldn't, she won't.[108]

Although death has brought physical separation, snapping their verbal life-line, Sandy and Beryl remain united in transcribed monologues of marriage and lingering images of infidelity, two snaps in a double frame, which Mieke Bal calls "double exposures" and Roland Barthes calls "une image sans code"[109] ("an uncoded image").

When Bal states that "conversations and dialogues are specific social events of a predominantly but not exclusively discursive nature, consisting of activities occurring in a particular time and place between people acting as subjects,"[110] she provides a definitive point for a view of Sandy's monologue as a postmortem event of a simultaneously verbal and imagistic nature, outside time and space – "so this is my Dreamtime"[111] – with the individual speech-actor. Sandy's image is "uncoded" precisely because, at the point of death, his genetic code, or DNA, broke down and became AND, like the computer search command <Sandy AND Stone>, which comes up blank, like a "sacred Site"[112] where Aboriginal inhabitants have gone and all their artifacts have become fictional.

Yet Sandy makes a "positively final appearance" in "A Letter from Limbo," from Humphries' Australian show *The Life and Death of Sandy Stone* (1990). Having dropped off the twig, Sandy now finds himself out on a limb in limbo as Humphries faces the narratological absurdity of how a dead person can narrate a story. Robertson Davies solves the problem handily in his novel *Murther and Walking Spirits* (1991) by allowing his narrator, the late murdered Connor Gilmartin, to be a ghost writer, telling the story of his premortem self. But Humphries accepts the narratological absurdity by casting Sandy as a hologram and setting his pen to paper. That he should write Beryl a letter "out of the blue" with no return address, and that he should "sign off"[113] when semiotics must surely be desystematized, emphasizes the absurdity of Sandy's existence without life.

Humphries clarifies Sandy's ambivalent position between word and image in his closing stage direction as the complimentary close of a letter becomes a *"photographic projection."*[114] The opening stage direction has prepared the spectator for this duality:

*A hologram. Sandy is writing. The hologram brightens and as suddenly, fades, as the audience becomes aware of an identical figure in suspension high above their heads, held in a spotlight.*[115]

Another duality is that Sandy is writing not just the letter but also the hologram itself. "A Letter from Limbo" is his holograph, a document written entirely in the handwriting of the person who has signed it, as in "Your ever loving, / Sandy."[116] He writes the hologram – his photographic projection in the theatre – through holography, as Gweneth Longmire sends Beryl the telegram, notifying her of Sandy's death, by telegraphy. His letter, the inscribed or typographic text, is Sandy's dead fall (his free fall outside the earth's gravitational field) from the theatrical spotlight through the remembrance of things past.

Of the monologue's nineteen paragraphs, eight begin with the imperative "remember" (in a bidding reminiscent of King Hamlet), one begins with the question "do you remember," and another begins with "Mind you." Sandy continues to exist after death but will "die" should his family and friends stop invoking his name and his image in thoughts, prayers, ceremonies, memories, and, indeed, holograms. Sandy knows the verb "remember" is his key to self-reflexivity. All his words reflect back on him, as when he recalls the bathroom tile pattern that he and Beryl designed and that the new owners of Kia Ora, the Cosmopolis, have altered: "I liked the beige mottled ones but you were dead set on the pale green."[117] This statement may remind spectators, readers, and listeners[118] that Sandy is set in death (in nominal stone) but also hanging above the stage (in holographic Limbo).

Sandy reminds Beryl of this stasis in life when he happens to recall "that melody was on the hit parade when we were trying for a family."[119] After reprising his and Beryl's old debate over the etiquette of whether or not, "in mixed company," to speak the idiom "to try for a family," Sandy remembers how their sex life came to an end. In one sense, he passes under the limbo Limbo pole (in another sense, he passes over it) from propriety to truth:

You reckoned it was O.K. to want a family or to *have* a family, but it was very uncalled for to *try* for one in mixed company. In point of actual fact, that was about the time we stopped trying funnily enough.[120]

The syntax of the phrase "to *try* for one in mixed company" (cf. Sandy's recollection of "playing mixed doubles"[121]) might explain why Sandy and Beryl had to give up having sex. However, more likely Humphries' treble entendre – (1) to utter the idiom in the company of men and women, (2) to have sex with other people present, and (3) to engage in a *ménage à trois* – reveals Sandy's ingenuousness (and something of his lingering bitterness).

Here his sexual innuendo is as innocuous as Dame Edna's is arch and tawny, and as Les Patterson's is brutal and filthy. (In fact, Patterson's sexual interdiscourse is not innuendo at all: it is just in your end.) In his remark on sexual performance "in mixed company," Humphries might also be alluding to what Dagmar Kift cites as "the London music-hall structure with its distinctions between socially mixed halls in the centre and working-class halls in the suburbs."[122] In British music hall audiences in the latter half of the nineteenth century, in London and especially in the regions, the social mix of egalitarianism was quite exceptional. Beryl and Sandy's "trying for a family" is a kind of music hall double-act or "two-handed sketch"[123] in that such acts often referenced unstable marriages and family disasters. Witness Les Patterson's parodic epithalamium odes "Genuine" (1981) and "My Old Lady" (1983), which document his ambivalence towards his wife, Meg, and his infidelities.

When the Stones stop trying, they signal the closings of the birth passage and of the music halls, and the opening of Humphries' one-man music hall revival (which he takes on because, like Sandy at his final curtain, music hall is in Limbo). His new presentation of an old theatrical genre is not a single act but, rather, the series of command music hall performances that make up his literary *oeuvre* and theatrical career.

Yet when the curtain comes down on his life, Sandy finds himself over the border of cultural difference, beyond the margins of Western cultures, which differentiate between life and death:

"culture" tells us blacks, Texans, and women under certain conditions are funny, and we laugh. As these examples indicate, unless we preserve the possibility of not accepting the joke as such, the possibility of seeing the joke as radically differing from itself even within the same situation, our definition of the joke becomes a form of coercion. It serves to institute the very culture within which it is judged by use to be appropriate. And this consideration is just as important in the case of the Texan as it is in the more sensitive cases of blacks and women, for one way culture is instituted is precisely by means of differentiations between innocent and touchy subjects.[124]

As subjects, Sandy is decidedly "innocent" and death is emphatically "touchy." By making a joke about Sandy's death, Humphries invites his audiences not to accept it – either the joke or the death, either Sandy's death or death itself. In refusing to differentiate between life and death, Humphries institutes a new culture: generically, it is theatrical; nationalistically, it is Australian.

Sandy's Dreamtime is the Australian centre, the living heart of Humphries' theatre, where life and death can be understood more as theatrical than as ontological events. In Limbo Sandy exists outside the boundaries of class and gender and, therefore in mixed, or mixed-up, company.

The move away from the singularities of "class" or "gender" as primary conceptual and organizational categories, has resulted in an awareness of the subject positions – of race, gender, generation, institutional location, geopolitical locale, sexual orientation – that inhabit any claim to identity in the modern world.[125]

In his Sandy Stone monologues, Humphries draws audience attention to all these issues. In "Sandy Comes Home" and "A Letter from Limbo," even from beyond the grave, Sandy worries about how the Cosmopolis, "a delightful multi-cultural ethnic minority Greek couple,"[126] are hellenizing Kia Ora, despite the fact that their name suggests they will merely help transform the middycosm of Glen Iris into what Melbourne already is – a world-class multicultural city.

Sandy also addresses the issue of race in "Sandy Claus," in his anecdote about David Cohen, who is excluded from the Yarradale Golf Club because he is Jewish. In most of the monologues Sandy emphasizes his and Beryl's childlessness; however, in "A Letter from Limbo" his chronicling of the end of their sexual relations – "that was about the time we stopped trying funnily enough" – reveals how they have transcended traditional gender roles (1) by recognizing that sex is funny and (2) by rejecting the sexual prerogative of the marriage construct and showing that asexuality may be essential to gender identities.

In "Sandy and the Sandman" he even rebukes genderized men, the kind of men who imagine they are helpless without women:

Some chappies' womenfolk skedaddle – toddle off – only for a few days perhaps, and they let themselves go to pack completely. I hope I couldn't be regarded as being such a type of grub and at the moment I've got three pairs of night attire soaking out the back in Beryl's yellow plastic bucket with a good old sprinkle of Bio-Ad.[127]

In "Can You Keep a Secret?" Sandy subjects the next generation, little Wayne and Marilyn, to in loco parentis scrutiny. In "Shades of Sandy" he discusses how "kids, bundling their old folks off to homes,"[128] betray the generation that gave them life. In "Sandy's Stone" he enters the "institutional locations" of the Repat(riation Hospital) and the Blamey Ward. In "Days of the Week," "Sandy Agonistes," "Sandy Soldiers On," "Shades of

Sandy," and "Letter from Limbo" he assesses, respectively, the "geopolitical locales" of the Returned Servicemen's League; 2a Pembridge Gardens,
Notting Hill Gate; the Garden of Rest mausoleum; the Holy Trinity Voluntary Helpers Opportunity Shop; and Purgatory; and, in all the other monologues, the "geopolitical locale" of 36 Gallipoli Crescent, and Unit 3, 7
Gallipoli Crescent, Glen Iris.

Sandy seems unaware of the issues of sexual orientation, yet in "Can You
Keep a Secret?" he seems to express his homophobia in reaction to Wayne
Nettleton,

all dressed up like Lord Muck – clopping around in a pair of Beryl's high-heeled
shoes, lipstick all over his chops, bangles and earrings and goodness knows what.
He was wearing everything but the kitchen sink and showing off something terrific
too, but we had to laugh! You should have seen his face. It was a picture no artist
could paint.[129]

In these ways Sandy Stone rejects "any claim to identity in the modern
world" and locates culture in speech-acts rather than in a bathrobe, a suit,
or even a Barry Humphries. Yet Humphries' monologues are localized in
modernity, in the pre-postmodern period of the 1950s, 1960s, and 1970s.
Indeed, Humphries has stated, "I would insist that I'm basically a regional
monologist,"[130] even though his apparently deliberate misuse of his de-
spised adverb "basically" and the fact that he made the statement to an audience of journos tend to qualify his admission.

Sandy Stone is his preeminent stage monologist, but Humphries has enacted several other remarkable speakers and speech-acts. One of his earliest monologues, "Jeff Pritchard: Seeing Australia First" (1959), in which
the speaker is a Pioneer Parlour-coachman whose glib commentary, part
travelogue and part history lesson, takes the passengers on a tour from
the Melbourne terminal to Mount Dandenong. Humphries performed the
piece on ABC television in Australia: "It was delivered to camera (there
was one) at high speed and with frenzied good humour by me wearing a
jaunty peaked cap and holding a steering wheel."[131] Within the context
of Humphries' monology, Jeff Pritchard's address is remarkable for his
guidance on the subject of "the garden suburbs of Hawthorn and
Camberwell"[132] (i.e., the middycosm) and for the music hall song that, at
the end of the tour narrative, he invites the passengers to join in singing,
"I'm Looking over a Four Leaf Clover" (1927) (music by Harry Woods,
words by Mort Dixon). Melbourne suburbs and music hall song would
become Humphries' preoccupation and the focus of his poetic and his
aesthetic.

Three other early model-monologues, "Buster Thompson," "Debbie
Thwaite," and "Colin Cartwright: The Battler," appeared, along with

"Sandy Stone: *Sandy Agonistes*," on Barry Humphries' first solo LP, *Sandy Agonistes* (1960).[133] Of Thompson's characterization, Humphries has noted:

This character was the prototype of my later comic strip invention Barry McKenzie. In fact it was after hearing this recording in New York in 1962 that Peter Cook, the actor and wit, invited me to devise a similar character for a comic strip in his magazine *Private Eye*. Although Buster and Bazza come from different social milieus, they are united by very similar views of life.[134]

The verb "to invent" means to find something that already exists, as in Dada *objets trouvés* and readymades, evident in Francis M. Naumann's phrase "the invention of the readymade."[135] In the sense that a prototype is an early form, Buster Thompson can be seen as a specious ancestor of Barry McKenzie: (1) an early form of the species "Australian character" and "very vulgar working-class character,"[136] and (2) a man with a McKenzie family resemblance yet, in the end, a stranger.

One imagines that Buster must have Bazza's jaw line, and, in the diction, idiom, and pacing of his monologue, one hears the uncommon protolinguistic pattern of Bazza's chin-wagging: "Paddy MacIlwraith and I ran the 'G over to the Down Under Club the other Saturday and had ourselves an absolutely fantastic night. Man, talk about birds; it was phenomenal!"[137] If the twenty-first-century London discourse (accent and dialect) is not Received Pronunciation but Estuary English, then Buster's discourse could be called "Australian (Pub) Crawl" as Buster and his mates taste the beverages and the everages[138] along the Thames estuary and the English Channel. In a monologue of just 1,020 words, Buster utters the word "fantastic" eight times and the word "phenomenal" seven times, taking care to alternate his intensives, as in "It's absolutely fantastic the phenomenal number of fellas whose people come over here," and to mix them up, as in "School's honour it was absolutely fan-bloody-tastic."[139]

Like Bazza-to-come, Buster demonstrates his understanding of women mainly in what men regard as women's discourse. He has seven different words for women (although he never uses "everage"): "talent," "lass," "physio," "bird," "piece," "she," "sweetie," and even the names Mrs Jameson-Beale, Judy-Anne Kershaw, Sandra Holt, and Di. The monologue is also a catalogue of automobiles: "the 'G," "bombs," "that 1960 Goddess," "cars," "Austin Healy," and "Jag." Sometimes the discourses of women and technology merge, as in Constantin Brancusi's sculptures *Mlle Pogany* (1913) and *Bird in Space* (1928?): Buster tells how "Paddy ... gave her the gun and bunged her up to ninety and we hammered her the whole way, and she went like a bird at eighty."[140] In Buster's phallocentric discourse, based on the simile "a car is 'like a bird,' " Humphries might be parodying the ideas of the car as phallic and vaginal symbol and men's sexualizing language of motion/rhythm. Thus, in addition to its literal meaning, according to Buster's figure of speech, the clause "and she went like a bird at eighty"[141] could mean: (1) at eighty mph the car performed (ran) like a woman; (2) the car performed (ran) like an eighty-year-old woman, or (3) given the narratological equation "A is like B, ∴ B is like A," the woman ("she") performed (functioned sexually) like a car going eighty mph (or, as Bazza McKenzie would come to say, "she bangs like a shit house door in a gale").[142]

Given the monologue's duration of 6:30 (on *Sandy Agonistes* and on *Dada Days*), Buster Thompson's patter can be paced at 157 words per minute, or about two and one-half words per second, which is, I would imagine, roughly equivalent to the pace of "a bird at eighty." Buster stutters through his words much as an MG ("the 'G'") that is in need of a carburetor adjustment sputters along the motorway. In their monologues from *Sandy Agonistes*, Debbie Thwaite and Colin Cartwright are also fast-talkers, at the pace of 125 and 133 words per minute, respectively. Because Humphries speaks her monologue in a falsetto, Debbie Thwaite resembles the early Edna Everage, whom Humphries performed in "a flutey falsetto" until he discovered how to train his voice to be her voice.[143] Her first three topic sentences announce the topicality of her mind: "I don't know whether I want to go back to Australia yet or not"; "I'm sharing a flat in London with a few other Australian lasses at the moment, and it's really superb"; and "Things have been a bit hectic in the flat just lately."[144] Debbie minds her monologue with a nominal sense of places, persons, and things. She speaks in fits and starts, about prices relative to Australia ("Now let's see, what's that in Australian money?"); about *la dolce vita alla città,* or the soft life in the city ("Anyway, if I don't get all my shopping organised soon I'll be in a real spot"); and about the guests coming and going around her flat ("I don't want to be in a spot like I was when Robyn and Gwenda descended on us out of the blue that time. We had to put sleeping bags down in the kitchen, and even then they stayed on for three and a half weeks"); and about thwaiting to return home ("It's funny to think I'll be back in Melbourne in such a short time. I don't know what I'll do. It'll be all so different").[145] And for Debbie th' wait will have been worth it. She has spent six months – "and six months *is* quite a long time, isn't it?"[146] – buzzing[147] around London but has emerged not as Deborah, a judge who helps the Israelites to victory in Canaan, but simply as Debbie, a deb, or debutante, who, despite her falsetto, will never debut as Tante Edna, either on stage or in joyous hearts.

As Buster's speech is marked by the stutter of hyperactivity[148] and Debbie's voice registers in the fitfulness of a woman who does not quite fit in, Colin Cartwright's discourse is interrupted by eructations of gas or, to use the medical term, acid reflux. His Sir Colin Belch act anticipates the refluences of the mature Dame Edna Everage and, his near namesake, Sir Leslie Colin Patterson. Cartwright's more immediate character model is

Table 4.1
Humphries' 1960s and 1970s Monologues Thematized

| Theme | Monologue | Show | Discourse |
|---|---|---|---|
| counter-culture 1: parodying Sydney beatnik coffee and bar scene of art, music, and literature | "Morrie Tate" | A Nice Night's Entertainment (1962) | beat vernacular |
| counter-culture 2: parodying Aussie folk-ways scene of Vietnam War protest and commu-nist sympathy | "Big Sonia" | Just a Show (1968–69) | folk vernacular |
| yartz culture 1: downing national-cultural stereotypes, manufactur-ing consent on identity | "Operation Oz-Image" | A Nice Night's Entertainment (1962) | expressionist propaganda |
| yartz culture 2: parodying Aussie expatri-atism and patriotism, bash-ing intellectual poseurs | "The Critic: Witchetty Grub Street" | A Nice Night's Entertainment (1962) | journalese du jour |
| yartz culture 3: parodying "tenth-rate aca-demics with chips on their shoulders" and chips off the old kafkaesque | "Neil Singleton: A Vignette of the Neskafka Society" | Excuse I: Another Nice Night's Entertainment (1965) | pseudo-intellects |
| yartz culture 4: parodying the elite of anti-elitists, and political cor-rectness, before it even had a name | "Neil Singleton: Would You Believe?" | At Least you Can Say you've Seen It: A Tragi-Farce in Two Acts, for Those too Drunk to Dance (1974) | pseudo-revolutionary discourses |
| yartz culture 5: pushing up underground cinema, putting down the coming 1970s film boom | "Martin Agrippa Down Underground" | Just a Show (1968–69) | "Woolloomooloo Yank" yank-your-chain metatalk |
| yartz culture 6: sending up the Australian paintings that Australians paint upon their walls | "Update Your Walls with Morrie O'Connor" | At Least you Can Say You've Seen It: A Tragi-Farce in Two Acts, for Those Too Drunk to Dance (1974) | art-talking bruitism: the noise of art |
| yartz culture 7: patronizing Gian Carlo Menotti's Il Telefono, or L'Amour à trois (1946) for grantees | "Brett Grantworthy: Talk to You Later" | At Least you Can Say You've Seen It: A Tragi-Farce in Two Acts, for Those Too Drunk to Dance (1974) | bureaucrat telephone chat |

Table 4.1
Humphries' 1960s and 1970s Monologues Thematized (*Continued*)

| Theme | Monologue | Show | Discourse |
|---|---|---|---|
| yartz culture 8: introducing music hall chairman, reintroducing music hall, and putting on the halls | "Les Patterson: Introducing the Yartz" | *Isn't It Pathetic at His Age"* (1978–79) and *A Night with Dame Edna* (1979) | dipso-diplomacy and phallotalking |
| yartz culture 9: trading punches with trade unionists on the leading edge of anarchy | "Lance Boyle Does His Block" | *"Isn't It Pathetic at His Age"* (1978) | language of negotiations |
| yartz culture 10: logging monologues, or, what to do with *il telefono* when Bob Newhart is not on the other end | "Lance Lets Off Steam" | *An Evening's Intercourse with the Widely Liked Barry Humphries* (1981–82) | no go scat |
| householding 1: discoursing father of the bride, or, what to do when King Lear will not shut up | "Rex Lear Requests the Pleasure" | *Just a Show* (1968–69) | speech speech |
| householding 2: outing Dad, or, how to turn round a poofter when he's got his back to the wall | "Brian Graham" | *Just a Show* (1968–69) | queer discourse |

*Note*: In his introductory note to "Neil Singleton: Would You Believe?" in R.F. Brissenden's edition *A Nice Night's Entertainment: Sketches and Monologues 1956-1961* (1981), Humphries states that this sketch "was chopped out of *At Least You Can Say You've Seen It* because of its technical difficulties – it requires a television set on stage on which the new Neil, now turned TV culture pundit, expatiates upon the modish topics of the day. The videotape machine failed on the first night and the sketch has been buried ever since." Of "Grett Brantworthy: Talk to You Later," which is listed in the program of *At Least You Can Say You've Seen It* under the title "Brett Grantworthy's Enterprises," Humphries notes that "this quaint period piece from the mid-seventies was performed once and probably deserved to be dropped." Humphries, *A Nice Night's Entertainment*, 153 and 148, respectively.

Sandy Stone, evident in his reference in *A Nice Night's Entertainment* to his expenditure on a new lawn, "something approximately in the vicinity of four hundred pounds."[149] But in *The Real Barry Humphries*, Peter Coleman likens Sir Les to Sir Toby Belch,[150] as does Barry Humphries.[151]

If Colin Cartwright were a music hall performer, then his turn would have to be a bilious turn, such are his bitter and disconsolate humours as he rants about his ungrateful children and raves about the cost of living, not the Australian domestic economy but the domestic economy of the Cartwright family home where the children – Christine, Andrew, Duncan, Stephen – are tied to daddy's purse strings as if to a Dada umbilical cord, and where Ange Cartwright, his wife, is scarcely mentioned and functions like an invisible angel. Thus Colin's references to his wife – "I let her [Christine] go to a dance the other night, and Ange and I were awake half the night waiting for her to get in"; "I had a big new Dishmaster DeLuxe built into the kitchen to save Ange, and what happens"; and "the wife drops her eternity ring down the new waste disposal unit in the sink. It wasn't insured, so guess who paid out for that little issue?"[152] – reveal her less as a woman under man's protection, or even as a child-wife under patriarchy, than as an angel of perpetual succor, signified by her "eternity ring."

Colin's final remark, "I've come to the conclusion you can give kids too much!"[153] for all its dramatic irony would have the eternal ring of truth if Colin could only have made a negative transfer and added a single word: "I've come to the conclusion you cannot give kids too much love." Then all he would need to do to rid his system of red and black bile would be to see Ange as a goddess (not to be confused with Rodney Jameson-Beale's "1960 Goddess" in "Buster Thompson"), or as an everage, and love her too much. One thing all Humphries' "women in the background," and even the foregrounded Dame Edna, have in common is that their men do not love them enough, or make love to them well enough, and that they themselves are love goddesses.

Humphries' other 1960s and 1970s monologues are best understood in their thematic series and show programs. In these monologues Humphries established several free-standing characters (Neil Singleton, Martin Agrippa, and Rex Lear); allowed a few others to wander off backstage (Morrie Tate, Big Sonia, Brian Graham); set up a platform for his nicest character (Sandy Stone); and cleared a space for autonomous characters (Les Patterson, Edna Everage) whose freedom is not limited to standing, or to the literary or theatrical state of characterization, who are free even to disavow Barry Humphries, to dispute his gender position (as Les does) or demote him to a managerial position (as Edna does). But, more important still, Humphries, as a writer and an actor, careered through monology into a theatrical career that, despite some fits and stops, like Debbie Thwaite's fits and starts, would seem unstoppable.

In the 1960s and 1970s Humphries used the theatrical form of the monologue to refine his talent for parody, which he continued to exercise in the Broadway run of *The Royal Tour*, which, in an interview with Charlie Rose (8 March 2000), he has called "a parody of celebrity," if only for the benefit of American audiences (excluding John Lahr), who are unable to discern a music hall turn. Humphries directed his parody at puffed up Australian attitudes towards culture: beat, folk, and hip counter-cultures; the cultural art forms of literature, film, music, painting, sculpture, and dance, which Les Patterson calls collectively "the yartz"; the cultural constructs of race, class, and gender; and the syndromic culture of complacency, the smug mug's game of being "world class." Through these monologues, Humphries encouraged Australian audiences to laugh at themselves not simply because the alternative, as Dame Edna is fond of saying, might be "to miss the joke of the century," but also to celebrate with British, Canadian, American, German, Dutch, Swiss, and Scandinavian audiences who have equated Australianness with *innocenti*, with a Blakean state (i.e., a mystical state, of innocent joy).

What might Humphries' other purposes be in parodying the Australian cultural (re)nascence? As a monologist, and through his speech-acting characters, Humphries can be attributed with what Susan Rubin Suleiman (1990) calls (a) "subversive intent." A subversive Dada artiste, he delves under the versions of Australian culture that other media, outside the fourth wall of his stage(d) reality, are bringing to view on screen (film screen, TV monitor, artistic canvas and pedestal, literary quarto and folio, journal broadsheet, stage boards, even the mirror into which one looks askance). His subversive stage acts are monologous[154] with "the Surrealists' predilection for punning and other verbal games, as well as for the humorous, often scatological or otherwise, 'scandalous' rewriting of traditional texts or images."[155] Thus, in the 1960s and 1970s Humphries engaged his audiences in verbal, visual, and participatory play; in the logic of scat (from chat to shit), or his characters' spoken and, at times, sung wit. His call to everyone in the theatre, "can you come out to play?" to Derridean play, Dadaist and Surrealist play, or just cheeky play, is an invitation to scandal and to the freedom that scandalizing sacred kangaroos may bring.

In contrast, the "yellow kangaroo" in "Wendy the One-Eyed Wombat" is scandalizing, not scandalized, bidding everyone come play – "Let's all go up the road and have a few" – but whose serious intent is to bring about a specious unity.

Was all this just child's play, the nose-thumbing antics of young boys drawing mustaches on the Mona Lisa? For the Surrealists of the 1920s, graffiti and defacement were more than "just play" – they were a veritable program for liberation.[156]

In effect, like Marcel Duchamp, and even Francis Picabia, Humphries was painting a mustache and goatee on the *Mona Lisa,* or on its antipodean counterpart, the *Mona Everage,* as an act of subversion, to free Australians not from their culture but, rather, from cultural stereotypes, from any construct of a culture (like Colin Cartwright), whose only sense of humour is the onset of yet another bilious turn.

Table 4.2
Humphries' 1960s and 1970s Monologues Programmatized

| Show | Program |
|------|---------|
| *A Nice Night's Entertainment* (1962) | "Edna Everage: The Latest Trends from Overseas" <br> "Sandy Stone: Can You Keep a Secret?" <br> "Operation Oz-Image" <br> "The Critic: Witchetty Grub Street" <br> "Morrie Tate" <br> "Dame Edna" |
| *Excuse I: Another Nice Night's Entertainment* (1965) | "Excuse I, with Edna Everage" <br> "Dod's Own Country" <br> "Jenny, Judy, and Felicity's Friend" and "Vicki, Robyn, and Sandra's Friend" <br> "Sandy Claus" <br> "Neskafka or Neil Singleton's Wake"* <br> "An Elegant Sufficiency" |
| *Just a Show* (1968–69) | "Relevantly Speaking" <br> "Rex Lear Requests the Pleasure" <br> "Lionel Stephen Denis Hunter" <br> "Pomme Frite" <br> "Big Sonia" <br> "Sandy's Stone" <br> "Down Underground with Martin Agrippa"* <br> "Brian Graham" <br> "Ednalogue" |
| *At Least You Can Say You've Seen It: A Tragi-Farce in Two Acts, for Those Too Drunk to Dance* (1974) | "At Least You Can Say You've Seen It" <br> "Edna's Dutch Treat" <br> "Polish Up Your Kiwi (with Madge Allsop)" <br> "Update with Morrie O"Connor"* <br> "Brett Grantworthy's Enterprises"* <br> "Alternative Bookshelf (THE BLUDGERMINDEE EXPERIENCE)" <br> "Would You Believe Neil Singleton?" <br> "At Least You Can Say There Was an Interval" <br> "Sandy and the Sandman"* <br> "Ol' Hazel-Eyes Is Back" <br> "Lorna's Secret Charity (An Old-Fashioned Monologue Rendered by Her Husband Sir Neville Creamer, K.B.E.)" <br> "Dream Time" <br> "A Tasteful Finale" <br> "At Least You Can Say It's Over" <br> "Car Park" |
| *"Isn't It Pathetic at His Age"* (1978) | "Les Patterson: Introducing the Yartz" <br> "Roger A. Nunn Offers Us the Good Oil" <br> "Lance Boyle Does His Block" <br> "Sandy Soldiers On" <br> "A Glimpse of LA EVERAGE" |

Table 4.2
Humphries' 1960s and 1970s Monologues Programmatized (*Continued*)

| Show | Program |
|---|---|
| *"Isn't It Pathetic at His Age"* (1978-79) and *A Night with Dame Edna* (1979) | "Les Patterson: Introducing the Yartz" "Roger A. Nunn Offers Us the Good Oil" "Lance Boyle Does His Block" "Sandy Soldiers On" "A Glimpse of LA EVERAGE" |
| *An Evening's Intercourse with the Widely Liked Barry Humphries* (1981–82) | "Les Looking Good" "A Fillup for Phil Philby Films" "Lance Lets Off Steam" "Shades of Sandy" |

*Note:* The program for Humphries' 1962 show, *A Nice Night's Entertainment*, is my reconstruction. Otherwise, monologue titles in show programs that differ from the titles in *A Nice Night's Entertainment: Sketches and Monologues 1956–1981* are designated with an asterisk.

By playing up and sending up cultural stereotypes, Humphries has encouraged Australians, and others, to laugh not only at him and his characters but also at themselves, at the negation of themselves on stage, and to come up on stage and join in the subversion of their images in the mirror. This is "subversive pleasure," in Robert Stam's phrase.[157] Thus, Humphries invites audiences to find pleasure in subversive things such as Dada, music hall, parody, theatre, kitsch, class, race, gender, and Australiana, as they play in the one-man show, and also to find the act of subverting pleasurable, even laughable.

The culture of real laughter (as opposed to canned or forced laughter) is absolutely central to Bakhtin's conception of carnival: enormous, creative, derisive, renewing laughter that grasps phenomena in the process of change and transition, finding in every victory a defeat and in every defeat a potential victory.[158]

Stam's phrasing here is highly pertinent to Humphries. In inducing a theatrical state of Bakhtinian carnivalesque, evident especially in his gender- and class-crossing costuming and his anti-authoritarian revelry and fantasy, Humphries makes people laugh, and even politicizes them; but the laughter that bursts out in his shows is an independent force.

Thus, in Stam's words, "laughter ... grasps phenomena in the process of change and transition." Humphries is not a political activist; he does not presume to understand the Australian nation or Australian identity. While he may be a satirist in many regards, he is not a political satirist. Nor does he foster political understanding in his audience; rather, he creates laughter as a cultural expression through which people might better understand their middycosm, wherever it is. In a sense, neither Humphries nor his audiences understand Australia. But his Laugh does, even independently of laughter, which tends to be spontaneous and ephemeral. Humphries' Laugh is like the *Kuntu*, or modality Laugh,[159] as distinguished from Skull, in Amos Tutuola's orative-novel *The Palm-Wine Drinkard and His Dead Palm-Wine Tapster in the Deads' Town* (1952):

we knew "Laugh" personally on that night, because as every one of them stopped laughing at us, "Laugh" did not stop for two hours. As "Laugh" was laughing at us on that night, my wife and myself forgot our pains and laughed with him, because he was laughing with curious voices that we had never heard before in our life. We did not know the time that we fell into this laugh, but when we were only laughing at "Laugh's" laugh and nobody who heard him when laughing would not laugh, so if somebody continue to laugh with "Laugh" himself, he or she would die or faint at once for long laughing, because laugh was his profession and he was feeding on it.[160]

In his monologues, and all his stage shows and writings, Humphries is "Laugh." Tutuola's comment, even though it comes from the vastly different context of 1950s colonial Nigeria, also describes Humphries and what he does (which are the same thing) better than any critical assessment by Peter Coleman, Peter Conrad, Jim Davidson, Ian Davidson, Ian Britain, Stephen Alomes, Geoffrey Dutton, Clive James, Patrick White, John Lahr, John Betjeman, John Allen, Katharine Brisbane, or even Paul Matthew St Pierre (who has presumed to explain Humphries' laughter through criticism, to force Laugh into a can, as if Humphries had never stepped out of his spot as Estragon).

Does Humphries the monologist, the music hall artiste, the Dada prankster, and, especially, the writer move his audiences to laughter, invoking the modality Laugh, even becoming Laugh himself, merely as a fetishistic act of exhibitionism? Janheinz Jahn has noted the philosophic connection between discourse and laughter: "And laughter itself, this special *Kuntu* force, is closely related to the word, to *Nommo*, for 'man' has not only the power of the word, but also the power of laughter."[161] John Lahr has observed, with reference to the comedic career of his father, Bert Lahr, "It is hard to imagine *the laugh* as an absolute value."[162] If Humphries' executive power is power *with*, not power *over*, then as a writer and a monologist he can be seen as sharing the power of the word, as distinguished from his own power over the word, with his audiences. Similarly, as a music hall comedian and a Dada prankster, or even, if you insist, as a fetishistic exhibitionist, Humphries invites his audiences to laugh with him, "to laugh with 'Laugh' himself," but he is always careful to give readers, hearers, and spectators the choice, to "roll it toward some overwhelming question,"[163] whether they should "die or faint at once for long laughing."

To die laughing is to reduce oneself to Skull, but to "faint at once" from laughing is to become Laugh, to elevate oneself to Humphries' level, as if one were to do the unthinkable and "ascend" Dame Edna's staircase, a fixture in her stage and television sets, as Dame Edna and Madge Allsop brazenly "go up your stairs" of the contestants on *Dame Edna's Neighbourhood Watch* (1992). All contestants in the game that Humphries plays as an artist, "because laugh was his profession and he was feeding on it," must choose between Skull and Laugh, much as in his novel *The Road to Mars* (1999) Eric Idle gives all comedians – that is, all people who are willing to laugh at themselves and laugh with Laugh – the choice between being "white face" ("Skull") and being "red nose" ("Laugh").

Now this complete gentleman was reduced to head and when they reached where he hired the skin and flesh which covered the head, he returned them, and paid to the owner, now the complete gentleman in the market reduced to a "Skull" and this lady remained with only "Skull." When the lady saw that she remained with only Skull, she began to say that her father had been telling her to marry a man, but she did not listen to or believe him.[164]

To laugh with Barry Humphries is to step up to his stage, to step into his artworld and to step onto Dame Edna's magnificent staircase. Each time Dame Edna comes down her staircase, making her grand entrance onto the stage or the television set, she re-enacts, "[d'après] Marcel Duchamp," *Nude Descending a Staircase*, whether No. 2 (1912), No. 3 (1916) or No. 4 (1918), without having to say so, and without having to be *nu*, except in the sense in which Rita Rudner (1992) is "naked beneath my clothes."

Humphries' purpose in referencing and replicating Duchamp is partly to call on the Dada muse without whom his show, it seems, cannot go on, and partly to call his audience into the readymade that is his *oeuvre*. It is as though Humphries on one side and the audience on the other side of the fourth wall were to adopt as their common motto Duchamp's Dada wisecrack, "*Peut-on fair des oeuvres qui ne soient pas 'd'art'?*"[165] which can be Skull-translated as "Can one make works out of non-artistic materials?" and Laugh-translated as "Can one make works which are not works of art?". Skull and Laugh are equal parts of Humphries' Lévi-Straussian/Derridean *bricolage*, in which each of his performances is the sum of all his performances, in intertextual relation to nineteenth- and twentieth-century works of art and art forms ranging from music hall and dramatic monologue to Dada and postmodernism. As Duchamp's nude is indistinguishable from her staircase and from her descent, so Humphries' *oeuvre* is at once work not made from artistic materials[166] and work that is art because it is made (written and staged), readymade (invented and named), alreadymade (intertext and *bricolage*), and in the process of being made (through Humphries' extemporaneity and audience participation). To enter Humphries' literary and stage *oeuvre*, to descend the staircase of Dame Edna Everage, people need only be willing to laugh at themselves and with Laugh, and to find their mark on the stage at which to become Laugh.

# Autobiography as Mockery, or Barry Humphries in a Mock-Turtle

Those who feel compelled, at some time in their life, to embark on autobiographical writing do so because they have no choice: they must do it, whatever the consequences.

> – Susan Rubin Suleiman, *Risking Who One Is: Encounters with Contemporary Art and Literature*

Autobiography is not a form which one would at first suppose comes naturally to the Australian temperament, either from a native circumspection or the covert suspicion that life in Australia may be too boring to merit a literary record.

> – Barry Humphries, Introduction to Graham McInnes, *Humping My Bluey*

Barry Humphries' stage shows have been one long suburban autobiography.

> – Humphrey McQueen, *Suburbs of the Sacred*

Where do I place autobiography in all this? After all, Es'kia Mphahlele has written more than one autobiographical account. It would be inappropriate in the present context to be side-tracked into a discussion of the theory of autobiography.

> – N. Chabani Manganyi, *Exiles and Homecomings: A Biography of Es'kia Mphahlele*

## THE GLASSY I OF BARRY HUMPHRIES

One consequence of Humphries' first autobiography, *More Please* (1992), was the 1993 J.R. Ackerley Prize for Autobiography. As Janet Frame says in her story "Prizes" (1963), "Life is hell, but at least there are prizes."[1] She should know: winning the Hubert Church Award for her story collection *The Lagoon* (1951) saved her from a forced leucotomy. For Frame the prize had a consequence, whereas for Humphries the prize was a consequence, yet each prize was a take in an Aristotelian absurdity of cause and effect. Whether Humphries' life is hell, only Humphries can say; but if Jean-Paul Sartre's character Garcin in *Huis Clos* (1947) was right when he observed "l'enfer, c'est les Autres" ("Hell is other people")[2], then Humphries has given other people enough joy to go around, to the last row of the balcony and the last page of the book.

His compulsion in writing *More Please*, as he has found expedient to preface it in "Alzheimer Remembers," is to steal the prize (to seize that which is seized) of a stalking and talking biographer (like Kenneth Grocock in Humphries' 1995 novel, *Women in the Background*) who will get the story all wrong, or possibly get it just right: "I am already the subject of two generous biographies, and it is only the fear that my adventures might for a third time be profitably chronicled by another man that prompts me to relate my own story."[3] Is Humphries afraid that writers and publishers will make money on his life, through identity-theft or by seizing his intellectual property? Or is he saying that, through their "generosity," biographers have profited him, by inspiring him "to embark on autobiographical writing"[4] and maybe even by putting a few bums in seats? As a critical writer, not a biographer, I hope this book, as well as revealing Humphries as a superb writer of literature, will help bring some of his books back into print and promote "Humphries Studies" at universities.

*More Please*, of course, is not Barry Humphries' only autobiography. In his second book-length autobiography, *My Life as Me: A Memoir* (2002), Humphries, in an otherwise conventional disclaimer in the Prologue, shifts his authorial fear from himself as subject to his own subjects in his writing: "I have changed the names of several of my dramatic personae who are still living, especially where their portrayal is of such accuracy as might inspire foolhardy litigation. I have honoured the dead by calling them by their real names."[5] Although worded ironically, his "dread of something after death" assumes a Hamlet-like edge in his closing words, as "Death strides whistling towards me"[6] from the middycosm, announcing, as one imagines Humphries' deepest-seated fear, a gush of scurrilous biographies of him, maybe to be issued by the Australian publisher who, in passing on my own manuscript, expressed disappointment I had not written more about Humphries' ex-wives and his children.

Humphries' other life-tellings are: "The Confessions of Barry Humphries" (1965); "The Confessions of a Conder Fan" (1977); his confidences to the (Melbourne) *Sunday Observer* (14 November 1971), which Keith Dunstan notes in *Ratbags* (1979); "Confessions of a Victoria Gentleman" (1981); "A Fugitive Art," his interview with Jim Davidson in *Meanjin* (1986); his confidences to Peter Conrad in his article "Barry Humphries on the Couch" (1994); *The Traveller's Tool* (1985), under the pseudonym Sir Les Patterson; and *My Gorgeous Life: An Adventure* (1989), under the pseudonym Dame Edna Everage. Together with his two autobiographies, these

works show, as well as their subjects and contents, that Humphries is neither a self-absorbed self-promoter, "happy to talk to them endlessly on my
favourite subject – myself,"[7] nor a natty narcissist, "the supremo of narcis-
sists", as John Lahr calls Edna in *Dame Edna Everage and the Rise of
Western Civilisation,*[8] preoccupied with "the friendly fellow who confronts
me from the shaving mirror, with his rehearsed and jaunty grin,"[9] but a
writer whose focus is on *les Autres,* and on bringing a little joy into their
hell, the hell which is they, or which is grammar.

Les Autres to Humphries are not just showpiece characters (Les and
Edna), intellectual specialties (Charles Conder), and sacred places (Melbourne and Victoria) but also all the little Garcins who make up his audiences, his public, who number among his biographical subjects just as
Madge Allsop plays Dame Edna's offsider: Dame Edna is the Duchampignon Bride and Madge is her Bachelor. My neologism "Duchampignon"
connotes a mushroom growing out of the remains of Marcel Duchamp. My
allusion is to Duchamp's drawing *The Bride Stripped Bare by Her Bachelors, Even* (1913) and to its series.

By writing his autobiographies[10] *More Please* and *My Life as Me,*
Humphries *risks who he is* (in Suleiman's phrase) for his public more than
for mere self-protection, knowing that he is old enough, writing in his fifties and sixties, to risk being taken for *risqué.*

When are you old enough to re-member who you "are"? The hyphen makes explicit and emphasizes what is always true about the activity of remembering: it is
not a passive reception of memories fixed forever like a series of faded images in a
scrapbook, but an active (re)construction, a putting together and shaping (the way
an artist puts together and shapes certain materials) of a life or part of a life. Similarly, the self is not a fixed entity but an evolving process, not something discovered
(or passively "remembered") but something made; which does not mean that it
does not exist, but that its existence is always subject to revision (re-vision). Whence
the quotation marks around the verb "to be," which indicate the necessary tenta-
tiveness, the necessary self-doubt, what Richard Rorty would call the necessary
irony, in every discourse about the self.[11]

Humphries' "Barry Humphries" in *More Please* and *My Life as Me* is, by
implication, an artistic creation, an ironic readymade and a processional
person: the implied author's implied narrator. He is the surreal Barry
Humphries, "a coincident ... personage from my earlier volume ... a cubist,
even a futurist, self-portrait,"[12] in a sense two-upping Peter Coleman's affectionate portrait of him (1990).

John Barry Humphries is like a little boy who, when his mother warns
him, "Stop playing tipcat, Sunny Sam, or you'll put your eye out,"[13] goes
on playing tipcat regardless. Barry Humphries, music hall artiste, Dada

artist, and writer, has played tipcat for his public and put his eye out, the eye that peers into his shaving mirror, the first person of the stage, and the "I" of autobiographical writing.

In this sense, the cool cat tipcat artiste Barry Humphries recalls (1) Stephen Dedalus, in James Joyce's *A Portrait of the Artist as a Young Man* (1916), whose schoolmates taunt him, "pull out his eyes, apologise";[14] (2) Samson from Milton's "*Samson Agonistes*" (1671) and from Judges (13: 6), who is blinded by the Philistines; and (3) the customer in the barber shop chair in Luis Buñuel and Salvador Dali's surrealist film, *Un Chien andalou* (1928), who has her eyeball sliced with a straight razor.[15] Humphries might be called "eyeless in Bazza," such are his commitments to the first person of telling and to letting his public catch a glimpse of him in his shaving mirror.

As his opening paragraph in *More Please* suggests, his surreality is to be found in Oliver, halfway between the characters Mr Sowerberry and Fagin:

I always wanted more. I never had enough milk or money or socks or sex or holidays or first editions or solitude or gramophone records or free meals or real friends or guiltless pleasure or neckties or applause or unquestioning love or persimmons. Of course, I have had more than my share of most of these commodities but it always left me with a vague feeling of unfulfilment: *where was the rest?* Is it possible that while still at the breast my infant gaze was fixed on the adjacent mound of nourishment fearing that it might be snatched away before I could clamp it with avid gums?[16]

Outside of his one-man shows, which, in his publication list ("By the Same Author") are called "One-Man Plays"[17] (suggesting how seriously Humphries takes them, and means them to be taken), Lionel Bart's musical *Oliver!* (1960, 1963, 1967, 1997) is his greatest stage triumph, a show that has become a measure of his career and by which he will undoubtedly be remembered. His title *More Please* is his deliberate acknowledgment of this fact. By glossing the words of the title as "*the author's first coherent utterance*,"[18] as well as being funny, he is saying that in *Oliver!* he made it as an actor, and he is deeply grateful.

But his opening paragraph reveals that, as in 1960 and 1963, when he played Sowerberry and was understudy to Fagin, when "Ron Moody looked discouragingly robust and I wondered if I would ever get a chance to take the leading role, even for a night,"[19] so throughout his career, even after playing Fagin at the London Palladium in 1967 and 1997, Humphries has wanted to show that he can do more. In the first paragraph of *More Please*, therefore, he puts on a show to announce that he is going to do "more" with words.

The second sentence of *More Please* is a rhetorical study in polysyndeton, as Humphries resists sequential (i.e., male) logic, spouting off his illogical litany of commodified desires, some of which carry his mystique ("money," "sex," "holidays," "first editions," "gramophone records," "guiltless pleasure," "neckties," "applause," "unquestioning love"), others simply creating the mystery ("milk," "socks," "solitude," "free meals," "real friends," "persimmons") of a truly private man. His query *where was the rest?* seems more philosophical than rhetorical, as if, after uttering his famous last words, "the rest is silence," Hamlet were to have propped himself up on one elbow and said, "yes, but where is it?" In the final sentence of the paragraph, Humphries allows his rhetoric to regain control, turning the contingency theorem "It is possible that" into a hilarious comment on the male gaze, on the narratorial figure of the eye/I, on the autobiographical fallacy ("When are you old enough to re-member who are 'are'?"), and on the presumption of David Copperfield's "I am born" in *David Copperfield* (1849–50).

The irony of "Alzheimer Remembers" is that Humphries is tutoring his readers and relying on them to remember all these seemingly inconsequential details, which are actually as important as are the melodies and motifs in an opera (or oratorio) overture, because readers will need to return to them in *More Please* and, indeed, throughout his *oeuvre* of texts.

Thus, some of Humphries' later references, in "Dirty Hair," to how the young man's "drives and juices" (the phrase is Edna's) began to move recall the "infant gaze" of the baby at the breast in the first paragraph. For example, he recalls how, while at the beach at Mornington

I noticed how her woollen bathing costume gaped at the place on her legs where her suntan stopped; and then I saw a kind of pleat, sutured with hair like a dark V-shaped darn. Soon she drew her knees together again and, sipping her tea, squinted out to sea where I hid in the white dazzle.[20]

Then he flashes forward to the Percy Grainger Museum at the University of Melbourne, and his recollection of

a young female archivist earnestly cataloguing the avalanche of letters to and from the composer, which Grainger had bequeathed to his own museum. It was a task for the stout-hearted, however, since Grainger's sexual vocation was, to say the least, exotic. Even as I entered the room, I observed the young woman holding an envelope at arm's length, and, with a pair of tweezers, disdainfully extracting from it a fibrous tangle of pubic hair.[21]

Perhaps significantly, Humphries has already made a link from Grainger to "the creator of *The Magic Flute*"[22] and perhaps to the immediacy of audience and overture. (Recall how, during the playing of the overture in his film of *The Magic Flute* [1974], Ingmar Bergman shoots the individual faces of the audience, listening intently.)

In another chapter on his youth, "Russian Salad Days," Humphries tells how in a class at George Bell's studio "I noticed that I was the only one who seemed to have devoted much care and attention to the rendition of pubic hair, and it was fairly clear that my work was still well out of line with George Bell's austere anatomical precepts."[23] All these references to pubic hair and sexuality point to Humphries' developing male gaze, the sexualizing gaze vilified in feminisms. But in recalling the "infant gaze" of a baby, Humphries invokes an absurd comic spirit, exposing the male gaze as infantile and the "infant gaze" as sexualizing, and also drawing an absurd and hilarious parallel between a man and a baby that suggests the futility of the autobiographer's attempt to make everything fit together (and perhaps also the randomness of life). Humphries' allusion to the "infant gaze" in young adult sexual experiences recalls V.S. Naipaul's comic turn of calling his infant protagonist "Mr Biswas" even at the start of his *ab ovo* novel *A House for Mr Biswas* (1961).

From these genital visions, the young artist Barry Humphries progressed from the pubic to the public, as later he transformed the middycosmic into the middycomic. (Consider, for example, Dame Edna's gynocentricity, and her preoccupation with gynaecologists, as in her famous quip, "Sometimes I think I give and care too much. In fact, my gynaecologist looked up the other day and said, 'Dame Edna, when will you ever stop giving?'")[24] These shifts from pubic-to-public and from cosmic-to-comic anticipate Humphries' personal transformation from Dame Edna Everage's creator to her (Mary Shelleyesque) creature, from her author to her manager. In his chapter entitled "The Birth of Edna," in *More Please*, Humphries recounts how he gave birth to Edna in 1955 at the back of the bus during the Union Theatre Repertory Company's tour of Victoria: "I usually sat at the back of the bus improvising, in a flutey falsetto, a speech of gratitude by some fictitious female factotum … It was only months later when we were preparing our end-of-season revue and Ray Lawler suggested that I revive the character that I decided to call her after my nanny, Edna.[25]" But in her autobiography, *My Gorgeous Life: An Adventure* (1989), which, of course, predates his by three years, Edna recounts a different nativity narrative. When she returns to Melbourne to visit her mother at Dunraven, precisely to retrieve the story of her birth, Gladys Beazley (neé Sloggertt),[26] inchoate (undoubtedly because she is under the care of Sister Choate), mistakes her daughter for her husband, Bruce: " 'Oh, Bruce,' she moaned, 'do you think Edna is really ours? Could there have been a mix-up at Bethesda?' " Edna leaves Dunraven without her birth narrative and in a state of confusion as the word " 'mix-up' tumbled around in my mind like undergarments in a

Zanussi drying cycle."[27] Gladys's "nonnarrated narrative" (see Prince) does nothing to refute Humphries' account in *More Please*.

Yet in *My Gorgeous Life* Edna distances herself from her Author in true Barthesian fashion, demoting him, albeit with reluctance, and eventually over protest, to the role of manager. Humphries gets the job only because of a telegram from Peter Cook, which reads in part "HAVE ASKED YOUR MANAGER BARRY HUMPHRIES TO BRING SHOW TO MY NEW LONDON CLUB THE ESTABLISHMENT."[28] Despite her indignation over Cook's mistake, Edna acquiesces to the managerial role: "Barry Humphries. Still my manager but under solicitor's thumb. His contributions to our show getting smaller by the year."[29]

At her Web site, <www.dame-edna.com>, Edna takes measures to keep her distance from Barry Humphries:

Dame Edna Everage appears on this website with her ex-manager Barry Humphries due to certain contractual obligations regarding Internet publicity rights. Dame Edna and Mr Humphries are currently engaged in heavy litigation over said contract and recent allegations involving the embezzlement of millions of pounds in donated money for the Prostate Olympics 2000, International Friends of the Prostate, and EdnaCare Switzerland, organizations for which Mr Humphries was Treasurer.

The comedy here is splendid, wonderfully arch and droll at the same time, but Barry Humphries and Edna Everage's "double life," like Sarah Bernhardt's (see Bernhardt) off-stage and on-stage, also rides a sharp (and serious) edge.

This doubleness is also evident in Dame Edna's remark in her *Bedside Companion* that "Sarah Bernhardt was my opposite number in the olden days" and in her instructions for "Sarah Bernhardt's Bath": "Cyield: one refreshed one-legged actress."[30] In playing up the variously twisted and severed identities of implied-Humphries and Dame Edna Everage, Humphries is playing up (again) as a Dada artist.

Dame Edna is Humphries' Rrose Sélavy: Barry Humphries is to Dame Edna Everage as Marcel Duchamp is to Rrose Sélavy, as La Gioconda is to Duchamp's mustachioed and goateed *Mona Lisa*, as Leonardo da Vinci is to Marcel Duchamp, as Marcel Duchamp is to Barry Humphries, as Barry Humphries is to Dame Edna Everage, and so on, and on, spinning like a Duchamp Rotary Demisphere or Rotorelief. Just as Marcel Duchamp is "Un Administrateur" ("An Administrator") and Rrose Sélavy, his female identity, alter-ego, and character, is "Le Président du Conseil d'Administration" ("President of the Administrative Council"),[31] so Barry Humphries is Dame Edna's administrator (from the Latin *ministrare*, meaning "to manage" and "to serve"): he administers all her presidential edicts and her speech-acts, and he serves in direct opposition to the *non serviam* of the devilish Les Patterson, who refuses to offer service (except of the sexual kind, which he extends – as he would say, "are you with me, ladies and gentlemen?" – to all his Girls Friday).

In allowing Dame Edna to discredit him, if only in his role as the implied author and as part of his ongoing theatrical Dada prank, Humphries engages his audience in his own autobiographical dialectic of "oneself as another." In *Oneself as Another* (1992), Paul Ricoeur discusses three positions on selfhood, which I find useful in interpreting the narratological and philosophical intricacies of the relationship of implicit Barry Humphries and explicit Edna Everage. These selfhood positions can be summarized as follows:

1 in its reflexivity, as in the French *soi-même*,[32] oneself is prior to subject position;
2 identity is a dialectic of "*idem*-identity" (sameness) and "*ipse*-identity" (selfhood);
3 "*ipse*-identity" is a dialectic of self as distinguished from other (other than self).

Thus, in casting himself (the implied author) as another (Dame Edna's manager), Humphries does more than characterize himself: he expresses the primacy of self-reflexivity – as in the autobiographical "I," the speech-actor, and narrating person – over his subject positions to which his act of speaking and narrating *More Please* and the "parallel memoir"[33] *My Life as Me* gives form: the constructs of misfit child, the public schoolboy icon-oclast, the precocious thespian, the Austral Dada-artist, the mummy-artist of Edna, the amnesiac actor, the alcoholic, the womanizer, the comedian, the artiste, the father, the husband, the collector, and the all-round show-man (among others), all of whom are no less fictional than Barry Humphries, whom Dame Edna casts and casts out as her manager, and the so-called "Brian Humphry," whom Les Patterson considers a *pédéraste manqué.*

Here Paul Ricoeur asserts the precedence of the speech-acting self:

By becoming the pivotal point of the system of indicators, the "I" is revealed in all its strangeness in relation to every entity capable of being placed in a class, charac-terized, or described. "I" so little designates the referent of an identifying reference that what appears to be its definition – namely, "any person who, in speaking, designates himself or herself" – cannot be substituted for the occurrences of the word "I."[34]

In this regard, Barry Humphries is the telling "I" prior to anything the "I" tells; *More Please* and *My Life as Me* disclose the "I" in his act of telling, perhaps even to the exclusion of what is told. Thus, Barry Humphries proves to be "I"; he is not the implied author, or Dame's Edna's manager, or Les Patterson's poofter, or the Camberwell toff, or the ABC Argonaut, or the music hall artiste taking a funny turn, and so on.

In *More Please* Humphries dares readers to venture beyond his first person,[35] yet he also cautions them that to go outside *soi-même* is to go beyond the frame of the mirror, the genre of autobiography, the only place where his "I" can be found in pub(l)ic nakedness. Still, compare his nude centrefold in *Cleo* magazine (November 1982) and Lewis Morley's 1994 publicity photograph of Dame Edna, wearing, to all appearances, only the back of a chair, pantyhose, and the iconography of Christine Keeler. Humphries uses the shot again in the *Remember You're Out* program and *My Life as Me*. He is referencing the swinging sixties, as in Morley's portraits of Keeler (1963) and also, in the Keeler pose, David Frost (1963), Joe Orton (1965), and Edina Ronay (1963).[36] He is also self-parodically exploiting the strategy of telling without investiture.

Humphries' *soi-même* autobiographical identity is a dialectic of *idem*-identity (sameness) and *ipse*-identity (selfhood), in which sameness has priority over selfhood. In identifying Humphries, I agree with Paul Ricoeur: "The weight of this comparative use of the term 'same' seems so great to me that I shall henceforth take sameness as synonymous with *idem*-identity and shall oppose to it selfhood (*ipseity*), understood as *ipse*-identity."[37] His autobiographical utterance, whether an individual assertion or *More Please* and *My Life as Me* as a whole, is not, *ipse dixit*, true because "he himself said it." It is true, *idem*, because it has been spoken previously: it is a speech or narrative readymade, a replica of Humphries' life-so-far. His identity, depicted, in a flash, as the mirror-image of "a round-shouldered, middle-aged man, dewlapped and disconsolate ... the *real* me,"[38] is about sameness not selfhood. Even though Humphries-himself (*lui-même*) is a man of kingly singularity – of whom I would say, if only the words were mine, "'A was a man, take him for all in all, I shall not look upon his like again,"[39] unless, that is, I happen to take in his next show – he is, *lui-même/soi-même*, the "same him/herself," the "same oneself" as everyone in his audience. In contradistinction to his mirror-image, his "I" is, *idem*, indistinguishable from that of any other *soi-même* person who has lived.

*More Please* and *My Life as Me* are Humphries' walk into the audience, and the audience's walk onto the stage: they are his admission, however subtle, that the "I" in the mirror, which, unlike the "round-shouldered, middle-aged man," or "the *real* me" of selfhood, is not reversed optically, is the surreal Barry Humphries – he who is before all the subject positions of mirror reality. In his surreality he rejects the dialectic, the binary opposition, of "*ipse*-identity" distinguished from other than self. As a man of the theatre – and an ethical man – Barry Humphries is selfless: his life-writing is marked by the samenesses of Dada replication and universality, and by the sameness of performer and audience, writer and reader, artist and spectator, in an Australian universe.

Dame Edna's quippy[40] "I'm an Australian, you know," given that punctuation is only implicit in speech, could be taken to mean "I'm an Australian [whom] you know [because I am the same as you]," or, in the words of the refrain from Dame Edna's song "Broadening My Horizons," from the TV show (1997) and the video (1997) *Dame Edna's Work Experience*, "God bless you, I'm just as good as you are – / And you're nearly as good as me."[41] People can recognize themselves in Edna Everage the prophet, just as they are able to make out Barry Humphries in Edna Everage the pantomime dame.

Similarly, they are able to recognize themselves in Barry Humphries, the autobiographical "subject,"[42] prior to subject positioning or characterization not through the identity-theft of appropriating his life through telling his autobiographies, or doing him or his characters at parties,[43] but, rather, through the "*idem*-identity" of knowing, or coming to know, oneself as another, an "I" also known as Barry Humphries, a.k.a. Dame Edna Everage, a.k.a. Sir Les Patterson, a.k.a. Sandy Stone, a.k.a. Barry McKenzie, a.k.a. Tid, a.k.a. *soi-même* because, as Humphries teaches – despite the appearance of self-promotion, his method is didactic, especially given that he is largely an autodidact – in the autobiographical exercise that is *More Please* and *My Life as Me*, everybody's "I," the body of every "I," is the same. He puts a laughing face on the grim-pose essentialization: "I," *ego sum*, is the essence of our existence. To Humphries I say, "*ta face, toi!*" ("your face, you!").

In *More Please* each time Humphries relates an anecdote illustrating his difference or his detachment from other people (*les Autres*), he seems to leave open the possibility of an association with other-than-self. For example, in the chapter "Dirty Hair" (83–95), he recounts how, because of his long hair,[44] he was singled out, and singled himself out, at the Melbourne Grammar School, as a painter in oils,[45] "as *Mr Humphries*,"[46] as a published poet and a member of the debating society,[47] as the founder of "a small subversive gang,"[48] as a communist,[49] and as a conscientious objector to school sports.[50] But perhaps the distinction of long hair stands out more than anything else he mentions because, for fifty years, his fringe, or forelock, has added the clearest definition to his personal and his professional images. Humphries' trademark[51] long hair, literally the mark of his trade as an artiste (painter, actor, writer), is also his distinguishing feature as *een persoon de stijl*.[52]

Yet "Mr Sutcliffe's peroration, delivered in tremulous pseudo-English Kiwi tones: LONG HAIR IS DIRTY HAIR,"[53] calls to my mind a parallel between Barry Humphries and Brendan Behan (1923–64), whose name,

"Brendan," means "stinking hair" in Irish,[54] and who, like Humphries, was an alcoholic of legendary (pro)portions, was influenced by Joan Littlewood,[55] was a leading figure in English theatre, and, of course, was a great writer. This LONG-HAIR-IS-BRENDAN association might remove the schoolboy Humphries from his isolation at the Melbourne Grammar School and place him in the *soi-même* company of borstal theatre folk and audiences. Also, within the name "Brendan" Edna is hidden – anagrammatically.

When Humphries describes his family's new house in Christowel Street, Camberwell (Melbourne), which had a trade entrance, and when he recalls "the hawker I imagined festooned with black birds like a sinister Papageno,"[56] he evokes for me his early rehearsals in the role of Papageno for Geoffrey Dutton's planned (but aborted) 1989 production of *The Magic Flute*.[57] This Papageno parallel could take Humphries, daydreaming at the Christowel Street trade entrance, into the *soi-même* company of Bernd Benthaak, Arthur Boyd, Yehudi Menuhin, Geoffrey Dutton, and Wolfgang Amadeus Mozart.

Finally, his disdainful allusion to Prokofiev's *Peter and the Wolf* – "[the film] *One Summer of Happiness*, a tedious Swedish idyll ... was to the Australian cinema of the early fifties what *Peter and the Wolf* was to music, and 'Sunflowers' to art"[58] – reminds me of his own (as Sir Les Patterson) parody "Peter and the Shark" (in his orchestral shows *Last Night of the Poms* [1981], *Song of Australia* [1983], and *Peter and the Shark* [1983]) and his own (as Dame Edna Everage) narration of Prokofiev's *Peter and the Wolf* on compact disc (1997). It might even take Humphries from the Savoy Theatre, in Russell Street (Melbourne), and place him in the *soi-même* company of Carl Davis, John Lanchberry, Sergei Prokofiev, and the Melbourne Symphony Orchestra. And (given that Dame Edna narrates *The Young Person's Guide to the Orchestra* and Humphries narrates *The Story of Babar, the Little Elephant*) it might put him in the company of Benjamin Britten and Francis Poulenc as well.

Although in "Alzheimer Remembers" Humphries promises that "in the illustrated section, the *here's me with* ... pictures will be mercifully few,"[59] he does cite some important *nous-mêmes* associations in the text. His encounter with Stephen Spender at Melbourne University[60] may have inspired him to become a poet and to "arrange" *A Garland for Stephen Spender* (1991), the eighty-second birthday tribute to Spender, by then his father-in-law. His meeting with Salvador Dali in New York in 1963[61] may have confirmed his status as a Dada (and Surrealist) artist and even helped him adopt a kind of Daliesque mien, and his encounters with Jack Kerouac definitely beat up his character Morrie Tate[62] from *A Nice Night's Entertainment*. His working relationships with Spike Milligan,[63] Peter Cook,[64] and Stanley Myers and Ian Davidson[65] in the 1960s in London helped establish lifelong friendships. His meeting with "the old and ailing Martin Boyd" in Rome in 1959 led him to assess Boyd as "Australia's greatest novelist."[66] These and many other associations helped move Humphries from *lui-même* to *soi-même* to *nous-mêmes* reality, to move far from his state of mind when he performed in Lionel Bart's *Maggie May* (1964) and was caught performing outside his marriage with Rosalind Tong, as "the theatre was reality; reality was theatre."[67] In *More Please*, he rises above this parallelism – compare Keats's parallelism in the phrase "Beauty is truth, truth beauty" in his "Ode on a Grecian Urn" (1820) – to take on the surreality of his life story.

Humphries' autobiographical surreality has to do with his candour about his failings (professional and moral) and with his specificity about his achievements (personal and professional). Although his self-portraits are as varied and revealing as are Van Gogh's, his "I" is not distorted by pigment or brush stroke but is as naked as he was on 17 February 1934, or at least on the day in November 1982 when he posed for the centrefold photograph of *Cleo*. It is the "I" one *soi-même* sees in the mirror, as the letter "I" is the same recto and verso.

Readers might even see themselves in his place from time to time, as when Humphries is "licking the beaters,"[68] either helping mum with the baking or imagining his revenge on Miss Jensen. I have licked the beaters, and the spatula, many times, and I only wish I could recall the name of the first-grade teacher who slapped the back of my head because I couldn't get an answer right on my first day at a new school, after my family had moved cross-country to Vancouver. Has anyone not passed a well dressed, well groomed man sheltering in a shop doorway in Lower Regent Street, fearing he might be having a heart attack?[69] Has anyone not felt him pulling (at) your leg, begging for your assistance? So why did I pull away and quicken my pace when, his emergency over, I learned that he was only trying to tell me that his funny turn was merely an attack of happiness? How could I have ignored Barry Humphries, after he has assailed me with happiness all these years?

The publication of three biographies on Humphries – Peter Coleman's *The Real Barry Humphries* (1990), John Lahr's *Dame Edna Everage and the Rise of Western Civilisation: Backstage with Barry Humphries* (1992), and Humphries' own *More Please* (1992) – around the same time hints at the possibility of a degree of cooperation between Humphries and his biographers. Peter Coleman has known Humphries for forty years; Humphries has served (1975–87) on the board of directors of Coleman's periodical *Quadrant*. John Lahr has been getting to know "the incomparable and elusive Barry Humphries"[70] since 1981, when he took in a performance of *An Evening's Intercourse with the Widely Liked Barry Humphries*, and his knowledge of the subject increased intensively in 1988, when Humphries allowed him to spend research time backstage during the run of his show *Back with a Vengeance* at the Theatre Royal, Drury Lane, in London. Stephen Alomes (dis)qualifies both Coleman and Lahr as "sympathetic" to Humphries,[71] but I believe they have been true to his story, even if with his cooperation, as true as his assemblage *Bicycle Wheel* (1913) was to Marcel Duchamp, who liked to spin it in his studio, if only because it spun truly. Just as Duchamp knew how to true a wheel, so Coleman and Lahr have shown that they know how to true a Humphries.

Still, Coleman's and Lahr's biographical contents at times do diverge from Humphries. The disparity may be simply an error, as when Coleman discusses Humphries' participation in "the BBC television's *The Late Late Show*, produced by Hugh Burnett in 1966 and Jack Gold in 1967,"[72] whereas Humphries says, "I was invited by the BBC to join the cast of a new weekly programme to be called *The Late Show*."[73] A proofreading or computer spell-check would have revealed in Coleman's reference to "*The Late Late Show*" a "repeated word" error and suggested deleting the second "late."

But another, more substantive disparity between Coleman and Humphries suggests that Humphries' life has been swept up in a black cape of legend (diction) and multiple narratives (contradiction). For example, consider the twinned-narrative of the origin of gladiolas in Humphries' shows and his tradition of throwing them to the audience in the finale. Coleman attributes the start of the custom not to Humphries but to Dame Edna in *Excuse I: Another Nice Night's Entertainment* (1965):

Above all, in 1965 she introduced the hurling of "gladdies" at the audience in the *finale*: it began originally in Adelaide before the Christmas shut-down as a way of disposing of surplus flowers. The audience was made to hold them up, quiver them and join in community singing. It was an enormously popular innovation and became the traditional *finale* of the shows, ultimately requiring over a hundred bunches, sometimes imported from Sicily or South Africa and kept warmed and watered in a special room. It also involved the audience, almost totally, in Edna's world: it was now impossible to laugh patronizingly at her from a great distance.[74]

Given that the monologue "Sandy Claus," with its Christmas theme, was prominent in *Excuse I*, and that Christmas falls in the height of the Australian summer, when keeping "surplus flowers" in show-quality overnight would be difficult, Coleman's version seems plausible. In his account in *More Please* Humphries also ascribes the origin to *Excuse I*, but he seems to invoke a Dada spirit:

It was during my extended season at the Theatre Royal in Sydney that Mrs Everage took pity on a woman in the front row who had been covetously eyeing the vase of "gladdies" on the piano all night. At last, in exasperation, Edna hurled the dripping blooms with full force at their sedentary admirer, who unselfishly passed them to her neighbours down the row. It was the sight of an audience spontaneously wagging these evocative flesh-pink spears in time to the final number that inspired Edna to "keep it in." No show of hers is now complete without ritualistic gladdie-waving in the finale, and sometimes as many as two hundred gladioli, imported from plantations as far distant as Brazil, Queensland, Malta and Mexico, are showered nightly on the stalls, or catapulted by giant slings or cannons into the dress circle.[75]

Although John Lahr confirms this story in *Dame Edna and the Rise of Western Civilisation*,[76] his evidence is mostly in "recalls Humphries" quotations.

But Edna Everage, in her autobiography, *My Gorgeous Life* (1989), which predates Humphries, Lahr, and Coleman's life-tellings, offers the earliest account (which is Humphries' and Lahr's most likely source) of how her gladioli-throwing rite started, when, according to her historicizing-I, she stole the show from Humphries at the Establishment Club:

While I was wittering away I noticed a little woman in the front row staring at the gorgeous vase of gladdies on top of Wendy's piano. They were beautiful flesh-pink specimens, with lovely ruffled and crimped florets. As you know I adore the gladiolus (whose name means "little spear" for my non-gardening readers), and as my talk drew to a close I yielded to a sudden impulse, and snatching the sheath of dripping stalks from its vase, hurled them with tremendous force at that mite in the front stalls who had so eagerly coveted them.[77]

Dame Edna also flashes forward from her failure at the Establishment Club to her triumph in *Housewife-Superstar!!*

It flashed into my mind one night in 1976 standing on the stage of London's beautiful Apollo Theatre in Shaftesbury Avenue, as the entire audience clutching its gladdies rose to its feet in a tumultuous standing ovation. This was the brilliant sunshine of success which I appreciated all the more keenly because I had known the shadow of rejection.[78]

Thus, Peter Coleman, John Lahr, and Barry Humphries date the gladdie origin as Adelaide 1965, Sydney 1965, and Sydney 1965, respectively, whereas Dame Edna dates it London 1962. She is the most reliable witness, however, given that the first gladiolus came from her hand. Nevertheless, to Dame Edna, the gladioli she casts into the audience have no origin, other than through the bio-imperative of "bisexual hermaphroditism," and certainly no narratological origin, as André Breton observes, as if in tribute to Edna: "Woman of mine with springtime buttocks / With gladiolus sex."[79]

Table 5.1
Edna Everage and Barry Humphries Speak and Are Spoken For

| Barry Humphries, More Please (1992) | Edna Everage, My Gorgeous Life (1989) |
| --- | --- |
| Mrs Everage took pity on a woman in the front row who had been covetously eyeing the vase of "gladdies" on the piano all night. | I noticed a little woman in the front row staring at the gorgeous vase of gladdies on top of Wendy's piano. |
| Edna hurled the dripping blooms with full force. | I yielded to a sudden impulse, and snatching the sheath of dripping stalks from its vase, hurled them with tremendous force. |
| covetously eyeing | eagerly coveted |

Yet, spookily, in its diction and idiom, Humphries' account echoes Edna's: phrases such as "my extended season," "took pity on a woman in the front row who had been covetously eyeing the vase of 'gladdies' on the piano all night," "exasperation," and "hurled the dripping blooms with full force" could have come from Edna's mouth, and of course the phrase "keep it in" is hers. Humphries out-Ednas Edna: his parallel phrases sound more like Edna than do her own! Perhaps, narratologically, Humphries is focalizing the story through Edna's consciousness: Edna is his focalizer here, and he, in a sense, is the man in her amanuensis.

But the discrepancy between Coleman's compost story – gladdies as rubbish – and Humphries' impost story – gladdies as "put upon" a member of the audience – is pronounced enough to demand explanation. Is Humphries covering up a simple story of housekeeping or stage management to glamourize a legend about a rite of spring, a priapic saturnalia, audience participation, or just gladioli? Or does Coleman merely make another "late late" slip, saying "disposing of surplus flowers," when he meant to say "hurled the dripping blooms with full force"? I believe Humphries' and Coleman's stories are complementary, in the main, not contradictory or exclusive (like the two creation myths in Genesis, if you will). Their interstice is stagecraft. Coleman explains the gladiola custom through techniques of theatre management. Humphries crafts a gladiola rite that, consistent with Dame Edna's account, has less to do with flower arrangement than with the arrangement between performer and audience: Humphries crafts a rite to explain every audience member's fervent, loopy desire to catch a gladdie, for Dame Edna to hear them singing and to be singled out like the covetous woman in the first row at Excuse I.

The factual differences between Lahr and Humphries are more muted than are those between Coleman and Humphries – muted, that is, as distinguished from spoken. First, Lahr focuses on Back with a Vengeance (1987–88), whereas in More Please Humphries recounts his life and career only up to 1977 and the fizzle of *Housewife! Superstar!!* in New York, after having dealt quite cursorily with his films *The Adventures of Barry McKenzie* (1972) and *Barry McKenzie Holds His Own* (1974), and the London production of *Housewife-Superstar!!* (1976) (despite the fact that after *Oliver!* it was his big break in West End theatre).[80] (Dame Edna also ends the curriculum vitae part of her autobiography by alluding to her own 1976 show at "London's beautiful Apollo Theatre in Shaftesbury Avenue.")[81]

While in Australia with his tour of *Remember You're Out: A New Barry Humphries Event* (1999), Humphries told Bryce Hallett of the *Sydney Morning Herald* that, following the tour, he would start writing a second autobiography, or a second volume of autobiography, to be titled *Are We Nearly There Yet?*[82] In *My Life as Me* (2002), in its single reference to John Lahr and *Back with a Vengeance*,[83] Humphries does not clarify Lahr's and his own versions of what happened backstage at *Back with a Vengeance*, except to hint that *Dame Edna Everage and the Rise of Western Civilisation* is "a book filled, it is true, with enough quotes from the show to entitle me to a generous royalty."[84] I compare several passages in *Dame Edna Everage and the Rise of Western Civilisation* and *More Please* in order to suggest that, when they were backstaging, Humphries fed Lahr with image-setting and legend-setting information.

In *More Please*, Humphries says of Les Patterson, who made his *début* (his "first turn," or music hall act) in *Housewife-Superstar!!*, "Deep within Les Patterson, I hoped at least one highbrow critic, whatever he thought of the show, might mention the persisting influence of Aristophanes' *Lysistrata* – or at least Brecht's Mr Punt."[85] Although I mention *Lysistrata* in Chapter 1, the statute of limitations on indebtedness disqualifies me from satisfying Humphries' hope: I am simply referencing *More Please* (and Les's Aristophallocentricity) not *Housewife-Superstar!!* But John Lahr, on the other hand, who published his book shortly before *More Please*, did not fall under the statute. Therefore, Lahr quotes Humphries, also with reference to Les Patterson.

"There are literary allusions in Les," says Humphries, "but you're not really meant to get them. He is a music-hall character, very much a vaudeville figure, related to Max Miller a bit. The phallus is Aristophanic. But then he's also related to Mr Punt, that figure in an otherwise very boring play by Brecht, and to certain sorts of Shakespeare drunks, like Toby Belch. He's also very like, whatever they might say, a lot of people in Queensland." Sir Les inspired a real sense of terror and elation in an audience.[86]

"It's the spirit of Aristophanes," says Humphries, about Sir Les's special power. "The priapic thing. Just as religious traditions become subterranean and re-emerge in other forms, the theatre has some traditions as old as religions and certain persistent themes have traditionally touched people. Perhaps Sir Les is the reincarnation of something significant. This may be fanciful, but you know what I mean. Kids who've never been to vaudeville or music hall come to my show and they *like* it. They like it not just because they like the characters. I think they even find it sexy, and I think there's a need in people for this kind of comedy."[87]

In the first quotation, consisting of ninety-one words, Lahr writes fifteen words ("says Humphries" and "Sir Les inspired a real sense of terror and elation in an audience") and Humphries speaks the rest. In the second quotation, consisting of 109 words, Lahr writes seven ("says Humphries, about Sir Les's special power") and Humphries speaks the rest. Lahr gives Humphries the floor, or the stage, to deliver a critical message. However, in a sense the speech is over, topically, as soon as Lahr interrupts him. In the opening sentence, paragraph one, " 'There are literary allusions in Les,' says Humphries, 'but you're not really meant to get them,' " Lahr's speech-tag gives stress to Humphries' brutally ironic comment on audience ignorance and to his pronouncement: "the phallus is Aristophanic." In the opening, topic sentence, paragraph two, " 'It's the spirit of Aristophanes,' says Humphries, about Sir Les's special power," Lahr's speech-tag finalizes his idea.

Both paragraphs satisfy Humphries' hope, as documented as a kind of last wish in *More Please*, about "the persisting influence of Aristophanes' *Lysistrata*," and thus Lahr also fills the role of "highbrow critic," particularly as a *New Yorker* columnist, even through he does not reference Aristophanes in his *New Yorker* article on Humphries ("Playing Possum" [1 July 1991], which is the source study of *Dame Edna Everage and the Rise of Western Civilisation*) or in any of his other published articles on Humphries.

Why does Humphries, at the end of *More Please*, voice his hope that "at least one highbrow critic ... mention the persisting influence of Aristophanes' *Lysistrata*" when Lahr has already fulfilled his hope by quoting him twice on the matter? Is Lahr not "one highbrow critic"? Does his quotation of Humphries not qualify as a "mention"? Did Humphries perhaps not read *Dame Edna Everage and the Rise of Western Civilisation* (or at least not page 111)? Or is he waiting for another critic (Me? Choose *me*, Barry!) to write on "Sir Les and Aristophanes' *Les Is Traitor*"?

Perhaps Lahr gave Humphries hope backstage at *Back with a Vengeance*, although throughout *Dame Edna* Humphries is conspicuous in his detachment from Lahr, who spends much of his backstage time not with Humphries but with his crew and staff. Lahr records his conversation with Harriet:

"Didn't Barry's secretary get you? He's got flu," she says. "He's a bit of a ratbag about interviews. He's always like this. It's not you." And then she adds, "It happens to the stage management too. He's known in certain circles as the 'megastar of hollow promises.' "[88]

Maybe Humphries' comment, quoted by Lahr, "but you're not really meant to get them," is directed at highbrow critics who do not *get* Aristophanes yet *like* Les, as distinguished from the kids who *like* Les but may not get Max Miller. But the most likely explanation is that Humphries and Lahr shared some of their ideas: perhaps Humphries made Aristophanic remarks backstage because the parallel had come up in his autobiography; perhaps the Aristophanic remarks come up in *Dame Edna Everage and the Rise of Western Civilisation* because Lahr was able to read some of Humphries' *More Please* manuscript and recognized how important the parallel was to Humphries. Perhaps Lahr's quotations fulfill Humphries' hope retroactively. But now I have come to believe that the statute of limitations may have expired on their retroactivity because, for example, Lahr's first Aristophanic quotation of Humphries – "There are literary allusions in Les" – is not a backstage citation at all but, rather, a quotation from an interview that Humphries gave to Ian Davidson in 1986 in the periodical *Meanjin*.[89]

One more comparison of *Dame Edna Everage and the Rise of Western Civilisation* and *More Please* is in order so as to reveal the possibility of the authors' collaboration. In 1970, in Melbourne, Humphries had two traumatic experiences: first, the police arrested him for public drunkenness, and then he was mugged, also while drunk. Because the publication of Lahr's book predates Humphries', Lahr recounts the arrest, one presumes, based on Humphries' testimonial evidence backstage at *Back with a Vengeance*.

In Melbourne in 1970 Humphries was charged with being drunk and disorderly. "You must have had a dull day," the papers reported Humphries saying to the police. "Didn't you have any old ladies to arrest! Hope you have a better evening, you pathetic bastards."[90]

Lahr makes a factual statement, specifying place, time, person, and event, and he offers supporting evidence in the form of published quotations.

Now compare this excerpt of Humphries' parallel arrest account, from *More Please*:

I returned to the car and was just about to turn the key in the ignition when two policemen appeared from nowhere. Some years before, in London, I had had brushes with the law, and I had once lost my licence for a year for driving in the wrong direction up the Tottenham Court Road in a state of chemical exaltation, but at least the London bobbies called one "Sir." Their Melbourne counterparts were less polite. I was hustled to the Camberwell police station, a stone's-throw from my parents' house, where I most unwisely muttered the word "fascists" within earshot of my apprehenders. Seconds later I was in a cell.[91]

If Humphries had told this story to Lahr backstage at *Back with a Vengeance* why would Lahr have quoted the newspaper report ("pathetic bastards") and not Humphries ("fascists"), trading insults with him, as it were? If Humphries' fabula were the same as what appears in this quotation, then why would Lahr not have ignored Humphries' at once cavalier and penitent tone (evident in the phrases "two policemen appeared from nowhere," "brushes with the law," "driving in the wrong direction ... in a state of chemical exaltation," and "most unwisely muttered") and accepted his slur "fascists"? Most likely, Humphries did not tell him.

Lahr's account of Humphries' mugging is, like his story of the arrest, factual, evidentiary, journalistic:

Three days later, drinking in the area of Richmond, Humphries was pulled into an alley where he was knocked unconscious and robbed. His bloated and bruised face filled the Melbourne papers the next day. As always, Humphries sidestepped public humiliation not by hiding from it but by admitting it with laughter.[92]

The phrase "as always" suggests Lahr might have taken Humphries' word "fascists," especially as a euphemism for "pathetic bastards," as part of his ironic structure.

Yet Humphries does not mug his way through his mugging story but, on the contrary, tells it straight-faced:

Two days later, my medication doubled, I was in town to discuss the possibility of writing a regular newspaper column for the Melbourne *Age*. I managed to slip out of a side door of the building and into a nearby bar frequented by journalists. Only very vaguely do I recall somebody saying, "There are some friends of yours in a car outside who want to talk to you." My next recollection is of distant lights and mud. It was night and for some reason I was lying face down in some kind of waste land surrounded by rubble and broken glass on which a fine drizzle descended. I tried to crawl, but there was an excruciating pain in my abdomen and I collapsed back into the mud. Slowly, however, I dragged myself towards the edge of a desolate road and, at length, attracted the attention of a passing car which dumped me off, like a severely damaged parcel, at St Vincent's Hospital.[93]

Note the time-line disparity between the two accounts. If Humphries had told Lahr the story backstage, would not Lahr, a model reporter and journalist, have recorded a two-day, not a three-day, interval between the arrest and the mugging? He would not likely make a mistake like Coleman's "late late."

Lahr's statement "his bloated and bruised face filled the Melbourne papers the next day" is detached, whereas Humphries' statement "I tried to crawl, but there was an excruciating pain in my abdomen and I collapsed back into the mud" is poignant, showing Humphries as he once was, *really*, without a "jaunty grin" and without moving the reading audience to laughter. That Lahr should, as it were, laugh off an assault story shows that he probably did not hear it from Humphries. Similarly, whereas Humphries attributes his accident partly to his being over-medicated ("my medication doubled"), Lahr places the blame, partly, on Humphries for "drinking in the area of Richmond."

Lahr and Humphries disagree, slightly, on one more matter: how arrest and assault changed Humphries' life. Lahr states: "But the incident proved a turning point in his life."[94] However, Humphries states, after a detailed three-page confession explaining how he moved from the gutter to Alcoholics Anonymous: "I wish I could say that my life changed immediately thereafter. In a sense it did, since, after a few meetings – and to Tony's alarm – I became a world authority on Alcoholics Anonymous."[95] The disparity of "a turning point in his life" and "I wish I could say that my life changed immediately thereafter" suggests Lahr and Humphries did not discuss post-trauma recovery data backstage; it also suggests that Lahr evidently relied on journalistic evidence more than testimonial evidence.

He might have based his information on the article on Humphries' arrest in the Melbourne *Herald* (7 September 1970) or, even more likely, on Keith Dunstan's account in the chapter "John Barry Humphries" in his book *Ratbags* (1979). The coincidence of Lahr's "Didn't you have any old ladies to arrest! Hope you have a better evening, you pathetic bastards" with Dunstan's "Didn't you have any old ladies to arrest! Hope you have a better evening you pathetic bastards"[96] reveals *Ratbags*, notwithstanding the intervention of a comma, as Lahr's likeliest source.

In his narrative of his arrest and how he hit the bottle and then hit bottom, Humphries documents the moment when the glassy-eyed man in "a state of chemical exaltation" meets the glassy I of the autobiographer who catches himself in "a lift or washroom, or some other chamber lined with mirror," such as the mirror-lined room *More Please*, from which "the *real* me,"[97] the *real* Barry Humphries, sends out an "envoy from mirror city"[98] to sue the audience for peace, mercy, understanding, and even love.

## BARRY HUMPHRIES PUTS OUT!

Barry Humphries has been not just putting out his eye/I but also putting himself out on stage for half a century, prolonging "an evening's intercourse with the widely liked Barry Humphries" to tantric lengths. It would appear, however, that his putting himself out in autobiography is of a different nature, almost an inconvenience, performed only recently (1992 and 2002) and under duress, out of fear the next biographer will get him. But, actually, Humphries has been putting out his "I" as an Andalusian dog-

and-pony show for most of his career. *More Please* and *My Life as Me* are just his most recent literary performances.

Humphries' "I" appears in six other glass shards that can be rearranged into a paradigm of *More Please* and *My Life as Me*:

1 "The Confessions of Barry Humphries" (1965)
2 "The Confessions of a Conder Fan" (1977)
3 "John Barry Humphries" (1979) by Keith Dunstan
4 "Confessions of a Victoria Gentleman" (1981)
5 "A Fugitive Art: An Interview with Barry Humphries" (1986)
6 "Barry Humphries on the Couch" (1994) by Peter Conrad

The resemblance of these passages, written some twenty-seven years apart, suggests that Humphries is telling the truth, that the incident is safely stowed, like Polonius's body, in his photographic memory, or that, in writing *More Please*, he relied on the evidence of his *Bulletin* article.

Humphries' account of his telephone conversation with Miss Amy Halford, which appeared in *Quadrant*, is more likely a transcription he made after putting down the phone than his recollection eleven years after the event. But his account in *More Please*, twenty-six years after the first event (telephone call) and fifteen years after the second event (article), is probably a paraphrase of the transcript.

Keith Dunstan's account is closely based on an article in the Melbourne *Sunday Observer* (14 November 1971). Its resemblance to Humphries' own account in *More Please*, like that of a fabula to a narrative, might suggest how, in the twenty-one years between the newspaper story and the autobiographical story, Humphries' Dada prank has remained quite constant and how, in the forty-odd years between the first Malouf encounter and Humphries' most recent curtain call, the prank has become an artistic legend, a kind of cargo cult.

Note how Dunstan stresses Humphries' lone execution of the initial prank and his leadership over his co-conspirators, whereas Humphries emphasizes the collective of practitioners and the camaraderie of their pleasure. Dunstan explains the prank minimally: "He gave Mr Malouf the money and he handed back the soap, plus the change"; "Humphries explained that he didn't want the soap, he had merely wanted to buy it." Humphries goes into the diegetic details of execution (in the manner of Juan Muñoz offering instructions on cheating at cards in Gavin Bryars' composition *A Man in a Room, Gambling* [1992]): "we would offer money that required change"; "When Mr Malouf put the change on the counter, we would take it and start to go, leaving the soap behind." Dunstan treats Mr Malouf as a figure in the historical past, whereas Humphries treats him as an almost willing artiste – as is evident in the construction "Mr Malouf ceased, at last, to mention our

Table 5.2
Humphries' Notes on His *Début* at Phillip Street Theatre

| *"The Confessions of Barry Humphries"* (1965) | *More Please (1992)* |
|---|---|
| Soon after this I went up to Sydney to work at the Phillip Street Theatre, and I found, to my great pleasure, that the Olympic hostess sketch was popular there and that Mrs Everage was by no means unknown in New South Wales. (21) | The Olympic Games sketch was still very topical and it went down astonishingly well. The character of Edna was not, it seemed, a uniquely Melbourne phenomenon and in this strange, new, raffish city, I began to feel a little more at home. (158) |

Table 5.3
Humphries' Stories on Being Mistaken for Charles Conder

| *"The Confessions of a Conder Fan"* (1977) | *More Please (1992)* |
|---|---|
| "I believe you were a friend of the late Charles Conder." <br><br> "*You* are a friend of Charles?" <br><br> "Pardon me, Miss Halford, but I understand you were a friend of Conder." <br><br> "Oh! So you also were a friend of Charles. I have a lot of things of his ... beautiful things." <br><br> Another voice now. Younger, sterner. <br><br> "Miss Halford has been quite ill and should not speak on the telephone. Who is this please?" <br><br> "It's a friend of Charles, Sister, just fancy, a friend of Charles!" The fainter, Edwardian voice may have enunciated into a bedside telephone extension. <br><br> "My name is Humphries ... I, er, I'm afraid, that is, I found to my surprise that your name was in the book and I hoped, perhaps, that I could meet you and talk about ..." <br><br> My voice trailed off. I was entirely disconcerted. The year was 1966, the city was London, I was speaking on the telephone to an old lady about a "mutual friend" who had been dead for over half a century! <br><br> "Miss Halford is not well enough to see anyone at present. She should not be using the instrument. I am very sorry. Goodbye." (39) | I had noticed in a contemporary book on this artist that many of the illustrations were reproduced by courtesy of their owner, a Miss Amy Halford. I looked in the telephone book and discovered to my amazement that there was one Amy Halford listed with a Kensington telephone number. Impulsively I dialled it and a very old lady answered the telephone. Slowly and quite loudly I explained the purpose of my call, but she had got hold of the wrong end of the stick. "Darling Charles!" came the Edwardian voice through my cream plastic receiver. "I haven't heard from you for weeks. How are you? The fan you painted for me looks glorious and Edmund Gosse was here with Ricketts for tea yesterday and thinks it is one of your best. When are you coming to see me?" Our conversation was rudely interrupted by a brisk modern voice, "This is Miss Halford's nurse. Miss Halford is not strong enough to speak on the telephone, I'm afraid. She should be having her rest. Good day." (207) |

Table 5.4
Humphries Turns a Dada Prank into a Double-Act

| Keith Dunstan, "John Barry Humphries," *Ratbags* (1979) | *More Please (1992)* |
| --- | --- |
| He also conducted a surrealist campaign against a Mr Malouf who had a small mixed business near Melbourne University. One day the young Humphries went into the shop and bought a bar of Lux soap. He gave Mr Malouf the money and he handed back the soap, plus the change. Humphries took the change and left the soap on the counter. Mr Malouf shouted to Humphries to come back, he had forgotten his soap.<br><br>Humphries explained that he didn't want the soap, he had merely wanted to buy it. Other Humphries friends called and went through the same ritual, paying for the cake of soap, but never taking it away until the hapless Mr Malouf began to wonder about his sanity; a grave fundamental principle was being undermined, that upon the exchange of money one should receive goods. (25) | For example, we selected s small shopkeeper near the campus called Malouf. He was chosen entirely for the euphony and novelty of his name. He was a typical, modest, corner-of-the-street tradesman who sold a variety of merchandise, and once a day, at a specific time, one of us would enter his shop and buy a cake of Lux toilet soap. For this we would offer money that required change. When Mr Malouf put the change on the counter, we would take it and start to go, leaving the soap behind. The shopkeeper would say, "Hey, you've forgotten your soap." To which we would make the standard reply, "I don't want the soap, *I just want to buy it!*" We would then leave and join our accomplices, convulsed with childish laughter. This simple but radical variation on a fundamental commercial principle was repeated countless times until Mr Malouf ceased, at last, to mention our failure to take the goods we had paid for. (115) |

failure to take the goods we had paid for" – complete with euphonious name, in a double-act: "The shopkeeper would say, 'Hey, you've forgotten your soap.' To which we would make the standard reply, 'I don't want the soap, *I just want to buy it!*'" Here a music hall audience would laugh, as indeed happens when Humphries adds: "We would then leave and join our accomplices, convulsed with childish laughter." Rather than misrepresenting the historical past or the factuality of the newspaper report or Dunstan's chapter, Humphries is merely pointing out the music hall element that has always been in this prank – and, it could be argued, in all his Dada performances, even textual ones.

Whenever Humphries comes home to Melbourne something magical happens, an evocative fragrance recalled in "Confessions of a Victoria Gentleman," an artistic vision transcribed in *More Please*. (Melbourne is also the site, as recounted in *More Please*, of his healing from the trauma of arrest and assault, and from the disease of alcoholism.) His Pittosporum narrative is plausible, even as a memory. His narrative about recovering Clifton Pugh's portrait of him is bizarre and incredible; thus, in order to enhance his own credibility as teller, he does not qualify it as a memory (of thirty-four years) but states it in the diegetic now.

Table 5.5
Humphries' Memories of the Evocations of His Home Town

| *"Confessions of a Victoria Gentleman"* (1981) | *More Please (1992)* |
|---|---|
| I remember an evening in late August several years ago when I revisited Melbourne after a long absence. Catatonic with jet-lag I sat in the taxi which carried me from the airport to my parents' home in Camberwell. We stopped at some lights in Hawthorn and I opened the window. A gale of Pittosporum of the most exquisite sweetness and potency enveloped me utterly. It was as though in that one magnificent *whiff* I re-lived all the joyful moments of my youth. (33) | In Melbourne not long afterwards, in yet another taxi, I experienced again that mysterious prompting to diverge from the normal route, which on that day took me from the airport to my mother's home. Motoring down an unfamiliar street I saw, outside a terraced house, a shingle that bore the legend ART GALLERY in sign-writers' gothic. I stopped the cab, got out and, still yielding to impulse, knocked on the door. It was opened by a bearded young man who, when he saw me, stepped back with a gasp. "Who told you to come here?" he asked rather rudely. "Is this some kind of joke?" |
| | \* \* \* |
| | "You'll see what I mean when you see the picture, Mr Humphries, but I still don't believe nobody put you up to this!" Together we entered a bare, recently decorated room. One large painting stood against the wall. It was a picture which I knew had been missing since 1958, and had long been thought lost or destroyed. When I recovered my composure I asked him his price, which was not, under the circumstances, extortionate. I paid it and, still in a great agitation of spirit, took the picture home. It was a portrait in oils by Clifton Pugh, of myself. It is the frontispiece to this book. (306–7) |

Like many mothers, Humphries finds the birth and the birth-narrative of his child unforgettable. After bringing Edna into the world at the back of the tour bus – she is born at the back of the bus; the warm bench seat over the engine is the world – he has his birth-fabula straight. Whether he recalls it after thirty-one years with *Meanjin* interviewer Jim Davidson or after thirty-seven years for his autobiography, he would appear to have near total recall.

About two years after the publication of *More Please*, in a meeting with Peter Conrad at the Freud Museum, London, Humphries expanded upon his explanation for his conscientious objection to physical training, suggesting that, suffering from what can now be named "dyspraxia," he was sicker than even "the sickliest boys" but had to execute a ruse to give his

Table 5.6
Humphries' Birth-Narratives on Edna Everage at the Start

| *"A Fugitive Art: An Interview with Barry Humphries" (1986)* | *More Please (1992)* |
|---|---|
| She was loosely based on all the people who surrounded me in my youth, surround most Australians in their youth; solicitous aunts ... let us say solicitous rather than solicitors' aunts, though solicitors' aunts would no doubt sound exactly the same as this early character. She spoke of the supper party which the major of the next town or the lady mayoress would offer us after the performance of *Twelfth Night*. A speech of gratitude for bringing Shakespeare to the town.<br><br>Ray said, when it came to be time for the annual revue, "Why don't you write a sketch for that character you did in the bus? What's she called?" I plucked a name out of the air: "Edna," I suggested, since I'd once had a kind of nanny called Edna, of whom I was very fond. (150) | As the tour progressed, my improvised burlesque of these poignant votes-of-thanks grew more elaborate and absurd. Sometimes the *actual* remarks of a headmistress or mayoress at the after-show reception bore an uncanny resemblance to my most fanciful parody and I prattled away on the back seat of the bus, grateful that I could, at least, amuse and entertain by day the actors whom I dismayed by night. My nice, well-meaning lady who was so thrilled that culture had finally come to her town, and who was convinced that Shakespeare's Anne Hathaway was fundamentally just like any ordinary Australian housewife with a growing family of kiddies had, as yet, no name. It was only months later when we were preparing our end-of-season revue and Ray Lawler suggested that I revive the character that I decided to call her after my nanny, Edna. (143) |

Table 5.7
Humphries Not "on the Couch," but in *écriture couchée*

| *More Please (1992)* | *Qtd. in Peter Conrad, "Barry Humphries on the Couch," Feasting with Panthers (1994)* |
|---|---|
| Only the sickliest boys escaped, on medical grounds, the ineluctable twice-weekly "turnout." (94)<br><br>Twice a week for several years I dutifully "turned out." No sooner was my name ticked off on the roll than I would furtively skirt the playing fields and vanish into a cubicle of the school lavatories. Minutes later, in response to a tapped signal on the door, I would open it, and my accomplice, now an advertising tycoon, for whom I performed a similar service on *his* turnout nights, thrust into my grasp a Gladstone bag containing my school uniform. A quick change, an all-clear whistle, and I was outside the school gates, off on a tram – to freedom! (95) | "It was a gift I found by accident I had. I mean that I was ridiculous. I found out at school that I had it. I made people laugh at athletics. I flapped when I ran – there's a name for it, dyspraxia – so they called me Granny Humphries. That was mortifying. But I learned how to use this talent to protect myself, and to get my own back. Comedy is largely about revenge." (283) |

Note: The French phrase *écriture couchée* refers to a sloping script in handwriting.

disease the recognition his schoolmasters would not. But *is* "dyspraxia" a disease, whether physiological or psychological?

Developmental dyspraxia, also called apraxia, is a phonological disorder affecting children's language acquisition. Its symptoms include a limited vocabulary, with few multisyllabic words. Even as a child, Humphries did not exhibit these symptoms but was decidedly sesquipedalian, as he remains, able in *More Please* to get away with words like "noctambulations"[99] without missing a beat, and without drawing suspicion to his role as a card-carrying abecedarian. In this regard, in disclosing that he suffered from dyspraxia, Humphries would seem to be putting Conrad on rather than putting himself out. He "flapped" when he ran because he did not want to run. (I imagine him flapping his arms and legs, as Dame Edna Everage does when she runs and dances, and as Sir Les Patterson, in his platform shoes, also does when he runs and dances.) Humphries' allusion to "dyspraxia" seems to make direct reference to his anecdote about cutting sports practice: due to his dyspraxia, his practice (*praxis*) was abnormal (*dys*). His word play here, a kind of Duchampignon pun, is hilarious.

But don't be too quick to laugh. Perhaps Humphries was not putting Conrad, and his readers, on. Dyspraxia can affect gestural as well as verbal development in children, particularly limb and facial mechanisms.[100] Humphries does not specify what parts of his body flapped (other than "I") when he was forced to run with the boys: one imagines him with his arms and legs flailing around the track or the pitch; one discerns a certain twist in the mouth, a numbness in the cheeks, and a boy whose abnormal (*dys*) practice (*praxis*) of hiding in the loo, and of course telling the story later, is also hilarious. The joke is that, while his practice may not have been cricket, it was practice: Humphries was practising for his Dada pranks, and he was rehearsing for the theatre.

Humphries might have pleaded "dyspraxia" in his bid for exemption from military service. As he explains in *More Please*, "At the medical examination I tried the Conscientious Objection tactic that had worked so well in the past, but it provoked only a derisory laugh."[101] At this point he might have turned from mockery to parody and, as a dyspraxic conscientious objector, sent them up.

These six tabular comparisons of passages from *More Please* and Humphries' remarks in journal articles and book chapters are shards of glass (mirror) forming an arrangement in black-and-white typography in which one can see a replica of Humphries, waiting for his cue to step on stage, to put out for his audience, to put his "I" out for readers, as in a staged mishap in a game of tip-cat. Recently, his urologist looked up from examining him and said, "Mr Humphries, will you ever stop putting out?"

## BARRY HUMPHRIES IN A MOCK-TURTLE

Has Humphries ever been pictured wearing a mock turtleneck jumper, or even eating mock turtle soup? He is a master parodist, and the author of mock-heroic monologues and poems. Shouldn't a mocking bard wear the suitable dress, and be pictured in it at least once, like Lionel Pinkhill in *Women in the Background* (1995) ("in jeans, Bally loafers and a black alpaca cardigan over a cream turtleneck")?[102] There have been several close sightings of Humphries *vêtu d'un chandail à col montant* ("dressed in a turtle-necked jumper"): in one of the "dressing up" boyhood pictures, Barry in a little peaked cap, an open overcoat, leggings, and boots; in Cecil Beaton's photograph of him in the program of *A Load of Olde Stuffe*; as Dame Edna in woollies in the program of *Tears Before Bedtime*; and in a Playbill photograph for the Broadway production of *The Royal Tour*. That Humphries is seen so infrequently wearing mock-turtleneck jumpers, however (and even then not so openly as to allow a positive identification), might suggest that his (auto)biographical art is less about mockery than about parody, less about voicing his derision for political correctness than about getting a rise out of his audience.

His fictional biographies – Sir Les Patterson's *The Traveller's Tool* (1985) and Dame Edna Everage's *My Gorgeous Life: An Adventure* (1989) – are pseudonymous travesties, burlesques of the genre of autobiography, parodies of authorship, and self-parodies. They are perhaps the funniest of Humphries' books, but they also feature his most character-driven writing: Les and Edna come alive in the costume of Humphries' language and as they clothe themselves in his flesh on stage and soundstage. Humphries allows Les and Edna their own first persons, a narratorial independence that extends to title page credits and authorship, and even to Humphries' authorial exclusion.

In the Introduction to *The Traveller's Tool*, Brian Malouf, professor at the "London Community Centre for Anglo-Australian Understanding," no doubt a relation of Mr Malouf, the Melbourne shopkeeper whom Humphries and his mates drove to a nervous breakdown with their (de)Lux(e) Dada prank,[103] makes a lofty case for the book's merit and the author's meretriciousness in what is, for Humphries, a brilliant parody of Les by a man like Les (only not as loose). When Brian Malouf notes that "there have been many attempts to get Sir Leslie to wet his nib" and alludes to "matters that the majority of readers will have in hand as they fondle the raunchy reading material,"[104] he introduces less Les Patterson's autobiography and travel guide than Humphries' shocking parodies of ocker phallocentricity and of Derrida's abstraction of phallogocentrism.

As an account of Les Patterson's sex life, and the male reader's guide to living sexually, *The Traveller's Tool* qualifies as an autobiography, especially given the etymological link (through the Latin word *genus*, meaning "kind") between the words "gender" and "genre." After all, most men have a touch of Les in them. When Brian Malouf ends his introduction "muttering my own Australian motto: *no worries*,"[105] he is really voicing his identification with another mutterer, Les, whose byword is "no worries."

Humphries seems to be suggesting not that Les has written his own introduction under the pseudonym "Brian Malouf" but, rather, that *Les, il est les Autres*: "Les is other people," or at least other men. Hence, you are Les Patterson, or you are Les Autres – or you are a poofter. It's that simple. For example, the first chapter title, "My Tool in Your Hands," suggests Les and his readers may be gay. Les even admits, in his second paragraph, "I'm a man's man,"[106] although he does qualify this kind of out-of-the-closet disclosure by chiding certain members of his audience:

so if you're a blue nosed wowser (q.v.), a stuffed shirt, a raving pillow-biter or a looney old lezzo with a face like a half-sucked mango,[107] I'd chuck this book away now, because in the pages that follow, I employ the direct no-holds-barred lingo of a senior Australian diplomat at the top of his profession and the height of his sexual powers. Between you and me I don't reckon this is a book for women neither.[108]

In the rest of his life-telling Les Patterson follows the pattern of heterosexuality many times, and his occasional allusions to homosexuality prove to be only a tease for queer theorists intent on outing Les as they outed Bazza.

His heterosexual tellings, or conquest narratives, form the base of his base autobiography and of what Humphries calls, in other contexts, "the dissemination of its message"[109] and the "seminal show."[110] Les Patterson's tellings, his ejaculations, are little bursts of seminal fluid, and his relationship with his audience, with Les Autres, is a seminar at which men exchange fluids and even put them on display as self-portraits of their *quiddity* (or liquiddity), like Marcel Duchamp's *hommage* (that is, his *homme-age*)[111] to patriarchy, *Paysage fautif* (1946), which consists of "seminal fluid on Astralon, backed with black satin."[112] Les has sexual discourse with his audience, "during the course of this publication,"[113] much as Humphries' singer does in his scandalous song "True British Spunk" (1969). Everything Les says is referenced in sex.

When R.F. Brissenden observes that "Sandy Stone and Edna Everage are full-blown characters with a life of their own,"[114] he makes a critical assessment of what E.M. Forster, in *Aspects of the Novel* (1927), calls a "round" character.[115] But if Les Patterson were to have made this statement it would have been immediately sexualized with associations to fellatio and cunnilingus. If Patterson-patter "is referenced in sex" and "immediately sexualized," then who is responsible for stimulating his discourse? Does Les charge his language with phallogocentric grandeur, or is perhaps the reader making the grand gesture, as if he or she (probably he) were blowing Brissenden's "full-blown" out of proportion?

For example, readers familiar with Patterson's sexual reputation with Girls Friday might see in his narratorial situation in *The Traveller's Tool* the circumstances for what Roland Barthes (1973) calls "le plaisir du texte" ("the pleasure of the text"): "In fact, if you were lying where I am, looking up the leather mini of the spunky little hornbag who's typing this out, I doubt if you'd be in a literary frame of mind either."[116] But, like Barry McKenzie, when he clarifies his point of telling, Les turns from foreplay to the play of the text:

Nerida Murphy's her name, from Tasmania, and she is blushing like a beetroot as I drag little personal touches like this into my bestseller. The Secretarial Agency sent her round this morning to do relief work, but she's a good Catholic and so far she hasn't taken off anything more then her ear-rings, which are of the chunky punky variety and a bit of a health hazard if you happen to be down on your knees with a senior Australian public servant holding onto your ears like grim death.[117]

Clearly, Les expects to wear down Nerida Murphy in her Catholic resolve, beginning with her removing her ear-rings, but his efforts to sexualize the situation through words like "spunky" (referring to semen), "Tasmania" (in the shape of women's pubes),[118] "beetroot" (with the suffix "root," Australian slang for sexual intercourse), and "punky" (archaic slang for "of a prostitute") are also efforts to distract the reader from Nerida's resolve.

Her resistance to Les is not only spiritual (Catholic) but also nominal: her name, Nerida, which derives from the Greek *Nereis*, meaning "a nymph,"[119] suggests that, as a nymph – as distinguished from the nymphet Les takes her for, and the nympha, or labia minoria, he desires in her – she is a beautiful young woman with the power of the sea, like the sea round Tasmania, which is the power of women: "The waters of the oceans are thus seen not only as the source of life but also as its goal. 'To return to the sea' is 'to return to the mother,' that is, to die."[120] Nerida Murphy has power over life and death, the power to say "no" to the sexual act, and the power of amanuensis (to take dictation), whereas Les Patterson has only the power of sexual force, the power of a man, to give dick. As Les puts it, "my current research assistant told me this morning that I'd put the dick back into dictation."[121] Les would have us believe he has had sex with his secretary, but she might claim only that Les thinks with his dick.

Later he says of another temp, Bronwyn, "she's got a pair of lips on her that could suck-start a Harley Davidson,"[122] which, of course, is high praise from Les, but his boast simply emphasizes the conditionality of his sexual discourse: nowhere does Les document her ("the young lady writing down these words as I speak at the rate of nine words a minute [eh, Bronwyn?])"[123] actually performing fellatio upon him. Bronwyn will take dictation from Les, but apparently she will not take any dick from him. With regard to her shorthand speed, perhaps it is nine words per minute only because that is the pace of Les's speech when he is plotting strategy (as distinguished from Buster Thompson, at 157 words per minute, Debbie Thwaite at 125, and Colin Cartwright at 133 [see Chapter 4], who perhaps speak more quickly than Les because they are not distracted by their sex plots). Excepting Les Patterson, Sandy Stone is Humphries' slowest talker. In "Sandy Agonistes," for example, he speaks thirty-nine words per minute. Even so, of course, Sandy cannot be said to have sex on the brain.

Although in Chapter 1 of *The Traveller's Tool* Les suggests that his point of distinction is his "appendage,"[124] in Chapter 2, "What Is Australian Style?" he notes that it is also his style, specifically "Aussie style": [125] thus, his autobiography seems to consist of appendage-adages of an Aussie. His commentary on style recalls his performance on *The Dame Edna Christmas Experience* (ITV, 1987) of the song "You've Either Got or You Haven't Got Style," with Roger Moore and Dennis Healey. Part of his style strategy is actually to evade discussing style: his digression is Gwen Patterson, whom he introduces not by name but generically, simply as "my wife (former model Bambi Dolan),"[126] thus categorizing her as an appendage and a parenthetical plaything. That she is an appendage related to Les's phallic appendage becomes apparent when he discloses that, "In her day, Gwennie was the highest paid hand model in Australia – though I always got it on the house." He adds injury to insult when he says: "But I guess Gwen's price might have dropped if the lens had travelled north of her wrist. God love her."[127] His invocation seems appropriate because surely the God of suffering loves the long-suffering Gwen, the short form of whose name means "blessed" in Welsh.[128]

Like Nerida Murphy, she is "a good Catholic,"[129] and, like a sea nymph, she knows how to drown a man when necessary. Les tends to equate Aussie style with events at the beach – "Let's face it though; style comes naturally to Australians. Look at our lifesavers"[130] – and he opposes the knockers who contend that the beaches are unsafe. He even offers an alternative theory (abduction by the Chinese Navy) for the death of Australian prime minister Harold Holt, who reputedly drowned off Cheviot Beach, Victoria, in 1967. He then concedes, with characteristic subtlety: "Thanks to our super-stylish shore squads, Aussie beaches are safe for everyone except swimmers and the occasional seventeen-year-old female sunworshipper who never guessed she had a surprise appointment with fifteen surf studs behind a changing facility."[131] But is the subtlety here Patterson's, or perhaps Humphries'?

I believe Humphries may be using Les, an unabashed woman-basher, or womanizer, not only to finger just such men as rapists but also to show the rapaciousness of men generally: he lists diplomats and judges, as well as lifeguards and himself, as engaged in "the shagging stakes."[132] But Les, after hinting that Australian beaches are safe, gives the finger to lifesavers who, while they are occupied with raping a young woman, taking her life, as it were, have left the beach unprotected for swimmers, for future Harold Holts. Les's mockery is evident in complimentary phrases such "super-stylish" and "surprise appointment." Both Humphries and Patterson point out the criminal irony of men's sexual behaviour. But the subtlety of their shared discourse arises out of the fact that both Nerida Murphy and Gwen Patterson, as sea nymphs, are protecting swimmers while lifesavers drive their stakes through an unsuspecting woman, who, because she is generic, unidentified except by incidence, age, and religion, might well be a sea nymph, whose style is to find a line of resistance to use against her rapists.

This line, or storyline, which might have recorded how the woman broke her appointment with rape, does not appear in Les's commentary on style. Yet, by deferring to "the occasional seventeen-year-old female sun-worshipper," whose story, Les seems to suggest, is her own to tell, he seems to regard her not, in the manner of the lifesaver gang-rapists, as a non-person but, rather, as a "non" person, *une femme qui dit "non"* ("a woman who says 'no'"), somewhat as Les says "no" in his appendage-adage "no worries." His assault account recalls his earlier stipulation, "between you and me I don't reckon this is a book for women neither,"[133] which now seems to have been made to save women from the occasion of rape, through the salvific intervention of Nerida and Gwen, who, by even their nominal presence, subvert men's rape fantasy. As nominally attendant nymphs, they save the woman from seamen/semen. As amanuensis, Nerida takes down Les (humiliating him) when she takes down his words and opens a space, however small, for women in male discourse. When Les concedes, "let's face it, Gwen's human,"[134] Nerida seems to conclude that, if Gwen is human and blessed, then men, in their rapacity, must be animals.

The chapter sequence of *The Traveller's Tool* is episodic, even picaresque, as Les, the picaroon, conducts the reader through his series of speech acts, sex acts. But, like Barry McKenzie, who constantly anticipates sex but never actually has it, Les Patterson constantly recalls sexual encounters in a reported past that, as story content, may always be adjudged "not to have been." Les Patterson's actual narratorial distance from sex, in an autobiography that purports to be about his sex life, first becomes evident in Chapter 3, which is about homosexuality in Australia.

While debating whether Sydney is a "Pooftah's Paradise," Les is careful to protest (and obviously a bit too much) his distance from gay men and sexual practice: "Well, all I can say is that I've knocked around the traps and I've lived in Australia man and boy for donkey's years, and in all that time nobody's every tried to slip their pollywaffle up my doughnut."[135] This very funny euphemistic language only emphasizes his distance from sex in general. *The Traveller's Tool* is about sex because its content is consistently sexual. Les, however, is about the sex act both because he is obsessed with sex and because he is all around sex (sniffing around it, as it were) more than he is engaged in it, in the Barthesian pleasure of telling, that of an Author who has died (i.e., climaxed) in the narratorial present. Even his disquisition on homosexuality in Sydney, his hometown, turns into a patriotic speech on Australia: "I hope, during the course of this publication, to explode many other myths and to provide a scholarly rebuttal to shithouse fallacies pertaining to my homeland."[136] Even his fantasies about women who "bang like a shithouse door," or like a changing room door at the beach, turn fallacious as he uses the discourse of sex to comment on everything "about" or around sex, from nationalism and marriage to tourism and language.

His commentary on Gwen and their family life, in Chapter 4, "The Home Front: The Woman Behind Me*" ("*At the time of writing, she's thirteen thousand miles behind me"[137]), is, in its surface meaning, a series of wife jokes, of mocking insults – for example "As a shag she might score zero, but she's ace at washing, ironing and keeping a man's tucker warm"[138] – but in its deep structure the commentary reveals much about Gwen: that she is dyslexic; that she refuses to sleep in the same room with Les when she has her period; that her former bridesmaid, Brigit, and her Auntie Kath are both nuns; that she rarely smiles in photographs; that her daughter, Karen, has a learning disability and a speech impediment; and that "Gwen's one of nature's givers."[139] Even though Les moves on to other subjects, leaving her "thirteen thousand miles behind me," Gwen remains in the reader's consciousness through these details about her, which not only give definition to her flat "Mrs Micawber" character but also define her own undoubtedly gynocentric narrative waiting to be told, the improbable narrative of a woman who puts up with the insufferable Les Patterson. But mainly the reader is enticed by the credible narrative of a nymph-woman whose story-content Les, and his readers, have never really known, except in her role as the long-suffering drudge and as the butt-end of Les's endless take-my-wife jokes. Gwen Patterson and Beryl Stone should really get together and write a book on their lives with, and without, their insufferable men.

In his address to prospective tourists to Australia, to his male-membered audience in "So You're Coming Down Under?" (Chapter 5), Les offers some advice that is as unreliable as is his advice on family and sexual matters: "Don't forget your bathers, or 'swimming togs' as we call them in Australia. The briefer the better if you've got a nice bit of hose-pipe to flash."[140] If Les had ever listened to the words of Eric Idle's "Penis Song (Not the Noël Coward Song)," which could easily be his signature tune, he would have heard some sage counter-advice, even endorsed with a phrase from Bazza McKenzie's sex-lexicon:

> So three cheers for your Willy or John Thomas,
> Hooray for your one-eyed trouser snake,
> Your piece of pork, your wife's best friend,
> Your Percy or your cock,
> You can wrap it up in ribbons,
> You can slip it in your sock,
> But don't take it out in public,
> Or they will stick you in the dock,
> And you won't come back.

So if tourists were to follow Les's advice, they might earn themselves a misdemeanor conviction, maybe on Mornington Beach in Melbourne or Avalon Beach near Sydney, and then be forbidden to "come back" to Australia, or, as Les prefers to phrase it, to "come Down Under."

Commenting on the film *Monty Python's Life of Brian* (1979), Robert Stam notes how "the Romans in this pseudobiblical epic have comic-phallic names such as Naughtius Maximus and Biggus Dickus, names that recall carnival's penchant for mocking the body's protuberances."[141] Les Patterson's phallogocentric haunts of strip clubs and massage parlours, and his trysts under desks and behind the water cooler, or in "a Dettol-scented Singapore motel room,"[142] conjure up a carnivalesque that, as in Stam's view of *Life of Brian*, parodies that which sticks out, especially in the minds of Humphries' readers. The phallo-parody is attributable to Patterson as much as it is to Humphries, both of whom are "latter-day echoes of Bakhtin's clown."[143] Patterson's sexual encounters are undoubtedly, in Stam's phrase, "subversive pleasures." As an invasive sexual player, Les always subverts his female partners.

For example, attempting to dispel the rumour, circulated by "a pommie women's magazine (probably run by a bunch of stoney-faced old skirt-lifters)," that Australian men do not go in for foreplay, he offers testimonial evidence: "That's a dirty lie. I've asked around my political colleagues and peer group, and every bloke I've talked to says he never gives his wife one without first asking if she's awake."[144] Nigerian-born British writer Buchi Emecheta has heard this sentiment before, from the mouth of her character Albert Okolo, one of whose domestic practices is noctambulatory sex (i.e.,

having intercourse with his wife, Kehinde, even while she is sleeping).[145]
Kehinde, who is pregnant, berates Albert:

How am I to know, enh? I always warn you not to bother me when I'm asleep.
Haven't I been warning you that it could happen? When you wanted to come inside
me earlier on in our marriage, you used to be so nice. You took the trouble to wake
me up with love. Now you're always impatient. You grip my breasts from behind as
if you're going to force yourself on me, and before I know what you're about,
you're done. I don't even know if you're using any protection or not. So I hope
you're not doing like Nigerian men and suggesting it's *my* fault.[146]

Les Patterson's joke about Australian men, which is also a joke played on
Australian women, conceals Humphries' serious comment on "gender
wars" – as Brian Fawcett negotiates them in *Gender Wars: A Novel and
Some Conversation about Sex and Gender* (1994) – and on offences ranging from sexual assault to domestic impropriety, which are offences against
love and niceness.

After offering detailed instructions on how to smuggle goods through
Heathrow customs under the ruse of breaking a bottle of whisky, Les turns
directly to his audience to implicate them not only in the smuggling strata-
gem but also in the sticky matter of his own DNA, dropping them through
the wet paper bag with the whisky bottle: "If you're anything like me – and
something tells me you are – every time you try to smuggle any gear
through the Green, you strike a luggage trolley with a dud wheel which
keeps veering in the direction of the dickheads in uniforms as though
drawn by bloody magnetism."[147] Humphries' "luggage trolley" conceit anticipates Dame Edna Everage's cheeky evocation of the actor Jack Palance
in her anecdote, which Edna recounts to guests Roseanne Barr and Tom
Arnold in the TV program *It's Edna Time* (1993), about having seen him in
a Hollywood grocery store: "You know, I was in a supermarket recently
and I saw Jack Palance, and he was lurching from one side of the aisle to
the other. I thought, 'He's got the cart with the wobbly wheel,' I thought. I
gave him the benefit of the doubt." This is one of Humphries' greatest wit-
ticisms, and a fine tribute to Mr Palance. Patterson's graphic "luggage trolley" image might distract readers from his conditional clause and his
dashed off realization, but they will eventually come back to the possibility
that they are "anything like" Les. Of course, Les makes up 33 and one-
third percent of Les Autres.

But even men who are better groomed and better behaved than Les – is
there anyone who isn't? – have spittle, semen, mucous, blood, urine, and fe-
ces in common with him, not to mention libidinous predilections. Each
male reader is a Dada replica of Sir Les Patterson; he may even feel inclined
to call Les a readymade Dada. And, like any good father, Les teaches his

boys how to be a cheat, a crook, a womanizer, a homophobe, and a racist. When he tells them "I'm not a regular church goer" and "if I've got a huge responsibility to my wife, the Lady Patterson, it's the responsibility of never letting her find out where I put it every night,"[148] they probably believe him, once they get over the shock: the shock of being told in the first place, and the aftershock of recognizing their Les-ness.

His Chapter 7, "Body Language: At Home and Abroad," a primer on how the male body, through cunning linguistic signs, can procure the female body, is also an exegesis of Les's male discourse in particular and sexual discourse in general. In the distinctive cadences of his speech, his peculiar idiom and syntax, and the text's heterodox typography, readers sense the movement of his body round the stage: how he sways his hips, how he swaggers and "flaps" when he walks, how he drops his jaw or twists his buttocks to let out wind, how he erupts into globules and drizzles of spittle. All his bodily movements, even his evacuations and ejaculations, are evident (in his scatological scat) to any reader who has seen Les Patterson's unforgettable performances onstage or on TV or video, his one-man shows, and his acts as *compère* without peer in Dame Edna's famous sharings before theatre and mediatized audiences.

As someone who claims to have "the Gift of Tongues,"[149] Les could prove to be either a disciple on whom the Holy Ghost has descended and who is intent on passing on his inspiration to readers, or a lecher who has sold his soul to the Devil (e.g., to Peter Cook as George Spiggott [Satan] in Stanley Donan's film *Bedazzled* [1967], in which Humphries played Envy) and is now intent on slipping readers the tongue. Given his male audience and his homophobia, gifting his male readers by slipping them the tongue seems unlikely, so it follows that Les would appear to be a disciple of the Holy Ghost.

I am joking, of course, but only by half. That Gwen is "a good Catholic" and Les admits to having had a "strict Mick upbringing"[150] suggests the probability that they received the Sacrament of Confirmation (whether in the Roman Catholic Church or the Church of England does not matter), when the Holy Spirit would have descended upon them. Whereas Gwen has remained close to the Spirit, no doubt relying on its cathartic power to protect her from Les's various contaminating fluids and stains, Les would appear to have wandered into sexual depravity. Yet the "maxicosm" is filled with depraved people, many of them confirmed as children, and no amount of depravity will ever exorcise the Spirit from them. Like the depraved and the blessed, Les is stuck with the Spirit. Perhaps the Spirit's cleansing action protects Les from contracting venereal diseases: the Spirit sticks with him, even as he "sticks" women. Perhaps the man who prides himself on his expertise in "coming Down Under" finds a moral balance in a Spirit that has deigned to come down upon him. The Spirit might even have inspired Les to compile his register of remedies for removing "travel stains."[151]

Sometimes Les Patterson seems capable of divining the beauty of life, as on his Cheese Board trip to Amsterdam: "To see attractive young girls on tandem bicycles with their boyfriends behind them moving quietly up their canals on a summer evening is soothing yet strangely stimulating."[152] Les, of course, like Edna, can be quite Socratic in scattering sexual innuendo. Their ironies are often so subtle that Les and Edna – I must apologize to Dame Edna for joining them in a sentence – seem not to realize that their utterances are shocking. But whereas Edna chastizes her audience, telling them to "get their minds out of the gutter," Les punctuates all his stories with the assurance "are you with me?" which seems to urge his audience to cock their ears for the overtone of *double entendre* and the undertone of *double entente* ("double understanding"). If one had any doubts about the tonality of his reference to Amsterdam cyclists, Les clarifies it when he adds: "Amsterdam is chock-a-block with Art Galleries too and there is no better place for picking up a nice bit of stray."[153] Are male readers still willing to count themselves among Les Autres, when Les turns cycling into a bestial sex act and refers to women as "stray" animals? Or have they misjudged Les?

Perhaps they could not dissociate themselves from Les if they wanted to. Humphries seems to be saying that every living thing in the universe, even the moral universe, is connected: a lecher to the Holy Spirit, his wife to a sea nymph, sex to cycling, animals to human beings, what is outside fiction to what is within it, even the squirmiest of readers to the slipperiest of characters. Thus, when Les tours Amsterdam's red light district and describes the prostitutes in their shop windows, he refers to these *tableaux* as "female installations."[154] The similarity of Les's wording and Humphries' (in reference to Dame Edna) in his interview at the Banff Television Festival (1997) – "In a sense, Edna is a sort of artistic creation. You might almost call her a living installation"[155] – suggests a moral bond, if only through art and autobiography, between a courtesan and a Dame at court, despite the obvious disparities of their society and class. Edna documents this bond in a photograph, snapped by her son Kenny, showing her and a courtesan at the door of the massage parlor where she has finally managed to track down her husband, Norm.[156]

If any readers feel uncomfortable being numbered among Les Autres, for example because Les is an incorrigible sexist womanizer, his autobiography offers a counter-argument. Once he recites his formula of political correctness, "I yield to none in my abhorrence of," he hoists himself on his own petard by documenting his sexual adventures. The self-contradiction is very funny. But his formula is not a political speech-writer's glib motherhood remark: it is Les's literal statement of his subject position as an unabashedly

Table 5.8
Methinks Sir Les the Lady-Killer Doth Protest Too Much

| "Body Language" | "Patterson's Blue Guide: Tokyo" | "Patterson's Blue Guide: Hamburg" | "Where I'm Coming From" |
|---|---|---|---|
| I yield to none in my abhorrence of sexism, but secretarial work, even at a senior executive level in the Commonwealth Government of Australia, can have moments of tedium and it behoves a senior public servant like myself to give the independent, liberated and randy young women who work under me an exciting and meaningful leisure incentive across the board at the end of the day, *are you with me?* (63) | I yield to none in my abhorrence of sexual discrimination in the workplace and there are even times when I let women walk all over me, especially in an up-market Tokyo bath house. A man lies flat on his face and those little yellow dolls go walkabout on your arse. It hurts like buggery at first but if you're still alive after the cold plunge and a little snooze in a cardboard cubicle, you come out of these joints ready for anything. (98) | I yield to none in my abhorrence of sexual discrimination in the workplace but, funnily enough, international conferences are invariably stag affairs. It's surprising how few ladies, God love them, sit on the Australian Cheese, Fillum, Opera and Disabled Puppet Boards for instance, but I guess someone's got to stay home and cook tea. That being so, I was amazed to see one solitary sheilah aboard the chartered jumbo taking our delegation to Hamburg for last year's Cheese Week. (107) | I yield to none in my abhorrence of chauvinism. I love women and women love me. I can't get enough of them, though I bet they sometimes wish they could accommodate a little less of me. But I don't give my all to the womenfolk, and if you don't believe me ask Geoff Bolton, the manager of my local sperm bank, to take you on a guided tour of the vaults and show you the Patterson Vat. Geoff reckons it's incredible the number of childless couples who specifically request a red-hot burst of L.P. Sauce. (136) |

sexual creature, whether monster or man. His "abhorrence" of "sexism," "sexual discrimination," and "chauvinism" as evils from which, in an etymological sense, he shrinks, is mild in comparison to the part of him that grows in the excitements at the office, in bath houses, on diplomatic flights, and at the sperm bank. His claim "I yield to none in my abhorrence of sexism [etc.]" is simply an equivocal double negative, as if he were to say, "I yield to everyone (every woman to whom I desire to give 'one') in my love of sexism [etc.] and I expect everyone to yield to me." His utterance is not just idiom but the formula of a lady-killer. And he knows his readers know it.

As a showman, not a womanizer but a music hall chairman intent on telling his own story, Les Patterson bears some resemblance to Dada showman Marcel Duchamp, specifically in 1966, on the eve of his eightieth birthday and a retrospective exhibition of his work at the Tate Gallery, to which organizer Richard Hamilton submitted a reconstruction of the famous *The Bride Stripped Bare of Her Bachelors, Even, or the Large Glass* (1915–16). In an interview at the time, Duchamp observed that, in the *Large Glass*, he had tried to make "something that wouldn't be anecdotal" but, rather, "something else where the grey matter would come in as an instrument of measure."[157] Duchamp's comment also marks out *The Traveller's Tool* as an autobiography and imprints Humphries as an autobiographer in a mock turtle.

Humphries would appear to agree with Duchamp as an artist who rejected what he called "retinal painting" (ranging from vanishing-point perspective representational art to Op art) in favour of painting that bypassed or surpassed the retinal eye for the "I" in "Intellect." In *The Traveller's Tool* Humphries seems to be encouraging his readers to bypass or surpass what appears to the eye: the typography of the page, his comic material, and the surface, the skinful, if you will, of his character's phallogocentric life. *The Traveller's Tool* is not about Les Patterson as he appears to the eye. It is about the "I" as it appears in the intellects of readers, the "I" not of Les Patterson's telling but of their knowledge and understanding of themselves, especially as Les Autres. Thus, each male reader looks beyond typography at his own mirror-image of *un vrai type* ("a guy"), *un drôle de type* ("a queer fish"), or just *un type* ("an individual").

*The Traveller's Tool* consists of seventeen chapters and two appendices ("Les's Large Appendage: A Glossary of Australian Language" and "Important Addresses for a Man on the Move"), and it includes more than fifty individual sections designated by titles and headings. Yet none of these divisions is an anecdote, even though the work as a whole appears to be anecdotal, recounting humorous incidents. Clearly, Les, who sees the mouth primarily as "laughing gear,"[158] wants to make his readers laugh: he knows he is funny; he knows his language and opinions are amusing; he knows his *escapades* (in French, the word can connote a boy's prank) are ridiculous; but he also knows that what he gives out is not anecdote, not narrative, but another matter.

What matters to him is not just funny material, in the sense that a stand-up comedian stands behind a microphone and does his or her material. What matters more to him is Duchamp's "grey matter ... as an instrument of measure," which, in his phallogocentric haze, Les would probably interpret to mean ejaculate: semen from the instrument with which he measures his life and measures out his autobiography. But, incredible as it might seem, Les is also concerned with the more obvious kind of grey matter – intellect – as measured out in the nerve tissue of the brain and spinal cord. Les would undoubtedly dismiss intellects as "ratbags," "pooftahs," and "arrogant dickheads," but for the intellect itself he seems to have a soft spot, a kind of "Lucky Spot," in Sandy Stone's language. Unlike Mordecai Himmelfarb, in Patrick White's *Riders in the Chariot* (1961), who observes, "The intellect has failed us,"[159] Les Patterson seems to have faith in the human capacity for knowledge and understanding.

For example, readers of *The Traveller's Tool* will increase their knowledge of such practical matters of Derridean phallogocentric etiquette as national beverages, sex holidays in international cities, and stain removal.[160] They will also come to two types of understanding: (1) a better understanding of their membership in Les Autres and of the company they may or may not keep with womanizers, lechers, and sexual predators; and (2) a fuller understanding of Sir Leslie Colin Patterson as an intellect, albeit a paradoxical music hall intellect, whose act is, by telling outlandish stories about the person audiences imagine him to be, to appeal to thinking people, people still capable of independent thought outside the checks of political correctness (which I prefer to call "political correctitude" and which Humphries has called "the new American disease")[161] and to hold a mirror up to their nature, the mirror into which Humphries also gazes in order to perceive himself.[162]

To be one of Les Autres, if only in one's capacity as a reader of *The Traveller's Tool*, even an unwilling reader, is to measure oneself against Les Patterson's instrument, and, just in case you think you will inevitably come up short, I hasten to add that I mean the instrument of his autobiography. If your life is not a series of sexual conquests – of sexist, racist, xenophobic, and alcoholic slurs, and of phallogocentric logos that would make even Jacques Derrida blush – then what is it? Les recounts his life in *The Traveller's Tool*, which will have to stand for Les Autres until they write their own lives.

Derrida, in fact, would not be embarrassed by Les's lascivious prose. As an intellect himself, Derrida would undoubtedly know how to understand Humphries' methodology in Les Patterson:

Because of the literary dimension, what "phallogocentric" texts display is immediately suspended. When someone stages a hyperbolically phallocentric discourse or mode of behaviour, s/he does not subscribe to it by signing the work, s/he describes and, describing it as such, s/he exposes it, displays it. Whatever the assumed attitude of the author on the matter, the *effect* can be paradoxical and sometimes "deconstructive."[163]

Derrida clearly categorizes Humphries' methodology in *The Traveller's Tool*: Les Patterson is a music hall foil who exposes the audience's gender, race, and class pretensions. As Humphries himself has said – in a Derridean mode if not exactly in Derridean terminology – "only a real dumdum believes that the bigotries of a fictitious character are shared by his inventor."[164] But, given that the by-line on the title page of *The Traveller's Tool* is "Sir Les Patterson" and that Les does not acknowledge

Humphries in his autobiography (not even on the copyright page), perhaps Les, and not (just) Humphries, is responsible for staging a Derridean show of phallogocentrism.

A mock turtlenecked Humphries, defending his character, would seem to agree: "Les Patterson's cheerful vulgarity is condemned on all sides in his homeland and is dismissed as a scurrilous anachronism. Les is by turns long-winded and laconic, and he has a knack of stating the obvious at length, which is particularly Australian."[165] As if in a double turn Les seems to agree with Humphries: "Whenever I talk in public I get laughs, particularly in the States and Pommieland where they seem to think the Australian turn of phrase is funny."[166] Les Patterson knows he is funny, but he seems indignant that, in the United States and England (and, one presumes, other places where people, non-intellects, only "seem to think"), not many people, excluding Les Autres, recognize his serious intent or even that he is capable of it. "Les Patterson, a serious parodist? A music hall clown? A Dada prankster? A card-carrying Derridean? You can't be serious!" (I imagine Dame Edna formulating these phrases.)

### DAME EDNA EVERAGE IN THE GARDEN OF DELIGHT

In conversation with Jim Davidson in 1986, Humphries summarized the connotations of the names "Edna Everage" and "Norman Everage": "Edna Everage as in 'average,' husband Norm as in 'normal.'"[167] But, given that the name "Edna" derives from the Hebrew *ednah*, meaning "pleasure" and "delight," and has associations with the Garden of Eden,[168] Edna can figure as Eve, or possibly even as Lilith (Adam's first wife, according to Jewish oral tradition), and her married name, Everage, can be seen as signifying the rage of Eve, which, of course, often comes out on stage. The name "Edna" derives also from the Pseudepigraphical Book of Enoch (ca. 200–150 BCE), a fragment, in Aramaic, from the Dead Sea Scrolls (Qumran Cave 4).[169] The Book of Enoch comprises three volumes. The sole reference to Edna, Enoch's wife, is in 1 Enoch 85:1–3, in Enoch's series of dream visions:

And after this I saw another dream, and I will show the whole dream to thee, my son. And Enoch lifted up (his voice) and spake to his son Methuselah: "To thee, my son, will I speak: hear my words – incline thine ear to the dream-vision of thy father. Before I took thy mother Edna, I saw in a vision on my bed, and behold."[170]

In *My Gorgeous Life* Edna tells Norm, right after their wedding ceremony, "I adore you just as you are, even if you're as old as Methuselah."[171] She is acknowledging her link with Methuselah's mother and conceding that, however much older Norman is than she, in Biblical time, she would have to have been one generation older than he.

Drawing on her ancient forebear – I can hear Dame Edna say, "In a previous life, I was Methuselah's mother!" – Edna Everage transforms the Qumran Edna from an obscure woman, taken by man, to *une grande dame* who can give without being taken, a "caring and sharing" woman who can be magnanimous without men, even the man Norman, and even when she calls herself "Mrs Norman Everage." Edna Everage is a visionary, not the wife of one. But, like Enoch of the Dead Sea Scrolls and the Old Testament Book of Genesis, Edna Everage, I reckon, will live to be 350 years old!

Edna Everage became Edna Mae Beazley only by back-formation, as, in the years since he gave birth to her in 1955, Humphries fleshed out her character, most fully in her autobiography, *My Gorgeous Life: An Adventure* (1989), published in the United States as *My Gorgeous Life: The Life, the Loves, the Legend* (1989). Humphries figures in her autobiography more than she figures in his, albeit only in the character of her irritating manager, somewhat as in Alex Xenophon Demirjian Grey's autobiography, *Memoirs of Many in One* (1986), Patrick White (the putative author, as is Humphries of *My Gorgeous Life*) figures as the editor.

Barry Humphries and Edna Everage's lives are intertwined in *My Gorgeous Life* so that sometimes their voices are barely distinguishable from each other. According to Lahr, even when backstage, Humphries may persist in speaking in Edna's voice.[172] For example, do you recall who said this? "I did not mind doctors so much, because it was their job to listen, and I was happy to talk to them endlessly on my favourite subject – myself." Does it sound, perhaps, like Dame Edna Everage? Actually, the speaker is Barry Humphries,[173] speaking, one presumes, in his own voice.

In titling his preface in *More Please* "Alzheimer Remembers," is Humphries not plagiarizing Dame Edna's title for Chapter 3 of *My Gorgeous Life* - "Oldtimer's Disease," – in effect identifying himself as a kidnapper not just of language but also of her first-born child, Lois, even though Dame Edna attributes the abduction to "a rogue koala," which she identifies by its "unmistakable footprints."[174] But everybody knows how easily koala footprints can be faked, especially by a person with a reputation for Dada pranks and replications. Even Dame Edna is aware that Barry Humphries read *My Gorgeous Life* (1989) before writing his own autobiography (1992) as she seems to send out a veiled message to him (as Lois's captor) when she says, "I know all women reading this book whose kiddies have gone off with marsupials will identify with me"; and when she says, "Perhaps somewhere in the world my lost daughter may be reading these words now."[175] In Dame Edna's account, Humphries is parodying the Australian news story of the disappearance of baby Azaria Chamberlain in 1980 from a campsite near Ayers Rock (Uluru) when the inquest ruled she had been abducted by a dingo. But her mother, Lindy Chamberlain, was later convicted, and then acquitted, of murder. The story was even the subject of an Australian film directed by Fred Schepisi, *A Cry in the Dark* (1988).

As Edna, Humphries extended his marsupial parody in his and David Mitchell's 1998 ABC television series, *Flashbacks*:

*When Azaria Chamberlain was abducted by a dingo – and I happen to know it was a dingo – I felt such a strong sense of identification because my own daughter, Lois, had been stolen from me. I'd missed the early-morning feed and Lois was taken from me by a rogue koala. They found the footprints on the verandah and in the bush nearby. My daughter has never reappeared – in the same way as Azaria. My theory and that of many zoologists is that she could still be with a caring koala family. I hope so, and I hope one of those koalas is watching this programme and that my daughter comes back to me. She will not be as she was, bless her heart. She'll be older and of course she'll be feral. She will reek, certainly, of eucalyptus leaves, but she'll be my daughter all the same and she'll be very, very welcome.*[176]

Phrases such as "a rogue koala," "a caring koala family," and "one of these koalas … watching this programme" are Dame Edna's coded message to little Lois's kidnapper. Clearly, no one fits the description "rogue koala" better than Barry Humphries.

Dame Edna's "Ode to Koala Blue" (1983), purportedly an occasional poem written for the opening of Olivia Newton John's boutique Koala Blue (in Los Angeles),[177] is really an appeal to the "rogue koala" Barry Humphries to release Lois. In the early 1980s, Dame Edna often wore frocks with koala patterns – notably her "Marsupial Dress," designed by Bill Goodwin[178] – undoubtedly to send a message to Barry the Rogue Koala, "LET LOIS GO!" I am disappointed that in his most recent book, *My Life as Me*, he does not reveal what he has done with Lois, nor whether Dame Edna has met his ransom demands.

To hear Edna's Mosaic outcry "let my daughter go!" is to enter her throat, not her digestive tract but her respiratory and vocal tract, the entr'acte of her speech performances, as though *My Gorgeous Life* were simply a spoken interlude between two of her stage shows, between, say, *Back with a Vengeance* (1987–88) and *Look at Me When I'm Talking to You* (1993). To read *My Gorgeous Life* is to hear Dame Edna's throaty voice, to get stuck in her throat. The word "gorgeous," as well as meaning "brilliantly beautiful" and "delightful," has connotations with the throat. The word's Old French derivation survives in the contemporary French *la gorge*, which means "throat" or "neck." As distinguished from Barry McKenzie, who is associated with disgorging himself, both in speech bubbles and through vomiting, Dame Edna Everage gorges her audiences, as if stuffing so many fowls in the *poulailler* (see Note 96, Chapter 1), and she also gorges on her audiences, devouring them through her delightful wit and charm, taking them into her throat, the site of her speech and song acts, and of Humphries' magical cross-gender vocalizations (and not, as he would undoubtedly have it, of a Les Patterson kissing or fellatio fantasy with the woman he has always desired – Edna). Ironically, Les Patterson does not mention Edna Everage in *The Traveller's Tool*, yet she touches on him several times in *My Gorgeous Life*.

Edna Everage seems to invoke Les Patterson, throat man, first through the objective correlative of her father, Bruce Beazley (or Beasley), who, she relates, had "always longed to be in ladies' underwear" before he became "your friendly Electrolux man," a travelling vacuum cleaner salesman who always gave "the lucky housewife a demonstration suck." Included among the "lucky housewi[ves]" was Edna's mother, Gladys Sloggertt, "as her inquisitive hands came to rest on her very first crevice nozzle," and they fell in love.[179] Edna Everage has another genealogical connection with Les Patterson. Karen-Lee and Craig, the children of her son Brucie and his wife Joylene, seem to have been named after Les and Gwen Patterson's children, Karen and Craig. One cannot begin to imagine what inspired this christening pattern.

Les makes his appearance in *My Gorgeous Life* when Edna, after recalling having "met him briefly at Ann Forbes's place,"[180] now greets him at the door as her date at what she has described as her "first big dance."[181] Les comes across as the original version of a man who now cannot stop replicating himself: "My heart sank. He was certainly a lot older than I thought and smoking too with the ash already sprinkled down the front of his slightly greasy dinner jacket."[182] Later, "He took a glass out of my father's hand to everyone's astonishment, helped himself to an enormous slug of port, some of which trickled on to his far from snowy shirt."[183] As well as introducing readers to early instances of Edna's censorious tone, Les serves the function of bringing Edna and Norman Everage together at the dance.

Just as in *A Time for Judas* (1983) Morley Callaghan makes a sympathetic case for Judas as a collaborator in Christ's redemptive sacrifice, so one might make a case for Les as a sympathetic figure who sacrifices himself for a greater good – the happiness of two other people. Edna seems to recognize his salvific role but only after she swallows her disgust and agrees to dance with him:

Les downed his lager in one gulp and dragged me on to the dancefloor still with a moustache of froth on his upper lip. In the hope that no one would recognise me I pressed my face to his soggy shirt front as he trundled me around the room pumping my right arm out of tempo. His other arm was locked around my neck and every now and then he would push his face over my shoulder and take a drag on the

Turf he had going in his right hand. No single experience of pain and anguish in my life ever seemed to last as long as that sickening circuit; not even my son Kenny's difficult birth or the time I nearly poisoned Prince Charles. But they are dramatic stories I must remember to tell you some other time.[184]

In its sexuality, the scene oozes with Les, and even ends with the birth of a child, but it is even more remarkable for how, like a choreographer, Humphries has contrived the scene, noting precisely how the dancers' bodies should be positioned in what is, in Edna's mind, a kind of obscene *pas de deux*.

But at the end of her dance with Les, as Edna runs off to the ladies' powder room, disgusted, ready to go home, "a little voice inside said, 'You're meant to be here tonight, Edna. Tonight is spookily special.'"[185] Is this the voice of conscience, the voice of Eros, or Rrose Sélavy? Or is it perhaps the voice of Les Patterson, "little" because whispered, and perhaps reminiscent of his "slightly common voice on the phone,"[186] reminding Edna that he has introduced her to Norman and is perhaps not so very different from her husband? "'Excuse I, remember me?' said a soft voice behind me,"[187] echoing the "little" conscientious voice of Les, as distinguished from his grating voice – *ca voix, c'est gratin* ("his voice is too much," i.e., like grated cheese.) Les developed this mode of address while chairman of the Australian Chapter of the International Cheese Board. He is an antithetical man of conscience.

Les appears again in *My Gorgeous Life* in the form of his heterodox typography, as Edna comes across a story in the "*Morning Murdoch*" reporting Les Patterson's appointment as "Australia's International Cultural Ambassador world-wide." Edna's double take, "the thought of that yobbo Patterson, whom I had known of old, stepping into *my* job, was chunderous!"[188] takes Les to task for his opportunism but also takes readers back, in the clause "whom I had known of old," to his kindness to Edna at the dance. In its surface meaning her word "yobbo" emphasizes that Les is a yob, or a lout, but in its deep structure it hints that, despite his perceived villainies, he remains that kind boy on the dance floor.

The other villain who lingers like a pustulant sore throughout the narrative is Barry Humphries, who, as a character in somebody else's autobiography, resembles not only Patrick White in *Memoirs of Many in One* but also Dr Meyer de Lamphrey, Humphries' alter ego in the Barry McKenzie comic strips, a helpful person whose kindnesses the autobiographer resents as intrusive. With Chaucer, and the canon's yeoman, Edna would say of Les Patterson and Humphries' assistance, "*profred servyse Stynketh.*"[189]

As Les makes his "positively final appearance"[190] in *My Gorgeous Life* typographically (or type-illogically), Barry Humphries makes his positively first appearance according to type, in the form of a cheeky letter from "a young actor in Melbourne" to Edna Everage, importuning her to "spare an hour or more of your valuable time to see me and perhaps help me in my research. I suppose I want to pick your brains."[191] But in disclosing his plan to stage "a kind of revue or variety show about Australian suburban life trying to point out its funny side," in which one of the characters is "a housewife who has just been on her first overseas trip,"[192] Humphries seems also to reveal his plot to "pick" not just her brains but every organ on her donor card and, in Stanislavskian fashion, to take over her life.

However, in her final reaction to his request, Edna reveals that she will always outmuscle Humphries, disemvowelling his name to reduce it to the interjection "Hmmph!"[193] By interrupting him here, she effectively scuttles his stage show by setting him the example of interference. Thus, when Humphries makes his stage debut at the Assembly Hall, Melbourne, Edna condemns his performance in peremptory, interjectory tones: "He delivered this in a high-pitched squeak and, to make matters worse, he kept interrupting himself to giggle at his own stupid 'jokes.'"[194] Then she proceeds to condemn Humphries right to his cheeky face:

"Pretty good, I *don't think*! Pretty awful, more like it. I have never seen such twaddle and hoo-haa on stage in my life and I have just been to the West End of London!"
The woman's voice was mine.[195]

Evidently, Humphries' performance – as Sandy Stone and as his *huisvrouw* character, Edna[196] – has been shocking enough to separate Edna from her voice, which is like splitting Laughter from Laugh within the Bantu modality *Kuntu* (see Chapter 4). Her statement "the woman's voice was mine" must be hyperbolical because Edna Everage is as inseparable from her voice as, in the parallel universe outside *My Gorgeous Life*, the writer and artiste Barry Humphries is from the voices of Sandy Stone, Sir Les Patterson, Dame Edna Everage, and, indeed, Barry Humphries.

The character Barry Humphries next enters Edna's life when an impresario invites him to take the show to Sydney, "but only," as Edna puts it, "on condition I headed the cast ... I was the toast of that harbourside city and Barry Humphries was having to like it or lump it."[197] Edna's mentoring story is credible: the parallel Humphries (writer/artiste) also has learned to be a great character actor by playing the character Edna.

The character Humphries' next entrance on Edna's stage is typographical or telegrammatical, when Peter Cook drops his name and lets slip the news of the gig in a cable inviting Edna to London to perform at his club:

Famous poet John Betjeman has lent me one of your early microgrooves stop you have many fans in England and will be a big star here or I'm a dutchman stop have asked your manager Barry Humphries to bring show to my new London Club the establishment where we take the mickey out of things with Zany Wacky and irreverent humour and satire stop godspeed stop Peter Cook.[198]

Peter Cook's phrase "your manager Barry Humphries" places in apposition what Edna Everage must have foreseen only in opposition: Barry Humphries in any kind of position in what was shaping up to be her "brilliant career," a career that would rival Sybylla Melvyn's in *My Brilliant Career* (1901), or Miles Franklin's, for that matter, provided that upstart Humphries would not upstage her. After Norman convinces her of the pragmatism of letting Humphries manage her career – "You need a manager right now if you're going to hit the big time overseas, and although Barry's a bit of a drongo, better the devil you know"[199] – Edna signs the contract with Humphries and Cook.

But does she sign on because of her husband's persuasion or because Cook has already inked in the deal in a cablegram? Print finalizes this business deal and professional relationship as print finalizes Edna's autobiography and her relationship with her readers. Peter Cook's appositive "your manager Barry Humphries" is as irretrievable as <email + send> on the Internet, and it is as hardened a transaction as enamel.[200] Peter Cook apposes Edna and Barry professionally, as at the Assembly Hall, Melbourne, Edna stands in for Barry; as in Sydney she works as his headliner; and, finally, as in London, at the Establishment, when she does her act to an empty room. When Cook encourages Edna, telling her "on the quiet that the audience had all been drifting out to the bar through the Humphries section and he thought my material would catch on eventually with discerning people,"[201] he also sets up a "side by side," not a film by Bruce Beresford (1975) nor a musical by Stephen Sondheim (1976), but a life-partnership between Edna Everage and her manager.

As they figure in her autobiography, and in Dame Edna's life, Les Patterson and Barry Humphries appear to be nuisances. But, etymologically, a nuisance is someone who causes harm, and, in fact, Les and Barry are quite harmless, most obviously because they are characters but also because they do Edna good. Les introduces her to Norman Everage at the dance hall and, outside *My Gorgeous Life*, plays compère at many of her stage and television shows. Barry sets the stage for her career on the halls and, outside *My Gorgeous Life*, writes her scripts, produces her shows, and makes her publicity appearances. In this way, Les and Barry often give good Dame Edna the goods.

The authorial/historical Barry Humphries uses *My Gorgeous Life* to flesh out Dame Edna Everage's character as well as to tell an amusing story, his funniest and most imaginative narrative by his most complex and engaging narrator. The details of her life, the biographical data that

Humphries has written, adding to what Edna Everage reveals about herself onstage, are the equivalent of antecedent action in the theatre. But, in the end, what Edna tells her readers is less important than how she tells them – in her own words and in her own voice. Like theatre spectators and television viewers who know intellectually that Barry Humphries is portraying the character Dame Edna Everage, yet in their unconditional imaginations accept her as a human being, readers of *My Gorgeous Life* know intellectually that Barry Humphries is the author, yet they can imagine only Dame Edna speaking. They read Humphries' words, but they hear Edna's voice, and, after they have read this chapter, they will trace its sonorities back to the unrecorded voice of Edna, wife of Enoch (also known as Norman) and mother of Methuselah (a.k.a. Kenny), by inscribing Dame Edna's antecedent action, particularly in her opening words, "I'm probably Jewish."

Humphries also enfleshes her Hebraic ancestor, Edna, and traces her Jewish line, through the mother, right to the Garden of Ednah, to Eve, Lilith, the goddess, and through them to all women. Edna's lineage has other important links. When Prime Minister (now Dame) Margaret Thatcher stepped down from office in 1990, Dame Edna Everage seemed to become ever so much more officious. When Dame Barbara Cartland died, 21 May 2000, Dame Edna's wisteria hair is said to have turned pink with the shock.

Dame Edna, as autobiographer, comes alive, in the sense that even readers who are not metaphysicians believe they hear her in the flesh, less through mimesis (the content of her story) than through diegesis (how she relates her story). Whether Edna is a reliable narrator; whether Les Patterson is really a predatory womanizer and Barry Humphries a predatory agent; whether Douglas Allsop really drowns at Rotorua (as I imagine it, to the chorus of Flanders and Swann's "The Hippopotamus Song" [1960]: "Mud, mud, glorious mud"); all the whethers of telling are less important than the reality of hearing them in Edna's own words and in her own voice, tones, and cadences. For instance, when she places professional achievements and family blessings in the balance, Edna seems to come out wanting morally, but readers come out wanting more:

A queue at the box office, a microgroove in the charts or record ratings for a TV spectacular are the *real* honours in my life, not forgetting of course the love of my family. I must confess however, that at this stage I sometimes went whole days without those little mites in Melbourne crossing my mind; it's awful I know, but that's how it was.[202]

Some readers might wish to condemn Edna for child abuse; others might wish to credit Humphries with confessing to his own neglect of wives and children in his pursuit of fame; but most, I believe, would simply like Edna

to go on in her protestations of cruelty not because Humphries is under-
mining her through authorial detachment but, rather, because they know he
is mocking them. Still, they love her voice and image – unconditionally.

Much of the humour of *My Gorgeous Life* arises out of what Dame
Edna does not divulge about herself, and through this omission Humphries
seems to comment on autobiography as a genre of concealment, of not telling. Thus, as Edna neglects telling readers about her family, so she neglects
to tell them about her professional success:

Over the next few years as my family grew up I had bursts of success, it is true,
which I need not describe in detail. "Why not, Edna?" I hear you women ask. Because, Possums, quite frankly I'm not in the business of making my Readers jealous;
that is not the purpose of this book, which is to educate, inform, and inspire. I'm
terribly sorry but it is.[203]

As well as being hilarious, this comment points to Dame Edna's McLu-
hanesque mediatization of her audience: the teller and her act of telling are
paramount, not what is told. In her stage shows, as in her recent Broadway
show, *Dame Edna – The Royal Tour (The Show That Listens)*, Edna has
been known to make vocative remarks such as:

1 educate: "I don't really look at this as a show – any more than you do. I
   see it as a lovely conversation between two people, one of whom is very
   much more interesting than the other";
2 inform: "This is a good show to take a senior to, because there's nothing
   to follow. There's no story";
3 inspire: "You may have to be politically correct. But I don't. I can tell the
   truth. And I bet it's been a long time since you've heard it."

Because I would steal an artist's intellectual property by surreptitiously tap-
ing or video recording a performance, I have relied on my memory and
notes for these quotations, which I have attributed to Dame Edna, based on
performances of *The Royal Tour* I attended in San Francisco (10 October
1998), New York (13 January 2000), and Seattle (3 May 2001). Her comments are what Dame Edna is all about, on stage, and in her autobiography, which is a kind of stage from which she addresses her audience.
Conversation is a lost art because people have forgotten how to listen: they
are too busy preparing what to say when a pause opens up. In her peremp-
toriness, Dame Edna revives the art of one-sided conversation.

Recall Peter Cook and Dudley Moore's brilliant two-hander as Pete and
Dud, in which Pete drones on and on until Dud complains that he can't get
a word in edgewise, so eventually Pete concedes him one word, the word
"edgewise." Cook and Moore reprised this act as the only performance

piece in their 1990 BBC retrospective *The Best of ... What's Left of ... Not Only ... But Also.*[204] Since Peter Cook's death in 1994, and Dudley Moore's death in 2002, the only character peremptory enough to take Pete's inimitable role would be Dame Edna Everage, and the only suitable Dud would be Sandy Stone. By not allowing her audience to get even the word "edgewise" in, Edna teaches them to listen, to look at her while she is talking to them; and Humphries, through comedy, revives the art of conversation, in which listening is an essential part in an alternating monologue of two interesting people.

Edna Everage is not a storyteller: she is, as she states throughout *My Gorgeous Life*, an autobiographer. While she undoubtedly has a following, she has never solicited or enlisted one. She does not presume to tell a story because there is none. There are only speaking and listening, voice and image. As a narrator, Dame Edna speech-(en)acts information about herself not her story. She informs her audiences that there is only information.

Political correctness is the great twentieth-century lie or, as Humphries calls it, "the new American disease."[205] Dame Edna Everage ushered in the twenty-first century with an us-her dichotomy and ultimatum: people can be one of "us" and perpetuate the lie, or they can be one with "her" and tell the truth. She inspires her audiences to tell the truth by saying what, but for the sway of political correctitude, they would like to say. *My Gorgeous Life* is her primer for telling the twenty-first truth. Through autobiography, Dame Edna Everage, like Barry Humphries, makes a piecework mockery of PC. He will undoubtedly come round to calling her "my own mock / me."[206]

# Barry Humphries:
# Scriptor or Descriptor?
# His *ficcionnes*

A mere list of confirmable singular existential statements does not add up to an account of reality if there is not some coherence, logical or aesthetic, connecting them one to another. So too every fiction must pass a test of correspondence (it must be "adequate" as an image of something beyond itself) if it is to lay claim to representing an insight into or illumination of the human experience of the world. Whether the events represented in a discourse are construed as atomic parts of a molar whole or as possible occurrences within a perceivable totality, the discourse taken in *its* totality as an image of some reality bears a relationship of correspondence to that *of which* it is an image. It is in these twin senses that all written discourse is cognitive in its aims and mimetic in its means.

– Hayden White, "Fictions of Factual Representation"

This brief biography includes a mixture of fact and fantasy about the life and death of the Rainbirds and you may not know which story to believe but it does not matter does it?

– Janet Frame, *The Rainbirds*

The house was in darkness.
Finding the front door locked, Watt went to the back door. He could not very well ring, or knock, for the house was in darkness.
Finding the back door locked also, Watt returned to the front door.
Finding the front door locked still, Watt returned to the back door.
Finding the back door now open, oh not open wide, but on the latch, as the saying is, Watt was able to enter the house.

– Samuel Beckett, *Watt*

TIME SEIZES UP: DEREK PETTYFER AS FOCALIZER

With the possible exception of his white-Beckett-fence little narrative "A Novel Called Tid" (1958), *Women in the Background* (1995) is Barry

Humphries' first novel. It is also, along with *My Gorgeous Life: An Adventure* (1989), *More Please* (1992), and *My Life as Me* (2002), one of the very finest of his finery of books, a wonderfully comic narrative in which Humphries stands back of all his characters, even the backgrounded women. Humphries has said of the novel, "It is not a serious book. Everything I do is meant for comedy. But it has some serious subjects treated lightly."[1] Rather than as a man of clay, a mutable human being, subject to decay and to silence, Humphries, on his own admission, figures in *Women in the Background* as a ghost.

In his "Disclaimer" he disavows any resemblance between his characters and actual people living or dead, not in a standard author's note or retraction but, rather, in an argument from the dead: "It is the custom sometimes of ghosts and demons to assume the form and likeness of real persons to achieve an evil purpose."[2] He seals the deal of incredulity, demanding readers suspend their belief, by warning, in a typographically centred line that seems to need no justification: "Do not be deceived." But his bidding echoes that of a magician to an audience that has come to the theatre precisely to be deceived. This is the premise of all fiction, to be deceived, as in *Hamlet*, by a ghostly lie.

Humphries is the self-proclaimed ghost[3] of *Women in the Background* in the obvious sense that, in its fabula – London television performer Derek Pettyfer (who has ex-wives in the background), creator of the beloved Mrs Petty, is trying to straighten out his life and to evade an unscrupulous biographer, Kenneth Grocock, who is trying to seize his identity in *carpe ipse / carpe idem* gestures (see Chapter Five) – Humphries' novel seems a mirror-image, complete with obverse distortions and ironic "flaws in the glass" (see Patrick White), of his life. In the ruse of discouraging readers from recognizing him in Derek Pettyfer and Mrs Petty, which he perpetuates in his interview with C. Lambert, insisting "Derek is always making critical remarks. That is the only autobiographical part of the book,"[4] Humphries may be identifying himself as a ghost writer and categorizing *Women in the Background* not as a *roman à clef* but as a *roman à terre*, about a man of clay, like Paul Ricoeur's "fallible man" (or a Patrick White-out *roman à "Clay"*).[5] Recently, Humphries has alluded to "my novel *Women in the Background*, which a few mischief-makers insisted on describing as a *roman-à-clef*, for it is true that I may have unconsciously woven some autogiographical material into this fiction."[6]

Like Derek Pettyfer, every man has at least one woman in his background: his mother. But, in fact, Humphries seldom mentions Derek's mother in the course of the narrative, except as a ghost. Perhaps, as a ghost writer, Humphries does not exercise narratological control over his protagonist's life. Certainly, the narrative suggests that Derek is at least taking control of it. While the narrative is often his indirect discourse, it is always his focalization. As focalizer, he filters in and filters out all the events of the narrative. Thus, he seems to filter his mother out of the narrative and out of the company of women in his background. But he seems unable to filter them out of his mind: consciousness, memory, conscience.

Given that he is a womanizer – not of the order of Sir Les Patterson but exercising a sexualizing agency all the same – his concern that these diegetic women, ex-wives, and ex-lovers may come to tell on him to his relentless biographer, Kenneth Grocock, seems justified. Grocock, however, is a professed brother in the Order of Les Patterson, to which the "authentic Australian dialogue" that he attributes to Derek Pettyfer in his creative biography of him attests, including signal discourse such as *"Give us another whisky Belinda or fair dinkum, I'll knock your teeth so far down your throat you'll have to put your toothbrush up your freckle to clean them"* and *"The last time I saw a face like yours Belinda, it had a hook in it!"*[7] In this dialogue, Barry Humphries derides Kenneth Grocock, he rides a cockhorse to the Court of St James, and he paints a parodic self-portrait, the most quick-witted self-parody anywhere in his *oeuvre bizarre*.

The most insistent woman in Derek Pettyfer's background is Mrs Petty, as the most resolute woman in Humphries' background is Dame Edna Everage, whose vanishing-point perspective on nonentities repeatedly foregrounds her. The opening words of *Women in the Background*, "Mrs Petty wondered what Vanessa would be like in bed,"[8] seem to open up the mind of the ironically named Pru Petty (as in *petite prudence*)[9] into girl-swirls of lesbian eroticism, until, a full three pages later, Mrs Petty steps into the background as readers learn she is really a character performed by a man, Derek Pettyfer.

This hilarious *trompe l'oeil*, in which the mind of Mrs Petty becomes the mind of Derek Pettyfer, reiterates the warning of the disclaimer, "Do not be deceived," as if Humphries were telling his readers, "Do not be deceived by gender, even your own, nor be deceived by genre, even this narrative."

As the novel's focalizing narrator, Derek can filter events through his consciousness and perception, but he also exercises an omniscient power as he moves in and out of character as Mrs Petty, who has a life of her own, a gender-shifting character reminiscent of Eddie in Patrick White's novel *The Twyborn Affair* (1979). The extent of his power to change his mind becomes evident at the end of Chapter 1, after he has had his first encounter with Kenneth Grocock, the journalist writing his obituary: "As he drove home Derek thought to himself: it's an odd sort of Ken who insists on Kenneth."[10] Is the idiom "to think to oneself" a colloquialism, a redundancy, or a hypercorrection? Or does it imply, in the narratological context of this novel, the focalizer's ability "to think to somebody else"?

For the first three pages of the novel, Humphries and his focalizer Pettyfer have taught readers to "think to somebody else," in that they have thought as Mrs Petty, they have thought as Derek Pettyfer thinking as

Mrs Petty, and they have thought as Barry Humphries thinking as Derek Pettyfer thinking as Mrs Petty: this *mise en abîme* of "thinking to somebody" is the essence of focalization. The sense within this essence is in Derek's ability to invoke the condition of anachrony, taking readers out of the present moment of narration and into the surrounding wormhole of time. His narratorial facility for taking people off is evident in his name: "Derek" is the English form of *Theodoric*, which in Old German means "ruler of the people."[11] His narratorial facility for invoking anachrony is evident in his proleptic and analeptic mind-shifts.[12]

In his first analepsis, he resets the party scene from the preceding chapter and sets the *mise en scène* of antecedent action:

Derek was thinking about Inge as he drove home. Why did she throw these ghastly parties for people she hardly knew? He supposed old Lionel encouraged it, probably on the advice of a neighbourhood analyst: something to do with giving her "her own space." It also probably took the focus off some of his own recreations. On tour he was supposed to be a bit of a "pants man," in a quiet way. Gerontophiles couldn't be as thin on the ground as most people supposed. But Derek had got off pretty lightly that night; still only ten o'clock.[13]

But this temporal, scenic, and narratorial analepsis also flashes a limelight into the back, the *focolare*,[14] of the focalizer's mind, showing how, as a ruling man, he manoeuvres people, especially women, as in his flashback to the first days of his courtship with Pam: "Was this the moment, he wondered, to put into effect Ross Gibb's allegedly foolproof 'photo in the briefcase' manoeuvre,"[15] which involves, as a conquest strategy, a man telling his girlfriend that his wife has found her picture in his briefcase.

But as the people's ruler, the antithesis of an anarchist, Derek manoeuvres language also. His phraseology and diction, notably "recreations," "pants man," "gerontophiles" and "thin on the ground," call attention to Derek as an inventor in language and story. His neologistic *parole* discloses meaning but also closes it off (i.e., in him): to understand his words, readers will have to determine who Derek Pettyfer is, to weigh his intentions as both a suitor and a focalizer. His life and his story might be seen as a series of analeptic fits, from "Derek thought back to that other party at Inge's, when she had introduced him to Pam"[16] to "as Derek drove home, he thought about May I. She was the first English girl he had ever slept with."[17] In other words, his life story moves from one memory of a "may I?" sexual episode to another.

But Derek Pettyfer takes proleptic fits also. Like other womanizers, and even like men who are not womanizers, he is always looking forward to sex. In fact, some of the novel's most wonderful broadly comic scenes have to do with Humphries' subverting the sexual intentions of Derek as an anticipatory man. At luncheon with Garryl Kurdish, for example, "Derek's heart was thumping; he had never impersonated a Lothario so boldly, so soon, while eating." Her response to him, "That is a proposition, isn't it? But I don't screw on the first date ... No, I'm afraid if we went to your place, I could only go down on you,"[18] is a star performance in a generic male fantasy, which Humphries seems to emphasize when, later at the Kemble Hotel, he has Garryl call Derek "Guy," which connotes both a typical man (*un type*, in French) and a grotesque, the freak of nature.

As Derek comments on Garryl's idea of man as guy-wire, " 'Guy?' Was it just a creepy Californianism, or did she prefer her lovers to be mere cyphers?"[19] Derek's prolepsis turns into prolepsis interruptus when Garryl first works "to remove his trousers, then his underpants, which she tugged off in spite of an inelastic obstacle," but "then, to his surprise, Garryl seemed to change her mind; for she suddenly abandoned him, and with a snap of her fingers and an exclamation of someone who has overlooked the obvious, she began rummaging in a shopping bag beside the bed."[20] Narratologically, the prolepsis lapses not as "he experienced that rare phenomenon: *pre coitus tristus*"[21] but, rather, when Pam phones to tell Derek that his mother has died.

Humphries undercuts the hilarity of Derek's sexual frustration, and the congenital comedy of the sexual act itself, when he matches Garryl, just emerged from the bathroom, a dominatrix all in rubber, with Derek, a ruler of women, whose mother has just left his background forever, "two hours ago,"[22] in an irretrievable analepsis. Here Humphries subverts his own comic ideas of a protagonist who has women in his past, a novel that takes its chapter structure from Derek's ex-wives and ex-lovers, and an antagonist (Kenneth Grocock) who structures his obituary notice on these women's subtexts.

In the non-narrated gap between Chapters 8 and 9, two hours and counting analeptically, the aesthetic background is the vanishing-point of death, which is the point – *le point*, the full stop – behind all "white face"[23] comedy. As death seizes Peggy Pettyfer, Derek seizes time in his role as an analeptic and proleptic focalizer. But he also seizes up in time, which draws him back from proleptic foreplay and foreshadowing into the deathless past of storytelling. Similarly, Kenneth Grocock, who, in the tumescent associations of his name, is proleptic, can focus only on the pre-mortem events of Derek's past.

Throughout *Women in the Background*, characters who venture into the future tend to be pulled back into the narratorial past through the present moment of narration and focalization. Even Peggy Pettyfer, who ventures into the ultimate futurity – death – is pulled back in the imagination of the reader, in my imagination, when I learn that Derek's mother was named not Peggy Pettyfer but Alison Peggy Quick,[24] and that the dead has become the quick, as happens only in narrative and imagination. I intend my passive mood phrase "is pulled back" to hint at the novel's unidentified omniscient/first-person narrator and implied author and his or her undisclosed presence in narratime. "Narratime" is my neologism for "narrative time," the non-linear duration of a narrative, either external reading time or internal episodic time, each of which is as indeterminate as is imagination. Narratime is to be distinguished from the construct of measured chronology.

In this regard, even Pam is pulled back from the appearance of class respectability when Ross Gibbo, who is Australian and therefore outside the British class paradigm, notices that her "accent was suddenly pure Birmingham."[25] Similarly, Denise, despite her efforts at "phonemic assimilation," feels the analeptic pull when, as Derek notices, "she still let slip a few Sydney giveaways: said 'Oo-er' if she nearly dropped something, 'haitch' for aitch, 'r-i-gh-t' for yes, and occasionally, when she wasn't thinking, enjoyed a 'fillum.'"[26] Even Sudesh Robinson is pulled back when Derek detects "a hint of something northern in her voice – Manchester?"[27] Derek even pulls himself back when he "assumed a mock Australian accent"[28] to make a point about expatriatism and when, at the Gibbs's home, "after all those years in tight-arsed, toffee-nosed Albion, he could be an Australian again."[29] Pam, Denise, Sudesh, and Derek's voice-breaks, their slipping out of character, are the accentual antithesis of comedienne Beryl Reid's transformation from her Brummagem character Marlene back to her own speech patter(n) as an actress from Hereford.

By pulling characters back from the futurities of sex, death, and appearance, Derek Pettyfer, as focalizer, and Barry Humphries, as implied author, draw the macrocosm of London to a close, perhaps Marvell Close or Eliot Close, squeezing the universe into the still point of narration: through their enduring analepses and scrapped prolepses, focalizer and scriptor tie a Frigian knot[30] in narratime and a slipknot for Samuel Beckett's syntactic package: "this refusal, by Knott, I beg your pardon, by Watt."[31] Knotted, too, are the novel's other focalizers, the competitive and intrusive focalizers Kenneth and Yvette.

## BARRY HUMPHRIES, SCRIPTOR OR DESCRIPTOR?

Humphries is a scriptor in the postmodern sense of an author after the Barthesian "death of the author." Given that he published "A Novel Called Tid" (1958) ten years before Barthes' essay, however, he would undoubtedly prefer literary critics to refer to him as a novelist. Yet Humphries is indeed a scriptor in two non-postmodern senses: he is the author of many superb stage, television, and film scripts; and, in *Women in the Background*, he describes the eponymous women of the narrative exactly and exactingly, foregrounding them not in Derek's foreplay but in a women's foreword to the male gaze, as in David Ireland's figuration of a "city of women" in his novel of the same name (1981).

In this sequence of portraits of women, Humphries eventually puts together a whole woman – Yvette – as invoked from the grave in the epilogue, through the analepsis of Derek Pettyfer into Derek Quick, who is the first- and last-person narrator of *Woman in the Background*, whose first act is as an Actor and whose second act is as the Author:

I will take up the story now in my own voice, for it is my story and there is still a little more to tell.

Till now, I have written it fancifully, rather like a novel, because the novel is a convenient form: it enables the author to reduce his own faults and follies and exaggerate the shortcomings of others.

I am, of course, strictly an Amateur, whose first profession is not authorship; and since I am also what used to be called a "colonial" I have indulged a lifelong taste for the sesquipedalian; that unerring giveaway of the Provincial.[32]

Derek Quick implies that he has been telling the story *Women in the Background*, through twenty-one chapters, in voices other than his own: in the voice of the apparent omniscient narrator; in the voices of the focalizers Derek Pettyfer, Kenneth Grocock, Inge Pinkhill, Bob Dooley, Yvette, and others; and in the voices of everybody who speaks and whose dialogue is designated by inverted commas and indirect discourse.

But who is Derek Quick, "over thirty years"[33] later, in an epilogue that revives at least the memory of his relationship with Yvette? He has told his readers very little about himself in the chapter that bears Yvette's name, where his self-disclosure is limited by young Derek Pettyfer's snide point of view. Yvette figures in Derek's focalization of the story of his esteem less for her than for the eighteenth-century Italian architect and artist Giambattista Piranesi: "How had his passion for this artist begun?" His fabula reveals these details:[34]

1 Derek met Yvette when he was nineteen years old;
2 they were students at the University of Adelaide;
3 he thought her name "absurd" for "a French girl";
4 she and her parents were immigrants from France;
5 unable to appreciate her French culture, he attributed it to "the Leslie Caron-Gigi École de Gallic Charme";
6 she was uninhibited sexually and in her sexuality;
7 they dated for three months and attended screenings of Ingmar Bergman films together;
8 Derek fell in love with Yvette, but she did not reciprocate his affection;
9 they would have sex in the back seat of Peggy's Vauxhall;

Table 6.1
Fetishizing Women: Derek, Kenneth, and the Male Gaze/Gays

| Ch. | Characters | Focalizers | Descriptions |
|---|---|---|---|
| 1 | Inge | Derek | Tonight, Inge's *décolleté* was especially inviting; a simple crossover of Fortuny pleated silk within which her large breasts loitered impatiently; but there was something different about her teeth. (7) |
| 2 | Pam | Derek | Yet did he really want Pam?, Derek wondered. It was the perfect moment to turn back. But it was surprising how quickly and with what a deep sigh and a whispered name she responded when he took her in his arms. Their lips met with a faint clash of teeth and he thought he felt the flick of her tongue. He noticed then, as he noticed hereafter, that her eyes were closed. Were always closed. (27) |
| | | | On the previous evening, Derek had observed that his wife's armpits, formerly rather titillatingly fronded, were now depilated to resemble the texture of chicken skin. (278) |
| 3 | Denise | Derek | Derek had liked Ross's girlfriend Denise, too. In those days she was like a beautiful yobbo, still dressed in the flattering mode of the sixties: backcombed Julie Christie hair, black mini and a big laugh. Not so much a dolly-bird, as a dolly-kookaburra. Now, years later and after two children, she was still attractive in a tough, wiry way, though her long hair was clipped short *au garçon* and coloured gold by Daniel Galvin in George Street. (31) |
| 4 | Belinda | Kenneth | With a sweep of her naked foot, Belinda cleared a pile of rubbish off a small chair and bade Kenneth sit down. The grime-mottled calf and ankle, which he had briefly glimpsed, were monumental; rather like the hefty terracotta limbs of Picasso's neo-classical bathing beauties. He noticed, too, that she had mauve feet. (45) |
| 5 | Yvette | Derek | She favoured cobalt stockings, short skirts, snug angora tops and black *grosgrain* chokers. One evening, after their first date, when Derek drove her back to her parents' home in a drab suburb, he had no sooner switched off the engine than she had methodically unhitched her bra and permitted him a systematic manipulation of her breasts, spasmodically lit by passing cars. (59) |

Table 6.1
Fetishizing Women: Derek, Kenneth, and the Male Gaze/Gays (*Continued*)

| Ch. | Characters | Focalizers | Descriptions |
|---|---|---|---|
| 6 | Vanessa | Derek, as Mrs Petty | Was she imagining it, or did Vanessa meet her gaze a little too directly with those grey, humorous eyes? Did her hands – smoothing in the Max Factor before a show – sometimes linger upon her face longer than was necessary? Mrs Petty felt an almost irresistible impulse to reach out and touch the younger woman; to knead a buttock, for example, or slide her hand in under her breast and feel the nipple graze her palm. (1) |
| 7 | Polly | Kenneth | "I could never understand why people rave about ballerinas anyway. No tits, skinny as scarecrows, scraped-back hair, pointy chins and they walk like ducks." To Kenneth's dismay, Polly burst into tears. |
| | | | "You're so cruel and beastly." |
| | | | "What's wrong, Poll?" |
| | | | "I was a dancer once, don't forget. I can't help the way I walk. And I like scraping back my hair, and I enjoy being thin and having a pointy chin and some men don't like boobs." She wept again. (93) |
| 8 | Garryl | Derek | Derek walked among the tables, saying a word to Alan Bates and another to Peter Hall, but he had already seen her at the corner table in a cool pistachio linen suit by Donna Karan, bare legs and strappy, high-heeled sandals. (98) |
| 9 | Bronwyn | Derek | Denise's "help" – they abjured the word maid – a New Zealand girl called Bronwyn, let them in. (118) |
| | | | "A few wee savouries," announced Bronwyn, taking one herself and munching it audibly. "Help yourselves, thanks." (120) |
| 10 | Peggy and Jill | Derek | He supposed all these embalmers felt on intimate terms with their cadavers. Certainly, in twenty-four hours they probably penetrated more orifices than the deceased husband had hoped to do in a lifetime. (123) |
| | | | And with that the old lady of forty-two at the wheel in a raincoat, gloves and a wildflowers of Tasmania headscarf who was his sister, burst into floods of tears. They pulled over to the side of the road while Jill recovered herself. Awkwardly, Derek put his arm around her shoulder. (125) |

Table 6.1
Fetishizing Women: Derek, Kenneth, and the Male Gaze/Gays (*Continued*)

| Ch. | Characters | Focalizers | Descriptions |
|---|---|---|---|
| 11 | [Polly, as] Antoinette | Inge | The miracle, however, was her face. Inge caught a final glimpse of it as she left the room. The resemblance was certainly uncanny. The hair, for instance, of an unreal brunette, was scraped back and secured in a tight chignon. The eyes, in that pale, almond-shaped countenance, were large, brown and emphasised with an abundance of kohl; even the celebrated mole, or *grain de beauté*, to the left of her aquiline nose, and recorded by Zoë Dominic in a famous photograph, seemed to be authentically located.<br><br>But she had given herself away completely when she scribbled her autograph in Melwyn's book. For Antoinette Diggins was left-handed, and this imposter was not. (149) |
| 12 | Doris | Derek | The plump little woman in tennis shoes, jeans and a paint-splattered, yellow tank top, held out her flabby freckled arms and pulled Derek's head into abrupt collision with her right ear. With his face buried in the grey undergrowth of her fulvous perm, and the smell of Anaïs Anaïs in his nostrils, Derek realised, with a sinking heart, that he was almost certainly in the embrace of his mother-in-law. (157) |
| 13 | [Pam as] Camille | Bob Dooley | "Camille Claudel was a nice little student who had a crush on Rodin." (178) |
| 14 | Estelle | Derek | Derek looked at those lips. Perhaps, long ago, they had been normal, even pretty lips. Now they had been grotesquely enlarged by some cosmetic surgeon who had done postgraduate studies with the Kichepo Tribe on the Ethiopian border. They had been implanted with a material similar, perhaps, to the shifting, squelchy substance in the beanbag beneath his bottom. She could have loudly applauded with them. To have actually smoked a cigarette with them was an admirable feat: it was akin to picking up a strand of spaghetti with a boxing glove. (197) |
| 15 | Ms [Coral] Fortune | Derek | He looked at the small, spinster-like figure across the desk. About forty-five, he reckoned, neatly got up in a grey suit and blouse, dull fair hair and a small, twitching face like a washed-out rabbit. Not his, or anybody's idea of a forceful, fearless private eye. (212) |

Table 6.1
Fetishizing Women: Derek, Kenneth, and the Male Gaze/Gays (*Continued*)

| Ch. | Characters | Focalizers | Descriptions |
|---|---|---|---|
| 16 | Karina | Derek | She was a pretty girl, he thought, tall, dark and olive skinned, with the ghost of a moustache pricked out with perspiration. She wore a purple sarong and a halter top, her spatulate toes divided by the raffia twine of her sandals. She smelled of Tuberose by Mary Chess. (227) |
| | | | Standing on tiptoe beside the bed in the dim room, his fingers resting lightly on her hips, Derek desperately sought some distracting and subduing image. He dared not look down at the girl who knelt before him like a cleft and sallow fruit; instead he fixed his eyes on that sinister image on the wall. (240) |
| 17 | Coral [Again] | Derek | Derek glanced up from the *Telegraph* and observed the small, bird-like woman in the Aquascutum raincoat, the green umbrella and the plastic over-shoes moving towards him. (252) |
| | | | Coral actually laughed as he eased the raincoat back over her bird-like shoulders. (260) |
| 18 | Polly Again | Kenneth | His flatmate, in tights, leotard and pointe shoes was doing strenuous *pliés* against the straight back of their Conran couch, as the stereo played the rather too sprightly scherzo from the *Divertissement* by Jean Françaix. (268) |
| 19 | [Roger Wainwright as] Whitney [Huston] | Derek | "We've got a terrific photo of me as Whitney at home – colour, of course – and you've got to see it, Derek. Matter of fact, I've just taken it to a reliable picture framer." |
| | | | ... Derek, feeling disembodied, withdrew a small notebook from his pocket and wrote three words therein: "reliable picture framer." (284–5) |
| 20 | [Pam as] Fanny [Mendels-sohn] | *tout le monde* | Pamela Pettyfer took her seat in the Birmingham Symphony Hall at twenty minutes past eight. She looked gorgeous. Several men, and women too, observed the green-eyed brunette in the black, Donna Karan backless dress and smiled appreciatively. (292) |
| 21 | Sudesh | Derek | Most of the space in the room was occupied by a conference table at which two people were seated: a man of about forty-five in a brown suit who introduced himself as Abbott, and a delicate looking Indian lady in an apricot-coloured sari. Derek thought she was called Sudesh Robinson. (310) |

Table 6.1
Fetishizing Women: Derek, Kenneth, and the Male Gaze/Gays (*Continued*)

| Ch. | Characters | Focalizers | Descriptions |
|---|---|---|---|
| Epilogue | Timothy | Derek | I stood there for a while, searching for the right words; the right way of thanking him; and he put his hand on my shoulder, that kind young man who must have reached out many times to comfort his mother. (326) |

10 Derek began to despair for Yvette's love;

11 Yvette gave him a birthday gift, from a second-hand book shop, of Aldous Huxley's essay on Piranesi's *Prisons*, which Derek left at his parents' home;

12 after this gesture, their relationship ended;

13 Derek began his search for works by Piranesi, but he misplaced Yvette's book and never recovered it.

These data reveal more about Derek than about Yvette – they do not even disclose her last name – and, in the end, they are insufficient to reconstruct an apparently minor character who turns out to have been, all along, the only enduring love of the first-person narrator and even the author. But Derek Quick does provide other data on Yvette for her narratorial reconstruction in the epilogue (in Derek Pettyfer's focalized descriptions of women and, to a lesser extent, in the focalizations of Kenneth Grocock and Robert Dooley).

Humphries' indebtedness for the idea of the cubist reconstruction of woman is probably to Salman Rushdie's *Midnight's Children* (1980). In recounting his own life, Rushdie's narrator, Saleem Sinai, goes back to the courtship of his grandparents. In the opening chapter, "The Perforated Sheet," Saleem describes how his grandfather, Doctor Aadam Aziz, paid a professional visit to perform an examination of Naseem, Ghani's daughter. For modesty, Ghani insists he examine her behind a sheet: "In the very center of the sheet, a hole had been cut, a crude circle about seven inches in diameter."[35] Initially, he examines Naseem's belly through the perforated sheet. Ghani invites Aziz back whenever Naseem has an ailment, until, although he has never actually seen her (that is, all of her at once), "gradually Doctor Aziz came to have a picture of Naseem in his mind, a badly-fitting collage of her severally-inspected parts. The phantasm of a partitioned woman began to haunt him,"[36] and eventually they get married. Like Naseem, Yvette is a cubist collage that readers of *Women in the Background* put together by examining Derek Pettyfer's performance as a focalizer: his male gaze, his fetishization of women, his way of looking through their holes.

If readers were to take Inge Pinkhill's breasts and teeth; Pamela Pettyfer's lips, teeth, tongue, and eyes; Denise Gibb's hair; Belinda Pettyfer's legs and feet; Yvette's breasts and hands; Vanessa's breasts, buttocks, hands, and eyes; Garryl Kurdish's legs and feet; Bronwyn's hands and mouth; Peggy Quick's "orifices"; Jill Pettyfer's hair, hands, and shoulders; Polly Garland's hair, eyes, nose, face, hands, feet, and shoulders; Doris Black's arms, ears, and hair; Estelle Weinglass's lips; Coral Fortune's hair and face; Karina Grocock's upper lip, skin, toes, hips, knees, and vagina; and Sudesh Robinson's "delicate" torso. If readers, impersonating Viktor Frankenstein or Aadam Aziz, were to fuse all these body parts, then they would have the body of a woman: hair, skin, face, nose, ears, eyes, mouth, lips, teeth, tongue, shoulders, arms, hands, torso, breasts, hips, vagina, buttocks, legs, knees, feet, and toes. Perhaps it would be the body of Yvette, who disappears in Chapter 5 and reappears in the epilogue, where Derek Quick confesses to having been present narratorially all along, as the author.

If these parts constitute her whole body, if only as a character in a fiction, then it would appear to be a fetishized body put together mainly by focalizer and male-gazer Derek Pettyfer and by the novel's other focalizers (Kenneth Grocock, Inge Pinkhill, and Robert Dooley). In this regard it is a sexualized "distortion" in a male fantasy having to do with (in both the referential and the sexual, even necrophilic, senses of the idiom "to have to do with somebody/some body," as in the current slang "to do somebody/some body") men's perceptual (even physical) dismemberment of women's bodies and with their marginalization of women to the background of narrative.

I intend my word "distortion" to have the connotations of Dame Edna Everage's usage in the first show of the second series of *The Dame Edna Experience*. Jane Fonda, an announced guest on the show, which is set in Dame Edna's luxury penthouse, is striving to gain entry into the building. As Fonda makes her plea on the video entry phone, Dame Edna interrupts her peremptorily: "Oh, Jane darling, lean back a bit. You're distorting in my entry phone system. You look a little bit like a reflection in a spoon." Derek Pettyfer distorts women's images as if they were reflected in what I imagine to be a recently recovered Barry Humphries Dada artwork from the 1950s, which I would entitle *Spoonscape*.

When Derek Pettyfer looks at women, even his mother, he festishizes them. His fetishes are usually sexual, but he tends not to sexualize women in positions of servitude, such as "Denise's 'help' – they abjured the word maid – a New Zealand girl called Bronwyn," and Coral Fortune, the private investigator to whom *"no one gives ... a second glance."*[37] Is this fetishist and womanizer the "real" Derek Pettyfer, corresponding in any way with "the real Barry Humphries" of Peter Coleman? Or with the "real persons" to whom Humphries refers in his disclaimer? When Brian McColl, Coral Fortune's partner, reveals that "Derek Pettyfer" is a stage name – "Also, Mr Quick, it's better to use your real name with us"[38] – readers may be reminded of Derek's response to Pam when she asks him if he has telephoned his sister Jill following the death of their mother: "Yes, but we couldn't hear each other. I'll use a real phone."[39] If a conventional telephone is real, then a cellular telephone must be unreal. Therefore, if Derek Pettyfer is a fetishist and a womanizer, Derek Quick, the real Derek, must not be. It must follow, therefore, that the real Barry Humphries, even as implied author, can have no correspondence with Derek Pettyfer.

What is Yvette's correspondence with Derek? Is it merely sexual and nostalgic? Or does it have to do with authorship? Has Yvette authored Derek's life? If Pettyfer rules the people, does Quick usurp his rule?

Quick corresponds with Pettyfer through authority and authorship. Quick usurps his male authority in part by calling into question his gender. As Garryl Kurdish remarks to Derek, "Gay? Aren't you a little bit gay?"[40] And Ross Gibbo advises him that "a nice media wedding would be one in the eye for a few ratbags out there who still reckon you're a poofter."[41] Just as Pettyfer disguises his male gender each time he dresses up as Mrs Petty (and risks the innuendo of a public that is less homophobic than simply ignorant of music hall, pantomime, and other cross-dressing traditions), so Quick takes on Derek as a man, allowing him to front his novel and even letting other characters queer the deal of Derek's hetero-masculinity.

By assuming the authorship of *Women in the Background* – openly in the epilogue but tacitly through the novel (by restricting Derek Pettyfer's role to that of focalizer and declining to identify the narrator either as to person or as to gender) – Derek Quick, in that he brings back to life his dead lover and, in a sense, becomes Yvette, draws on the female-maling tradition of Ella Shields, Vesta Tilley, Bessie Bonehill, Gertie Gitana, Sarah Bernhardt, Fanny Robina, Millie Hylton, and Hetty King and may even anticipate the performance of Hilary Swank in the film *Boys Don't Cry* (1999). Derek Quick's female-maling narratological performance as Derek Pettyfer is antithetical to Derek Pettyfer's male-femaling performances as Mrs Petty.

The name "Yvette" derives from the Germanic *Ivo*, which means "yew wood,"[42] which, in a playful Dada spirit, could be homophoned, using a "real phone," of course, to mean, syntactically, "you would." In Chapters 1 through 21 of *Women in the Background*, Yvette conceals herself in a yew wood, and she shrouds Derek in the "you would" of conditional action, effectively turning him into her narratee and addressing him as "you." Even her appearance as a character (58–60) is conditional upon what Derek ("you") would have her say and do (in the sense that Derek loves her, tells her he loves her, and would have her love him back). As a character, Yvette is appearance, contingent upon Derek's focalization of her. She lingers in a yew wood/you would until the epilogue, when she becomes a reality: Yvette helps to deliver the epilogue, the afterword, like the book that her son Timothy delivers to Derek, in which she reveals something of what happens after the events of the novel.

She seems to speak to Derek from the yew wood of death, when Timothy says of Yvette's card, "You could easily miss it if you didn't expect to find it."[43] Yvette is also the epilogue, the performer of the epilogue. She speaks after everyone else has had their say; she speaks when male discourse has come to an end (albeit an arbitrary end through the narratological invocation of closure). Derek Quick's discourse is so radically different from the fetishizing, womanizing, dismembering discourse of the male focalizers of Chapters 1 through 21 that the epilogue seems to be outside patriarchy altogether. It might be protolinguistic, stemming from Eden, in that Yvette is a kind of Eve; or it might be *écriture féminine*, in that Yvette now contains the eye of focalization and of first-person narration.

Yvette is an epiloguist as Sandy Stone is a monologist, except that her words are less about herself than about what comes after the story: after patriarchy, *écriture féminine*; after dismembered women, a whole woman; after remembered narrative, a proleptic narrative; after *Women in the Background*, a new woman who takes the foreground; after Derek dies, (in a way) he becomes Quick.

In signing off the epilogue, Derek gives his readers a sign pointing to the novel's composition and narrativity:

Chalet Claire-fontaine
Gstaad
*February-March 1995*[44]

With reference to composition, these data may reveal that

1 Derek Quick wrote the novel in Gstaad, Switzerland, while staying at Chalet Claire-fontaine;
2 He wrote the novel in a two month period,[45] in as few as twenty-eight days (1 February – 1 March 1995) or as many as fifty-eight days (1 February – 31 March 1995).

What inferences might be drawn from these data? Despite Derek's insistence that he is a "colonial," he may in fact be *un Suisse romande* ("a francophone Swiss"). His stay at the Chalet Claire-fontaine, in the resort village of Gstaad, suggests a leisure as well as a work retreat, even though "I remained there still, for a long time in the empty flat, soon to be sold."[46] If the Chalet Claire-fontaine were in a novel, it might suggest Derek Quick's clarity of expression and his flow of ideas; but it is a geographic rather than a literary setting, and it has only literal associations. Derek Quick wrote the novel quickly, perhaps because he had Derek Quick in mind, writing, on average, as many as eleven pages per day or as few as five. He may have been able to complete the novel at this swift rate because he had researched it thoroughly or because the events were sharp in his memory, like "the fly-leaf; the blank page that had so wounded my adolescent heart over thirty years ago."[47] He proves himself the scriptor of *Women in the Background*, and, in the end, he demotes Derek Pettyfer to the navvy role of a descriptor of women.

In its narrativity, Derek Quick's novel *Women in the Background* represents two stories: (1) the story of Derek Pettyfer's unrequited love for Yvette and (2) the story of Derek Quick's struggle to break out of Derek Pettyfer and Derek Pettyfer's struggle to break free of Mrs Petty.

According to Gerald Prince, "narrativity" is "the set of properties characterizing narrative and distinguishing it from nonnarrative."[48] Within this paradigm, *Women in the Background* is a narrative characterized by chapter portraits of women: Inge Pinkhill, Pamela Pettyfer, Denise Gibb, Belinda Pettyfer, Yvette, Vanessa, Garryl Kurdish, Bronwyn, Peggy Quick and Jill Pettyfer, Polly Garland, Doris Black, Estelle Weinglass, Coral Fortune, Karina Grocock,[49] Sudesh Robinson, and even Dame Antoinette Diggins (through Polly Garland), Whitney Huston (through Roger Wainwright), and Fanny Mendelssohn (through Lionel Pinkhill). *Women in the Background* is distinguished from non-narrative, however, in the epilogue, where Derek Quick quickens the pace of telling the truth and exercises his narratorial power "to make the past not to have been"[50] by turning the preceding twenty-one chapters from narrative into non-narrative.

Prince sets out some other conditions of narrativity, which the appropriat(iv)e narrator Quickly violates:

The degree of narrativity of a given narrative depends partly on the extent to which that narrative fulfills a receiver's desire by representing oriented temporal wholes (prospectively from beginning to end and retrospectively from end to beginning), involving a conflict, consisting of discrete, specific, and positive situations and events, and meaningful in terms of a human(ized) project and world.[51]

The narrativity of *Women in the Background* would seem to be muted not only because Derek Quick renders narrative non-narrative (thus assigning it zero-degree narrativity) but also because the novel fails to meet receivers' expectations, replacing the construct "whole time" with "splintered time" in unpredictable analepses and prolepses. Even the novel, Chapters 1 through 21, is not a temporal whole because, in the epilogue, Derek Quick counts out a thirty-year prolepsis; nor is it a spatial whole (because he relocates his receivers with him to Gstaad, Switzerland).

The receiver, who negotiates narrative meaning in its deep structure, may (or may not) be the reader, or the audience; but, according to Prince, the receiver "is the one who (eventually) receives the object looked for by the subject." Thus, Derek Pettyfer, as subject, whose focalizations are his subjectivities or subject formations, looks for the objects of love and identity; and the receiver finds these objects in Yvette and Derek Quick, in the epilogue. The reader, in contrast, may not have recognized in Chapters 1 through 21 that Yvette is Derek's one true love[52] and that Derek Pettyfer has been Derek Quick all along; the reader probably knew only that Mrs Petty was "really" Derek Pettyfer when, in fact, Derek Quick is the "real" Derek Pettyfer. Thus, in the epilogue, the receiver emerges, with Derek Quick and Yvette, as a negotiator of the deep structure of meaning.

Prince also distinguishes between the receiver and the addressee: "A distinction is sometimes made between the addressee and the mere receiver (who may not be the addresser's intended addressee)."[53] If Derek Quick, who, by saying in the epilogue "I will take up the story now in my own voice,"[54] implies he has narrated *Women in the Background* in voices other than his own, is the addresser of the novel, then the addressee would seem to be anybody who has recognized the addresser as Derek Pettyfer (in company with the novel's other focalizers). Thus, in the epilogue four transformations occur, which, in turn, change the narrativity of *Women in the Background* from traditional linear novel to a music hall telling and change Barry Humphries from scriptor into artiste:

1 Derek transforms from Pettyfer to Quick;
2 Yvette transforms from quick to dead;
3 reader and addressee transform into receiver;
4 surface meaning (Chapters 1 through 21) transforms into deep structure (epilogue).

Humphries seems to signal his music hall turn by placing Yvette's message on "a Lautrec reproduction on a postcard, the one of Aristide Brouant (sic)."[55] Aristide Bruant, of course, was a great *chansonnier* at the Folies-Bergère.

In its trick ending, *Women in the Background* recalls several of the fictions of Janet Frame, notably *Scented Gardens for the Blind* (1963), where, in the final chapter, Vera Grace turns out to have been the narrator all along; and *The Carpathians* (1988), where, in the final chapter, John Henry Brecon turns out to have been the author all along. In its end-game of giving the narrator asylum in Switzerland, *Women in the Background* also closely resembles Robertson Davies' novel *Fifth Business* (1970), in which the narrator, Dunstan Ramsay, walks away from the act of telling, taking refuge in Sankt Gallen, whence, we learn, he has recounted the entire narrative.

As a music hall artiste, Humphries works some stage magic into the epilogue, loosening credibility, so that receivers might believe that Timothy would travel from London to Gstaad just to return a book that was thirty years overdue. This also frees receivers to find the objects of love and identity – a requiting lover for Derek Quick and an identity for Derek Pettyfer. When Derek reads Yvette's inscription on the card he missed in the book thirty years ago, "*To Derek, / With all my love / Yvette*," he takes an analeptic fit, making "the past not to have been," as he realizes his love for Yvette was always requited. In repeatedly reading her message from the grave, from one ghost to another – "But I remained there still, for a long time in the empty flat, soon to be sold, reading that message of love, borne back to me out of the past"[56] – Derek Pettyfer becomes Derek Quick again, and the novel teeters between the memory of what seemed a casual affair and the causality of endless love.

The epilogue, as the last word, like the inscription on the card, demonstrates that, despite appearances to the contrary, there has never been a love conflict between Derek and Yvette, and there has never been an identity conflict between Derek Pettyfer and Derek Quick. The only narratological conflict in *Women in the Background* is between readers who assume they are addressees and receivers who find the artistic commodities of love and identity. This narrativity seems to exclude even the ultimate existential and ontological conflict, that between the living and the dead. If Derek Quick is a ruler of living people, might Derek Pettyfer then be seen as a ruler of dead people? His name seems to carry these colourations. Pettyfer is feral, less in the sense that he is a wild animal (like Les Patterson) than in the sense that he presides over the dead: he conducts a f(un)er(e)al rite, reconciling the living and dead in Derek and Yvette, much as Patrick White does in his early novel *The Living and the Dead* (1941).

If the word "Pettyfer" is broken down to *petit fer*, it reveals several playful associations with language, books, and freedom. Thus, the *Oxford English Dictionary* cites "fer" as an "apparently meaningless" word (i.e., a nonsense word), or what Humphries might see as a Dada word. So, as a narrator Derek Pettyfer is a teller of little inanities. The *OED* also cites the word "fer" as an "obsolete form" of the words "far," "fear," and "fire." In these regards, Derek Pettyfer could be seen as a narrator who makes distant things present, who assuages receivers' fears of death, and whose prose is sometimes inflammatory. In French, the word *fer* denotes a bookbinder's tool, which could suggest that Derek Quick uses Pettyfer as a little tool for binding his book, for linking all the women in the background. The French word *fer* also denotes "iron," as in *chemin de fer* ("railroad"), and in the plural form, *fers*, "irons" or fetters. Thus, Derek Quick can be seen as liberating Pettyfer from his *petits fers*: *Derek Quick brise les petits fers à Pettyfer* ("Derek Quick sets Pettyfer free").

The two Dereks (Pettyfer and Quick), like the two Barrys (Humphries and McKenzie), are not in conflict but conjoined in a diversity of languages in the Bakhtinian conditions of heteroglossia (in Russian, *raznorecie*):

Heteroglossia, once incorporated into the novel (whatever the forms for its incorporation), is *another's speech in another's language*, serving to express authorial intentions but in a refracted way. Such speech constitutes a special type of *double-voiced discourse*. It serves two speakers at the same time and expresses simultaneously two different intentions: the direct intention of the character who is speaking, and the refracted intention of the author. In such discourse there are two voices, two meanings and two expressions. And all the while these two voices are dialogically interrelated, they – as it were – know about each other (just as two exchanges in a dialogue know of each other and are structured in this mutual knowledge of each other); it is as if they actually hold a conversation with each other. Double-voiced discourse is always internally dialogized. Examples of this would be comic, ironic or parodic discourse, the refracting discourse of a narrator, refracting discourse in the language of a character and finally the discourse of a whole incorporated genre – all these discourses are double-voiced and internally dialogized.[57]

Without, of course, having read *Women in the Background* – he died in 1975 – Bakhtin describes its narrativity with feral precision. It is demonstrably heteroglossic, consisting of two narratives by self-consciously hetero-male-tellers: the focalizer Derek Pettyfer (Chapters 1 through 21) and the author Derek Quick (the epilogue, plus Chapters 21 through 1). As tellers, the two Dereks speak different languages, *deux langages*, in the Saussurean sense: *paroles*, as distinguished from *langues* (specifically, *la langue australienne* as Sidney J. Baker systematized it in *Australian Language* [1966] and *The Australian Language* [1978]).

Derek Pettyfer speaks a fetishizing, womanizing, dismembering phallogocentric male discourse; Derek Quick speaks a factual, womanist, remembering, gynocentric discourse: "factual" in that it is not factitious or fetishizing; "womanist" in that its focus is on the matrilineal Yvette, mother of Timothy, who honours God[58] by drawing Derek into his mother's line, her line(s) of inscription; "remembering" because, analeptically, it puts Yvette back together, piece by piece; "gynocentric," perhaps in the spirit of Dame Edna Everage, because its centre is not the back seat of Peggy Quick's Vauxhall, where Derek and Yvette carried out their "erotic rituals,"[59] or his villa in Barbuda, where "almost violently [Karina Grocock] scrambled on to her knees across the bed and thrusting one hand between her legs, roughly guided him in"[60] but, rather, the site of love, where an "Amateur,"[61] a woman who with "one hand" signs herself "*With all my love / Yvette*," and a "kind young man who must have reached out many times to comfort his mother"[62] (as he is now reaching out to Derek

Quick), form a kind of ghost family, including even the implied author, Barry Humphries, whose bond is not Sex but Love.

When Derek notices, and makes note of, "a rectangular 'ghost' off-set on the page where it had lain all those years,"[63] he reinvokes the ghostly presences that have haunted the novel from the point of the disclaimer, where Humphries casts personages and characters "as ghosts." Humphries, even though his name appears on the title page and his book is categorized as "a novel by Barry Humphries," must be considered the ghost writer of *Women in the Background* because, in the epilogue, Derek Quick identifies himself as the storyteller and takes possession of the story when he says, "I will take up the story now in my own voice, for it is my story and there is still a little more to tell." He also identifies himself as the writer of the story, the pseudo-novelist and the author: "Till now, I have written it fancifully, rather like a novel, because the novel is a convenient form: it enables the author to reduce his own faults and follies and exaggerate the shortcomings of others."[64]

According to Humphries' disclaimer, all the characters in *Women in the Background* are ghosts. Peggy Quick and Yvette, because they die, become ghosts – ghosts for the second time. Mrs Petty is a ghost many times over in that she dies each time Derek Pettyfer removes her wig, makeup, and costume and "takes up his own voice." Similarly, Derek Pettyfer becomes a ghost when Derek Quick utters the words "I will" in his own voice, in contrast to the "you would" conditional clause of Pettyfer. Yet his "I will" also marries him with Yvette, whose "yew wood" is reminiscent of the dark wood that Dante enters in *Inferno*, Canto 1 of which begins, "Nel mezzo del cammin di nostra vita / mi ritrovai per una selva oscura" ("In the middle of the road of our life / I found myself in a dark wood" [my translation]). As the only person in *Women in the Background* who is not a character, and the only person to keep quick, Derek Quick corresponds with Dante, as if, in the Bakhtinian sense, "they actually hold a conversation with each other," which creates similar correspondence between Yvette and Beatrice, and between Timothy and Virgil.

With Timothy's guidance, Derek Quick, under the appearance of a ghost, descends into an antipodean underworld,[65] "the empty flat, soon to be sold,"[66] to find his beloved, Yvette. His remark to Timothy about the postcard, "I never found it at the time,"[67] might suggest he has found it (the receiver's "object looked for by the subject," Yvette) now. In this regard, Derek has supplanted receivers, turning them into ghosts and conscripting them in the descriptive (Chapters 1 through 21) and postscriptive (epilogue) company of ghosts, which the novelist Amos Tutuola calls "the bush of ghosts," beginning with his orative *My Life in the Bush of Ghosts* (1954).

According to Bakhtin, who, in so far as his critical reputation in the West is posthumous, speaks as a ghost, the focalizations of Chapters 1 through

21 constitute Derek Quick's speech (*parole*) in Derek's Pettyfer's language (*langue*, the male discourse of fetishists, womanizers, and dismemberers). Derek begins his association with *la langue* shortly after his introduction to Pam Black at Inge Pinkhill's party, when "their lips met with a faint clash of teeth and he thought he felt the flick of her tongue."[68] Afterwards, *il tire la langue aux femmes* ("he sticks out his tongue to all women" / "he has his tongue hanging out for all women"). Through his *langue*, his language and his tongue, Derek has the power to turn women into ghosts.

From the beginning he notices that Pam "diffused a tantalising aura. When they met she rarely spared him more than the ghost of a smile and when she finally slept with him after the third sitting, she was compliant yet curiously detached and silent."[69] When Derek Quick quickens Yvette in the epilogue, he rescues from the underworld all the women Derek Pettyfer has ghosted. Like Horatio, Quick knows how to speak ghost,[70] the language of a moribund patriarchy. His exchanges with Pettyfer, "refracted" through the narratological device of focalization, are a "double-voiced discourse," at once patriarchal (Pettyfer) and matriarchal (Yvette), with Mrs Petty assisting him occasionally as a kind of cross cross-gender interpreter.

This discourse speaks two intentions: (1) Pettyfer's is to sexualize and (2) Quick's is to "refract" phallogocentric discourse through the medium of the epilogized novel, as it were, altering the light in which one reads *Women in the Background* so that it seems (if only in the music hall limelight of Barry Humphries) to read as *Women in the Foreground*. The Pettyfer-Quick dialogue is a conversation between two people, one of whom, Derek Quick, is much more interesting than the other.

As implied author, Humphries seems to be saying that the man who turns away from patriarchy will be rewarded with love, a kind of metaphysical love that transcends the grave. In his closing mood, "reading that message of love, borne back to me out of the past," Derek Quick may not seem transcendent, but he does hint at a transition from "the empty flat" to having the *objet d'amour* "borne back," which implies the rebirth of love in his life.

The "comic, ironic or parodic discourse" that Bakhtin cites as features of "double-voiced discourse" resounds throughout *Women in the Background*. For example:

1 *broad comedy*, in the narratives of Polly Garland's outrageous impersonation of Dame Antoinette Diggins, and the camp revengers' tragedy of Drs Pinky and Perky;
2 *blistering irony*, in the narratives of Derek Pettyfer's obsessions with sex and taxes, and Kenneth Grocock's confusion of obituary and biography;
3 *pin-prick parody*, in the narratives of Derek and Woody as collectors and their mutable collectibles, and Humphries' surtext of self-caricature.

In comedy, irony, and parody Humphries double-voices appearance and reality, as the postcard of Aristide Bruant double-images (or ghosts) in the Huxley book. This interplay of voices and images is the novel's narrativity.

## BROAD COMEDY:
### BARRY WANTS TO BROADEN HIS HORIZONS

Kenneth Grocock gets his idea for Polly Garland to impersonate Dame Antoinette Diggins after he drops her name in between insults about Polly's dancer's body and *mienne* (all that she calls "mine"): "You know, Poll, you're a dead ringer for Antoinette Diggins. Did you know that?"[71] A "dead ringer" is an exact double, or *doppelgänger*, a figure with ghostly associations. But a ringer is also a dishonest contestant or a plant in the audience, so the phrase "dead ringer" foreshadows that Polly will be exposed as an imposter. The adjective "dead" confirms that Polly is among the company of the ghosts.

Inge Pinkhill is the first to notice Polly's imposture:

Inge's eyes followed the prima ballerina with more than an idle curiosity. She observed the shabby Lotus sling-backs, the bulging calves, the navy garberdine [sic] skirt. Her gaze took in the rather short navy bolero jacket with its cheap gold buttons, beneath which the woman had chosen to wear an old-fashioned peach blouse, fastened with a necktie. It was an ensemble which a famous dancer might easily have worn who cared little for worldly things, or the exigencies of fashion, but it was not what Antoinette Diggins would have been seen dead in.[72]

As a focalizer, Inge Pinkhill is brilliant. Her purpose is to expose identity theft, not, as is so often the case with Derek Pettyfer, to win a sexual favour. Her sharp perception is reflected in her subtle syntax: when she observes, "It was an ensemble which a famous dancer might easily have worn" she uncovers Polly as a fraud, as if divesting her of her quite meticulous costume. Polly gives herself away as a ghost because, in a sense, Antoinette Diggins is caught dead in her. Her makeup and her signature also give Polly away, "for Antoinette Diggins was left-handed, and this imposter was not,"[73] but Inge elects not to give her away: "It seemed inappropriate, even cruel, Inge decided, to rob Pinky and Perky of this roseate illusion."[74] Her eventual cooperation with Polly in her identity theft may show the extent of her immorality, yet it also sets the stage for two broadly comic events: Polly's deadly liaison with Lionel Pinkhill and her lover's appointment with revenge, which Pinky and Perky ex(tr)act from him.

With threats of informing on her to the police and of inevitable lesbian assaults on her when she is in prison (all because, by playing Antoinette, she fraudulently procured dental treatment from Pinky and Perky), Inge blackmails Polly into performing a sexual favour for her. As Polly observes, like an Aristotelian refugee from *Oliver!* " 'I'll do anything – anything!' re-peated the reprieved mimic."[75] All she need imitate is the line that Inge, as prompter, feeds her, "It's me, Antoinette, here at last, Lionel. Can you get it up?"[76] But at feeding time receivers can only guess how Polly as Antoinette will ever manage to deliver the line. The wait between rehearsal and show-time is brief, however: two chapters.

At the beginning of Chapter 2, entitled "Fanny," Inge gives Polly some last-minute direction, blocking out the scene in which, as Antoinette, she will simply go to Lionel's room, "dead on eleven thirty,"[77] remove her coat, and deliver the line. Inge's final encouragement, " 'You'll be brilliant, Polly dear,' said Inge. 'You'll kill them,' "[78] along with her "dead on," is broad-minded foreshadowing from the implied author, Barry Humphries. The brilliance of his broad comedy is that he makes it peak in Polly's preview performance, which she gives to Pam after promising to show her Lionel's birthday gift: "Inge walked a few steps away from their table in the direc-tion of the bar, then looking quickly to either side she turned towards Pam and opened her fur coat. Except for her faintly lewd Ferragamo shoes and another mink-like shadow, she was completely nude."[79]

At show-time, Humphries cleverly underplays Polly's play. Other than the door-knock and the one-liner, the whole scene is reaction, like a reaction shot in the cinema: "First, rather absent-mindedly, he seemed to give himself a funny little hug. Then, still looking at her oddly, he had just toppled forward on to his knees and rolled very, very slowly backwards. She had closed the door then, as Inge had told her to."[80] Here the curtain comes down on com-edy, as the idiom "knock 'em dead" becomes literal, yet the audience persists in its laughter: after all, nothing is funnier than a man dropping dead from cardiac arrest, if the man is Lionel Pinkhill, a personification of pomposity and pretension. Lionel may not get it up, but he does get the last laugh. And Humphries broadens his readers' comic horizons.

As with Polly's pseudo seduction of Lionel, Hugh Bremner and Trevor Watson's revenge on Kenneth Grocock for ruining their business occurs outside of Derek Quick's circle of telling. Like Humphries in *More Please*, Kenneth discerns his imperfect self in a mirror:

Kenneth ran to the loo and coughed a quantity of crimson syrup into the basin. He peered at the mirror. His face was white; ashen. His mouth ... his mouth was just a black hole – *and where were his teeth?* He darted back into the waiting-room, as though he might have left them there by mistake, but Raewyn was standing rather impatiently holding the door.[81]

Here Humphries turns Grocock into an emblem of the obituarist's mis-printed page (white face, black hole), a parody of the white-faced come-dian, yet another ghost in the novel's company, and an asshole sucking all the energies and truths of decent people into its absence. When they read that "Kenneth made feral noises of incomprehension and distress with the wound he once used to talk with,"[82] receivers may sense the presence of the feral Derek Pettyfer stuffing up this hole of mendacity. When Raewyn hands Kenneth the bill, adding, "I hope they've charged you an arm and a wee leg,"[83] receivers may realize little Kenny has been dismembered, countering Yvette's re-dismemberment in Derek Quick's consciousness.

BLISTERING IRONY:
CAN BLISTERING PAINT BE FAR BEHIND?

Sex and tax are Derek Pettyfer's undoing, but dying seems not to be a problem for him, given he turns Quick. Actually, sex would seem to be his doing, and Derek is intent on doing as many women as will accommodate him. But sexually transmitted diseases, or STDs, are another matter, the matter of being sexually overdone or done over. In his focalization Derek Pettyfer describes his "minor but disagreeable inflammation in a vulnerable place which had troubled him once before that morning"[84] and even self-diagnoses it as herpes, ironizing it by recalling "a grisly heading in *Cosmopolitan*: MANY HERPES RETURNS![85] This is one of a series of puns that Humphries might invoke to commemorate the Dada puns of Duchamp.

Derek's herpes vesicle bursts in the blistering irony of his encounter with "his subjacent neighbour, Mr MacDermott," whom, while riding a kind of farcical built for two, Derek mistakes for a dermatologist because "Mr MacDermott's name had lodged in his mind because someone, Amerika perhaps, had said he was a dermatologist, and Derek was always amused to find a clue to a man's calling in his surname."[86] By focalizing the rather heterodox word "subjacent," Derek seems to want to distract receivers from his own nominal associations as *compère* over a death rite in "the bush of ghosts"; that is, until "Kenneth made feral noises of incomprehension and distress with the wound he once used to talk with" and exposes him from under his life-mask.

For Humphries, the purpose of this tactic of distraction seems to be to ensure that receivers have the same shock as Derek and that everyone – including Alan MacDermott, accountant, the *doppelgänger* of the real Dr MacDermott, who lives in another flat – falls off their farcical at once. The theme of mistaken identity was old even in Shakespeare's day, but has it ever before turned on the bird not in the bush, a protagonist "holding his cock in a trembling hand"? Alan MacDermott's horror arises not out of a prurient homophobia but out of his wounded sense of propriety:

To his amazement, the old man uttered a hoarse cry of horror, leaped out of his chair and ran for the door. "What the hell do you think you're up to, man? What the devil do you take me for, you dirty bugger? Put it away man, put it away and get the hell out of here, sir! Get out of this flat, and God help you, sir. God help you!"[87]

Mr MacDermott's "amazement" and "horror," his invocations of God and the devil, even his accusation that Derek is a sodomite, pale in comparison to his handling of the word "it," the same pronoun that Mieke Bal uses to refer to the narrator. His "put it away man, put it away," recalling Othello's "put out the light, and then put out the light,"[88] is also Humphries' nod to the phallogocentricity of Pettyfer's focalization. To Derek, narration is a series of rude gestures in which he puts narrative out, puts it away, puts it out, puts it away. Yet, other than noting that "Derek was immobilised" by MacDermott's tirade, the narrative makes no reference to Derek's having put it away. Perhaps it is in hand still.

Herpes, however, may not be Derek's disease (as it is Abu-Nivea's disease in *Les Patterson Saves the World*) but only the symptom of another disease. In one of his most confessional chapters, "Vanessa," comparable in its self-revelations to the opening pages of the novel (where he focuses his male gaze, albeit through Mrs Petty, on Vanessa), Derek diagnoses his disease as sexual addiction:

It was a miracle, Derek reflected, that he had reached the age of fifty without ever getting any of those nasty little bugs which afflicted people far less promiscuous than he. Twelve years ago, at the nadir of his drinking, there had been a period of satyriasis which he preferred not to think about.[89]

Within the context of this confession, "satyriasis" can mean only ferine licentiousness; that is, Pettyferine sexual addition. The euphemism "nasty little bugs," the projection "people far less promiscuous than he," and the distanciation "twelve years ago, at the nadir of his drinking" do little to separate Derek from his overactive libido. Satyriasis is the men's disease that haunts him still, evident in the fact that "it was an hour before he slept"[90] and that, for the duration of the novel, he has lusted after Vanessa, Mrs Petty's makeup artist, even when he is in the guise of Mrs Petty, whose seldom-mentioned first name, Pru, suggests her association with prudence. In the end, however, Derek's satyriasis and his suspected herpes may not have a causal relation: satyriasis is a sexual disease but not a sexually-transmitted disease; therefore, it cannot cause an STD like Derek's form of herpes. Promiscuity, of course, would have increased Derek's chances of contracting herpes from one of his sexual partners (who had active-phase genital herpes when they had sex).

But to Humphries, at least as the implied author, satyriasis is not sexual addiction but satire, although not the satire of 1960s London, as at the Establishment. Humphries' satire is that of the satyr, the goat-man of the woods, specifically, the "yew wood" with which Yvette is associated and the burlesque wood of Greek *satyros*. His satire is fiery enough to blister paint: with irony and wit, he directs it less at vice and folly (which in theatrical and narratological contexts can hardly be deemed faults), than at pretension, meanness, and falsehood (especially as embodied by Kenneth Grocock's pursuit of Derek Pettyfer's ghost and his life story).

## PIN-PRICK PARODY LEAVES A MINOR WOUND: AN OPEN MOUTH

Both Derek Pettyfer and Woody Weinglass are collectors, Derek of drawings by Giambattista Piranesi (1720–78) and of Roman glass works, Woody of Christmas kitsch. Derek's collection of "serried Piranesis" would be perfect if not for his missing book, Yvette's gift of Aldous Huxley's commentary on Piranesi's *Prisons*. His glass collection would also be perfect but for one flaw in its principal object, a funerary flask from Koblenz, formerly a Roman settlement:

The flask was intact, except for one small chip in its rim, a few strain-cracks in the body, pin-prick bubbles, a flaky iridescence and a trace of incipient crizzling on the foot. It was miraculous to think that this delicate object, except for the patina of age, had survived unbroken for 1,700 years.[91]

Recall the similar language Derek uses to reflect on his evasion of STDs: "It was a miracle, Derek reflected, that he had reached the age of fifty without ever getting any of those nasty little bugs which afflicted people far less promiscuous than he." He cannot be accused of not believing in miracles! Out of these "pin-prick bubbles," like the bubbles through which Barry McKenzie speaks, Barry Humphries, equipped with only a pin and a prick, imparts a parody on collectors, collections, and collectibles.

His ridicule is not derisive but gentle, even celebratory. It begins with the idea of the perfect collection and the reality that no collection is ever perfect (because it is never complete) and that no collector is ever satisfied (because he or she is always seeking an elusive or unavailable piece).[92] Both Derek and Woody strive to amass their collections to perfection, but, in the end, comically, their collectibles are reduced to ruin.

Chapter 14, "Estelle," named after Woody's wife, begins with a forthright statement: "Woody Weinglass was a Collector."[93] Like an apolitical collectivist, like a priest reading the Collect at Mass, and like Terence Stamp in William Wyler's film *The Collector* (1965) (based on John Fowles' novel [1963]), he amasses commodities: "nineteenth-century farming implements" and "Christmas." Derek Pettyfer focalizes Woody's collections with pin-prick parody, holding Weinglass up to the light of ridicule and holding him down until he says "Father Christmas":

> He owned an example of the first commercial Christmas card, printed in 1846 by Sir Henry Cole and J.C. Horsley. He possessed a first edition of Charles Dickens's *A Christmas Carol* of 1843. He cherished the original artwork by Norman Rockwell for a 1938 *Saturday Evening Post* cover, depicting children unwrapping presents while their parents peeked ecstatically around the door. In a glass case lay the shooting script of *White Christmas*, autographed by Bing Crosby, Danny Kaye and Rosemary Clooney, whilst beside it reposed Irving Berlin's signed copy of the eponymous song. A life-sized dummy was apparelled in the tuxedo Mel Torme wore when he first sang about Chestnuts Roasting on an Open Fire, and in pride of place, in a gold frame discreetly spotlit, was a "Dear Santa" wants list from little Ronnie Reagan, obtained from a private source in Washington D.C.[94]

This travesty of collecting is disguised not in derisive language but in the accumulation of things, each valuable in itself, yet in combination, like a "dummy," quite silly.

The kicker is the end Derek focalizes to this collectibles account: "These were just, as collectors say, the 'highlights.' There were hundreds, perhaps thousands of lesser items, indexed and catalogued."[95] He is then emboldened to call Woody simply "The Collector," suggesting that every collector is at once generic and exclusive, or, as the narrator pinpoints it in parody: "The reason why a group of persons in the same world – a peer group – assemble the same things, is to show off to each other."[96] They exhibit themselves to one another in a voyeuristic group, in a phallogocentric universe, as Derek Pettyfer shows off his prize item – it has only one flaw, the possibility of disease, herpes – to Mr McDermott.

Like the males of the species, who, if only because of an evolutionary imperative, prefer to distribute their genetic material liberally as collateral against the collateral damage of mutability and death, so collectors, it seems, gather insignificant things around them – Piranesis and Roman glassware, while precious, have only modest significance philosophically; archaic plows and Christmas kitsch hardly have meaning within the secular urban paradigm – to inoculate themselves against absurdity. In the Aristotelian cause-effect universe that Humphries favours, in which funny remarks cause laughter, things are insignificant when they are inconsequential. *Women in the Background* is an antigene allowing receivers to make antibodies to immunize themselves against the absurdity that lurks outside it – a prophylactic against the STDs of reading.

Throughout *Women in the Background*, Derek Pettyfer expresses his disgust with collecting, collectors, and collectibles, including, eventually,

himself (possibly because he knows Kenneth Grocock is compiling an obituary file on him). Knowing their death notices have already been written
and have been reduced to standing type must be a burden to celebrities, including Humphries. Often in newspaper obituary articles the only phrase
that has meaning is "who has died," as in "Paul Matthew St Pierre, who
has died, was a professor of Australian literature and an expert on Barry
Humphries." In the Salopean dialect, the saying "I know a man what's
dead" means "I know something as a fact," or "I am *gnarus*, the one who
knows knowing." This is the message Timothy delivers in the epilogue, as
though he were saying, "I know a woman what's dead." Outside of the in-
controvertible fact of death, it seems, everything is meaningless: illusion,
construct, theory, dogma, or premise, all is absurdity. As Groucho Marx
philosophized, "outside of a dog, a book is a man's best friend; inside of a
dog, it's too dark to read." In this sense, Humphries proves himself to be an
epistemologist of the dark wood of death – and of laughter.

Every collectible – in other words, everything: everything that has been
collected, everything that could be collected – is a *memento mori*. Witness
the transition in Coral Fortune's fortunes for Derek, when by chance she reveals she is a collector:

> "I have a confession to make. I'm a bit of a collector."
> "A collector?" he said.
> "Yes. Georgian Silver. There's a sale in half an hour across the road at Bonhams
> and I have my eye on a salt cellar. When you talk in terms of Harrods, and then the
> Georgian Restaurant, I regarded it as a happy omen."[97]

Her jargon ("in terms of") and the fact that, although she is (C)oral, she is
a poor listener are enough for Humphries to condemn Coral Fortune in
parody. But condemnation is more difficult for Derek because, in her collective unconscious, he is starting to perceive himself, as if in a mirror, as
another unscrupulous dick. Derek does not have long to debate condemn-
ing himself because, by the end of the scene, Coral does it for him:

> Derek looked around. "Is this really a good place to meet? I mean, people seeing
> us together."
> Coral actually laughed as he eased the raincoat back over her bird-like shoulders.
> "Not to worry. They'll think we're a couple of scheming silver collectors, hatching
> something." She peered at her unhappy client. "*You look just like an antique dealer!*"
> Derek felt, on reflection, that Coral's observation was the single most insulting
> thing that anyone had ever said to him in his entire life.[98]

This passage might be interpreted as parodying Coral Fortune for her lack
of decorum. By noting how "she peered," the focalizer aligns her with all

collectors in peer groups, including Kenneth Grocock, who, after having had all his teeth extracted, "peered at the mirror." Derek's "reflection" here seems hardly serious: his irony merely dismisses Coral as an inarticulate, indecorous fool.

Yet by enlisting Derek in her peer group, by casting him as an antique dealer, Coral seems to force him into a serious *doppelgänger* crisis. In this regard, Derek's reflection is to be taken literally: it is the most telling utterance Derek has ever heard. It forces him to rediscover Derek Quick and to recover Yvette. When, in an act of revenge against him, Doris destroys his Roman glass collection, putting it through the dishwasher cycle, she also deconstructs his identity as a collector:

Derek was disinclined to turn it off, let alone open it. With a water pressure at ten bars, a temperature of seventy degrees celsius and a big scoop of Finish, it would have been a miracle if fifteen irreplaceable pieces of two-thousand-year-old, unannealed glass had survived Doris Black's thoughtful farewell gesture.[99]

Whereas Derek has considered it "a miracle … that he had reached the age of fifty without ever getting any of those nasty little bugs which afflicted people far less promiscuous than he," here he makes the miraculous conditional upon Aristotelian cause-and-effect.

The ironic statement "it would have been a miracle if fifteen irreplaceable pieces of two-thousand-year old, unannealed glass had survived" could suggest the impossibility, at least in a world that does not believe in miracles (see Appendix 10), of finding fifteen pieces unbroken. A miracle would cause them to survive. But, more likely, the statement suggests Derek's decision to renounce collecting, and it marks his transformation, signalled in the word "disinclined" (which connotes a change of will), from Derek Pettyfer to Derek Quick. His reference to the "thoughtful gesture" is ironic not because Doris's gesture is obviously not thoughtful (rather, it is negligent and cruel) but because it has made Derek think (as in "it was a miracle, Derek reflected") about his identity, chiefly as a collector. Doris's rude gesture is cause for reflection.

Whereas Derek Pettyfer would have risked personal injury to salvage as many as fifteen precious glassworks, Derek Quick has elected to leave the dead to collect the dead. He has distinguished himself from the "rich banker who, in the early forties, had created deep below his London house a bomb-proof museum to protect his collection of eighteenth-century drawings."[100] He has already left behind the dead collector, Woody Weinglass, consumed in his house fire, possibly in his attempt to salvage his kitsch. But in the epilogue, Derek Quick, who as Pettyfer has renounced collecting dead things, *memento mori*, now takes up not a collectible but, in the form of a morphemic postcard, "that message of love, borne back to me out of the past," a mnemonic of Yvette.

All people are either collectors or, like Derek Quick, reformed collectors. One of the first things people collect is first teeth. Children collect them first in their jaws and their mouths. Then, as permanent teeth grow in and push the first teeth out, they collect them, one after another, under their pillows and in canisters and the corners of drawers. But in *Women in the Background* no teeth are permanent, certainly not Kenneth Grocock's teeth. Might Humphries have a tooth fetish? His tooth motif is as prominent as the teeth of the Bee Gees before their "many trips to the orthodontist."[101]

According to Cirlot, "Loss of one's teeth ... signifies fear of castration or of complete failure in life, or inhibition."[102] Does Humphries have this fear? Only he, or his analyst (his psychoanalyst, not his literary analyst!), could say. In *More Please*, he seems to express a fear of failure but never of "complete failure in life," and certainly not of "inhibition," given that, to him, "Success is 80 per cent effrontery and 20 per cent talent."[103] Therefore what is the occasion for the toothy smiles of so many characters in *Women in the Background*?

Cirlot offers another clue in "the Gnostic concept ... in which the teeth constitute the battlements, the wall and the fortifications of the inner man."[104] Thus, when Bob Dooley tells Kenneth Grocock that Derek Pettyfer "dangled his credit cards in front of our Pamela and kicked me in the teeth," he discloses his interiority, or, as the narrator puts it, "The jilted sculptor grimaced again, revealing the necrose dentition in question."[105] Similarly, only when he has had his teeth removed can Kenneth reveal his inner man, the bio-graphed Derek Pettyfer, to whom he attributes the tasteful utterance, "*Give us another whisky Belinda or fair dinkum, I'll knock your teeth so far down your throat you'll have to put your toothbrush up your freckle to clean them.*"[106] In contrast, Pinky and Perky build up the battlements of "interesting people from the world of art and entertainment" with "dazzling teeth,"[107] allowing them to conceal their inner persons behind flashy smiles.

Humphries parodies the binary opposition of human beings as toothed and toothless, notably when Kenneth tries to

identify with the world's great Toothless; the edentate heroes of history. There was Churchill, for instance, whose teeth had never been seen. In spite of being frequently likened to a bulldog, he had never revealed to the camera so much as a glint of porcelain. How superior Churchill was, thought Kenneth. How much more appropriate a role model than the Kennedys![108]

Perhaps a person who never revealed his teeth to the camera cannot be said to be either toothed or toothless and is, therefore, outside the binary. Derek

Quick, who, in the epilogue, is the embodiment of Derek Pettyfer's inner man, is not seen to flash a smile and is therefore outside both the novel's tooth motif and the human binary of toothed and toothless.

Like the ghost of Old Hamlet, who appears on the battlements of Elsinor Castle, the characters in *Women in the Background* move in and out of their toothy battlements like the ghosts of inner people. But Derek Quick, who is never known to haunt the battlements of teeth, dispels the ghosts and, through pin-prick parody, exposes not just pretense but also interiority as he reveals the inner woman of Yvette. In the end, when life gets grave, teeth, along with bones and hair, are one of the few things "left" of the body.

Perhaps the battlements that we erect between ourselves and other people, *Les Autres*, come down only in death. But in the meantime, Humphries seems to say, the minor wound of an open mouth, the orifice of narratorial telling (not of bitchy obituary lying, so blatant as to make your cock grow) is the opening to the inner person. By taking "up the story in my own voice" Quick says that the return to interiority starts not in death, not even with mutability in life, but with the act of telling, which is so simple anyone can perform it: you just open your mouth and blow.

Humphries reveals something of his own interiority here as well, in a wide-open self-parody, a kind of acting-up, an outing, an airing on a Sunday in the park with Barry. The parallels between Derek Pettyfer and Barry Humphries are blatant, like those between the unnamed first-person narrator of *The Enigma of Arrival* (1987) and V.S. Naipaul. Readers are certain *The Enigma of Arrival* is really about Naipaul because the narrator is a Trinidad-born, Oxford-educated author resident in Wiltshire, who has written the same books Naipaul has written. But because the narrator is never named, the reader cannot be certain the novel is a not about a person who is almost identical with Naipaul and that Naipaul is not having the reader on.

Similarly, in *Women in the Background* Humphries appears to have written a kind of displaced autobiography, much as *My Gorgeous Life* (1989) is an autobiography only once removed from *More Please* (1992) and *My Life as Me* (2002). But the reader can never be certain that Derek Pettyfer, or Derek Quick, is really Barry Humphries and not just a person who resembles him on many points, maybe even his *doppelgänger*. Derek resembles Barry, who dissembles himself.

That Derek Pettyfer should be an Australian-born showman and the star of a London television show and of TV commercials; that his principal character should be a pantomime dame and an outspoken harridan who is larger than his own life; that he should be a womanizer and an alcoholic; that the death of his mother should mark a traumatic turning-point in his life; that he should have a pathological suspicion of critics, agents, ex-wives, and other (as he sees them) hangers-on; that he should be a collector of art, books, kitsch, and arcana; that he should be a meticulous dresser and a fastidious cross-dresser; and that he should be a friend of Michael Palin and other comedians and actors – parallels for all of which can be found in *More Please, My Life as Me,* and other accounts of Barry Humphries' life – is less important than the simple fact that Barry Humphries, the historical person, as distinguished from the implied author, never appears in *Women in the Background.* This is (1) because it is a novel, a work of imagination; (2) because having written two volumes of autobiography (*More Please* and *My Life as Me*), he has no need to boil his cabbages thrice; and (3) because Humphries fictionalizes himself as the managerial persona "Barry Humphries" in Dame Edna Everage's act, as the authorial persona "Brian Humphry" in Sir Les Patterson's act, and as "Dr Humphries"[109] in his theatre program blurbs, and has no need to cast himself as Derek Pettyfer Quick (except as a Naipauline Dada prank on prying Grocockeral readers, audiences, and fans; as a pin-prick parody of them, pinning them to the page and pricking the speech bubble in which, through interpretation, they try to trap him).

In *Women in the Background* Humphries parodies Grocockeral readers (as distinguished from receivers), who insist on reading him into every line he writes. Sue Armstrong, for example, in her book *Star Palms* (1988) reads his fortune from two handprints. Humphries cooperated with Armstrong by giving her handprint samples (although, one trusts, not by "Mrs Palm and her five daughters") because she is qualified in palmistry and because, in this instance, she does not take her art too seriously. As she explains: "Because this book leans towards the light-hearted rather than the more serious aspects of the art, these guidelines for interpreting palms are kept to a minimum."[110] Humphries tends not to cooperate with biographers and other interpreters (such as English professors) because so often they take their arts of identity theft and of meaning appropriation, or criticism, much, much too seriously.[111]

Is *Women in the Background* a good novel? Did it make you laugh? Did it move you to ponder every aspect of human nature, except the one that prompted you to laugh? Did it make you wonder whether the story was anything more than the well-turned words on the page? Did it call to mind Malcolm Lowry's assessment of his collection of interrelated short stories, *Hear Us O Lord from Heaven Thy Dwelling Place* (1961) – "it seems to be shaping up less like an ordinary book of tales than a sort of novel of an odd aeolian kind itself, i.e. it is more interrelated than it looks" – and perhaps inspire you to assess it as "a sort of novel of an old music hall kind, i.e. it is more theatrical than it looks," or as Derek Quick calls it, "fancifully, rather like a novel"[112]? If you answered "yes" to any of these questions, even just the first one, then *Women in the Background* is a good novel for you. Of course, I must answer "yes" to my own rhetoric, but I also regard *Women in the Background* as a good novel because Humphries has taken women from the background and foregrounded them in Yvette, who lives on in Derek Quick's remaining "there still, for a long time in the empty flat, reading that message of love, borne back to me out of the past," not as the object of the male gaze but as a woman subject whom the novel is mostly about.

*Women in the Background* passes what Hayden White calls "a test of correspondence":[113] it is "an image of something beyond itself" (a human comedy beyond the life of Barry Humphries), and thus it can "lay claim to representing an insight into or illumination of the human experience of the world" (not Barry Humphries' experience as much as receivers' experiences of the world, the micro-, middy- and macrocosms, of the novel). As discourse, *Women in the Background* "taken in *its* totality as an image of some reality bears a relationship of correspondence to that *of which* it is an image."[114] In that it is "rather like a novel," *Women in the Background* corresponds to a novel: it is an image of a novel, a double, as Derek Pettyfer is Derek Quick's *doppelgänger*. It is more *ficcionnes*, in the ghostly spirit of Jorge Luis Borges and Aritha Van Herk,[115] than fiction in the manner of *les Autres*.

# Humphries' Occasional Texts,
# or One Good Man's Miscellany

There are many good rôles, but there are none that would attract the ordinary actor to want to play them. The other rôles are little ones; they can be written on one sheet of paper.

— Constantin Stanislavski, *My Life in Art*

Let me play all parts
There are no small parts
Only small actors my friend

— Stan Freberg, "Show Folk"

I had now found another outlet for my work: cartoon books. These were simple to put together since the work had already been done. Just grab a year's supply of cartoons, throw them between a couple of covers and there you have it: a book. It was a hit with Christmas shoppers and so I vowed to do a book a year for as along as people bought them.

— Ben Wicks, *Master of None: The Story of Me Life*

Apart from and in addition to their genius I wonder what quality it was they possessed that made them outstanding? Certainly they had authority. Authority in work is important. But they also had something else – a tremendous love of humanity which came right through their work.

— Clarkson Rose, *With a Twinkle in My Eye*

## COMEDIAN, HEAL THYSELF

In *More Please* (1992) Humphries is candid (frank) and *candide* (ingenuous) in recounting his adventures with alcohol in the 1960s and his misadventures with alcoholism in the late 1960s (Dr Lászlo Zadór, Harley Street specialist, London, 1967; Elm Hill Nursing Home, London, 1967) and the early 1970s (St Vincent's Hospital, Melbourne, 1970; Alcoholics Anonymous, Melbourne, 1970; Delmont Hospital, Sydney, 1970). In contrast, Richard Ouzounian, in "An Audience with … Dame Edna and Barry Humphries," has noted that "Humphries has been candid with other journalists up to this point [2000], but he has never discussed his actual recovery."[1] Yet, in fact, Humphries has been alluding to "his actual recovery" since his creation of Les Patterson in 1975. In one example, from the TV show *Dame Edna's Christmas Experience* (1987), Dame Edna, having just activated a button that has turned her stairs into a slide to propel Les Patterson down a chute and out of the television studio, observes, while also moving into a commercial break, "He's on a chute now. He's on a chute. He's going to the London Weekend psychiatric department. He is. It's going to be cold turkey for Les Patterson this Christmas. We'll take a break while they dry him out." That Humphries could utter these words for a laugh at Les Patterson's expense when they cut so close to the bone of his own experience is a mark of his professionalism – and a sign of healing.

Humphries' (mis)adventures with alcohol are (Malcolm) Lowryesque both in pathos and in mythos, with the obvious exception that Humphries has survived his, gaining control over his disease when he was thirty-six, whereas Lowry died at forty-seven, in 1957, choking on his vomit, his demise ruled "death by misadventure." Like Lowry, who, despite his misfortunes, alcoholic and otherwise, saw life as a Dantesque *divina commedia*, Humphries, even with *delirium tremens*, has viewed life as a comedy but in Balzac's encyclopedic sense of *comédie humaine*.

Therefore, at least within the construct of autobiographical telling, Humphries has seen humour in his most abject experiences. In the words of Eric Idle's composition, from the film *Monty Python's The Meaning of Life* (1983), Humphries almost always looks on "the bright side of life." His output of twenty-nine books – novels, autobiographies, fictional biographies, comic books, poetry, dramatic sketches, film scripts, editions, and several unclassifiable works – identify him as a singularly important comic writer, a daring postmodern generic deconstructionist, a Dada prankster in language, and a master of grotesqueries. But his more than forty articles, introductions, and forewords, in contrast to his haughty theatrical image, reveal him as a generous patron of the arts, willing to give young Australian and British painters, writers, and photographers his endorsement.

Consider how, in these passages from *More Please* – which contrast with his italicized dream passages, like "*a remembered story by Kafka*"[2] – humour may have inspired his kindness, niceness, philanthropy, and humanitarianism, even while Humphries was facing down despair and death:

The last example, from Delmont Hospital, which Humphries recalls two years later, while filming *The Adventures of Barry McKenzie* (1972), is more telling than funny. It is an epiphany of Joycean proportions. Dr John Moon's question, "How about gratitude, and concern for others?" touches Humphries deeply. His narratorial comment, "At the time, they were the most novel concepts I had ever encountered," seems ironic, self-parodic, pointing to his reputed self-absorption, to which he alludes in his memory of St. Vincent's: "I did not mind doctors so much, because it was their job to listen, and I was happy to talk to them endlessly on my favourite subject – myself."[3]

Notwithstanding his false bravado here, if indeed his favourite subject is himself, then his second favourite subject must be other people not by default, which would point to logic, but by empathy, which points to niceness and kindness, and, of course, *Les Autres*. In the period between 1965 and 2003, Humphries contributed more than forty articles to books and periodicals. Some of his writing is, understandably, self-centred, such as his confessional articles "The Confessions of Barry Humphries" (1965) and "Back in the Decadent Dump, or, How to Desert a Cultural Renaissance" (1984), and self-serving, such as his promotional and retrospective essays on Bruce Beresford's film *Barry McKenzie*: "Why Bazza Is a Virgin" (1973) and "The Last Australian Hero: The Filming of *The Adventures of Barry McKenzie*" (1981). But most of his writing during this period is on his second favourite subject, other people, twenty-four other-centred articles in all.

He wrote seven forewords: for Keith Dunstan's *Knockers* (1972) and *Ratbags* (1979); for Robert Aickman's *Night Voices: Strange Stories* (1985); for Charles Osborne's *Max Oldaker: Last of the Matinee Idols* (1988); for Glenn A. Baker's *Perpetual Motion: Travels with Glenn A. Baker* (1993); for Rob Johnson's *The Golden Age of the Argonauts* (1997); and for Charles Osborne's novelization of Oscar Wilde's *The Importance of Being Earnest* (1999).

In the same patronal spirit he wrote five introductions to other people's books: to *The Penguin Leunig: Cartoons by Michael Leunig* (1974); to the Louise Whitford Gallery's catalogue *Dreamers and Academics* (1981); to *The Art of Dominic Ryan* (1984); to the paperback edition of Graham McInnes's novel *Humping My Bluey* (1986); and to a new edition of Arthur Machen's story collection *Ornaments in Jade* (1997). He contributed articles to the Government of Victoria tourist book *Victoria with Love: Some Personal Views of Life in Victoria, Australia* (1981); to Geoffrey Dutton's *The Australian Bed-Side Book* (1987); to the Art Gallery of New South Wales catalogues *Francis Lymburner 1916–1972* (1992) and *Margaret Olley* (1997); and to the tribute books *Spike Milligan, a Celebration* (1996), *Spike Milligan: His Part in Our Lives* (2002) and *Australians on Arthur Boyd* (1998).

Table 7.1
Unbottling Humour and Kindness, Humphries Misses Bottom

| Site | Year | Humor in More Please |
|---|---|---|
| Dr László Zadór's office, Harley Street, London | 1967 | I told the doctor a long and rambling yarn which I felt sure would amuse him, and he took copious notes. At the end of the interview, in his strong Hungarian accent, he asked me only one question: "Have you ever thought of going to Alcoholics Anonymous?" I felt soiled and degraded. It seemed to me a disgrace that one should actually *pay* to be insulted. (267) |
| Elm Hill Nursing Home, London | 1967 | "Ahem, twenty, er, no, forty Dunhill please ... and, er, a couple of boxes of matches, thank you." The Irishman smiled again and put the cigarettes on the counter, and the matches, and then a package containing six miniature bottles of Smirnoff Vodka. What are these for?" I asked, flabbergasted. "You're up at Elm Hill, aren't you now?" he asked. I nodded. "*That's what they all order.*" (270) |
| London | 1970 | A doctor told me that my liver was inflamed and asked me how much I drank. It was a difficult question to answer. Did he mean, for example, before or after breakfast? Did he mean wines or spirits? How could a professional man expect me to know how much I drank, when much of my drinking was performed unconsciously and in those reaches of the night that were becoming increasingly blank. (285) |
| Dymphna Ward, St Vincent's Hospital, Melbourne | 1970 | I learned that I was in the psychiatric section of the hospital and a very softly spoken doctor saw me daily for a chat. I was constantly being woken up and given tablets of various colours and quantities, but they did little to alleviate my self-pity. (290) |
| Dymphna Ward, St Vincent's Hospital, Melbourne | 1970 | One morning a man in a suit [Tony] walked straight into my room without knocking, and sat on the end of my bed. I assumed he was a new psychiatrist, and I prepared to launch into another impressive monologue of self-justification, but he cut me short. He explained that he was a prosperous real-estate agent. It occurred to me that he was probably another psychiatric patient, and possibly dangerous. (291) |

Table 7.1
Unbottling Humour and Kindness, Humphries Misses Bottom (*Continued*)

| Site | Year | Humor in More Please |
|------|------|----------------------|
| Dymphna Ward, St Vincent's Hospital, Melbourne | 1970 | I wish I could say that my life changed immediately thereafter. In a sense it did, since, after a few meetings – and to Tony's alarm – I became a world authority on Alcoholics Anonymous. At the drop of a hat I would stand up at a meeting and give everyone the benefit of my insights – at length. I discharged myself from St Vincent's Hospital, and I decided that it was time to resume my trade as a comedian; time to do another show. (293) |
| Delmont Hospital, Sydney | 1970 | Two years before, after a meeting at Delmont Hospital, I remembered asking Dr Moon a question over which I had long agonized: "Now that I have stopped drinking, John, what am I going to do with my time?" He had smiled patiently. "As you get well, a person like you will find more than enough to do. The danger is getting too busy." But I had persisted: "What takes the place of alcohol in a man's life?" Dr Moon said, "How about gratitude, and concern for others?"<br><br>At the time, they were the most novel concepts I had ever encountered. (299) |

In addition, he delivered a speech in *The Power of Speech: Twenty-Five Years of the National Press Club* (1989); allowed excerpts of his autobiography to appear in the collections *Great Southern Landings: An Anthology of Antipodean Travel* (1995) and *Autographs: Contemporary Australian Autobiography* (1996); wrote occasional poems for the anniversary collections *A Garland for Stephen Spender* (1991), a book that he also compiled, and *Paeans for Peter Porter: A Celebration for Peter Porter on His Seventieth Birthday by Twenty of His Friends, 16 February 1999* (1999); and selected a "favourite" poem for a collection commemorating the late John Betjeman (1906–84) – Anthony Kilmister and Donald Lenox's edition *My Favourite Betjeman: A Selection of His Poems by a Selection of His Admirers* (1985).

Why would Humphries devote so much of his creative time and energy over the last thirty years to contributing these works, albeit mostly for friends, writers, artists, and causes he believes in, when he could easily have turned down all these offers by simply offering the excuse of having to write his next show? Is the answer that Humphries is put upon, that he should be more discriminating in agreeing to make literary endorsements? Or is it that, like Edna Everage, he puts out, that he is willing to put his niceness and kindness down on the page, even when the page is somebody else's?

When he was in San Francisco with *The Royal Tour*, I wrote to Humphries about starting a correspondence on the topic of art and artists, with an eye to publication. I received the following note, by fax, dated 17 November 1998, from Humphries' Private Secretary, Rebecca Nestle:

It was very kind of you to write to Barry, who appreciated your letter, but apart from his work at night and the odd publicity call he is absolutely in communicado [sic], trying to write a new show which is to open early next year in Australia. I fear that any meetings have to be postponed until he returns to the States in the middle of next year. I'm sure you understand.

I was delighted to learn Barry Humphries wouldn't waste his time with a nonentity and thrilled to fantasize about my small part in his writing of *Remember You're Out, A New Barry Humphries Event* (1999). Indeed, I did (and do) understand. Yet I also appreciate that Humphries, like the Artful Dodger, is often willing "do [almost] anything at all" as a personal kindness or as a professional courtesy.

When I was awarded tenure as an English professor in 1998, one of my senior colleagues advised me that, now that I had job security, I should turn my attention away from students, from writing new courses and supervising directed studies courses and graduate degrees, and concentrate instead on myself and my career, on writing books and getting promoted. I was shocked to hear this advice from a colleague I greatly respected. I became a university professor so I could devote my life to serving other people. I am writing this book not out of opportunism but out of community service, as a note of thanks to Barry Humphries and as an offering to his squillions of fans.

## THE POLEMICS OF PUT IN HUMPHRIES' SMALL ACTS OF WRITING

Dame Edna Everage puts out (just ask her gynecologist) and, as "the megastar who won't go away," she stays put. Sir Les Patterson puts down some members of his audience and puts away Johnny Walker and Chardonnay. Sandy Stone puts up with Beryl's absences and puts off death and the afterlife. Barry Humphries puts lyrics to music and puts on his audiences. But is he put upon by his friends and colleagues? I believe he writes forewords, introductions, and articles as acts of kindness and niceness for people, out of "gratitude, and concern for others," to Moon them.

He is not put upon. On the contrary, he puts out like Dame Edna! What does Humphries put out? He puts out the modality Laugh. He makes laughter the currency of theatrical and social exchange; he is concerned with modalizing audiences, if only for the duration of the performance of watching in the theatre or reading a text, reminding them of what configures them as in space and time: Laugh. He shows his gratitude to audiences for giving him their attention and their love by making them Laugh: by moving them to laughter, of course, but also by transforming them from mutable human beings, Yeatsian "dying animals," into a modality of sound and imagination beyond decay, as if the laughter of a theatre audience were never to fade out, or as if, in a Monty Python spirit, audiences were literally to die laughing, but their laughter itself were never to die out, so the modality Laugh would endure for all other generations.[4]

Humphries' puttings are polemical because they engage audiences and readers in discussions and arguments, much as in the theatre Edna and Les are known to put audiences in their place, notably latecomers, people who arrive conspicuously late for the show and people who stand out in the crowd because they are new to Humphries' shtick. Whether on stage or in print, his polemics have to do with the nature of niceness and kindness, and with the interplay of the bizarre and the shocking with what I call political correctitude.[5] In his introductions and forewords, especially, he puts down his polemic for all to consider.

In his introduction to *The Penguin Leunig: Cartoons by Michael Leunig* (1974), collected from the Melbourne *Age* and other Australian newspapers and magazines, Humphries performs his introductory task well, citing Leunig's ironic themes ("World cataclysm, The Flood, loneliness, cruelty, lust and greed")[6] and his absurd scope ("A man in a boat rows out of his apartment window towards a distant moon. His wife is concerned but shares his fantasy. 'You've forgotten your pond' she cries. There is the joke; there is the Leunig poetry").[7]

But here, as in an opening anecdote about a dinner host who abandons him at table to watch him on TV, he polemicizes certain issues of mediatization as they have rubbed him the wrong way:

A claret-faced Melbourne hack recently reproached me for presenting a theatrical revue in which, so it seemed to him, I exhibited "a sorry unawareness of how much life had changed." Grub Street prigs expect jokes to somehow justify themselves by being "satirical" or up-to-date: *relevant* in short. Interpretative artists – even vaudeville artistes – are not newsagents or telex machines thank God, yet they are suspect by drab minds if they fail to assert a "point of view."[8]

Similarly, in Janet Frame's novel *The Carpathians* (1988), when the protagonist, Mattina Brecon, dies from cancer, "a malignant tumour so deep-seated that excision would sever an artery in Mattina's chest,"[9] the narrator reports her death narratologically: "Mattina died in February, surrendering at last her point of view."[10] With his sharp diction, which stops just short of the pin-prick point of satire, Humphries puts "hacks" and "prigs" in their place, under the rubble of black type.

But to Michael Leunig he pays a high compliment: "I hope this book will bring Leunig's art to the attention of a wide international audience. He deserves his country's honour because he is the only artist I know working for newspapers who seems to me to have a truly inspired comic gift."[11] Perhaps Humphries is being a good little penguin here, winning a few sales for the publishers, but he has also been a bit of an angry penguin in his artistic career, and, in the end, he proves himself an upright penguin, doing a good turn out of concern and gratitude.

If to Dame Edna Everage "a talk show is a monologue, interrupted by total strangers," to Barry Humphries an introduction is prelusive, too brief to be allusive. His introduction to *The Art of Dominic Ryan, 1979–81* (1984) is a mere 116 words, but it is the soul of brevity. He focuses less on Ryan's greatness as an artist than on his originality: "Strange, even alarming, images of Dominic Ryan recall the work of no other artist. For this reason criticism may find him an uncomfortable specimen to pin down neatly."[12] By electing not to pin Ryan down, Humphries indirectly distinguishes his introduction from art criticism. Rather than qualifying Ryan's art, he shocks readers by recommending Ryan as an original artist who is *not* worth watching: "Mr Ryan is not an artist to be watched, but an artist to beware of."[13] Because in his sur-surreal paintings Ryan exploits tropes of bondage and torture, Humphries complements his introduction with a photograph of himself, purportedly at the dentist, with an elaborate orthodonitic apparatus (worthy of Pinky and Perky at their sadistic worst) attached to his mouth and head.

His anecdote about the self-portrait reveals his concern and gratitude for a daring young artist: "It was only after a recent visit to my dentist's surgery that I realised I was turning into a painting by Dominic Ryan. It is not an enviable destiny, but I hope it guarantees me a place in the pantheon of art."[14] Readers may wonder which is more bizarre: that Humphries should have himself photographed having a procedure at the dentist or that he should stage an "S & M Lady" picture just for a book occasion. Prompting this reflection, Humphries leads readers less into his own mood of self-deprecating humour than into the *viseur bizarre* ("bizarre viewfinder") of Ryan's paintings, and he initiates Ryan into his company of visionary painters.

Humphries' other principal introductions form a pattern of his personal anecdotes combined with his compliments to the author. They suggest that Humphries has used his success as a performer, painter, and writer, and his fame as an Australian ambassador at and writ large, to further the careers, reputations, and memories of fellow artists.

In his introduction to *Ornaments in Jade*, which is a brief publishing history of Arthur Machen's fiction and a personal tour through antiquarian book shops and rare first editions (which knowing readers will infer is his own tour), Humphries introduces himself as "we," as one of the company

Table 7.2
Permit Me to Introduce the Author by Introducing Myself

| Humphries' Introduction to: | Humphries' "Permit Me to Introduce Myself" | Humphries' "My Compliments to the Author" |
|---|---|---|
| Graham McInnes, *Humping My Bluey* (1986) | A couple of my suburban sketches appeared on a small "microgroove" (quaint period word) and when I first read the McInnes autobiography in the mid-sixties I was flattered to find that my privately circulated "Wild Life in Suburbia" records had earned a generous footnote. (5–6) | The precise observation, the humour, and the author's apparently flawless powers of recollection have produced an absorbing and joyous narrative, as fresh and direct as Sassoon or Isherwood, and, thank God, free of those arch autobiographical mannerisms which have long given sensitivity a bad name. In short, you feel you are reading a classic. (6–7) |
| Arthur Machen, *Ornaments in Jade* (1997) | The reputation of Arthur Machen has suffered many vicissitudes, amongst them shameful neglect and disproportionate praise. Those of us who admire him will readily forgive the latter. (vii) | Pervading all these stories is the author's sexual morbidity, the more intriguing for being expressed in Machen's limpid latinate prose. The "decadent" elements attain their unique zest because we know they were not contrived by some enervated Enoch Soames, but that they sprang from the imagination of an Inverness-cloaked trencherman of pipes and punchbowls. (ix) |
| Charles Osborne, *The Importance of Being Earnest* (1999) | Then my mind flew back, as I find it increasingly does, to Melbourne, Australia, in the fifties, and to an encounter I had there with a very old English actor called Gaston Mervale, who had appeared in a touring production of *Earnest*, long whiles ago. He recounted having met Oscar Wilde in Naples, Italy, and being told by the playwright himself that he had toyed with the idea of novelizing *The Importance of Being Earnest*. (vii) | Dr Osborne has not just "joined up the lines": he has translated the play with immense sympathy into a Handbag-sized composition much more reader-friendly than a bald theatrical script (a literary form with which even some thespians of my acquaintance have difficulty). I for one am grateful. (viii) |

of Machenites. But a Publisher's Note suggests that his introduction is a personal endorsement: "The text of this centenary edition is based on Machen's revised typescript, reproduced by kind permission of the President of the Arthur Machen Society, Mr Barry Humphries."[15] This note identifies the text as an introduction both to Machen's short story collection and to Barry Humphries as president of the Arthur Machen Society.

By putting life-tellings into his introductions, Humphries enacts Judeo-Christian charity because, of course, no one has greater love than he who puts down his life for his mates. If Les Patterson is the king of audience put-downs – his rudest audience put-down, like a poke in the eye with a sharp stick, recorded in *Les Patterson Has a Stand-up: Live and Rampant* (1996), is: "What's so fuckin' funny about that?" – then Humphries is king of puttings-down, of putting down his life-tellings for his fellow artists.

A foreword serves a different function from that of an introduction (to announce a book's themes and range). Usually, an author writes his or her own introduction. Humphries may have written introductions to other people's books because of his special admiration for the subjects' works (*The Penguin Leunig* and *The Art of Dominic Ryan*) or because the subjects were no longer around – Graham McInnes died in 1970, Arthur Machen in 1947 – to write their own introductions to new editions of their works. By convention, someone other than the author of a book usually writes its foreword. Exceptions to this rule of publishing are many, of course, but one exception especially pertinent to Humphries is the first edition of *Humping My Bluey* (1966), which contains no introduction and to which the author, Graham McInnes, contributed his own foreword.

Barry Humphries has been this "someone else" seven times of note, always for people in whom he believes, or has believed: Keith Dunstan, Robert Aickman, Charles Osborne (and Max Oldaker), Glenn A. Baker, Rob Johnson (and the Argonauts), and Oscar Wilde. His forewords are of a different design from the anecdotal-complimentary pattern of his introductions, although they do succeed in introducing the work at eyes' length. In his forewords, Humphries' pattern is to place himself in the company of the people who are the books' subjects: knockers and knocked, ratbags, gothicists, Phillip Street Theatre revue artistes, world travellers, the Argonauts, and Ernest and Bunburry. He writes forewords to books in which he believes, but which also happen to be partly about him.

Thus, in his foreword to Keith Dunstan's *Knockers* (1972), Humphries enumerates some of the hard knocks he has had to take – mostly from critics, as an Australian performer who is known to humour his compatriots, "to crack a few unsporting jokes about Australia"[16] – and even some of the knocks he has given out. "Am I not a knocker myself," he asks, "for knocking knockers?"[17] Similarly, in his foreword to Dunstan's *Ratbags* (1979), Humphries puts forward, almost verbatim (letting his monologue do double-duty), the words of his performance piece "Barry Humphries at Las Vegas," from the LP *Barry Humphries' Savoury Dip* (1971) (see Appendix 11). The speaker on the recording has an American accent so is only "implied Humphries," but the foreword is both by-lined and signed "Barry Humphries." The speaker begins by asking "What is a Ratbag," goes on to list some of the types in the company of Ratbags (whose personality traits include folly, churlishness, fastidiousness, timidity, pretension, superstition, political correctitude, presumption, archaism, and irksomeness), and concludes by announcing, "And friends this story is true ... I AM THAT RAT-BAG!"[18] Thus, he joins the company of Ratbags, as he has joined the company of Knockers.

In his foreword to Robert Aickman's posthumous short story collection *Night Voices* (1985), Humphries keeps company with a more "savoury dip" of people: bibliophiles and, in particular, collectors of arcane literature:

I still ascribe rare intuitive gifts to the best booksellers, although I know that like their brethren the gypsies[19] and fortune tellers, they combine an innocent knavery with their clairvoyant faculties. Nor is the power of retrocognition uncommon amongst bibliopoles who regularly press upon me expensive editions of recondite works I had enjoyed and discarded many long years before.[20]

Humphries may be the only writer since Gutenberg who has managed to link the words "retrocognition" (surely, his neologism) and "bibliopoles" in fluent syntax.

What is the nature of this accomplishment? It identifies Humphries as sesquipedalian, lexicographical, and bibliophilic; a word-freak; somebody with one-and-a-half feet, who has committed the English lexis to memory (not to CD-ROM), and who knows the Barthesian *plaisir du texte*. It also identifies him as a grateful and concerned person who knows when to invoke the language of gratefulness, when to speak and write *gratis* – without taking payment but also freely, of his own free will, out of kindness, in a foreword or an introduction: "I have to thank Ellis Bird, proprietrix of a once famous Melbourne book shop, for introducing me, some 35 years ago, to the Gothic novelists; or at least, for divining that a schoolboy might relish the charnel-house eroticism of 'Monk' Lewis."[21] His gesture of thanks to Ellis Bird, in 1985, shows that Humphries took seriously Dr John Moon's counsel to him, in 1970, that he show his "gratitude, and concern for others."

His expression of gratitude has continued right to the present, as in his closing words in his introduction to Charles Osborne's novel(ization) *The Importance of Being Earnest*: "I for one am grateful,"[22] and in the opening and closing words of identity in his foreword to *Perpetual Motion*: "Glenn A. Baker is a Sydney writer" and "Barry Humphries is a Melbourne writer."[23] In addition, all his introductions and forewords are expressions of his gratitude not only to authors for their books but also to the gods for having healed him, in particular women in the background (Diana, Artemis, Ishtar, Hathor, and Anaitis, who, of course, are the patronal lunar goddesses of Dr Moon).

Keeping company with a goddess was nothing new to Humphries, who, in 1956, as a young struggling actor made the transition from sitting in the gods at the theatre to performing on stage with the gods of Australian revue. His first successful show at the Phillip Street Theatre was the revue *Around the Loop* (1956–57), which starred Max Oldaker, June Salter, and Gordon Chater, and which featured, along with Pat Pearson, Wendy Blacklock, and Shirley Regan, a young Barry Humphries. The program to *Around the Loop* describes Oldaker as an actor "so well known in Australia that it seems impossible to enumerate all his successes," whereas of Humphries it says only "he divides his time between Radio and Phillip Street Theatre,"[24] which suggests he was beginning to move about among theatre divinities.

That Humphries went on to experience his own apotheosis in the theatre is evidenced in his having been chosen to write the foreword to Charles Osborne's biography, *Max Oldaker: Last of the Matinée Idols* (1988). In his characteristic up-front foreword style, Humphries recounts how he joined the company of Phillip Street Theatre and kept company with Oldaker. He gives credit to Oldaker for his own career:

In 1956, soon after I had been fired by the Union Theatre Repertory Company, (now the Melbourne Theatre Company) I was invited to join the Phillip Street Revue Theatre in Sydney. News of this enterprising and energetic company had percolated to Melbourne, and I was already persuaded that my talents were better suited to the Music Hall than they were to the rigorous discipline of the conventional Repertory Theatre.[25]

In the foreword he acknowledges Oldaker not only as "the last of the Australian Matinée Idols" but also, in another of his lunar gestures of "gratitude" and "concern," as a music hall artiste who gave him a leg-up onto the boards.

Ever observant of theatre etiquette, Humphries is careful to take second-billing, even thirty-two years after he and Oldaker first worked together:

The show in which I had been invited to appear [*Mr and Mrs*] was short-lived but my contract was renewed for the subsequent revue, *Around the Loop* starring Max Oldaker and the gifted young English comedian, Gordon Chater, and featuring quite a large cast of pretty, talented girls. The best material was carved up between Max and Gordon. I, who shared their small subterranean dressing room, had to content myself with the leftovers; excellent training for a young revue artiste.[26]

Clearly, Humphries esteems having kept company with Max Oldaker and Gordon Chater, and he regards the run of *Around the Loop* as his tenure in RADA – not the Royal Academy of Dramatic Art but the Revue Artistes' Dramatic Academy.

In his foreword to *Perpetual Motion*, he politely anticipates keeping company with author Glenn A. Baker on a "desolate beach" (reminiscent of the site of his *Desert Island Discs* appearance on BBC Radio 4, 17 July 1988):[27] "One day in the future we well meet on a desolate beach in the Bahamas or some Corsican cove. He striding along the shingle, I in my wheelchair."[28] Notwithstanding the intervention here of Dame Edna Everage, who claims to have healed some nonambulatory members of her audiences, Humphries' positioning himself in a wheelchair, as well as being hilarious and self-parodic, references

1 his age: even now, at age seventy, Humphries can kick up his heels as Dame Edna, and shows few signs of slowing down and none of retiring;
2 his ageism: Edna's exposure of "seniors" in her audiences, while keeping her own age (and even Humphries' age) indeterminate;
3 the age: Humphries' periodicities, as insular as the "desert island" Australia, are decidedly *fin de siècle*, music hall, and Dada;
4 mutability: the transitoriness of the theatrical stage and of the human body, and the ephemerality of the book, of publication, and, ultimately, even of Humphries' *œuvre*.

In his forewords Humphries recalls an even earlier company than that of the Phillip Street Theatre and an even more fantastic circle than that of a desert island. In Rob Johnson's study of the popular and successful children's radio program *The Argonauts Club* (ABC, 1941–72), *The Golden Age of The Argonauts* (1997), Humphries confesses, with nostalgic pride, "I was an enthusiastic Argonaut between the age of 10 and 13."[29] He even credits *The Argonauts Club* with helping him start his careers as a painter: "When I was a fully fledged club member and I had sent off to far-flung Sydney endless packages containing my entire creative output of verse and painting, I received an art prize signed by all three of my idols."[30] And as an author: "In about 1945 [Humphries was age eleven] a group of my caricatures was reproduced – badly out of register – on the Argonauts page of the ABC *Weekly*."[31]

Throughout the foreword, Humphries expresses his loyalty to the Argonauts, to the archive of the radio show and the memory of the members of the club. But he also conducts himself as an Argonaut still, as a Wordsworthian child who has fathered a man, a comedian with the ability to heal himself as well as *Les Autres* through laughter, by invoking the modality Laugh and through memory, making the past "to have been" again as it once was in imagination.

Humphries has also shown his "caring and sharing" spirit in several of his articles. For example, he contributed extensive notes (in the form of a letter) on his Phillip Street Theatre days and the 1950s Sydney art scene to Geoffrey Dutton, who was writing *The Innovators: The Sydney Alternatives in the Rise of Modern Art, Literature and Ideas* (1986). Dutton cites two excerpts from Humphries' notes in *The Innovators*[32] and a much longer extract, under the title "In Search of Bohemia," in his edition *The Australian Bed-Side Book: A Selection of Writings from* The Australian Literary Supplement (1987).[33] In his acknowledgments in *The Innovators*, Dutton says, "Also I am most grateful to Barry Humphries, who wrote me a long letter about his early days in Sydney,"[34] but, of course, Humphries may have contributed his letter in gratitude to Dutton for his many years of friendship.

Humphries has written two important articles supporting exhibition catalogues of fellow artists Francis Lymburner and Margaret Olley. In "Lost at Life: A Recollection of Francis Lymburner" (1992), he pays tribute to Lymburner as a painter and a friend, in part by giving him a role in his own Notting Hill theatrical mythos, the mythos that informed his finest poem, "Sandy Agonistes": "Although I had no money and my wife and I lived in a small basement flat in Notting Hill Gate we found ourselves falling for Francis's hard luck story and offering him our spare bedroom for a new nights."[35] Even though "the 'few days' he was staying with us became weeks, the weeks months. Resentment set in,"[36] Humphries' article is *un hommage* to a "to have been" friend who is no longer *un homme*, whose past seems "not to have been."[37]

His article on Margaret Olley, "A Note of Exclamation" (1996), is also *hommage* but to a living artist. Here his gesture of friendship is more reserved than it was with Lymburner in that Humphries does not present Olley as his houseguest but, rather, himself as a passive visitor to her home: "A visit to Margaret Olley is certainly an unforgettable experience. Her house is a series of studios, filled – burgeoning – with the furniture, textiles and objects which she incorporates into her ravishing *natures mortes*."[38] He continues his house tour in the passive mood – "as the artist conducts her visitor through the rich labyrinth of her magically transformed terraced house"[39] – albeit with a curator's eye. Only in the article's final sentence does he activate himself: "What a fortunate man I am to know Margeret Olley!"[40] With the deference of an acolyte, he expresses his "gratitude" to Olley as a great artist and his "concern" that she get a proper critical recognition.

Humphries is considerably more familiar in his tribute to his old friend in Roger Sawyer's compilation *Spike Milligan, a Celebration: The Best of Milligan* (1996): "It was in Sydney in the early sixties that I first met Spike Milligan. At the time, I was performing my first one man show [*A Nice Night's Entertainment*] in a small theatre, when I was told the famous Goon was in the audience. He came backstage later and we soon became friends."[41] But does his assessment of his friendship with Milligan, "I regard myself as a fortunate man to know him,"[42] which is the last sentence of the article, seem a hollow turn of phrase in its familiarity? Or does Humphries reserve this idiom for only the very greatest artists, Milligan and Olley? In fact, Humphries uses the complimentary closing yet again, in his untitled posthumous tribute in *Spike Milligan: His Part in Our Lives* (2002): "What a fortunate man I am to have known Spike Milligan."[43] Here it is poignant, a clown's mark of respect to a fellow of infinite jest. The truth is that a cogent remark bears repeating, just as my own comment, "I regard myself as an unfortunate man not to know Barry Humphries," is one I hope never to have to utter again.

## ODDS, SODS, PODS, AND BODS

Barry Humphries' first pseudonymously written book is *Dame Edna's Coffee Table Book: A Guide to Gracious Living and the Finer Things of Life by One of the First Ladies of World Theatre* (1976), a kind of recipe book (the Table of Contents replaced with an "Ingredients" page) for Kafkaesque starvation artists. It features a commendation page (with tributes from Patrick White, Dudley Moore, Sidney Nolan, and others); a genealogy; a family photo album; a curriculum vitae; a letter to the reader; etiquette, sex, and beauty manuals; a glossary and pronunciation guide; a photo gallery; a cook book; a gardening book; a poetry book; a scandal sheet; and a photomontage of Dame Edna Everage, masked and unmasked.

Edna categorizes her book *qua* book in her title but also referentially, "as I write this wonderful book for the famous firm of George G. Harrap & Co. Ltd."[44] She also distinguishes herself as author and from Barry Humphries: "The joke is, of course, that some critics, poor baffled little things that they are, think Barry and I are one and the same person simply because we have never been photographed together! This is not in actual fact true as you'll have seen in the pickie overleaf."[45] The photograph, in the manner of medieval iconography, shows Edna twice as large as Barry, clearly because she is twice as important. Humphries used the photograph again inside the *On Stage* program for the 1977 production of *Housewife! Superstar!!* at Theatre Four, New York, where it is credited to John Timbers. The photo first appeared in *Harpers & Queen* in October 1973. Of the legerdemain, Timbers says: "I did some trick photography and had Barry presenting her with a bunch of gladioli. It was a very fawning, deferential Barry – I printed him smaller – set against the towering, formidable Edna. I've never analysed it, to be honest. It was just a joke."[46]

Timbers' picture anticipates another playful shot of Edna and Barry, a News Limited photograph reprinted in *Barry Humphries' Flashbacks*,[47] showing them together on the doorstep: this time the legerdemain of trick photography is revealed not in the clash of bodies but in the ragged line of mismatched floor tiles. Like Luis Buñuel and Salvador Dali in *Un Chien andalou*, Humphries is always careful to make a clean cut in his *coups d'oeil*, such as his cutting remarks to literalists who insist on seeing him in Edna, and his cutting down to size of any complacent readers of his books. Yet the mismatched tiles may well have been not a photo editor's error but Humphries' deliberate Dada prank.

The word "prank" derives from the Middle English "pranken," meaning "to show off." In this regard, Humphries might be showing off not only his Dada sense of humour, by creating a Montgomery Clift (i.e., "rift") between Dame Edna and her tenacious manager, but also his knowledge of Dada history. His allusion might be to the greatest Dutch Dada artist Theo van Doesburg, who, with the Dutch architect J.J.P. Oud, designed "De Vonk (1917–18), a seaside hostel for young women, which featured vibrant and oscillating tile floors and wall mosaics designed by van Doesburg."[48] In his picture-perfect Dada prank, Humphries does Van Doesburg and Oud well, and visualizes the fracture that is the ironic distance in all comedy.

His second pseudonymous book is *Dame Edna's Bedside Companion* (1982), despite the fact that the by-line qualifies its authorship as "crafted by Dame Edna Everage." Indeed, the book, although it features some fine writing, is a kind of hand-crafted Dada assemblage consisting of narratives (including a "MICRONOVEL"), poems, photomontages, drawings, memoranda, advice columns, medical articles, catalogues, recipes, formulae, diet books, quizzes, a crossword puzzle, biographies, a letter, a scrapbook, and household hints, all in/as an entertaining prank. It establishes Humphries' series of comedic bibliophilic challenges to the literary construct "book."

Technically, any written or printed document, record, or set of pages is a book. Yet my English department tenure committee would hardly count an unpublished or uncontracted manuscript, or even a published article, as a book when considering a professor for tenure, promotion, or merit. And in the so-called "information age" the construct "book" has become as fugitive as a power surge of deconstructive electrons. Yet Humphries, like an artiste peeling a banana on the music hall stage, was deconstructing the book back when, in the period between 1976 and 1979, he turned out our Edna Everage as a heterodox authoress.

The book in which he does most to deconstruct the book is *Les Patterson's Australia* (1978), beginning with the by-line "extolled by Barry Humphries," in which Humphries gives praise to Australia, albeit through Les Patterson's ironic le(n)s. If any written or printed record is a book, then *Les Patterson's Australia* is a bookish book. In his foreword, Patterson truly confides to his readers:

If you ask me what I'm proud of, more than anything else I'd say it in one word – TRACK-RECORD. Although I say it myself – mine's a beauty. The rest is history. Hopefully this sumptuous volume by my goodself will find its way into an in-home library situation, not only in terms of Australia, but also Overseas where interest in our superlative life-style is arguably nil.[49]

Les is absolutely right, of course, if not about outside interest in Australia, then that "TRACK-RECORD" is one word. But if *Les Patterson's Australia* is a book because it is a "TRACK-RECORD," then I suppose a junkie's punctured arm is also a book because it is a track-record, often the cause of his or her being booked on a criminal offence.

Les Patterson's book comprises pictures and captions and some captious text (fifteen poems, a letter, and a newspaper clipping). Of the seventy-six pictures, including those on the covers, seventy-five show, and show up, Les, and the other is of "Patterson Pie,"[50] which is an entrée consisting of two sausage rolls, seasoned with ketchup, on a piece of toast. This picture solves a riddle I have been pondering: "Why is Les Patterson like a sausage?" The answer? "Because they are both bangers." Humphries boldfaces the sexual overtones of Patterson's Pie in his description of it as "Sir Leslie's favourite after-theatre snack – the secret of his incredible energy," as if "energy," like every other prop of impropriety in his life, were double entendre rhyming slang for libido. The other pictures – the camera loves Les – are anathema to reading, yet *Les Patterson's Australia* is a comic book that the reader can get (understand and generate) without reading. It is enough to make readers give up reading. It is the deconstruction of "book," the declassification of the book as a class-distinctive artifact or commodity in that, as the pictures show, its putative author clearly has no class.

Humphries turned from Les Patterson's bad taste bite of Australia to his own kitschen-sink delicatessen in *Barry Humphries' Treasury of Australian Kitsch* (1980). In his introduction Humphries classifies (categorizes and puts manners on) his book, observing that "no single art book, let alone one which surveys the total panorama of the Australian aesthetic achievement, has addressed itself to so immense a public" and that *Australian Kitsch* "is essentially an art book and a work of original scholarship."[51] He even replaces the Table of Contents with a "Catalogue," organizing the content taxonomically rather than sequentially.

Humphries' scholarship has involved research and compilation, and the invitation he extends to readers to share in his "treasures" of Australian popular art, of odds, sods, pods, and bods: oddities, sodomites, podites, and bodies. His photographic selection of Australian *objets d'art* is imposing, many of them framing Humphries' continual performance as a Dada *poseur.* Consider these examples:

1 odds: a picture of a pineapple-shaped building, "Sunshine Plantation," with the caption "A typical Queensland home,"[52] and portraits of two bonneted women, an unidentified model in a hat made of a crab,[53] and Dame Edna Everage in her 1976 Royal Ascot chapeau, shaped like the Sydney Opera House;[54]

2 sods: pictures of a men's street urinal, with the subtle caption, "The sensuous nature of the Australian renders him peculiarly susceptible to texture, and the pragmatic and aesthetic qualities of exposed aggregate,"[55] and of two transvestites, whom the caption places among "a race of young men and women whose sophistication and wholesome sexuality are the envy of lands outside the A.D.R."[56];

3 pods: a picture of a kangaroo paw flower, with the caption, "Marsupial foot-fetishists with an horticultural bias are keen cultivators of this curious bloom which rivals the Gladiolus as Australia's national flower,"[57] and a picture of a woman who has just pulled a foot out of her slippers because, as the caption notes, " 'environments for the feet' are a favoured nesting place of the fecund funnel-web, or deadly slipper spider";[58]

4 bods: a postcard made from kangaroo hide,[59] two pictures of an old Holden, showing its tail fins nudging the arches of the Sydney Opera House,[60] and a group shot of the contestants at the 1979 Miss Universe pageant, which was held in Perth.[61]

In addition to the public urinal, which recalls Duchamp's readymade *Fountain* (1917), Humphries makes several telling Dada allusions. He shows a hand-painted tea towel, depicting the Sydney Opera House and quasi Aboriginal motifs, which bears the caption: "Utilitarian Art. This beautiful textile, hand-painted with evocative native scenes, is here displayed on the most successful piece of mobile sculpture ever wrought by an Australian hand – Hills's 'Rotary Clothes Hoist' (*circa?*)."[62] Humphries thus declares an umbrella clothes line a readymade *objet trouvé.* In another Dada declaration, he lines up seven media award show trophies, with the gloss: "These coveted and striking statuettes in metal and perspex are also a boon to Australian-based sculptors, offering them a welcome chance to liberate themselves from the influences of Henry Moore, Barbara Hepworth and Lyn Chadwick."[63] These trophies look like sculptures that Constantin Brancusi (1876–1957) would have made today.

## BARRY HUMPHRIES, A WIDO IN THE AUSTRALIAN INTELLIGENTSIA

In one of his photo captions in *Barry Humphries' Treasury of Australian Kitsch*, Humphries subtly identifies himself as another kind of person often marked up and out in Australia – other, that is, than the tall poppy (or tall pansy) and the expatriate, as he has been stigmatized. The photograph is of Tom Bass's fountain sculpture, situated in the façade of the Peninsular and Orient Line building, on the corner of Castlereagh and Hunter Streets in Sydney. Although Humphries does not name the fountain, he does allude to its history: "The allure this functional free-form fountain holds for Sydney's nocturnal fontaphiles has necessitated round-the-clock surveillance by the New South Wales hard-pressed water police."[64] This allusion may be immediately recognizable to Sydney-siders and other Australians, but to the book's other readers, the speakers of "some thirty-seven languages ... in Western Europe, the Americas and the South-East Asian continent ... two thirds of the world's literate population,"[65] it is surely an obscurity.

Of course, Humphries is alluding (1) to the cover of the February 1964 issue of *Oz* magazine, which depicts three men urinating into the fountain, of which one Mr Polonius has observed, "By th' mass and 'tis, like a urinal indeed"; and (2) to the censorship controversy that exploded in Australia when "the editors [Richard] Neville and [Richard] Walsh, and the artist, [Martin] Sharp, were charged under the Obscene and Indecent Publications Act."[66] His allusion to "nocturnal fontaphiles" hints at Humphries as that object and subject of dread in some Australian traditions: an intellect.[67]

Despite all appearances of folly, frivolity, absurdity, and niceness; despite his act of eschewing intellectual properties such as satire and meaning, Barry Humphries is an intellect, a person of singular knowledge, conviction, understanding, thought, and perception – an Australian, like Mordecai Himmelfarb and Dame Leonie J. Kramer, whom the intellect has not failed and who does not fail it. He is the very model of an Australian intellectual gentleman.

The author of a foreword (1999) to *The Importance of Being Earnest*, he even recalls Oscar Wilde, most obviously in his dandyism but also in his intellectual sharpness:

In dark times an intellectual is very often looked to by members of his or her nationality to represent, speak out for, and testify to the sufferings of that nationality. Prominent intellectuals always are, to use Oscar Wilde's description of himself, in symbolic relationship with their time: in the public consciousness they represent achievement, fame, and reputation which can be mobilized on behalf of an ongoing struggle or embattled community. Inversely, prominent intellectuals are very often made to bear the brunt of their community's opprobrium, either when factions within it associate the intellectual with the wrong side (this has been quite common in Ireland, for instance, but also in Western metropolitan centers during the Cold War years when pro- and anti-Communists traded blows) or when other groups mobilize for an attack. Certainly Wilde felt himself to be suffering the guilt of all avant-garde thinkers who had dared to challenge the norms of middle-class society.[68]

Although Edward Said (1935–2003) does not cite Barry Humphries by name – his company of intellects includes Bertrand Russell, Noam Chomsky, Antonio Gramsci, Jean-Paul Sartre, Elie Wiesel, and Virginia Woolf – he seems to invoke his spirit in his references to the role of the intellect within an at times hostile community and when he singles out Oscar Wilde.

For nearly fifty years Australians have looked to Humphries to represent them on stage, in print, on canvas and even abroad during the "dark times" and the "sufferings" of British and American cultural domination. He maintained a "symbolic relationship" with Dame Edna Everage throughout the second half of the twentieth century: Edna is a symbol of the age and "in the public consciousness." Humphries is an artist and a citizen of "achievement, fame, and reputation" who has fought for his community, notably to preserve heritage architecture. He has also felt his community's "opprobrium" when people, including Sir Les Patterson, have accused him of letting down the side, of giving his art to the Poms, and "tipping the bucket on his superlative homeland for an easy quid."[69] Finally, like Oscar Wilde, Humphries is an "avant-garde thinker" who dares "to challenge the norms of middle-class society," of every Norm Everage (not just Edna's husband).

Dame Edna Everage is a symbol of her age, of ever(y) age. Her bizarre hats, whether contoured like the Sydney Opera House, moulded like a crown, squeezed into a pillbox, or scattered into veils and flowers, are her trademark coverings for her peculiar intelligence. Similarly, Humphries' own akubras, fedoras, and panamas are the marks or symbols of his role as an intellect of the age. Edna Everage and Barry Humphries, it might be said, are at once millinery and millenary (see Appendix 9).

As J.E. Cirlot points out, "According to Jung, the hat, since it covers the head, generally takes on the significance of what goes on inside it: thought ... The choice of a hat – associated with a particular social order – denotes the desire to be admitted to that set or to partake of its inherent characteristics."[70] Thus, Edna's wearing a Sydney Opera House hat at Royal Ascot symbolizes her membership in the house of Australia,[71] and her wearing a crown at her backstage meeting with Queen Elizabeth the Second symbolizes her loyalty to the British monarchy.[72] Humphries' wearing of hats, always of the broad-brimmed, low-crowned variety, symbolizes his fellowship with Australian men (akubra), his dedication to leisure and pleasure (panama), and his role as a theatrical player (fedora).[73]

Whereas Dame Edna Everage is a widow,[74] Humphries is a wido – in my own Sapolean dialect a person of wide knowledge, understanding, thought, and perception: an intellect. He has taken the saying "to keep something under one's hat" literally, using hats, and other costume properties (flying buttress spectacles, improbable monocles, gorgeous frocks, sleek Savile row suits) to cover his intellect; and he has taken it idiomatically, tipping his hats to audiences around the world and sharing with them his knowledge of Australia and Britain, art, literature, comedy, nostalgia, and obscurantia; his understanding of human pretension, hypocrisy, kindness, and cruelty; his thoughts on everything that comes to the top of his head and the tip of his tongue; and his perceptions of all that is bizarre, from Les Patterson and Edna Everage, who on stage are proper sights, to original ideas that have never before found a way into books and non-books (such as his remark that Melbourne should be coloured orange):

The benevolent Authorities have insisted that as many objects as humanly possible should adopt an orange hue or related shades of rust, shrimp, mango, ochre, pumpkin, terra-cotta, mustard, mimosa, paw-paw, auricular wax or marmalade; and it is not surprising that this directive (inspired by a sloughed citrus rind) should also dictate the colour of the national sweetmeat, or *jaffa*, as well as the accoutrements and appurtenances of the Australian-based telecommunications system.[75]

In conversation with Max Bell in 1985 Humphries would observe peremptorily, "Australia is orange."[76] Anyone visiting Melbourne after reading this caption, and poem, will forever see orange as a primary Australian colour and as a symbol of Humphries' primary importance to all Australians.

Orange is a symbol of "fire and flames"[77] and is thus associated with "the Heraclitean notion of fire as 'the agent of transmutation,' since all things derive from, and return to, fire. It is the seed which is reproduced in each successive life (and is thereby linked with the libido and fecundity)."[78] Needless to say, Les Patterson is a seedy character with libidinous leanings and risings so regular (as regular as the sun, in fact) that you could set your watch by them. Edna Everage is also a character known for her fecundity, for still having "all her drives, all her juices." But Barry Humphries is not a character at all. Nor is he a "clone": he is an original performer. He is a person who does not need to stage a proof of his reality by inviting the audience (including John Lahr) to come backstage after the show and, Thomas-like, touch his body to test its veracity, to probe his holes, as it were.

As a wizard,[79] I can attest to Humphries' transmutative powers, not an alchemical power to transmute base metal to gold but an artistic power to primatize orange from red and yellow; a linguistic power to rearrange the alphabet into unimagined configurations; and a magical power, to be found only among wizards, to mutate audiences from their normality into the bizarre, to deform them from the mode "Norm" to the modality "Laugh."

To Humphries, laughter is the colour orange. Just as laughter arises from the modality "Laugh," so orange is the only generic colour. Orange is called "orange" because it is the colour of oranges, the reddish-yellow fruit of an evergreen citrus tree, and, as such, it is different from all other colours. Barry Humphries is a prism that refracts white light not into spectral colours but, rather, into the spectacle of orange, which is his performative (and which is a special quality of Australian light). Then he refracts orange into the achromatic pairing of black and white, in which his books are printed. As a prism, Humphries is a transparent body: he allows audiences to see through him to his characters Edna, Les, Sandy, and many others, to see through the appearance of the performer, including the performative writer, to the reality of his idea, the kernel of his ideation, which is that *Laugh Is It*, as in the French, and Pythonesque, idiom *mourir de rire* ("to die laughing").

### COKE WAS IT, LAUGH IS IT

Humphries is a great Australian comic writer, to be distinguished, for instance, from the American comedians who, in recent years, have turned to writing, usually after they have turned to television situation comedies and secured large audiences. For example, he is not, like Jerry Seinfeld, Tim Allen, Paul Reiser, Ellen DeGeneres, Drew Carey, Kelsey Grammer, Garry Shandling, Jon Stewart, Janeane Garofalo, and Ben Stiller, a joke writer and stand-up comedian who has taken a turn (in most cases a bad turn) at writing a book.[80] Rather, he resembles Woody Allen, whose early books, *Getting Even* (1971) and *Without Feathers* (1975), have led to a brilliant writing career, consisting mostly of original screen plays,[81] informing his career as actor and director; Steve Martin (as a stand-up sitting down), whose *Picasso at the Lapin Agile* (1996) is a thoughtfully funny play, which probably marks the start of his career as a playwright,[82] and whose novella, *Shopgirl* (2000), shows his narratorial skill for writing a postmodern comedy of manners; and Roseanne Barr, whose autobiography, *Roseanne: My Life as a Woman* (1989), demonstrates why her calling to be a writer took precedence over even her calling to be a comedian and deserves her further attention.[83]

But unlike Woody Allen, Steve Martin, and Roseanne Barr, Humphries has never been a stand-up comedian. He has, however, inspired audiences around the world to stand up and cheer his performances. Unlike most American comic writers who have secured book contracts because of their success on television sit-coms, Humphries started as a writer in "A Novel Called Tid" (1958), *Bizarre* (1965), and the *Barry McKenzie* comic strip (from 1964), well before his first television show, *The Barry Humphries Scandals* (1970).

In his Preface to *Feel This Book* (1999), co-written with Janeane Garofolo, Ben Stiller makes light of sit-com privileging: "First off, a few disclaimers. I do not presume to be an expert in any area regarding self-help, relationships, personal growth, or anything else that I have been asked to write about. I have no medical degree, I am not a father, and I am not married. Nor do I have my own sitcom."[84] Similarly, in his *Confessions of a Late Night Talk Show Host: The Autobiography of Larry Sanders* (1998), Garry Shandling sends up celebrity authorship in his own sit-com character: "Why am I writing this autobiography now? Because I'm Larry Sanders. I'm famous. Actually, I'm very, very, very famous, but the publisher said that title wouldn't fit on the cover of the book."[85] Once it was established, Humphries' writing has been concurrent with his career as a stage and TV performer but owes nothing to theatrical privilege or sit-comedy success. Humphries has always been primarily a writer, extending an invitation to an evening's discourse with him.

If Clara Bow is the "It Girl" and Michael Palin, in character as the shipwrecked survivor in the opening sequences of *Monty Python's Flying Circus*, is the " 'It's' Man," then Barry Humphries is the "It Kid," or *het kindje*,[86] concerned as he is throughout his writing with "It."

So, what is It? A few years ago, the Coca-Cola company had the slogan "life goes better with Coca-Cola," which prompted the Canadian writer Dave Godfrey to title his first collection of short stories, an interrelated sequence similar to the early collections of Australian writer Frank Moorhouse, *Death Goes Better with Coca-Cola* (1967). Then Coca-Cola shortened the slogan to "Coke adds life," then encrypted it to "Coke is it," meaning "life goes better with Coca-Cola" (major premise); "Coke adds life" (minor premise); therefore "Coke is it – Coke is life" (conclusion).

But Godfrey argued that Coke, as the nectar of the gods of American imperialism, is death. Is Humphries, as the "It Kid," concerned, authorially and philosophically, with the "It" of life or the "It" of death? (I am assuming, for the moment, that his primary concern is not with Coca-Cola!) Throughout his writing, Humphries has addressed fundamental philosophical issues of life and death in the manner of Patrick White in *The Living and the Dead* (1941) (see Chapter 6). His "It" is the modality Laugh, which mediates between life and death, an ontological mediation that is too often ignored in criticism about literature, especially comic literature.

In reference to the performance art of American comedians Andy Kaufman and Sandra Bernhard, Philip Auslander observes that

conceptual art was "about art" partly in the sense that, following dada, it treated the concept of "art" (visual art in particular) primarily as a context then investigated the conditions and limits of that context largely by placing within it objects traditionally excluded from it (e.g., texts, declarations of intention, documentation), often objects that self-reflexively raised questions about the nature of the context and their own participation in it.[87]

In his nearly unclassifiable assemblages, installations, and narratives – *Dame Edna's Coffee Table Book* (1976), *Dame Edna's Bedside Companion* (1982), and *Barry Humphries' Treasury of Australian Kitsch* (1980) – Humphries introduces elements out of the generic contexts of "book" and "literature," such as faux genealogies, photograph albums, and tabloid *exposés* in the *Coffee Table Book*; arch recipes, a celebrity picture gallery, an exhibition of doctored masterpieces, and a 117-page "*MICRONOVEL*" ("reproduced micrographically"[88] to two pages), in the *Bedside Companion*; and an opportunity shop of kitsch to tickle (*te kittelen*, in Dutch) the fancies of his readers, especially readers who may have forgotten that books are supposed to be fun.

Whereas Monty Python told "The Funniest Joke in the World,"[89] so funny that anyone who read it, or heard it, literally died laughing, Humphries, who does not tell jokes, invokes a modal Laugh to assure his audiences that they are indeed alive. By becoming Laugh, audiences can put down life and put off death, at least for the duration of the book or performance (but perhaps also beyond). This artificial possibility, not of laughing until you die but of living as long as you laugh, is, of course, the most important part of his humoresque, his comic poetic, as *het kindje*.

Anyone can tell a joke, just as "any idiot can reproduce himself."[90] Anyone can deliver a line trippingly, like the players in *Hamlet*. Most people can even elicit illicit laughter. But precious few writers, outside of Amos Tutuola and Barry Humphries, can invoke Laugh, and Humphries is possibly the only living writer who can make audiences Laugh: not just move them to laughter but transmute them from normality to modality.

This transformation is to be distinguished from both conventional and avant-garde comedy's subversion of the status quo. Philip Auslander correctly observes that

the disappearance of the "normal" under postmodernism is not at all a bad thing: traditional stand-up comics generally assumed the heterosexual, white male as the "norm" and often singled out women, gay people, and ethnic minorities as the butts of jokes. Since the 1980s, comics who would themselves have once been the disempowered objects of comedy are the ones making the jokes, often at the expense of that canonical heterosexual, white male.[91]

But Auslander does not describe Humphries' subversion of the norm, even though, it might be argued, Humphries has toned down his satire a little recently (e.g., in his characters' confrontational takes on homosexuals and

Japanese people). Auslander's "postmodern" comedians simply displace one norm to replace it with another, as if, after the death of her husband, Dame Edna were to marry another man named Norm and immediately set off in him a prostate explosion.

On the contrary, Humphries is subverting the norm of earnestness in human conduct, regardless of political correctness, of whether straight white males occupy the centre or are relegated to the margins of art and culture. Humphries seems to see life as a Derridean-Wildean play, a work in progress that could be entitled *The Importance of Being Laugh*. This life is neither hedonistic nor frivolous; it is less about the phenomenon of laughing than about the propensity to laugh and the potential to be Laugh.

When I read, for example, Garry Shandling's *Confessions of a Late Night Talk Show: The Autobiography of Larry Sanders* (1998) and Ben Stiller and Janeane Garofolo's *Feel This Book: An Essential Guide to Self-Empowerment, Spiritual Supremacy, and Sexual Satisfaction* (1999), I never laughed once. I recognized what was supposed to be funny and recalled that one of the least funny things in the entire comic universe (as, for instance, Eric Idle envisions the universe in *The Road to Mars* [1999]) is somebody trying to be funny. But when I read *My Gorgeous Life: An Adventure* (1989), I recognized in Dame Edna Everage somebody who is Laugh, despite the construct of herself, either as "woman" or as "character."

A joke is a construct. A stand-up comedian is the construct of the jokes he or she tells. Dame Edna, because she is not a joker but Laugh, deconstructs the earnest norm by virtue of her comic nature. As a reader of *My Gorgeous Life* – I read the book in a single sitting – I found myself transmuted to Laugh: I became Edna Everage and I felt not "this book" but, in a sense that can only be described as "spooky," alive.

Humphries has the intellectual power to move people to laughter and transmute them to Laugh, for the duration of the book, the show or the recording, but perhaps also, as in my case, for the beyond that is life outside of books, theatres, and technologies. Thanks to God, my ontology is human being, but, thanks to Humphries, my modality has become Laugh, and the human comedy of living has become decidedly less Existential than before. If you should shudder at my placing God and Humphries in a single sentence, then please remember that they are both song-and-dance men and that their common property is "exclusivity":

Dieu, étant toute l'existence, ne peut permettre à rien d'exister aussi, qu'à la condition de s'exclure à sa mode de Lui. L'homme, ce témoin vertical, ne peut constater, en fin d'analyse de la matière, que le fait pur mathématique, le mouvement. Tout *périt*. L'univers n'est qu'une manière totale de ne pas être ce qui est. Que disent donc les sceptiques et quelle n'est pas la sécurité de notre connaissance! Certes, et nous avec, le monde existe; certes, il est, puisqu'il est ce qui n'est pas. (God, being the whole of existence, cannot permit anything else to exist also, except as it is excluded from Him, each in its own way. Man, this upright witness, can see, in the final analysis, only the purely mathematical fact, movement. Everything perishes. The universe is just a total manner of not being what is. So let the skeptics keep saying how secure our knowledge is! Most certainly, and together with us, the world exists; indeed, it is, since it is what is not. [my translation])[92]

Just as Paul Claudel argues that every being is excluded from God, so I argue that, compared to Humphries, every artist and reader-spectator is, exclusively, among *Les Autres*.

Humphries is a tall poppy that will never be topped! Coke was It. Laugh is It. Humphries is the It Kid. He gets It, when so many comedians-turned-writers do not. He gives It to readers and audiences indiscriminately, including his detractors, for example reviewers of the New York run of *The Royal Tour*, such as Ben Brantley in *New York Today* (18 October 1999), who mistakenly places his act in the stand-up traditions of Jackie Mason and David Letterman. And Humphries does you a good turn, by turning your human being, your "you," into It (as Mieke Bal [1985] neutralizes narrators as "it"), into Laugh.

## BARRY HUMPHRIES, *ÉCRIVAIN, AUTEUR, ARTISTE*: AN ASSESSMENT

All Humphries' books are occasional texts not because he wrote them to commemorate events, or because he has published them infrequently, but because his books are occasions for celebration, for celebrating Australia and for celebrating Laugh, as in the flight and the song of a kookaburra. The appearance of a new Humphries book – notably his second volume of autobiography, *My Life as Me: A Memoir* (2002) (the work-in-progress of which Humphries had entitled *Are We Nearly There Yet?*[93]), and his devoutly-to-be-wished-for second novel, *Women Dancing Backward*[94] – is a great publishing event.

Much of his writing is beyond classification: if "A Novel Called Tid" is a novel, then the novel called *Women in the Background* seems a narrative of a different order; if *More Please* is an autobiography and *My Life as Me* is a memoir, then *My Gorgeous Life* must indeed be "an adventure." By venturing outside genre, Humphries scores an anarchist circle around his originality. The League of American Theatres and Producers and the American Theatre Wing recognized his originality when they awarded Humphries a 2000 Special Tony Award for a Live Theatrical Event, for *Dame Edna: The Royal Tour*, a Broadway show in a category of its own:

neither a play nor a musical, and certainly not a revival, but still an important occasion for a public show of recognition.

Humphries has also been recognized publicly for his career as a painter and sculptor, as at the retrospective exhibitions *Irreverent Sculpture*, held 1–30 August 1985 at the Monash University Gallery; and *Surrealism: Revolution by Night*, held 12 March-2 May 1993 at the National Gallery of Australia, Canberra.[95] But no one has yet made a public show of recognizing Humphries' literary output, his *oeuvre bizarre*. So I have taken "It" upon myself, as a professor of Australian literature, to act as his curator and to make a spectacle of Humphries by writing this retrospective study of his writing and his performative.

Is Humphries an original, innovative, talented, credible, heterodox writer? Or is he a celebrity comedian writer like Ben Stiller and Janeane Garofolo, unable to translate their considerable skills as stand-up comedians and comedic actors on printed pages? Or is he perhaps a writer like cartoonist Ben Wicks, whose formula was once "Just grab a year's supply of cartoons, throw them between a couple of covers and there you have it: a book"?[96] Was this Humphries' strategy, in collusion with Nicholas Garland, in putting together and putting out *The Wonderful World of Barry McKenzie* (1968); *Bazza Pulls It Off! More Adventures of Barry McKenzie* (1971); *Bazza Comes into His Own: The Final Fescennine Farrago of Barry McKenzie, Australia's First Working-Class Hero* (1979); and *The Complete Barry McKenzie* (1988)? Might not this comic strip sequence suggest to a Humphries-detractor that his entire *oeuvre bizarre* is *bricolage*, a self-indulgent exercise in intertextuality? Did Humphries not set off this pattern of bricolage in his first book, the compilation *Bizarre* (1965)? Is he not, therefore, not an author at all, but a helper, literally a handyman?[97]

On the contrary, the semantic content and the reader connotations of the Barry McKenzie books are entirely different from those in the original strips in *Private Eye*. Through republication they are new works of art, because of Humphries and Garland's methodology in compiling them in the manner of a retrospective exhibition rather than as a marketing strategy of mercantile capitalism. Similarly, Humphries' other books are works of art on exhibition, almost, one might say, on loan to readers: as Humphries owns the copyright on his books, so he also maintains a proprietorship over the content; by purchasing his books, readers, as it were, have been entrusted to borrow them from his private library, to lease their content.

Although this propriety-proprietorial paradigm could, of course, be applied to any relation of book-author-reader, it has a special significance in the *oeuvre bizarre* of Humphries in that his writings, in drawing on his personal life and his stage scripts, are like personal papers that he has deigned to make public (now, as opposed, say, to fifty years after his death) not for purposes of exhibitionism, publicity, or narcissism but for the express purpose of transmuting audiences from It Kiddiness into Laugh.

Each book is like a reader's ticket[98] to Humphries' private library, into the sancta of his home and his life (although clearly not into the sanctum sanctorum of his privacy). By exploring this space of language, readers discover that Barry Humphries is an original, innovative, talented, credible, albeit very heterodox, literary writer.

He is *un auteur*, "an author" of twenty-nine books, and he is also – specifically in his role as a neologist and a sesquipedalian (like a mad organist hammering out impossible cadences with his hands and feet) and as a brother to the Nyoongah – "the founder of a race" of Aboriginal and Euro-Australians (people who speak the Australian tongue). He is also *un écrivain*, "a writer" of (ab)original prose, whose delicate hand inscripts *une écriture australienne*, and whose books point to his handiwork as a bookmaker, making *bricolages* reminiscent of the revolutionary Dada assemblages of the 1910s, 1920s, and 1930s.

Indeed, Humphries' entire *oeuvre bizarre* is *bricolage* but not in any self-absorbed intertextual Wicksian sense. First, his *bizarrerie* has to do with true heterodoxy and originality. The eclecticism and avant-garde daring of his books show up even in simple generic classifications.

Given the common etymology of the words "genre" and "gender," from the French word "gen(d)re," one can see that, using the passport of poetic licence, Humphries has crossed the boundaries of genre, much as, using a backstage pass to the music hall, he has crossed the boundaries of gender. His cross-border ventures in gen(d)re are in character: Humphries has always been known to cross the line.

Just as Johnny Cash (1932–2003) walked the line,[99] so Humphries has crossed the lines of poetry, fiction, drama, and prose; the lines of political correctness and snobbish decorum; the lines of people queuing up for his shows; and the lines of the conventional occupations "writer" and "actor," respectively; the ruled paper of literary convention; the arbitrary codes of societal and socialized conduct; the picket-lines of fans and protesters; and sanctioned roles in the capitalist workplace, including the theatre.

And just as Johnny Cash crossed the gender line in "A Boy Named Sue,"[100] so Humphries has crossed the gen(d)re line in theatre and literature, as if his signature tune were not "Niceness" but "*Het Kindje Heet Edna*" and his motto not "a joyous heart always" but "*Wanneer zij lachte, wij lachten.*"[101] By crossing the line as a laughing dandy, Humphries has identified himself with both the Australian avant-garde of the 1950s and 1960s, and the European Dada avant-garde of the 1910s-1930s.

But is Humphries part of the avant-garde of the twenty-first century? Or has he been relegated *à l'arrière-garde des artistes anciens qui sont allés à l'arrière scène* ("to the rearguard of old artists who have gone backstage").

Table 7.3
Humphries Looks Down His Nose at Generic Classification

| Genre | Work |
| --- | --- |
| assemblage | *Bizarre* (1965); *Dame Edna's Coffee Table Book* (1976); *Les Patterson's Australia* (1978); *Barry Humphries' Treasury of Australian Kitsch* (1980); *Dame Edna's Bedside Companion* (1982). |
| comics | *The Wonderful World of Barry McKenzie* (1968); *Bazza Pulls It Off!* (1971); *Bazza Comes into His Own* (1979); *The Complete Barry McKenzie* (1988). [all co-authored with Nicholas Garland] |
| scripts | film scripts: *The Adventures of Barry McKenzie* (1972); *Barry McKenzie Holds His Own* (1974); [both co-authored with Bruce Beresford] theatre scripts: *A Nice Night's Entertainment: Sketches and Monologues 1956–1981* (1981); *Shades of Sandy Stone: The Reveries of a Returned Man* (1989); *The Life and Death of Sandy Stone* (1990); *Single Voices* (1990) [co-authored with Roy Clarke, Sheila Hancock, Carla Lane, Bob Larbey and John Sessions]. television scripts: *Flashbacks* (1999) [co-authored with David Mitchell and Roger McDonald]. |
| songster | *The Sound of Edna: Dame Edna's Family Songbook* (1979) [co-authored with Nick Rowley and Stanley Myers]. |
| anthology | *The Penguin Private Eye* (1965); *The Barry Humphries Book of Innocent Austral Verse* (1968); *"Punch" Down Under* (1984); *The Humour of Barry Humphries* (1984); *A Garland for Stephen Spender* (1991). |
| poetry | *Neglected Poems and Other Creatures* (1991). |
| autobiography | *More Please* (1992); *Less Is More Please* (1996); *My Life as Me: A Memoir* (2002). |
| fictional autobiography | *The Traveller's Tool* (1985); *My Gorgeous Life* (1989). |
| fiction | *Women in the Background* (1996). |

Sir Les Patterson, who is known to regard women's derrières, would be a member of the *derrière-garde*.

Like the needle of irony – "Why is irony like a needle? Because its eye looks both ways." – he looks both ways, back to music hall (and beyond) and straight ahead into futurity. His novel *Women in the Background* (1995) is a *roman à clef* only in its surface meaning. In its deep structure it is a daring experiment in life-telling, an imp(r)udent parody of journalists dedicated to defaming the famous. As a mock autobiography, mocking both biographers and the genre of autobiography, it is an accomplishment of the order of V.S. Naipaul's *The Enigma of Arrival: A Novel in Five Sections* (1987). *My Gorgeous Life* (1989) is a fictional autobiography only in its surface meaning. In its deep structure it is Dame Edna Everage's assault on readers, like her assaults on her stage show audiences. As her send-up of her "manager," Barry Humphries, it is an accomplishment of the order of Patrick White's *Memoirs of Many in One* (1986), which is, in part, Alex Xenophon Demirjian Gray's send-up of her "editor," Patrick White.

But ever *en avant-garde* to shock, to say shocking things, Humphries out-Naipauls Naipaul and out-Whites White. He is such a wild Dada artist – he has been performing Dada pranks for fifty years, helping to keep Dada alive – that he could manage to put *le choc* even in *le chocolat*! His ability to evoke the cry "*quelle drôle de surprise!* ("what a shock!")," followed by the sigh of relief "*quelle bonne surprise!*" ("what a pleasant surprise!"), is unsurpassed on stage and in literature.

In Salman Rushdie's *Midnight's Children* (1980) the narrator, Saleem Sinai, ever self-conscious about constructing his narrative, notes how storytelling is dominated by "what-happened-nextism."[102] But in Humphries' *oeuvre bizarre* spectators and readers need have no "nexist" worries – with Les Patterson, they can sign themselves with the phrase "no worries" – because "next" is not a retail space where the merchandise is the same from one shop to another but a place, like Oz, either Emerald City or Australia, where anything can happen; where the merchandise, or content, is always changing; where what-happened-next is always a surprise; where there is no "nextism" because there is no next (not even "over the rainbow"). As Rushdie puts it elsewhere, "It is a celebration of Escape, a grand paean to the Uprooted Self, a hymn – *the* hymn – to Elsewhere."[103] Atemporal narrative without "next" may seem an anachronism, but it indefinitely exists in the "now" of performative:

In performative writing, the writer makes no pretense at absenting herself from the process of criticism. Instead, gestures that are at least "autobiographical," in the sense of simulating self-reference, provide shadow commentaries that keep the writing subject in the reader's peripheral vision – when she does not assume center stage. The staging of the writing subject not only blurs the boundary between subject and object; it also implicitly argues that words solicit identifications and psychic performative writing implies that understanding is always highly personal, even idiosyncratic, and that it is an outcome of recognitions and deferrals that are not simply linguistic.[104]

In both *Women in the Background* and *My Gorgeous Life*, Humphries plays the critic by making autobiographical "gestures" and "simulating self-reference" to lure critical readers, like passers-by in a 1950s Melbourne street where he is performing a Dada prank, into misclassifying the narratives as veiled autobiographies.

Yet he maintains a prominent place on the periphery of these narratives, as in all his writing, like a patron on the edge of an Italian Renaissance painting, reminding readers that, to find meaning, they will have to go through him, not his personal and private life but his role as "the writing subject," the intellect who mediates between the subject of semantics and the object of textuality in a complex performative that spills over (like a gobful of Russian salad or of Les Patterson's spittle) from books and articles to stage and TV shows, to audio recordings, films and videos, all of them forming *l'oeuvre bizarre de Barry Humphries*, and stemming from "a youthful folly" – his first book, *Bizarre* (1965). This *oeuvre* is, finally, *un paradoxe dadaïste*, a dadadox.

On the one hand, Humphries' lifework is substantive enough to be called an *oeuvre*, comprising theatre, television, and video programs; audio recordings; essays; life-tellings; and literature. His literary lifework alone is of substance: *c'est une oeuvre, pas un oeuf!* ("It's an oeuvre, not an egg!"). It is remarkable for its abundance and variety. It is *une bibliothèque et un libraire* ("a library and a bookseller") of genres, forms, modes, and packages: fiction, autobiography, verse, drama, music, comic strip, and essay; monologue, travelogue, sketch, assemblage, short story, photomontage, recipe, cultural history, coffee table book, and drawing; irony, satire, mockery, parody, burlesque, comedy, romance, nostalgia, subversion, music hall, and Dada; large-format picture books, hard and "limp" editions, retrospective catalogues and anthologies, and, in his own titular words, "a novel called TID," "a world," "Australia," an "entertainment," "an original photoplay," "a guide," a "final fescennine farrago," "confessions," "ruminations," "a note," "a recollection," "letters," a "family songbook," a "treasury," a "companion," a "tool," "reveries," "an adventure," "creatures," "a garland," and "flashbacks."

On the other hand, his *oeuvre* is as ephemeral as *un objet perdu* in the sense that many of Duchamp's *objets trouvés* – the original *Bicycle Wheel* (1913), the original *Bottle Rack* (1914), the original *Fountain* (1917) – seem to get lost forever. Humphries' *oeuvre* is *perdu* because it is "lost" and because it is "ruined," both by chance and by his own dadadox design: it might even be entitled *À la recherche de l'oeuvre perdue*. It is "lost" by chance because most of his books are out of print and, by Humphries' dadadox design, because his readers lose themselves in his ideas and become Laugh. It is "ruined" by chance because it is the remains of an artiste who has dashed his own identity (e.g., he would have made a dashing barrister and solicitor) and, by Humphries' dadadox design, because it is focused on the deconstruction of the construct of the book and of pompous art aesthetics.

Humphries' *oeuvre* is a "treasury of Australian kitsch," at one end treasure and at the other end kitsch. The word "kitsch" usually connotes maudlin art in bad taste. But Humphries' dadadox is best evident in the French synonym for kitsch, *art pompier*, which references "traditional" or "conventional art" but that literally means "fireman's art" or the kind of art that the fire brigade would "pump." *Art pompier* is Humphries' ongoing dada prank, which Barry McKenzie, Les Patterson, Edna Everage, Sandy Stone, and others pump onto audiences. Imagine Humphries in a fireman's uniform, like music hall star Horace Kenney, the "Fearless Fireman," pumping out his books to solve the dadadox of the universe. (Merely to *write* his books would be just too conventional.) His *oeuvre pompière* is the solution to the dadadox.

Through *kétainerie*[105] ("kitsch") Humphries has helped to keep music hall and Dada alive; he has deconstructed the book; he has turned his readers into Laugh; he has shown his "gratitude" and voiced his "concern for others"; he has distinguished himself as *écrivain, auteur,* and *artiste*; he has confronted Australians with negative stereotypes and taught them, like as many kookaburras, to laugh at themselves as well as the world; he has brought distinction to Australia (Melbourne, in particular); he has pumped out *une oeuvre bizarre* that could put out the most purposeful Australian bush fire; he has contributed original and enduring characters to Australian theatre and hilarious and shocking performative texts to Australian literature; and he has used language so inventively, so spunkily, as to inspire every Laugh in his audience to take on the stage name Hilarious.[106] For all these accomplishments, and in his own person, Barry Humphries is a great writer and a great Australian!

His greatest act as a writer has been no less than to reveal the secret of the dadadox of the universe, which is the paradoxology or heterodoxology of Laugh: if you are not *bizarre*, if you are not *hétérodoxe*, if you are not Laugh, if you are not It, you may be missing out on the joke of two centuries and on the most original and provocative Australian stage performer and comic writer ever, the It Kid.

My last points pumped out on his *oeuvre bizarre* are:

1 he oughta get on;
2 he oughta sell out;

3 he oughta turn your naughty human being into the aught of Laugh;
4 you oughta read Humphries, one good man's miscellany;
5 if you read Humphries, he will make you laugh/he will make you Laugh;
6 if you read Humphries and modalize into Laugh, you will become an honorary music hall artiste, Dada artist, intellect, and comedian;
7 if you read Humphries, you may help to bring all his books back into print and reinforce the imprint of his genius in Australian literature.

But I would like to devote the last section of this book to expressing my gratitude to Humphries for converting millions of people ("squillions" of "nonentities," I would like to say, if only the words were mine) to the modality Laugh, for entertaining them and especially for making them think. *Wel bedankt* is a Dutch expression of thanks, a variation on *dank je wel* ("thank you very much"): the use of the anticipatory past participle suggests that the person is already thanked. To Barry Humphries I say *wel bedankt* because in this book I have already thanked you.

Finally, with a nod and a wink to Dr John Moon, I would like to express my concern for Humphries, to encourage him to go on pumping out words and putting out bush fires of ignorance, pomposity, seriousness, complacency, provincialism, and political correctness around the world. Barry Humphries, who has played all the parts of a writer – autobiographer, poet, novelist, dramatist, essayist, editor, book-maker and deconstructionist – and played them exceedingly well, merits a lead role in Australian literary history, for which, I hope, this book might be his casting call.

# APPENDICES

# Graduate English Course Proposal, Simon Fraser University

ENGLISH 806–983 PROPOSAL: PAUL MATTEW ST PIERRE
The Many Faces of Barry Humphries:
*A Portrait of the Australian Artist*
*As a Cross-Dressing Parodist*

For forty years, Barry Humphries (1934-) has been parodying class and gender pretensions in front of Australian, English, and international audiences: in theatre reviews, sound recordings, one-person shows, comic strips, poetry, film scripts and films, television programs, fiction, and events of comedy and satire.

This multi-media course examines the life and work of Barry Humphries, both as a literary figure (whose entry in *The Oxford Companion to Australian Literature* [1985] runs to 1½ pages) and as a figure of popular culture (whose mass audience is listening around the world). The thematic focus is on Humphries' stage personae, such as Sandy Stone, Bazza McKenzie, Sir Les Patterson, and Edna Everage, and on methods of parody and customs of cross-dressing culture, all with reference to the theatrical revue.

The literature component of the course comprises verse parody, mock biography and autobiography, and narrative fiction, and will be complemented by commentaries on Bruce Beresford's early films, *The Adventures of Barry McKenzie* (1972) and *Barry McKenzie Holds His Own* (1974), and on the film *Les Patterson Saves the World* (1987), by the sound recordings *Moonee Ponds Muse* (1991), *The Sound of Edna: Dame Edna's Family Songbook* (1993) and *More Please* (1993), and by clips from Humphries' television appearances, often as Dame Edna Everage, the suburban Moonee Ponds housewife who in 1955 began satirizing Australian society and who is now a DBE and world megastar, the preeminent voice of parodic satire.

The theory component of the course examines four recent (1996–98) works on gender and gender reversal, cross-dressing in theatre and in culture, and the hisandherstory of dress(ing up).

This discussion-based course views gender, costume and voice as parodic badges, and cross-dressing as a decodifying strategy.

REQUIRED TEXTS

Ekins, Richard. *Male Femaling: A Grounded Theory Approach to Cross-Dressing and Sex-Changing* (Routledge)          ISBN 0-415-10625-7

Everage, Dame Edna (pseud.). *My Gorgeous Life: The Life, the Loves, the Legend* (Bantam)          ISBN 0-440-50614-X

Griggs, Claudine. *S/he: Changing Sex and Changing Clothes* (Berg) ISBN 1-85973-916-4

Humphries, Barry. *Flashbacks* (HarperCollins)          ISBN 0-00-255896-3

– *More Please* (Penguin)          ISBN 0-14-023193-5

– *Neglected Poems* (HarperCollins)          ISBN 0-207-17212-9

– *"Punch" Down Under* (Robson)          ISBN 0-86051-296-7

– *Women in the Background* (Heinemann)          ISBN 0-434-00356-5

Ramet, Sabrina Petra, ed. *Gender Reversals and Gender Cultures: Anthropological and Historical Perspectives* (Routledge)   ISBN 0-415-11483-7

Solomon, Alisa. *Re-Dressing the Canon: Essays on Theater and Gender* (Routledge)          ISBN 0-415-15721-8

RECOMMENDED TEXT

Hutcheon, Linda. *A Theory of Parody: The Teachings of Twentieth-Century Art Forms* (Methuen)          ISBN 0-416-37090-X

REQUIREMENTS

A 4000–5000 word research paper (80%) and a 20–30 minute oral presentation (20%), both assignments on the life, work, and/or characters of Humphries, or on gender and/or cross-dressing theory. The course will culminate in a graduate-faculty symposium on Humphries, parody, cross-dressing, gender-crossing.

# Barry Humphries Recalls The Establishment

Dame Edna's response to Ned Sherrin shows Humphries' brilliance as a speech-actor:

NED SHERRIN: Dame Edna, in the early sixties, when you played the Establishment with an audience of about seven and only one dress, were times very hard for you then?

DAME EDNA: You've got a memory like an elephant, haven't you? [LAUGHTER] You know, many years ago there was this little place called the Establishment in London. It was ... what was it? A little cubby hole, wasn't it, designed by Sean Kenny. It was a long narrow thing. You thought it was the passage to something, but that was it. [LAUGHTER] And goodness me, what a passage to success it was, wasn't it? Because little Ned Sherrin struggled along there for many many moons. [LAUGHTER] Before he became the ubiquitous figure he is today. And David Frost, of course, started off there. And you know it was one of my first little starting places, as you first said. And how right you are, Ned. But my following was pitifully small.

NED SHERIN: Have you still got the dress?

DAME EDNA: I've still got the frock, as I prefer to call it! "Frock" is Australian for dress. I've still got it. As a matter of fact, the Victoria and Albert Museum, viewers, have asked for a lot of my old cozzies, and they're going to have a beautiful section showing fashions ... Australian women's fashions through the ages, as exemplified by my gorgeous frocks, Ned. So just as well I didn't give them to you, as you once requested. [LAUGHTER] I don't forget much either, Ned. [LAUGHTER]

– *An Audience with Dame Edna* (1980)

That Ned Sherrin went on to act in the film *Orlando* (1992), based on Virginia Woolf's 1928 novel about an androgynous character who cross-dresses and gender-crosses over four centuries, suggests that he may have yielded to Dame Edna's censorious memory and suggestive powers.

# Article and Letter to the Editor, the *National Post*

ME, MYSELF AND EYE
*Shinan Govani*

A couple of nights ago I had a date with Dame Edna. Well, to be exact, I went to see the Australian satirist-in-drag in her new show on Broadway, *The Royal Tour*, a jolly, sloppy jumble of caricature, wit and song. And notwithstanding the quick-witted, lynx-eyed brand of humour of The Dame, not to mention her mauve hair and bubble-gum-pink frock, the most indelible image I came away with was that of rhinestone-coated eye-glasses.

If you've seen this loopy comedian on TV, you know what I'm talking about. She's made a virtual career out of her eyewear, and it's somewhat difficult to figure out if she's wearing her glasses or the glasses are wearing her. But yet, when you think about it for a moment, she's part of a grand old traditional [sic]: one of those people who've made a virtual spectacle out of their spectacles.

Think Gloria Steinem, with her aviator frames, or John Lennon with his small, round, black-rimmed glasses, or even Malcolm X with his rectangular-shaped specs. This is eyewear as political arsenal. Even our own Stéphane Dion, Minister of Intergovernmental Affairs up in Ottawa, is impossible to imagine without his rather homey, but nonetheless potent, wire-rimmed glasses. Would he be as successful fighting separatists without them? Probably not. His glasses are face furniture, confirmation of a somewhat dry yet working Confederation.

And if you doubt the power of eyewear, consider for a moment the great American villainess Linda Tripp. One of the reasons I think the American public never took warmly to her, and why she was in many ways the greatest gift to the Clinton camp, was her ghastly glasses. Yes, not only did Tripp have a tense and iron-jawed face, but a pair of vulture eyes that were only magnified by her poor choice of eyewear. That, my friends, is what they call the power of television.

In the world of celebrity, of course, eyeglasses have often been an inspired handiwork of personality. Elton John and his string of campy frames. Jacqueline Kennedy Onassis and her outsize sunglasses. Buddy Holly and his portly, nerdy pair. Looking at their lives through the lens of history, their glasses are an indispensable part of their iconographies.

And this is hardly a new phenomenon. As an exhibition at the New York Historical Society a few years ago showed, famous Americans are almost as old as famous eyeglass designs. Benjamin Franklin, for example, invented bifocals, and the owl-eyed versions he wore were widely copied. Thomas Jefferson introduced oblong lenses for reading glasses that he considered more efficient than the conventional round or oval ones. And the scientist-inventor Peter Cooper wore glasses with side flaps long before rock stars did.

In antiquity, the Inuit perfected goggles to reduce the glare from snow, and in the late Middle Ages the elite in China and Italy wore spectacles to sharpen their sight, by the eighteenth century, eyeglasses had improved to the extent that most people who had to wear them were able to see better, to look better or, in the case of tinted lenses, not be seen at all. But it has only been in this century that eyewear has moved so dramatically from prosthetic device to personality signature item.

And thank God for that. Where, after all, would the surrealistic Edna be without her eye accessories? There is, after all, nothing like a Dame with gladiator glasses.

*Shinan Govani is a Toronto writer*
*– National Post,* 26 October 1999, A18

RE: ME, MYSELF AND EYE, OCT. 26

Shinan Govani credits Minister of Intergovernmental Affairs Stéphane Dion's separatist-busting power partly to his "face furniture." I must point out that it was Dame Edna Everage herself, a subject of Mr Govani's article, who coined the phrase "face furniture" as a signifier of eyeglasses, allowing everyone to make spectacles of themselves. I am inclined to gripe that, by leaving the telling phrase out of quotation marks, Mr Govani has not properly acknowledged his indebtedness to Dame Edna, whose manager, Barry Humphries, also uses the phrase brazenly, as if it were his own. After all, "face furniture" comes up in Dame Edna's current Broadway show, *The Royal Tour,* so Mr Govani, who claims to have seen the show, has no excuses.

But how can I take Mr Govani to task, really? John Lahr, in his book *Dame Edna Everage and the Rise of Western Civilisation* (1992), has already taught me that Dame Edna's many neologisms have become part of everyday usage. They are in my linguistic code, and no doubt in Govani's as well. As discourse "face furniture" signifies that we in the West may still have a spectacular civilization.

*Paul Matthew St Pierre*
*Burnaby, BC*
– *National Post*, 1 November 1999, A19

# Paul Matthew St Pierre, letter, *National Post* [Toronto], 3 November 2000, A19

TRACING ELTON

Re: Eye of the Credit Card Holder: Is Elton John's Photo Collection Worthy of an Exhibit? Nov. 1 [2000].

In his article on Elton John's contributions to the photographic exhibit at the High Museum of Art in Atlanta, John Bentley Mays calls "middlebrow rocker Elton John, the love-child of Liberace and Dame Edna, and an occasional Atlanta resident." I dismissed the remark as meretricious patter, until I recalled that Dame Edna Everage, who is a prolific composer of serious music, as well as a megastar, co-wrote, with Nick Rowley, the song "Every Mother Wants a Boy Like Elton," for her 1978 album *The Sound of Edna*, and published the sheet music in *The Sound of Edna: Dame Edna's Family Songbook* (1979). The refrain includes the telling lines: "Every Mother wants a boy like Elton, every girl deserves the very best. / Every Mother wants a boy like Elton to press against her breast."

This is as close to a formal confession of maternity as you'll get from the close-lipped Dame Edna. Still, it's common knowledge in show biz circles that little Elton is her bubba. What has never been known, however, although there have always been whispers, is the identity of the father. But now the cat is out of the bag (which calls to mind another Everage-Rowley composition from *The Sound of Edna*, "S & M Lady"). In a shocking scoop that will surely inspire a glut of tell-all books, John Bentley Mays has now exposed Liberace as the father of Elton John. Imagining Liberace and Dame Edna together gets my drives and juices flowing. But picturing the ménage of "Liberace and Dame Edna, and an occasional Atlanta resident" takes me even further. It makes my syntax boil.

*Paul Matthew St Pierre, Vancouver*

# Barry Humphries, "Broadening My Horizons," from *Dame Edna's Work Experience* (1996, 1997)

I want to broaden my horizons.
I want to meet my public face to face.
However humble you are,
There's a hands-on megastar,
A friend of the Queen
Who's terribly keen
To invade your space.
When they all say I'm not coming,
I don't think of it as slumming:
I'm striking a blow! You know what? For Me!
God bless you, I'm just as good as you are –
And you're nearly as good as me!

I want to get out in the workplace.
I want to grab my possums by the paw.
It isn't meant to tease,
But I love nonentities.
No it isn't a joke,
You're the kind of folk
I really do adore.
I'd trade my penthouse on the top floor,
For a corner of your shop floor:
I could live without a carpet or a view,
God bless you, I'm just as good as you are –
And we're nearly as good as you!

I want to lay myself wide-open.
I want to give you total access to my web.
Although my fortunes rust,

I'm putting something back at last.
I'm an easy touch
And I've got so much
To give each little pleb.
When the Queen says in a quarrel,
"I want you at Balmoral"
When she heard I was going to visit this factory,
I said, "Bless you, Ma'am, I'm just as good as you are –
And you're nearly as good as me!
I said, "You can keep your Scottish scenery,
Give me a Lancashire Baked Beanery
Cause that's good enough for me!
That's good enough for me!"

# Selected Publications of the Poets in *The Barry Humphries Book of Innocent Austral Verse*

Aston, Tilly. *Songs of Light*. Melbourne: Lothian, 1935.

Boake, Barcroft. *Where Dead Men Lie and Other Poems*. Ed. A.G. Stephens. Sydney: Angus and Robertson, 1897.

Carew, Elsie. *The Passing Pageant: Poems and Prose*. Sydney: Wentworth, 1970.

Gillespie, Douglas. *Leaves of Gold*. Sydney: Lothian, 1952.

Hardwicke, Elizabeth. *Poems*. Melbourne: Davison, Duncan, 1894.

Lawson, Will. *The Three Kings and Other Verses*. London: Angus and Robertson, Sydney: Penfold, 1914.

Mack, Louise. *Teens: A Story of Australian Schoolgirls*. Sydney: Angus and Robertson, 1897.

Major, A.G. *Wayside Elegies, Dreams and Scraps*. Melbourne: Cole, 19[?].

Moses, Jack. *Nine Miles from Gundagai*. Wollstonecraft: Pollard, 1972.

Price, Hannah [Mrs Hannah Fisher]. *Original Poems: Dedicated by Kind Permission to Lady Loch*. Ballarat: Pinkerton, 1889.

Storrie, Agnes L. *Poems*. Sydney: n.p., 1899.

Turner, Ethel. *That Girl*. London and Melbourne: Ward, Lock, 1912.

# The Middycosm

A "middycosm" (my neologism), neither big enough to be a macrocosm nor small enough to be a microcosm, is the middle world of Australian suburbia that, throughout his career, Humphries has graphed with the steady hand of a cartographer (or a young gynecologist). This is an Aristotelian place of no beginning and no end – just middle.

In his annotation to "Dear Beryl" Humphries observes, "In the early years of this creation, admittedly, I had not sought to precisely locate him anywhere but in a suburban limbo."[1] Yet Sandy's posthumous monologue, entitled "A Letter from Limbo," raises the prospect that Glen Iris is not limbo but middycosm. Humphries' middycosm derives in part from the late 1950s Antipodean movement in Australian art, comprising manifesto signatories of the artists John Perceval, Arthur Boyd, David Boyd, Clifton Pugh, John Brack, Charles Blackman, and Robert Dickerson as well as the critic Bernard Smith: "The Antipodeans found themselves on their own, in a society without passions or ideals, the very world that Barry Humphries soon began to satirize in the persona of the suburban housewife, Edna Everage."[2] The aesthetic link between Humphries and the Antipodeans is further illustrated in Pugh's portraits *Barry Humphries* (1958) and *Barry Humphries* (1966), Brack's portrait *Barry Humphries in the Character of Mrs Everage* (1969), and Humphries' poem "The Ballad of Charles Blackman" (1961).

# Barry Humphries, Actor

Humphries has appeared in more than twenty films. He has starred in *The Adventures of Barry McKenzie* (1972) and *Barry McKenzie Holds His Own* (1974), both directed by Bruce Beresford; and *Les Patterson Saves the World* (1987), under the direction of George Miller. Of his other film appearances, his greatest comic roles have been as Envy in Stanley Donen's *Bedazzled* (1967), with Peter Cook and Dudley Moore; as Bert Schnick in Jim Sharman's *Shock Treatment* (1982); as three characters simultaneously – a grocery store clerk, the store manager, and Dame Edna Everage as a shopper – in *Pterodactyl Woman from Beverly Hills* (1994), directed by Philippe Mora; and as Kevin McMaxford in *Spice World* (1997). His finest character roles have been as Humphrey Beal in *The Leading Man* (1996), directed by John Duigan; as Mrs Crummles and Mr Leadville in Dickens' *Nicholas Nickleby* (2002), directed by Douglas McGrath; and, on television, as Richard Deane in *Doctor Fischer of Geneva* (1984) by Graham Greene; and as Rupert Murdoch in *Selling Hitler* (1991) by Howard Schuman. His cameo appearances have been spotty, but he steals the show as an art agent in Joe McGrath's *The Bliss of Mrs Blossom* (1967) and as the voices of an animated kangaroo in *Napoleon* (1994), directed by Mario Andreacchio, and an animated shark in *Finding Nemo* (2003), directed by Andrew Stanton. But his acting career is perhaps most distinguished by his serious roles, as Reverend Strachey in Bereford's *The Getting of Wisdom* (1977) and as Clemens Metternich in *Immortal Beloved* (1994), directed by Bernard Rose. For complete details on Humphries' film and TV appearances, see my Appendix 12.

# Barry Humphries: Clothes and the Man

When he appears out of character and costume, Barry Humphries is rarely seen (at least before photographers and camera operators) out of a suit, the matched outfit of jacket, trousers, sometimes a waistcoat, with a matching shirt and tie. (He has never been seen "in mixed company" in Sandy Stone's costume of pyjamas, housecoat, slippers, and a hot-water bottle.) It is always a nicely tailored suit, of fine fabric with an assertive twill yet delicate lines, including creases in the trousers (from pressing, never wrinkling). Humphries is nothing if not a natty dresser.[1] In a review of Anne Hollander's book *Sex and Suits: The Evolution of Modern Dress* (1994), David Livingstone, fashion columnist for the Canadian newspaper the *Globe and Mail*, observes, "It could be argued that the suit is about nothing but power and that its real, enduring force is as the material representation of the tyranny of class and gender."[2]

Humphries' suits are mainly about style, but they are partly about (one type of) power. His sartorial style (his own, of course) is that of a dandy or swell, specifically the *lion comique* of the halls, not to be confused with the "counterfeit swell"[3] who emerged from music hall audiences in imitation of the proprietor.

But does Humphries wear a power suit? Power may be of two kinds: power *over* and power *with*. Although Dame Edna Everage and Les Patterson might be seen as exercising power *over* their audiences, to the point of crushing them sometimes, if only in "a kind and caring way," Barry Humphries asserts his power *with* audiences: in a postmodern sense, he empowers them. He shares with them his estimable powers of speech, wit, voice, song, gesture, movement, humour, and persuasion as well as his power base of effrontery (80 percent) and talent (20 percent).[4] Patrick White might have felt this sartorial power when he and Manoly Lascaris entertained Humphries at a power lunch: "He arrived an hour late, after two more telephone calls announcing himself, and a taxi driver at our door to ask whether I still expected to see Barry Humphries. Barry, in a grazier's hat and monocle, was looking rather strange."[5]

Whether White felt the power more of Humphries' outfit or of his fit out of his alcoholism recovery program is debatable, but Humphries' decision to include this letter as an "aside" at the conclusion of *More Please*[6] – which was two years before it appeared in David Marr's edition of White's letters (1994), and then as Humphries' choice[7] – shows his pride in all things bizarre, notably his *hauteur-couture*. White may well have appreciated the power of Humphries' flair for clothes; Geoffrey Dutton relates that White's cousin "Peggy [Garland] recalled Patrick as a young dandy in the South of France with an opera cloak and a gardenia."[8] Yet White might also have found Humphries' *hauteur-couture* more than a little daunting. Dutton recalls how

Patrick, always an admirer of Barry, had often said how much he would like to see him again, so I rang and asked if he would come along to the lunch. There was a long pause. Then Patrick said, in his slowest voice, "Oh no, dear me, definitely no. It would take me at least a fortnight to get my act together for Barry Humphries."[9]

Perhaps in invoking the idiom "to get my act together" White meant putting together a music hall turn, complete with tailored costume, that would be equal to Humphries'.

Whereas Malcolm Lowry was engaged in a cold war with his clothes – "How else explain the continual painful conflict that went on between him and reality, even him and his clothes. 'There is a continuous cold war between me and my clothes.'"[10] – Humphries elects to share his power, in a fashion. His suit (including his hirsute image), rather than tyrannizing audiences into the binaries of class and gender liberates them from the tyrannies of class and gender binaries. As a music hall artiste, he gives his "joyous heart always" to people of all classes, even by parodying the class divisions of theatre seating arrangements. Dame Edna Everage truly cares if paupers fall out of the balcony. She also admits that she finds gender-crossing offensive. In his suits and investments in clothing and costumes, Humphries dresses up to meet his public face to face.

### MY IMPRESSIONS ON FIRST MEETING BARRY HUMPHRIES

On Wednesday, 9 March 2001, I met with Barry Humphries at 10:15 PM, after his performance of *Dame Edna – The Royal Tour (The Show That Listens)* at the Moore Theatre, Seattle. I was sitting in the front row of the theatre, waiting, when Humphries, dressed in his street clothes, entered the stage, announcing in a burst of enthusiasm and uninhibited charm, "Well, hello, Paul. I am so pleased finally to have a chance to meet you." He descended the stairs from the stage, stood very close to me, looked me directly in the eyes, and we shook hands. He seemed to hold my hand, and I his, longer than social decorum required (but not the decorum of dramaturgy).

Humphries was dressed in a light brown sports jacket and trousers, with a pale open-necked shirt, and tan-coloured moccasin-stitched dress loafers. He seemed shorter than his reputed six feet one inch, in part because his posture is stooped, as is apparent also when he is in character as Dame Edna and Sir Les. He has a good head of hair, with a bit of his trademark fringe, and very good skin.

I told him he performed with agility and must have great stamina, and he seemed pleased. I reported that, from where we were in the foyer earlier, the audience reaction to the finale had been uproarious. Humphries led me up the stairs onto the stage, where we continued our conversation at the piano. He asked me about my discipline, if I were a historian. When I told him I was a professor of English, he was curious about my specialty, and, when I said I specialized in Australian literature, he was greatly interested and suggested we talk about that.

"Which writers do you like?" he asked. When I told him Martin Boyd was the greatest Australian writer, after him, of course, he immediately concurred, adding that he had met Boyd once in Rome (as he recounts in *More Please*). Humphries mentioned that he also likes Randolph Stow and Hal Porter, and we talked briefly about them. I presented Humphries with a 9 March 2001 Gary Larson "Farside" calendar cartoon, depicting Ed's dingo farm next door to Doreen's nursery, with the caption "Trouble Brewing." I told Humphries I had brought the cartoon in honour of Dame Edna's daughter Lois, who was abducted by a "rogue koala." He laughed. Next I gave him a vinyl envelope containing tearsheets of two letters to the editor of the *National Post* (which I wrote defending him against inaccurate commentary) and a copy of my Dada prank letter to Professor Paul Budra. I told him that I am trying to follow his lead as a music hall artiste and a Dada artist. Finally, I gave him another vinyl envelope, with typescripts of the prospectus, title page, table of contents, preface, Chapter 6, and addendum of my book *A Portrait of the Artist as Australian:* L'Oeuvre bizarre de *Barry Humphries*. He was delighted with everything I gave him, especially the manuscript. After introducing me to his wife, Lizzie Spender, the daughter of Sir Stephen Spender, Humphries held up the envelope to her and said, with glee, "Do you know what this is? It's the book about me!" Humphries told me he is writing his second volume of autobiography, which he will complete two months from now. He intends to send me what he has written, from which I surmise either the manuscript or an advance copy. He also promised to send me some unpublished scripts of Sandy Stone. Throughout the meeting, Humphries was very friendly and gracious. He seemed genuinely interested in my book and supportive of it. As we walked off stage and up the aisle of the theatre, he named Elizabeth Jolly as another writer he likes, adding, "but I don't think she's from Australia, is she?" "No," I said, "I believe she's from Birmingham."

Then I introduced Humphries to my colleague Joan, who all along had been sitting near the back of the theatre. He was very gracious to her also, even apologizing for having neglected her there. When he shook her hand, he held it for a long time (just as he had mine). As we walked out of the theatre I wished that he would "break a leg" on the rest of this tour, and, thanking him for his kindness, shook his hand again. As we slipped out the front door of the theatre, Humphries and Lizzie Spender joined a group of about eight fans who had been waiting for him on the sidewalk and proceeded to walk down the street with them, while Joan and I returned to our car in the parking lot across the street. Humphries was the personification of kindness, gentility, and intelligence.

# Dame Edna Everage and the Miraculous

In Canada, even the Roman Catholic Church does not believe in miracles. It its current English translation of scripture, it calls miracles "deeds of power." Now it categorizes the miracles of Jesus Christ with other deeds of power, such as persecution, enslavement, and despotism. But Dame Edna Everage believes in miracles. She expressed her belief in January 1997 in her ITV special *Dame Edna Kisses It Better*, in which, with Errol Brown, she sang the Brown/Wilson composition "You Sexy Thing," whose chorus features the lines "I believe in miracles / Where you from / You sexy thing." Not only does Dame Edna believe in miracles but she also performs them.

Throughout *Dame Edna Kisses It Better* she performs healings, and at one point she even offers to heal the viewing audience: "Tonight, you've seen me perform miracles, medical miracles you never thought possible. Have you felt a little out in the cold at home? I bet you have. 'Can Edna help me?' I hear you ... whine. Well, I've taken pity, and luckily I'm interactive, and not just on my own Web site, which incidentally is ww.edna.prostatemiracle./ [sic], but also through your own TV set. Yes, I can kiss you better at home, darlings. So this is the moment. Don't be afrightened. Place those hurty bits to the TV screen. Press them to that little pink dot. Make sure they're nice bits. Respect my lips. Nearer ... nearer ..." Edna then kisses the pink dot from the other side of the TV screen.

Dame Edna performs healings at many of her stage shows as well as on her real Web site, http://www.dame-edna.com, which is "An Online Healing Centre" inviting visitors to "press your afflicted bits on this gorgeous snap to begin healing. (*Please remember to wipe your monitors off afterwards Possums!*)." In *My Gorgeous Life*, she confesses: "What a vain woman I would be if I set myself up as a one-woman Lourdes! But spooky things *have* happened during my performances and barely a night goes by after one of my shows when the cleaners do not discover, in the aisle or under a seat, a pair of crutches, a Zimmer frame or a prosthetic device. I make no greater claim than that."[1] She also observes, "I am not a saint. At least not yet, though I have had a rather flattering tip-off from my little Polish pal."[2] Dame Edna is also fond of saying she has it on the authority of a very highly placed person that she is to be canonized soon. She cannot reveal her source, however, except to note that he's single, he's Polish, and he lives in Rome. A candidate's association with at least two miracles is one condition of canonization in the Roman Catholic Church.

# What a Ratbag Is and Isn't

The disparities between "Barry Humphries at Las Vegas," from his LP *Barry Humphries' Savoury Dip* (1971), and his Foreword in Keith Dunstan's *Ratbags* (1979) are apparently minor: the line "transferring Virginian cigarettes into an old menthol packet to save himself an expensive round" becomes "... to save an expensive round"; "He hates pillows, central heating, champagne, James Bond movies, other Ratbags and black jelly beans" becomes "... and jelly beans"; "They have their ancestry traced, their faces lifted and they eat Chinese food with chopsticks" becomes "They have their ancestries traced, their faces lifted and eat Chinese food with chopsticks"; "If you're a vegetarian Jehovah's Witness birdwatcher" becomes "If you're a vegetarian, a Jehovah's Witness birdwatcher"; "have ghost-written the autobiography of a surf rider" becomes "have just ghost-written ..."; "A Ratbag is a curious blend of King Lear, Rasputin, Lady Godiva, Doctor Timothy Leary, the Emperor Nero, Albert Schweitzer and Yoko Ono" becomes "A Ratbag is a curious blend of Rasputin, Lady Godiva ..."; "He's a fascinating composition with the arms of the Venus de Milo, the head of John the Baptist, the thoughts of Mao Tse Tung, the feet of Dr Christian Barnard and the ear of Vincent Van Gogh" becomes "He's a fascinating composition with the arms of Venus de Milo, the head of John the Baptist, thoughts of Mao Tse Tung, the heart of Dr Christian Barnard and the ear of Vincent Van Gogh"; and "He's always lending you books you won't read" becomes "... books you don't read." These disparities might be between Humphries' original script and his recording or between his recording and his Foreword.

# Barry Humphries' Theatrical and Artistic Works, 1952–2002

### STAGE PERFORMANCES

Humphries, Barry, perf. *Call Me Madman!* The Melbourne Dada Group. Union Theatre, Melbourne. 1952.
- *You Never Can Tell*. Union Theatre, Melbourne. 1953.
- *Hamlet*, by Shakespeare. 1954.
- *Le Malade imaginaire*, by Jean Baptiste Molière. 1954.
- *Love's Labour's Lost*, by Shakespeare. 1954.
- *Twelfth Night*, by Shakespeare. Union Theatre Repertory Company Tour, Victoria. 1955.
- "Edna Everage: Olympic Hostess," by Humphries, Noel Ferrier, Bill Donaldson, and Gordon Chater. *Return Fare*. Union Theatre, Melbourne 1955. (Edna Everage's first stage appearance, 13 December 1955.)
- *Tram Stop Ten*. Union Theatre, Melbourne. 1956. Phillip Street Theatre, Sydney. 1956. (Including "Edna Everage, Olympic Hostess," by Barry Humphries.)
- "Olympic Hostess," by Humphries, Dudley Goldman, and Eric Rasdall. *Mr and Mrs*. Phillip Street Theatre, Sydney. 1956.
- *Alice in Wonderland*. Phillip Street Theatre, Sydney. 14 December 1956.
- "Maroan," by Humphries. *Around the Loop*. Phillip Street Theatre, Sydney. 1956–57.
- Untitled Performances, by Barry Humphries. Granville Returned Servicemen's Club, Sydney. 1957.
- *Pygmalion*, by George Bernard Shaw. Directed by Peter O'Shaughnessy. Phillip Street Theatre, Sydney. 1957.
- *Waiting for Godot*, by Samuel Beckett. Directed by Peter O'Shaughnessy. Arrow Theatre, Melbourne. 1957. Independent Theatre, Sydney. 1958.

- *The Bunyip and the Satellite*, by Barry Humphries and Jeffrey Underhill. Directed by Peter O'Shaughnessy. National Theatre, Melbourne. 1957–58. Independent Theatre, Sydney. 1958.
- *Lunch Hour Theatre Revues*, by Peter O'Shaughnessy. Melbourne. 1958.
- "Dramatic Recital," by Barry Humphries and Peter O'Shaughnessy. Sixth Wangaratta Arts Festival. 9–18 April 1958.
- "Days of the Week." *Rock 'n' Reel Review*, by Barry Humphries and Peter O'Shaughnessy. New Theatre, Melbourne. 1958. National Theatre, Melbourne. 1958.
- *Peter O'Shaughnessy and Barry Humphries, Testimonial Performance*, by Barry Humphries and Peter O'Shaughnessy. Assembly Hall, Sydney. 20–2 February 1959.
- *The Demon Barber*, by Donald Cotton. Lyric Opera House, Hammersmith, London. 1959.
- *Mumba Jumba and the Bunyip*, by Barry Humphries. New Theatre, Melbourne. 1959–60. Russell Street Theatre, Melbourne. 1960–61. Unley Town Hall, Adelaide Festival of the Arts. March 1964. St Martin's Theatre, Melbourne. 29 December 1965. New Theatre, Sydney. January 1968.
- *Oliver!* by Lionel Bart. Wimbledon Theatre, London. 1960. New (Albery) Theatre, London. 1960.
- *A Nice Night's Entertainment*, by Barry Humphries. Assembly Hall, Melbourne. Australian tour. 1962. Revised as Untitled Performances. Establishment Club, London. May 1963.
- *Oliver!* by Lionel Bart. Imperial Theatre, New York. 1963.
- *The Bedsitting Room*, by Spike Milligan and John Antrobus. Duke of York's Theatre, London. 1963. Comedy Theatre, London. 1963.
- *A Nice Night's Entertainment*, by Barry Humphries. The Establishment Club, London. May 1963.
- *The Merry Rooster's Panto*, by Peter Shaffer. Wyndham's Theatre, London. 1963.
- *A Kayf Up West*, by Frank Norman. Theatre Royal, Stratford East, London. 1964.
- *Maggie May*, by Lionel Bart. Adelphi Theatre, London. 1964.
- *Excuse I, Another Nice Night's Entertainment*, by Barry Humphries. Theatre Royal, Sydney. 1965–66. Australian tour. 1965–66.
- *Oliver!* by Lionel Bart. Piccadilly Theatre, London. 1967. London Palladium, London. 1967.
- *Treasure Island*, by Robert Louis Stevenson. Mermaid Theatre, London. 1967.
- *Just a Show*, by Barry Humphries. Tivoli Theatre, Sydney. 1968. Australian tour. 1968. Fortune Theatre, London. 1969.

- *A Load of Olde Stuffe: A Divertissement in Two Acts, for Those Too Drunk to Dance,* by Barry Humphries. Playbox Theatre, Sydney. 1971. Australian tour. 1971.
- *At Least You Can Say You've Seen It: A Tragi-Farce in Two Acts, for Those Too Drunk to Dance,* by Barry Humphries. Elizabethan Theatre, Sydney. 1974. Canberra Theatre, Canberra. 1974. Comedy Theatre, Melbourne. 1974. Her Majesty's Theatre, Brisbane. 1974. Theatre Royal, Hobart. 1974. Australian tour 1974. Her Majesty's Theatre, Melbourne. 1975.
- *A Poke in the Eye with a Sharp Stick,* performed by Barry Humphries, Alan Bennett, John Bird, Eleanor Bron, Tim Brooke-Taylor, Graham Chapman, John Cleese, Carol Cleveland, Peter Cook, John Fortune, Graeme Garden, Terry Gilliam, Eric Idle, Neil Innes, Des Jones, Terry Jones, Jonathan Lynn, Joe Mella, Jonathan Miller, Bill Oddie and Michael Palin. Her Majesty's Theatre, London. 1, 2 and 3 April 1976.
- *Housewife-Superstar!!* by Barry Humphries. Apollo Theatre and Globe Theatre, London. 1976. Theatre Four, New York. 1977. (At Theatre Four, the play title was punctuated *Housewife! Superstar!!*)
- *"Isn't It Pathetic at His Age,"* by Barry Humphries. Her Majesty's Theatre, Sydney. 1978. Comedy Theatre, Melbourne. 1978. Australian tour. 1978–79.
- *A Night with Dame Edna, and a Handful of Cobbers (Not So Much a Show as an On-Going, Open-Ended, In-Theatre Entertainment System Situation),* by Barry Humphries. Piccadilly Theatre, London. 1978. UK tour: Newcastle, Coventry, Norwich, Leeds, Stratford on Avon, Oxford. 1979. Australian tour. 1979.
- *The Secret Policeman's Other Ball,* performed by Barry Humphries, John Cleese, Graham Chapman, Alan Bennett, Tim Brooke-Taylor, Neil Innes, John Fortune, John Bird, Rowan Atkinson, Pamela Stephenson, Griff Rhys Jones, Chris Langham, Clive Anderson, Martin Bergman, Jasper Carrott, Jimmy Melville, Alexei Sayle, John Wells and Victoria Wood. Theatre Royal, Drury Lane, London. 9, 10, 11 and 12 September 1981.
- *An Evening's Intercourse with the Widely Liked Barry Humphries,* by Barry Humphries. Regent Theatre, Sydney. 1981. Her Majesty's Theatre, Melbourne. 1981. Theatre Royal, Drury Lane, London. 1982.
- *The Last Night of the Poms,* by Barry Humphries and Carl Davis. Conducted by Carl Davis. Royal Albert Hall, London. 1981. Then as *Song of Australia.*
- *Song of Australia,* by Barry Humphries and Carl Davis. Conducted by Carl Davis. Regent Theatre, Sydney. February 1983. Melbourne Concert Hall, Melbourne. February 1983.
- *Peter and the Shark,* by Barry Humphries and Carl Davis. Conducted by Davis. Melbourne Concert Hall, Melbourne. 12 March 1983.

- *Carl Davis in Croydon*, by Barry Humphries and Carl Davis. Conducted by Carl Davis. Croydon. 1983.
- *Tears Before Bedtime*, by Barry Humphries. Australian tour. 1983. Then as *Back with a Vengeance*.
- *Dame Edna's Australian Walkabout*, by Barry Humphries. Australian tour. 1985.
- *Back with a Vengeance*, by Barry Humphries. Strand Theatre and Theatre Royal, Drury Lane, London. 1987–88. UK tour. 1989.
- *Sunday with Sondheim*. Shaftesbury Theatre, London. 27 March 1988.
- *A Royal Gala in Aid of the Prince's Trust: An Evening of Contemporary Music and Comedy Celebrating 21 Years of London Weekend Television*. London Palladium, London. April 1989.
- *Noël Coward's Semi-monde*, by Noël Coward. Royalty Theatre, London. 13 September 1989.
- *Back with a Vengeance: The Second Coming*, by Barry Humphries. Theatre Royal, Drury Lane, London. 1989.
- *The Life and Death of Sandy Stone*, by Barry Humphries. Australian tour. 1990–91.
- *Look at Me When I'm Talking to You!* by Barry Humphries. London. 1993. Australian tour. 1993–94. Palace Theatre, Manchester. October 1995. Empire Theatre, Liverpool. November 1995. London and UK tour. 1996.
- *Dame Edna uber Deutschland*, by Barry Humphries. German tour. 1996.
- *Juste pour rire/Just for Laughs Comedy Festival*. Montreal. 1996. (Dame Edna Everage as gala host)
- *Jack in Review*. London Palladium, London. February 1997.
- *Dame Edna Everage in an Evening of Innocent Austral Verse*. Wigmore Hall, London. October 1997.
- *Oliver!* by Lionel Bart. London Palladium, London. 1997.
- *New Edna – The Spectacle*, by Barry Humphries. Theatre Royal Haymarket, London. 1998.
- *Sondheim Tonight: A Gala Concert Celebrating the Music of Stephen Sondheim for the Benefit of the Alan Jay Lerner Fund for Cancer Research at the Royal Marsden Hospital*. Barbican Centre, London. 17 May 1998.
- *Dame Edna – The Royal Tour (An Appropriate Show)*, by Barry Humphries. Theatre on the Square, San Francisco. 1998.
- *Remember You're Out, A New Barry Humphries Event*, by Barry Humphries. Australian tour: Canberra Theatre, Canberra; Newcastle Civic Centre, Newcastle; Parramatta Riverside Theatre, Parramatta; Sydney State Theatre, Sydney; Melbourne Princess Theatre, Melbourne; Adelaide Her Majesty's, Adelaide; Perth Regal Theatre, Perth. March – May 1999.

- *Sir Les Patterson's Australia Night*, by Barry Humphries. Royal Festival Hall, London. June 1999.
- *Dame Edna – The Royal Tour (The Show That Listens)*, by Barry Humphries. Booth Theatre, New York. 1999–2000. North American tour: State Theatre, Minneapolis; Royal Alexandra Theatre, Toronto; Parker Playhouse, Fort Lauderdale; Royal Poinciana Playhouse, Palm Beach; Ruth Eckerd Hall, Clearwater; Wilbur Theatre, Boston; Music Hall, Detroit; Shubert Theatre, Chicago; Orpheum Theatre, Phoenix; Moore Theatre, Seattle; Shubert Theatre, Los Angeles; Auditorium Theatre, Denver. 2000–01.
- *A Night with Dame Edna (The Show That Cares)*, by Barry Humphries. North America tour: Jackie Gleason Theatre, Miama; Tampa Performing Arts Center; Colonial Theatre, Boston; Shubert Theatre, New Haven; The Centre in Vancouver for Performing Arts, Vancouver; State Theatre, Minneapolis; Fox Theatre, St Louis; Merrill Auditorium, Portland, ME; National Theatre, Washington, DC; Forrest Theatre, Philadelphia; Bushnell Center, Hartford; Curran Theatre, San Francisco. 2002–03.
- *Back to My Roots and Other Suckers*, by Barry Humphries. Australian tour: Union Theatre, Melbourne; Canberra Theatre, Camberra; Lyric Theatre, Brisbane; State Theatre, Sydney; State Theatre, Melbourne; Adelaide Her Majesty's, Adelaide; Perth Regal Theatre, Perth. 2003.
- *A Night with Dame Edna (The Family Show)*, by Barry Humphries. American tour: Heinz Hall, Pittsburgh; Fox Theatre, Atlanta; Morris A. Mechanic Theatre, Baltimore; Murat Centre, Indianapolis; Majestic Theatre, Dallas; Performing Arts Centre, Providence; Barbara B. Mann Performing Arts Hall, Fort Myers, FL; Louisville Palace, Louisville; Palace Theatre, Columbus, OH; Playhouse Square, Cleveland; Arnonoff Center for the Arts, Cincinatti. 2003–04.

### SOUND RECORDINGS

Humphries, Barry. *Wild Life in Suburbia*. Performed by Barry Humphries. Score POL 014. 1958. EP.
- *Wild Life in Suburbia, Volume Two*. Performed by Barry Humphries. Score POL 018. 1959. EP.
Bart, Lionel. *Oliver!* Performed by Barry Humphries and others. Decca LK 4359, Decca SKL 4105, Decca SPA 30. 1960. LP.
Humphries, Barry. *Sandy Agonistes*. Performed by Barry Humphries. Score POL 024. 1960. LP.
- *A Nice Night's Entertainment*. Performed by Barry Humphries. Parlophone PMCO 7519/PMEO 9613. 1960. LP.
Humphries, Barry, Peter Cook, Dudley Moore and Richard Ingrams. *I Saw Daddy Kissing Santa Claus: A Special Christmas Record Issued by Lord Gnome*. Performed by Barry Humphries, Peter Cook, Dudley

Moore, and Richard Ingrams. Lyntone LYN 758 (*Private Eye* [December 1964]). 1964. 7".

Bart, Lionel, *Maggie May*. Performed by Barry Humphries and others. Decca LK 4643. 1964. LP.

Humphries, Barry. "Earl's Court Blues" and "Old Pacific Sea," performed by Barry Humphries. On *Private Eye's Blue Record*. Performed by Barry Humphries, Peter Cook, Dudley Moore, and others. Transatlantic TRA 131. 1965. LP.

Humphries, Barry. *Chunder Down Under: Snow Complications; The Old Pacific Sea*. Performed by Barry Humphries. Bulletin MX 19053. 1965. 7".

– *Ulysses Rag (Pianola Honeymoon)/Love's Old Sweet Song*. Performed by Mr Stanley Myers and the West Hamstead Tea Room New Orpheans with Vocal Refrain by Master Barry Humphries and the Noveltones. RCA Victor RCA 1579. 1967. 7".

Humphries, Barry. "The Little One-Eyed Trouser Snake," performed by Barry Humphries. On *The Abominable Radio Gnome*. Performed by Barry Humphries, Peter Cook, Dudley Moore, John Wells, Willie Rushton, John Bird, Richard Ingrams, Barry Fantoni, and Eleanor Bron. Lyntone LYN 1345 (Private Eye). 1967. Flexi.

Moore, Dudley. *Bedazzled*. Performed by Dudley Moore. London MS 82009, Decca LK 4923. 1968. LP.

*The Naked Bunyip*. Performed by Barry Humphries. Big Time Records/Bunyip BUN 069. 1970. EP.

Humphries, Barry. *Barry Humphries*. Performed by Barry Humphries. Parlophone PMEO 9616. 1970. LP.

– *Barry Humphries' Savoury Dip*. Performed by Barry Humphries. Parlophone PMEO 9716. 1971. LP.

– *Freedom from Hunger Campaign*. Performed by Barry Humphries and others. AWA Custom Recording AW32962A. 1971. 7".

– *Freedom from Hunger Campaign*. Performed by Barry Humphries and others. AWA Custom Recording AW32963A. 1971. 7".

– *The Barry Humphries Record of Innocent Austral Verse*. Performed by Barry Humphries. Philips 6357 011. 1972. LP.

Humphries, Barry, and Dick Bentley. *A Track Winding Back*. Performed by Barry Humphries and Dick Bentley. Philips 6205 019. 1972. EP.

Humphries, Barry. *Is 'E an Aussie, Is 'E, Lizzie*. Performed by Barry Humphries. Philips BF 480. 1972. 7".

Humphries, Barry, and Nigel Butterley. *Barry Humphries at Carnegie Hall in First Day Covers: A Philharmonic Philatelia*. Performed by Barry Humphries and Nigel Butterley. Philips 6357 010. 1972. LP.

Humphries, Barry, Peter Best and Barry Crocker. *The Adventures of Barry McKenzie*. Performed by Peter Best, Julie Convington, Smacka Fitzgibbon and others. Fable FBSA 026. 1972. LP.

Humphries, Barry. *Bazza McKenzie Party Songs*. Performed by Barry Crocker. Festival FL 34733. 1972.

– *Ricky Roo/Sandy Sings Sacred Songs*. Performed by Barry Humphries. Philips 6037 021. 1972. 7".

Humphries, Barry, Peter Cook, Dudley Moore, John Wells, Willie Rushton, John Bird, Richard Ingrams, Barry Fantoni, and Eleanor Bron. *Private Eye's Golden Years of Sound: The Collected Christmas Records 1964–1970*. Performed by Barry Humphries and others. Lynton LYN 2745/6. 1973. LP.

Humphries, Barry. *The Adventures of Barry McKenzie*. Performed by Barry Humphries. Bell S 228. 1973. LP.

Bart, Lionel. "Ballad of the Liver Bird," performed by Barry Humphries. On *Calvacade of London Theatre*. Performed by Barry Humphries and others. Decca D140D1/4. 1973. LP.

Humphries, Barry. *Housewife, Superstar!* Performed by Barry Humphries. Charisma CAS 1123. 1976. LP.

– *The Sound of Edna*. Performed by Barry Humphries. Charisma CAS 2240, Gladdy Records/Charisma 9124 027. 1978. LP.

Humphries, Barry, and others. *Best Sellers Recorded Session at the Writer's Week at the Adelaide Arts Festival*. Performed by Barry Humphries and others. ABC Radio. 1978. Audiocassette.

Humphries, Barry. *Disco Matilda*. Performed by Barry Humphries. Charisma CB 336. 1979. 7".

Humphries, Barry, and Carl Davis. *The Last Night of the Poms*. Performed by Barry Humphries and Carl Davis. EMI EMC 2742/3, EMI EDNA 81. 1981. LP.

Hartley, Richard, Richard O'Brien, and Jim Sharman. *Shock Treatment*. Performed by Barry Humphries and others. Ode R271678 1981. Compact sound disc.

Humphries, Barry, Peter Cook, Dudley Moore, John Wells, Willie Rushton, John Bird, Richard Ingrams, Barry Fantoni and Eleanor Bron. *Private Eye Presents Golden Satiricals*. Performed by Barry Humphries and others. Springtime HAHA 6002. 1981. LP.

Humphries, Barry. "The Royal Australian Prostate Foundation," performed by Barry Humphries. On *The Secret Policeman's Other Ball*. Performed by Barry Humphries, Rowan Atkinson, Alan Bennett, John Bird, Tim Brooke-Taylor, Jasper Carrott, Graham Chapman, John Cleese, Billy Connolly, John Fortune, Neil Innes, Chris Langham, Griff Rhys Jones, Alexi Sayle, Pamela Stephenson, John Wells, and Victoria Wood. Springtime HAHA 6003. 1981. LP.

– "Les Patterson" (*Housewife Superstar!*), performed by Barry Humphries. On record two of *We Are Most Amused*. Performed by Barry Humphries and others. 2 records. Ronco RTD 2067. 1981. LP.

Humphries, Barry, and Nick Rowley. "Niceness" (*The Sound of Edna*), performed by Barry Humphries. On record two of *We Are Most Amused*. Performed by Barry Humphries and others. 2 records. Ronco RTD 2067. 1981. LP.

Humphries, Barry. *12 Inches of Les, The Album*. Performed by Barry Humphries. Liberation/Towerbell Records LIB 5064 1985. LP.

– *The Les Patterson Long Player*. Performed by Barry Humphries. WEA 254779-1 1987. LP.

– *G'Day*. Performed by Barry Humphries. Powderworks POW 03876, 1987. 7".

– "G'Day," performed by Barry Humphries. On *World Expo 88: The Songs*. Performed by Barry Humphries, Rick Price, Julie McKenna, and Normie Rowe. EMI 8801. 1987. LP.

Humphries, Barry, and Tim Finn. *Les Patterson Saves the World*. Performed by Barry Humphries, Tim Finn, and others. WEA 254779.1. 1987. LP.

Finn, Tim, and Michael J. Kenny. *You Saved the World*. Performed by Tim Finn and others. WEA 7-258352. 1987. 7".

Humphries, Barry. *Theme from Neighbours (Caring and Sharing Mix)*. Performed by Barry Humphries. Epic 654503 6. 1988. LP.

– *Spooky Christmas*. Performed by Barry Humphries. Epic 654503-7. 1988. 12".

– *The Dame Edna Party Experience*. Performed by Barry Humphries. Epic 463235-1. 1988. LP.

– *Barry Humphries Self-Indulgently Presents "The Life and Death of Sandy Stone."* Performed by Barry Humphries. 1990. Audiocassette.

Everage, Dame Edna [Barry Humphries]. *My Gorgeous Life: The Life, the Loves, the Legend*, read by Barry Humphries. Dove Audio. 1990. Audiocassette.

English, Jon, David MacKay, and others. "Inside Outside," performed by Barry Humphries, Francis Rossi, and Demis Roussos. On *Paris*. By Jon English, David MacKay, and others. 2 records. WEA 903172072-1. 1990. LP.

Everage, Dame Edna [Barry Humphries]. *My Gorgeous Life*. Read by the author. Collins Audio. 1991. Audiocassette.

Humphries, Barry. *Barry Humphries on Patrick White*. ABC Radio. 1991. Audiocassette.

– *Moonee Ponds Muse, Vol. 1*. Performed by Barry Humphries. Raven Records Australia RVCD-17. 1991. Compact sound disc.

– *Dada Days: Moonee Ponds Muse, Vol. 2 (1951–1983)*. Performed by Barry Humphries. Raven Records Australia RVCD-34. 1993. Compact sound disc.

Humphries, Barry, Nick Rowley, and Stanley Myers. *The Sound of Edna: Dame Edna's Family Songbook*. Performed by Barry Humphries. Dove Audio. 1993. Audiocassette.

Humphries, Barry. *More Please*. Read by the author. Penguin Audiobooks PEN 4. 1993. Audiocassette.

– "Cultural Attaché." Performed by Barry Humphries. On *The Silver Tongued Years, Vol. 3*. Virgin CAS BOX 1C. 1993. Compact sound disc. (*The Famous Charisma Box: The History of Charisma Records 1968– 1985: Charisma's Purple Patch, Vol. 1; Carry on Charisma, Vol. 2; The Silver Tongued Years, Vol. 3; The Terminal Years, Vol. 4*. 4 discs. Virgin CAS BOX, 1A, 1B, 1C, 1D. 1993. Compact sound discs.)

– *Women in the Background*. Read by the author. Reed Audio 152. 1996. Audiocassette.

Patterson, Les [Barry Humphries]. *Les Patterson Has a Stand-up: Live and Rampant*. Performed by Barry Humphries. MCI Spoken Word GAGSDMO 053. 1996. Audiocassette.

Tchaikovsky, Piotr Ilyich. *Peter and the Wolf*. Read by Dame Edna Everage [Barry Humphries]. Melbourne Symphony Orchestra. Naxos. 1997. Compact sound disc.

Humphries, Barry, Peter Cook, Dudley Moore, John Wells, John Bird, Willie Rushton, Richard Ingrams, Eleanor Bron, and Barry Fantoni. *The Best of Private Eye: Golden Satiricals Presents ... Volume One, The Famous Flexies!* Performed by Barry Humphries and others. MCI Spoken Word GAGDMC 085. 1998. Audiocassette. (Contents: eleven 7" flexi-discs, plus lost EP "Private Eye Sings.")

– *The Best of Private Eye: Golden Satiricals Presents ... Volume Two, The Swingeing Sixties*. Performed by Barry Humphries and others. MCI Spoken Word GAGDMC 087. 1998. Audiocassette. (Contents: *Private Eye's Blue Record* and *Mrs Wilson's Diary*.)

– *The Best of Private Eye: Golden Satiricals Presents ... Volume Three, The Sarcastic Seventies!* Performed by Barry Humphries and others. Audiocassette. MCI Spoken Word GAGSDMC 093. 1998. Audiocassette. (Contents: the lost LP *Ho-Ho! Very Satirical* [1971].)

Humphries, Barry, comp. *Barry Humphries' Flashbacks*. Sony. 1999. Compact sound disc.

Humphries, Barry. "Dame Edna Everage." Performed by Barry Humphries. On disc one of *Sondheim Tonight, a Gala Concert to Celebrate the Music of Stephen Sondheim*. Performed by Barry Humphries, Michael Ball, Len Cariou, Maria Friedman, Dominic John, David Kernan, Cleo Laine, Millicent Martin, Julia McKenzie, Julia Migenes, Clive Rowe, Ned Sherrin, Elaine Stritch, Christina Sunnerstan, and Stephen Sondheim. 2 CDs. JAY. 1999. Compact sound discs.

Sondheim, Stephen. "The Ladies Who Lunch." Performed by Barry Humphries. On disc one of *Sondheim Tonight, a Gala Concert to Celebrate the Music of Stephen Sondheim*. Performed by Barry Humphries, Michael Ball, Len Cariou, Maria Friedman, Dominic

John, David Kernan, Cleo Laine, Millicent Martin, Julia McKenzie, Julia Migenes, Clive Rowe, Ned Sherrin, Elaine Stritch, Christina Sunnerstan, and Stephen Sondheim. 2 CDs. JAY. 1999. Compact sound discs.

Humphries, Barry, comp. *So Rare*. Bilarm BAC 11–2 1999. Compact sound disc.

– *So Rare 2, a Second Selection by Barry Humphries of His Favourite Gramophone Records*. Bilarm BAC 12–2, 2000. Compact sound disc.

Humphries, Barry. "Dear Beryl" and "Lament for Maid Melbourne." Performed by Barry Humphries. On *Funny Business Down Under*. Laugh Radio. 2000. Compact sound disc.

– "Les Patterson, Cultural Attaché." Performed by Barry Humphries. *The Best Comedy Album in the World ... Ever!* 3 CDs. Circa. 2000. Compact sound disc.

Everage, Dame Edna [Barry Humphries]. *Edna's Show Songs*. Performed by Barry Humphries. Tamarin TAM205. 2000. Compact sound disc.

– *Color Me Edna: Songs of Co-Dependency*. Performed by Barry Humphries. Tamarin TAM206. 2000. Compact sound disc.

Humphries, Barry. "Special Message from Dame Edna Everage." Performed by Barry Humphries. On *Private Eye's CD-Romp*. Performed by Barry Humphries, Eleanor Bron, Jon Culshaw, Harry Enfield, Ian Hislop, Lewis MacLeod, Kate Robbins, and John Sessions. Pressdram. 2001. Compact sound disc.

FILMS: BARRY HUMPHRIES, PERFORMER

– *Bedazzled*. 104 min. Directed by Stanley Donen. TCF, 1967. (Envy)
– *The Bliss of Mrs Blossom*. 93 min. Directed by Joseph McGrath. Paramount, 1968. (art dealer)
– *The Naked Bunyip*. 136 min. Directed by John B. Murray. 1970. (Edna Everage)
– *The Adventures of Barry McKenzie*. 114 min. Screenplay by Barry Humphries and Bruce Beresford. Directed by Bruce Beresford. Columbia/Longford, 1972. (Aunt Edna Everage; Hoot)
– *Barry McKenzie Holds His Own*. 93 min. Screenplay by Barry Humphries and Bruce Beresford. Directed by Bruce Beresford. Satori, 1974. (Aunt/Dame Edna Everage; Dr Meyer de Lamphrey; Englishman; Senator Douglas Manton)
– *Percy's Progress*. 90 min. Directed by Ralph Thomas. EMI Elstree, 1974. (Dr Anderson)
– *The Great McCarthy*. 106 min. Directed by David Baker. Stoney Creek, 1975. (Col Ball-Miller)
– *Side by Side*. 84 min. Directed by Bruce Beresford. GTO, 1975. (Rodney)

- *Pleasure at Her Majesty's.* 70 min. Performed by Barry Humphries, Alan Bennett, John Bird, Eleanor Bron, Tim Brooke-Taylor, Graham Chapman, John Cleese, Carol Cleveland, Peter Cook, John Fortune, Graeme Garden, Terry Gilliam, Eric Idle, Neil Innes, Des Jones, Terry Jones, Jonathan Lynn, Joe Mella, Jonathan Miller, Bill Oddie, and Michael Palin. Directed by Roger Graef. 1976. Released in America as *Monty Python Meets Beyond the Fringe.* 1977. (Dame Edna Everage)
- *The Getting of Wisdom.* 101 min. Directed by Bruce Beresford. Southern Cross/AFC/Victorian Film Corporation, 1977. (Reverend Strachey)
- *Sgt Pepper's Lonely Hearts Club Band.* 113 min. Directed by Michael Schultz. RSO, 1978. (Dame Edna Everage)
- *Shock Treatment.* 94 min. Directed by Jim Sharman. TCF, 1982. (Bert Schnick)
- *The Secret Policeman's Other Ball.* 88 min. Performed by Barry Humphries, Rowan Atkinson, Alan Bennett, John Byrd, Tim Brooke-Taylor, Graham Chapman, John Cleese, Billy Connolly, Griff Rhys Jones, Alexei Sayle, Michael Palin, and others. Directed by Roger Graef and Julien Temple. Amnesty International (UIP), 1982. (Various roles)
- *A Toast to Melbourne.* 1982.
- *Les Patterson Saves the World.* 98 min. Screenplay by Barry Humphries and Diane Millstead. Directed by George Miller. Humpstead, 1987. (Les Patterson; Dame Edna Everage)
- *Howling III.* 94 min. Directed by Philippe Mora. Baccania, 1987. (Dame Edna Everage)
- *Pterodactyl Woman from Beverly Hills.* 97 min. Directed by Philippe Mora. 50th Street Films, 1994. (Bert; lady shopper; store manager)
- *Immortal Beloved.* 120 min. Directed by Bernard Rose. Entertainment/Majestic/Icon, 1994. (Clemens Metternich)
- *Napoleon.* 81 min. Directed by Mario Andreacchio. Australian Film Finance Corporation/Harold Ace/Film Australia/Furry Feature Films, 1994. (Voice of Kangaroo)
- *The Leading Man.* 100 min. Directed by John Duigan. J&M, 1996. (Humphrey Beal)
- *Welcome to Woop-Woop.* 97 min. Directed by Philippe Mora. 50th Street Films, 1997. (Blind Wally)
- *Spice World.* 93 min. Directed by Bob Spiers. Columbia, 1997. (Kevin McMaxford)
- *Nicholas Nickleby.* 108 min. Directed by Douglas McGrath. United Artists, 2002. (Mrs Crummles and Mr Leadville)
- *Finding Nemo.* 100 min. Directed by Andrew Stanton. 2003. (Voice of Bruce)

VIDEOS

Humphries, Barry, perf. *Bedazzled*. Directed by Stanley Donen. 1967. 105 min. 20th-Century Fox, 2000. Videocassette.

– *The Bliss of Mrs Blossom*. Directed by Joe McGrath. 1968. 93 min. Paramount, 1992. Videocassette.

– *The Adventures of Barry McKenzie*. Screenplay by Barry Humphries and Bruce Beresford. Directed by Bruce Beresford. 1972. 117 min. Magna, 1986. Videocassette.

– *Barry McKenzie Holds His Own*. Screenplay by Barry Humphries and Bruce Beresford. Directed by Bruce Beresford. 1974. 93 min. VidAmerica, 1985. Videocassette.

– *Percy's Progress*. Directed by Ralph Thomas. 1974. 97 min. Thorn EMI, 1974. Videocassette.

– *Side by Side*. Directed by Bruce Beresford. 1975. 90 min. Showcase, 1975. Videocassette.

– *The Great McCarthy*. Directed by David Baker. 1975. 96 min. Filmpac, 1989. Videocassette.

– *The Getting of Wisdom*. Directed by Bruce Beresford. 1977. 100 min. Fox Lorber, 1997. Videocassette.

– *Shock Treatment*. Directed by Jim Sharman. 1982. 95 min. Fox Video, 1993. Videocassette.

– *Dr Fischer of Geneva*. Directed by Michael Lyndsay-Hogg. 1984. 97 min. VCI, 1990. Videocassette.

– *Dame Edna, Back with a Vengeance, The Second Coming*. Directed by Ken O'Neill. 90 min. Virgin Vision, 1989. Videocassette.

– *Howling III*. Directed by Philippe Mora. 1987. 94 min. Vista, 1987. Videocassette.

– *Les Patterson Saves the World*. By Barry Humphries and Diane Millstead. Directed by George Miller. 1987. 105 min. CBS/FOX 1987. Videocassette.

– *The Very Best of The Dame Edna Experience*. By Barry Humphries. 65 min. MSD, 1988. Videocassette.

*The Best of ... What's Left of ... Not Only ... But Also ...* Performed by Barry Humphries, Peter Cook, Dudley Moore, and others. 90 min. BBC Video, 1990, CBS/Fox, 1991. Videocassette.

*Barry Humphries*. Performed by Barry Humphries, Melvin Bragg and Nigel Watts. LWT, 1989, ABC-TV (Australian Broadcasting Commission), 1992. Videocassette.

*An Intercourse with Barry Humphries*. Performed by Barry Humphries, Phillip Adams and Sally Loane. Directed by Kevin Ryder. SBS, 1992. Videocassette.

Humphries, Barry, perf. *Pterodactyl Woman from Beverly Hills*. Directed
   by Philippe Mora. 1994. 90 min. Troma, 1997. Videocassette.
– *Napoleon*. Directed by Mario Andreacchio. 1994. 81 min. Orion, 1994.
   Videocassette.
– *Immortal Beloved*. Directed by Bernard Rose. 1994. 121 min. Columbia
   Tristar, 1995. Videocassette.
– *Les Patterson Has a Stand-up: Live and Rampant*. By Barry Humphries,
   Ian Davidson, and Laurie Holloway. Directed by Brian Klein. 72 min.
   VCI, 1996. Videocassette.
– *Dame Edna's Work Experience*. By Barry Humphries and Ian Davidson.
   Direct by Brian Klein. 49 min. DLT, 1997.
– *Spice World*. Directed by Bob Spiers. 1997. 93 min. Columbia, 1997.
   Videocassette.
*Pleasure at Her Majesty's*. Performed by Barry Humphries, Alan Bennett,
   John Bird, Eleanor Bron, Tim Brooke-Taylor, Graham Chapman, John
   Cleese, Carol Cleveland, Peter Cook, John Fortune, Graeme Garden,
   Terry Gilliam, Eric Idle, Neil Innes, Des Jones, Terry Jones, Jonathan
   Lynn, Joe Mella, Jonathan Miller, Bill Oddie, and Michael Palin. Di-
   rected by Roger Graef. 1977. 70 min. Rhino, 1998. Videocassette.
*The Secret Policeman's Other Ball*. Performed by Barry Humphries, John
   Cleese, Graham Chapman, Alan Bennett, Tim Brooke-Taylor, Neil
   Innes, John Fortune, John Bird, Rowan Atkinson, Pamela Stephenson,
   Griff Rhys Jones, Chris Langham, Clive Anderson, Martin Bergman,
   Jasper Carrott, Jimmy Melville, Alexei Sayle, John Wells, and Victoria
   Wood. Directed by Julien Temple. 1982. 88 min. Rhino, 1998. Video-
   cassette.
Humphries, Barry, perf. *Barry Humphries' Flashbacks*. By Barry Humphries
   and David Mitchell. Directed by David Mitchell. 2 videos. 184 min. ABC,
   1998. Videocassettes.
– *The Leading Man*. Directed by John Duigan. 1996. 96 min. WinStar,
   1999. Videocassette.
– *Dame Edna's Neighbourhood Watch*. Volume 1. By Barry Humphries
   and Ian Davidson. 60 min. Arts & Design Q Connection, 1999. Videocassette.
– *Dame Edna's Neighbourhood Watch*. Volume 2. By Barry Humphries
   and Ian Davidson. 60 min. Arts & Design Q Connection, 1999. Videocassette.
– *Dame Edna's Neighbourhood Watch*. Volume 3. By Barry Humphries
   and Ian Davidson. 60 min. Arts & Design Q Connection, 1999. Videocassette.
– *Dame Edna's Neighbourhood Watch*. Volume 4. By Barry Humphries
   and Ian Davidson. 60 min. Arts & Design Q Connection, 1999. Videocassette.

- *Dame Edna's Neighbourhood Watch.* Volume 5. By Barry Humphries and Ian Davidson. 60 min. Arts & Design Q Connection, 1999. Video-cassette.
- *Dame Edna's Neighbourhood Watch.* Volume 6. By Barry Humphries and Ian Davidson. 60 min. Arts & Design Q Connection, 1999. Video-cassette.
- *Dame Edna's Neighbourhood Watch.* By Barry Humphries and Ian Davidson. 149 min. Image, 1999. DVD.
- *The Leading Man.* Directed by John Duigan. 96 min. Fox Lorber, 1999. DVD.
*Party at the Palace: The Queen's Concerts, Buckingham Palace.* Performed by Barry Humphries and others. Directed by Geoff Posner. BBC, 2002. Videocassette.
Humphries, Barry, perf. *Les Patterson Saves the World.* By Barry Humphries and Diane Milstead. 86 min. Prism Leisure, 2002. DVD.
- *Nicholas Nickleby.* Directed by Douglas McGrath. 132 min. Metro Goldwyn Mayer, 2002. DVD.

TELEVISION

Humphries, Barry, perf. *Wild Life and Christmas Belles.* By Barry Humphries. Melbourne. 1958.
- *Trip-Tease and High C's.* By Barry Humphries. Melbourne. 1959.
- *Tonight We Improvise.* By Barry Humphries, Spike Milligan, Maggie Fitzgibbon, Maggie Charmon, and Barry Stanton. Performed by Barry Humphries, Spike Milligan, Maggie Fitzgibbon, Marigold Charman, and Barry Stanton. BBC. 12 July 1959.
- *Comfort Station.* By Barry Humphries. Melbourne. 1966.
- *The Late Show.* By Barry Humphries, John Bird, John Fortune, Eleanor Bron, Michael Palin, and Terry Jones. Perf. John Bird, Eleanor Bron, John Wells, Anthony Holland, and Andrew Duncan. Performed by Barry Humphries, John Bird, John Fortune, Eleanor Bron, Michael Palin, and Terry Jones. Perf. John Bird, Eleanor Bron, John Wells, Anthony Holland, and Andrew Duncan. BBC-1. 15 October 1966 – 1 April 1967.
- *Strangers in the Night.* By Barry Humphries and Ian Davidson. BBC-2. 12 July 1969. One-off special show that became *Barry Humphries' Scandals.*
- *Barry Humphries' Scandals.* By Barry Humphries and Ian Davidson. 5 episodes. BBC-2. 12 January – 9 February 1970.
*Not Only – But Also.* Performed by Barry Humphries, Peter Cook, Dudley Moore and others. ABC-TV (Australian Broadcasting Commission). 8 and 15 February 1971. BBC-1, 18 and 25 June 1971.
Humphries, Barry, perf. *HurRah.* BBC-2. 4 June 1971.

- *The Barry Humphries Show*. By Barry Humphries and Ian Davidson. 3 episodes. BBC-2. 3 March 1976, 26 September 1977, 5 December 1977.

*Pleasure at Her Majesty's*. Performed by Barry Humphries, Alan Bennett, John Bird, Eleanor Bron, Tim Brooke-Taylor, Graham Chapman, John Cleese, Carol Cleveland, Peter Cook, John Fortune, Graeme Garden, Terry Gilliam, Eric Idle, Neil Innes, Des Jones, Terry Jones, Jonathan Lynn, Joe Mella, Jonathan Miller, Bill Oddie, and Michael Palin. BBC-1. 29 December 1976.

Humphries, Barry, perf. *A Summer Sideshow*. London. 1977.

- *La Dame aux Gladiolas*. By Barry Humphries. BBC-2. 19 March 1979.

- *An Audience with Dame Edna*. By Barry Humphries. ITV (LWT). 26 December 1980.

- *The Last Night of the Poms*. By Barry Humphries. ITV (LWT). 3 January 1982.

- *A Birthday Tribute to Dame Edna Everage, la Dame aux Gladioli: The Agony and Ecstasy of Edna Everage*. By Barry Humphries. BBC-2. 17 February 1984.

- *Another Audience with Dame Edna*. By Barry Humphries. ITV (LWT). 31 December 1984.

- *An Aussie Audience with Dame Edna*. By Barry Humphries. Melbourne. 14 August 1986.

*Doctor Fischer of Geneva*. By Graham Greene. Performed by Barry Humphries and others. BBC-2-Consolidated Productions. 1 October 1984.

Humphries, Barry, perf. *The Dame Edna Experience!* By Barry Humphries. First cycle, 6 episodes. ITV (LWT). 12 September – 17 October 1987.

- *Dame Edna's Christmas Experience!* By Barry Humphries. ITV (LWT). 26 December 1987. Part of *The Dame Edna Experience!* series.

*A Night of Comic Relief*. By Barry Humphries and others. Performed by Barry Humphries, Lenny Henry, Griff Rhy Jones, Jim Davidson, Rod Hull and Emu, Harry Enfield, Syd Little, Eddie Large, Rory Bremner, Victoria Wood, Julie Walters, Stephen Fry, Hugh Laurie, Ernie Wise, Ronnie Corbett, Warren Mitchell, Michael Palin, Phil Cool, Dawn French, Jennifer Saunders, Bel Elton, Gareth Hale, Norman Pace, Tommy Cannon, Bobby Ball, Pamela Stephenson, and Matt Frewer. BBC-1. 5 February 1988.

Humphries, Barry, perf. *One More Audience with Dame Edna*. By Barry Humphries. ITV (LWT). 25 December 1988.

- *The South Bank Show*. Interview by Melvyn Bragg. ITV (LWT). 1989.

*A Night of Comic Relief 2*. By Barry Humphries and others. Performed by Barry Humphries, Robbie Coltrane, Dawn French, Matty Freweer,

Stephen Fry, Lenny Henry, Maichael Palin, Jennifer Saunders, Mel Smith, Emma Thompson, and others. BBC-1. 1989.

Hummphries, Barry, perf. *The Dame Edna Experience!* By Barry Humphries. Second series, 6 episodes. ITV (LWT). 4 November – 16 December 1989.

– *The Dame Edna Satellite Experience!* By Barry Humphries. ITV (LWT). 22 December 1989. Part of *The Dame Edna Experience!* series.

– "Sandy Comes Home." On *Single Voices*. 6 episodes. BBC. April 1990. ("Sandy Comes Home" was recorded 27 February 1989 in studio TC8 at the BBC Television Centre, London.)

– *A Night on Mount Edna.* By Barry Humphries. ITV (LWT). 15 December 1990.

*The Best of ... What's Left of ... Not Only ... But Also.* Performed by Barry Humphries, Peter Cook, Dudley Moore and others. 6 episodes. BBC-2. 4 November – 9 December 1990.

*Selling Hitler.* By Howard Schuman. Performed by Barry Humphries and others. Directed by Alastair Reid. 5 episodes. 11, 18, and 25 June, and 2 and 7 July 1991.

Humphries, Barry, perf. *Dame Edna's Hollywood.* By Barry Humphries and Ian Davidson. 3 episodes. ITV (LWT). 21 December 1991, 26 December 1993, 24 December 1994. NBC. 2, 9, and 16 May 1992.

– *The Life and Death of Sandy Stone.* By Barry Humphries. 1991.

– *Late Lunch with Sir Les.* By Barry Humphries. C4 (LWT). 27 December 1991.

– *Dame Edna's Neighbourhood Watch.* By Barry Humphries and Ian Davidson. First series, 6 episodes. ITV (LWT). 19 September – 24 October 1992.

– *Dame Edna's Neighbourhood Watch.* By Barry Humphries and Ian Davidson. Second series, 6 episodes. ITV (LWT). 18 September – 23 October 1993.

– *Vicki!* Interview by Vicki Lawrence. FOX. 23 October 1992.

– *It's Edna Time!* By Barry Humphries. FOX. 1993.

*Some Interesting Facts About Peter Cook.* Performed by Barry Humphries, Alan Bennett, John Bird, Eleanor Bron, Stanley Donen, David Frost, Ian Hislop, Jonathan Miller, Dudley Moore, Trevor Nunn, Ned Sherrin, Mel Smith, and others. 1995.

*A Gala Comedy Hour – Best of the Prince's Trust.* Performed by Barry Humphries, Russ Abbot, Rowan Atkinson, Michael Barrymore, Steve Coogan, Richard Digiance, Griff Rhys Jones, Rita Ruder, and Mel Smith. ITV (Carlton). 3 July 1996.

*Seriously Funny: An Argument for Comedy.* Performed by Barry Humphries, Howard Jacobson, Patch Adams, Roy "Chubby" Brown, John Lahr, Bernard Manning, Roseanne Barr, and others. 1996.

*Comic Relief*. Performed by Barry Humphries, Lenny Henry, Stephen Tompkinson, Dawn French, Jennifer Saunders, Jonathan Ross, Griff Rhys Jones, Harry Enfield, Kathy Burke, Steve Coogan, Robbine Coltrane, Paul Whitehouse, Jo Brand, Rowan Atkinson, Angus Deayton, Ben Elton, and others. BBC-1. 14 March 1997.

Humphries, Barry, perf. *Dame Edna's Work Experience*. By Barry Humphries and Ian Davidson. BBC-1. 3 April 1997.

– *Sir Les and the Great Chinese Takeaway*. By Barry Humphries. BBC-2. 28 June 1997.

– *Dame Edna Kisses It Better*. By Barry Humphries, Ian Davidson, and Jez Stephenson. ITV (LWT), 26 December 1997.

– *The Roseanne Show*. Interview by Roseanne Barr. SHOW1003. 15 August 1998. Transcript.

– *Barry Humphries' Flashbacks*. By Barry Humphries and David Mitchell. 4 episodes. ABC-TV (Australian Broadcasting Commission). 1998.

*A Royal Birthday Celebration*. Performed by Barry Humphries, Rowan Atkinson, Stephen Fry, Geri Halliwell, Desmond Llewelyn, Elle Macpherson, Spike Milligan, Robert Moore, Prince Charles, Mel Smith, Peter Ustinov, Robbie Williams, and others. 1998.

Humphries, Barry, perf. "The Two of Us." Interview by Liz Hayes. On *60 Minutes*. Nine Network. 28 February 1999.

– "Artist of the Week." Interview. On *Arts and Minds*. BRAVO! 31 October 1999. (Repeat broadcast)

– *Charlie Rose*. Interview by Charlie Rose. Show 2634. PBS. 8 March 2000. Transcript.

– "Nothing Like the Dame: An 'Australian Housewife' Is a Hit in New York but She Is Really a He." Interview by Bob Simon. On *60 Minutes II*. CBS. 25 April 2000.

*The Talk Show Story*. Performed by Barry Humphries, Michael Parkinson, Andrew Sachs, Steve Allen, Clive Anderson, Bill Carter, Simon Dee, David Frost, Clive James, Sue Lawley, Jay Leno, Jonathan Miller, Graham Norton, Conan O'Brien, Des O'Connor, Joan Rivers, Terry Wogan, and others. 2000.

*The 100 Greatest TV Characters*. Performed by Barry Humphries and others. 2001.

Humphries, Barry, narr. "RuPaul." On *Biography*. A&E. 9 July 2001.

– "Stone Cold Steve Austin." On *Biography*. A&E. 10 July 2001.

Humphries, Barry, perf. "Dame Edna." Narrated by Harry K. Smith. *Biography*. A&E. 11 July 2001.

Humphries, Barry, narr. "Liberace." *Biography*. A&E. 12 July 2001.

– "Phyllis Diller." *Biography*. A&E. 13 July 2001.

Humphries, Barry, perf. "Judge Ling." On *Ally McBeal*. Performed by Calista Flockheart and others. FOX. 5 November 2001.

- "Neutral Corners." *Ally McBeal.* Performed by Calista Flockheart and others. FOX. 12 November 2001.
- "Woman." *Ally McBeal.* Performed by Calista Flockheart and others. FOX. 18 February 2002.
- "Homecoming." *Ally McBeal.* Performed by Calista Flockheart and others. FOX. 25 February 2002.
- "Heart and Soul." *Ally McBeal.* Performed by Calista Flockheart and others. FOX. 4 March 2002.
- "Love Is All Around." *Ally McBeal.* Performed by Calista Flockheart and others. FOX. 15 April 2002.
- *The Tonight Show with Jay Leno.* NBC. 17 April 2002.
- "Tom Dooley." *Alley McBeal.* Performed by Calista Flockheart and others. FOX. 22 April 2002.
- "Another One Bites the Dust." *Ally McBeal.* Performed by Calista Flockheart and others. FOX. 29 April 2002.
- "What I'll Never Do for Love." *Ally McBeal.* Performed by Calista Flockheart and others. FOX. 6 May 2002.
- "All of Me." *Ally McBeal.* Performed by Calista Flockheart and others. FOX. 13 May 2002.
- "Bygones." *Ally McBeal.* Performed by Calista Flockheart and others. FOX. 20 May 2002.
- *Party at the Palace.* BBC. 3 June 2002.
- *Vicky Gabereau.* Interview by Vicky Gabereau. CIVT (Vancouver). 28 October 2002.
- *The Tonight Show with Jay Leno.* NBC. 14 January 2003.
- *Micallef Tonight.* ABC. 12 May 2003.
- *The Tonight Show with Jay Leno.* NBC. 2 October 2003.
- *The Sharon Osbourne Show.* AND Syndicated Productions. 21 October 2003.
- *Dame Edna Live at the Palace.* BBC 1. 30 December 2003. 4

ART EXHIBITIONS

*The First Pan-Australasian Dada Exhibition.* University of Melbourne, Melbourne. 1951.
*The Second Pan-Australiasian Dada Exhibition.* University of Melbourne, Melbourne. 1953.
*Barry Humphries.* Victorian Artists Society Gallery, Melbourne. 1958.
*Ten Little Australians.* Myer Mural Hall, Melbourne. 1958.
*Barry Humphreys* [sic] *Retrospective.* Bonython Galleries, Sydney. 20 – 28 August 1968.
*Dame Edna and Friends: Photographs by John Timbers.* Royal Photographic Society National Centre of Photography, London. 13 June 1988.

*Dame Edna Regrets She Is Unable to Attend: Humour and Satire in Australian Sculpture*. Heide Park and Art Gallery, Bulleen. 7 July – 6 September 1992. Australian tour. November 1992 – January 1994.

*Barry Humphries, Dada Artist*. National Gallery of Australia, Canberra. 12 March – 2 May 1993.

*Humphriana: The Alter Egos of Barry Humphries*. Gallery 3, Victorian Arts Centre, Melbourne. 27 March – 27 June 1999.

*Dame Edna's Frock-a-Thon: A Journey from Cardigan to Couture*. George Adams Gallery, Victorian Arts Centre, Melbourne. 3 April – 30 May 1999.

*Favourites: Margaret Olley and Barry Humphries Choose from Australian Collections*. S.H. Ervin Gallery, Melbourne. 15 January – 27 February 2000.

*Rarely Everage: The Lives of Barry Humphries*. Victorian Arts Centre, Melbourne. 2 July – 24 August 2003.

RADIO

Everage, Dame Edna [Barry Humphries]. Interview by Sue Lawley. *Desert Island Discs*. BBC Radio 4, London. 17 July 1988.

# Addendum

## THE BARRY HUMPHRIES COLLECTION
## AT THE PERFORMING ARTS MUSEUM,
## VICTORIAN ARTS CENTRE, MELBOURNE

In October 2000 I went on a research field trip to the Performing Arts Museum, Victorian Arts Centre, Melbourne, to inspect the Barry Humphries Collection there. In contrast to "the Everage Archives at the University of South West Virgina (apply: Miriam K. Benkowitz),"[1] the Barry Humphries Collection is a material site managed by dedicated and talented curators and archivists such as Catherine O'Donoghue and Joanna Leahy, although it does come under the protection of the goddess PAM.[2] Humphries formally initiated the collection in 1981 when he donated manuscripts, costumes, programs, posters, props, letters, and other documents to the museum through its director, Janine Barrand. Over the past twenty years[3] Humphries has continued to contribute to the collection, which has come to number over 1,200 items, including forty-two pairs of Dame Edna's *diamanté* eyeglasses (donated in 1981 and 1985) and twenty-two of her mauve and other-coloured "synthetic" wigs (donated in 1983). Enough, no doubt, to invoke a spectacle of mass wisteria.

The 1,248 items in the collection would be enough to reintegrate Humphries' theatrical and literary career, in the manner of Saleem Sinai, who, in Rushdie's *Midnight's Children* (1981), disintegrates into all the children born at the precise moment of India's independence in 1947. This synthetic Barry Humphries, like a synthetic wig, would represent Australia, the country of his birth and which he represents (and some would say "misrepresents," as in the vulgarian characters Bazza McKenzie and Sir Les Patterson) professionally around the world.

Most of the items in the Barry Humphries Collection are literary: manuscripts; typescripts and transcripts of theatrical scripts and running orders;

film scripts; articles and essays; song lyrics and sheet music; memos, notes, scrapbooks, folders, lists, and interviews; speeches and poems. The collection also comprises first editions of many of Humphries' books, journal articles (both by Humphries and about him), greeting cards and postcards, personal and business letters, and telegrams. All these materials, including the costumes and other non-scribal performative items, have been meticulously documented in the two-volume archive *Barry Humphries Collection, Performing Arts Museum* (June 1998). I have noticed only one possible anomaly, and it is surely attributable to Humphries rather than to the curators of the Performing Arts Museum or to the goddess PAM. The collection features three typescripts, all dated 1984, of the film *Les Patterson Saves the World* (1987) by Barry Humphries and Diane Millstead, but no revised versions of the script.

The script went through four revisions (dated February 1986, March 1986, April/May 1986, and 30 June 1986) before the film went into production.[4] I have in my possession a typescript of the final revision, signed by Humphries on the cover and on the title page, and which he has inscribed (in purple felt pen ink) "ONLY COPY TO SURVIVE."[5] Humphries probably means the only copy of the fourth revision. But if he means the only copy of the film script, the only one extant, then the three copies at the Performing Arts Museum, which Humphries donated as recently as 1997, would seem to contradict his inscription.

The title page of my copy of the fourth revision calls collateral attention to the Barry Humphries Collection for another reason. After the byline "BARRY HUMPHRIES / and / DIANE MILLSTEAD," Humphries has written in two question marks, apparently calling into question Millstead's co-authorship. But in his further interpolation on the title page, Humphries clarifies his position on the Barthesian "Death of the Author." Following the "??" he prints: "(I'D PREFER NOT TO SHARE THE BLAME FOR THIS SCREEN PLAY)." Rather than distancing his co-author, he records a *memento mori* on the screenplay itself, exonerating his collaborator from responsibility in what he may have anticipated would produce a modest film.[6]

In fact, of course, *Les Patterson Saves the World* proved to be the antithesis of *The Adventures of Barry McKenzie* (1972), one of the most popular and commercially successful Australian films until then,[7] which has been widely credited with leading off the Australian cinematic renaissance of the 1970s.

*Les Patterson Saves the World* presents a curious case study. Much publicised before its release, it "bombed" at the box office within six weeks, and was damned by virtually all reviewers, who evoked the inevitable unfavourable comparisons and associations. Australian cinema was returning it seemed, in the unsubtle hands of actor-writer-satirist Barry Humphries, to the "ocker" comedies it had left behind with the advent of *Picnic at Hanging Rock* (Peter Weir, 1975).[8]

Perhaps Humphries does have "unsubtle hands": after all, satirists rarely let their left hand know what their right hand is doing. But his subtle tonalities, both in his speech-act exempting Diane Millstead from authorial blame and in his screenplay of *Les Patterson Saves the World*, are, in the nature of things subtle, mistakable. That the screenplay might read better than the film looks is a possibility that has been lost on film critics and Humphries critics alike. In fact, *Les Patterson Saves the World* features some of Humphries' most incisive comic dialogue and absurd theatrical scenes, which, far from invoking the ocker, evoke the rocking hobby-horse of Dada farce.

Consider, for example, Edna Everage's exchange with Neville Thonge, a career diplomat, who in this scene informs Edna that Col Richard Godowni, president of the Republic of Abu-Nivea, is enamoured of her. With subtle tonality, Edna softens the male gaze into flirtation.

THONGE   I don't think he's ever met a more sophisticated and cultured woman before.
EDNA   (coyly) Oh Neville! Flattery will get you everywhere – well almost! I'd like to make you my honorary possum. Here, wear this little possum badge, it's a prezzie!

She pins brooch in the form of a possum on THONGE's lapel.

THONGE   (extremely touched and suddenly boyish)
Oh, thank you Dame Edna. I'll never take it off.

He gives Edna a peck on the cheek.[9]

In its mock sentimentality, this spare dialogue, along with its alternately thin and fat stage directions, is as smooth as Nivea-Abu. The gap between "brooch in the form of a possum" and "this little possum badge" emphasizes Edna's characteristic direct discourse, her bluntness and rudeness, and reveals how Humphries, here with Millstead, exploits Australian emblems as signifiers of prestige.[10]

Just as, here, Humphries and Millstead share a screenwriting credit that seems to have made a quick dissolve into Australian cinematic history, so the Barry Humphries Collection is a hiding place for other curious collaborations. For example, Humphries co-wrote a script with David Smilow, "The Dame from Down Under – An American Docu Comedy,"[11] dated 6 May 1984, which is a kind of "dancing backward" false start towards *Les Patterson Saves the World*. This notes-towards approach is typical of Humphries' modus operandi. The collection is littered with his jottings, lists, and mementos;

preliminary, tentative, and interrupted scripts and sketches, all pointing to his operative ("unsubtle" hands-on) aesthetic and his perfectionism as a writer whose "death of the author" strategy seems to be willing to let conditional scripts die, when necessary, at the pre-scriptive stage.

Does the Barry Humphries Collection have anything to do with the "Death of the Author"? Undoubtedly, part of Humphries' purpose is to put his theatrical and literary house in order so that his remains – I am reminded of Malcolm Lowry, who would refer to his *oeuvre* as his "corpus" – might lie in situ rather than be scattered around the world. Humphries has provided some precedent for this interpretation, when in "Alzheimer Remembers," his preface to *More Please* (1992), he observes that "I am already the subject of two generous biographies and it is only the fear that my adventures might for a third time be profitably chronicled by another man that prompts me to relate my own story."[12] In the Barry Humphries Collection, which recalls other eponymous ventures, such as *The Barry Humphries Book of Innocent Austral Verse* (1968), *Barry Humphries' Treasury of Australian Kitsch* (1980), and *Barry Humphries' Flashbacks* (1999), Humphries both asserts his ownership of his intellectual property, securing it in a vault, and, in contrast to "Sandy Agonistes" (see Chapter 3), surrenders his authorial control over it, distancing himself as Author and giving executant, interpretive "play" over to the reader because, as Barthes has dictated, "the birth of the reader must be requited by the death of the Author."[13] An alternative translation (by Stephen Heath) of this famous passage hints at another of Humphries' motives in donating his papers and costumes to the Performing Arts Museum: "the birth of the reader must be at the cost of the death of the Author."[14]

The "cost" to Humphries of giving away his art, if only to ensure its preservation and to secure his place in Australian history, is enormous. As a collector, I well know the exact(ing) cost of "the exceedingly rare first edition"[15] of *Paston's Melbourne Quarterly: A Journal of Literary Pleasantry for the Entertainment of the Public and the Edification of the Young* (Spring 1958), which features Humphries' first publication, the Dada narrative "A Novel Called Tid." PAM features the first edition of *Paston's*, along with a rare reprint of "A Novel Called Tid" in *Gambit* (Spring 1961), an Edinburgh University review.

The monetary cost to Humphries as donor and patron is inestimable. From Dame Edna Everage's lovely frocks to six tubes of Nivea face cream in a bag (1985.202.029), from Humphries' own copy of Henry Popkin's review of *Housewife! Superstar!!* at Theatre Four, New York (1977), to a batch of scribblings that Humphries made as a Melbourne schoolboy in the 1940s (1981.202.872), these items are priceless artifacts (even though, of course, they can be evaluated as commodities, as for insurance purposes). Yet Humphries' offering of these and a kilobyte of his other properties to the goddess PAM is not primarily a monetary gesture but a philanthropic, humanitarian, theatrical, intellectual act, a Dadact (see Chapter 2): part Dada (Humphries' provocation about just what to do about so many seemingly inconsequential things), part act (his institutionalization of his performative), and part didacticism (a final lesson on Humphries as a good man, a *very* good man, a very *good* man, currently on show at PAM).

The Barry Humphries Collection, his gift to the people of Australia, is the possum badge of their uncommon cultural heritage.

# Notes

## PREFACE

1 Britain, *Once an Australian*, 81.

2 Humphries, *More Please*, 282.

3 Humphries, *A Nice Night's Entertainment*, 74.

4 Humphries and Garland, *The Complete Barry McKenzie*, v.

5 Huelsenbeck, "Dada Lives!" 281.

6 Qtd. in Dunstan, *Ratbags*, 30.

7 Humphries, "Barry Humphries," interview by Murray Bramwell, 40.

8 See Note 79, Chapter 7.

9 The cover of the sheet music adds "and Sung by Mess^rs J.F. Wilfred, Harry Clifford, Walter Stanley, Charles Willoughby, &c &c &c," and it also pictures the singers in a lithograph by H.G. Banks.

10 Leighton, *We're Australians but Still Britannia's Sons*, 2–4.

11 James, "Approximately in the Vicinity of Barry Humphries," 30.

12 Humphries, "The Real Barry Humphries," interview by Andrew Olle, 80.

13 Humphries, "The Book," e-mail to the author, 5 July 2001.

14 See Tomkins, *Duchamp*, 447.

15 Humphries and Garland, *The Complete Barry McKenzie*, 100.

16 Humphries, *My Life as Me*, 217.

17 Cabanne, *Duchamp & Co.*, 194.

## CHAPTER ONE

1 Humphries, *More Please*, xii.

2 Ibid., 128.

3 See, for example, Conrad, "Superstars and Others," 7–16, and Lahr, "Notes on Fame," 231–43.

4 Humphries, *More Please* 216–18; Lahr, "Barry Humphries," 89; Thompson, *Peter Cook: A Biography*, 151.

5 Wilmut, *From Fringe to Flying Circus*, 83.

6 Humphries, *More Please*, 278–9.

7 Coleman, *The Real Barry Humphries*, 115–17; Humphries, *More Please*, 274.

8 Derrida, *Acts of Literature*, 323.

9 Idle, *The Road to Mars* 228–9.

10 Humphries, *More Please*, 301; Humphries, *My Life as Me*, 172; Humphries and Garland, *The Complete Barry McKenzie*, x.

11 Humphries, *More Please*, 229. See also Humphries, *More Please*, 300–1; Humphries, comp., *"Punch" Down Under*, 7.

12 Humphries and Garland, *The Complete Barry McKenzie*, 11.

13 Humphries, *Neglected Poems and Other Creatures*, 4–5.

14 Humphries, *More Please*, 301.

15 Ibid., 129–33.

16 Humphries, *Neglected Poems and Other Creatures*, 107.

17 Humphries and Garland, *The Complete Barry McKenzie*, x.

18 Morgan, *Monty Python Speaks!* 25.

19 Eric Idle toured North America with this show, which included performances in Vancouver on 12 and 13 May 2000.

20 Beaver, *The Spice of Life*, 29.

21 Idle, *The Road to Mars*, 146.

22 Rose, *Red Plush and Greasepaint*, 59; Leslie, *A Hard Act to Follow*, 177.

23 Humphries, "A Recollection," 61–2; Humphries, *More Please*, 197; Humphries, *My Life as Me*, 168–9; Thompson, *Peter Cook*, 137–8.

24 Wilmut, *From Fringe to Flying Circus*, 59.

25 Thompson, *Peter Cook*, 137.

26 Carpenter, *A Great Silly Grin: The British Satire Boom of the 1960s*, 188.

27 Ibid., 150 and 299, respectively.

28 Humphries, *My Life as Me*, 330.

29 Coleman, *The Real Barry Humphries*, 65.

30 Rutherford, "'Managers in a small way': The Professionalisation of Variety Artists 1960–1914," 116.

31 See also Coleman, *The Real Barry Humphries*, 8.

32 Humphries, *More Please*, xii. Cf. Peter Coleman's search for "the real Barry Humphries" (1990).

33 Lahr, "Edna Takes Manhattan," 6.

34 Adair, "La Dame aux Gladioli," 98–9.

35 Humphries, "Barry Humphries," interview by Murray Bramwell, 42 and 38 respectively.

36 *Just a Show* (Tivoli Theatre, Sydney, 1968), 7. *Just a Show* (Fortune Theatre, London, 1969), 15.

37 Bell, "Return to Oz," 77 and 73, respectively.

38 Humphries, foreword to *Max Oldaker: Last of the Matinée Idols*, n.p.

39 Beaver, *The Spice of Life*, 114.

40 Minogue, "What's the Big Idea?" B7.

41 Rose, *Red Plush and Greasepaint*, 34.

42 See Appendix 4 for my case for Dame Edna's liaison with Liberace.

43 Kift, *The Victorian Music Hall*, 34.

44 Rose, *With a Twinkle in My Eye*, 241.

45 Humphries, *More Please*, 59.

46 Dessau, *Rowan Atkinson*, 150.

47 Humphries, *Neglected Poems*, 28.

48 Humphries, *More Please*, 59.

49 Humphries, *My Life as Me*, 13.

50 Wilmut, *Kindly Leave the Stage!* 100.

51 See Lahr, *Dame Edna Everage and the Rise of Western Civilisation*, 72.

52 See Robinson, "Tray Bong! *Godot* and Music Hall."

53 Humphries, *More Please*, 193.

54 Ibid., *More Please*, 193.

55 Ibid., *More Please*, 194.

56 See Jahn, *Muntu: The New African Culture*.

57 Rose, *Red Plush and Greasepaint*, 127.

58 See Leslie, *A Hard Act to Follow*, 185; Harding, *George Robey and the Music-Hall*, 190.

59 Leslie, *A Hard Act to Follow*, 230.

60 Harding, *George Robey and the Music-Hall*, 75.

61 Rose, *Beside the Seaside*, 73.

62 Delfont, *Curtain Up! The Story of the Royal Variety Performance*, 203 and 205 respectively.

63 Leslie, *A Hard Act to Follow*, 235.

64 Humphries, *More Please*, 329.

65 See Leslie, *A Hard Act to Follow*, 182.

66 Kilgarriff, *It Gives Me Great Pleasure*, 3.

67 Humphries, *Neglected Poems and Other Creatures*, 142.

68 Leslie, *A Hard Act to Follow*, 122.

69 Humphries, *More Please*, 308.

70 Harding, *George Robey and the Music-Hall*, 9, 23.

71 Humphries' colloquialism "the yartz" may point to his affinity for Dada. Compare Beverley Keith and G. Legman's 1953 translation of Alfred Jarry's *Ubu Roi* (1896), the first English version of the complete three-play *Ubu* cycle. For example, Papa Turd tells Stanislas Leczinski, "Well then, hornstrumpot, listen carefully or these gentlemen will cut off your years. So are you going to listen to me?" Later he wakes from a dream, uttering the threat, "And get Mama Turd! Cut off her years!" See Jarry, *King Turd*, 47 and 74, respectively. Perhaps after reading this edition, Humphries attributed Ubu Roi's elision to Patterson. Humphries has turned H.W. Fowler's stricture (in *A Dictionary of Modern English Usage*) against "speaking words as they are spelt" into his own obloquy

in Les Patterson's predilection for "spelling words as they are spoken." In this regard, Humphries' usage resembles the phoneme-poetic of Canadian poet bill bissett, as in *Th influenza uv logik* (1995).

72 Humphries, *Tears before Bedtime*, n.p.

73 See Alomes, *When London Calls*, 219.

74 Bailey, "A Community of Friends," 36.

75 Humphries, *Neglected Poems and Other Creatures*, 56. See also Barry Crocker's performance of "Washed Down the Gutter," on *Bazza McKenzie's Party Songs*.

76 Humphries, Rowley, and Myers, *The Sound of Edna: Dame Edna's Family Songbook*, 3.

77 From the film *Robin and the Seven Hoods*, directed by Gordon Douglas, Warner/PC, 1964.

78 Leslie, *A Hard Act to Follow*, 36.

79 Humphries, *More Please*, 309.

80 Patterson's taxonomic wild flowing mane may invoke the leonine in music hall just as insistently as does his padded thigh.

81 Solomon, *Re-Dressing the Canon*, 8.

82 Duchamp, *The Writings of Marcel Duchamp*, 117.

83 *More Please*, 309.

84 Leslie, *A Hard Act to Follow*, 120; cf. 115.

85 Ibid., 41.

86 Harding, *George Robey and the Music-Hall*, 40.

87 Ibid., 21.

88 Leslie, *A Hard Act to Follow*, 57.

89 Gifford, *Entertainers in British Films*, 104; see also Busby, *British Music Hall*, 83.

90 Karpel, "Did Dada Die? A Critical Bibliography," 321.

91 Humphries, *Barry Humphries' Treasury of Australian Kitsch*, 13.

92 Leslie, *A Hard Act to Follow*, 127.

93 Humphries, *More Please*, 142–4.

94 The tour, 24 October 2000 – 29 July 2001, consisted of shows in Minneapolis, Toronto, Fort Lauderdale, Palm Beach and Clearwater (Florida), Boston, Detroit, Chicago, Phoenix, Seattle, Los Angeles, Houston, Denver, Atlantic City, and Dallas.

95 Humphries, *More Please*, 252.

96 Leslie, *A Hard Act to Follow*, 138–9.

97 Barry Humphries and Mark McKinney co-starred in the film *Spice World* (1997).

98 But a link with the music hall/variety performer Edna May is more likely.

99 Humphries, *More Please*, 284.

100 Bailey, "A Community of Friends," 36.

101 Ibid., 34.

102 Leslie, *A Hard Act to Follow*, 19; see also Scott, *The Early Doors: Origins of the Music Hall*, 42–5.

103 Wilmut, *Kindly Leave the Stage!* 14. See also Felstead, *Stars Who Made the Halls*, 20–4; Kift, *Victorian Music Hall*, 17–21; Mander and Mitchenson, *British Music Hall* (13–19); Harding, *George Robey and the Music Hall* (15–17); Bailey, "Introduction" (ix–x). In American vaudeville, the originary chairman was the comic monologist Frank Fay; see Lahr, "Bob Hope," 207.

104 Humphries, *More Please*, 309.

105 Ibid., 276.

106 The British actor Arthur Treacher (1894–1975) was active on the London stage between 1918 and 1926 before moving to the United States, where he appeared in Broadway plays and off-Broadway revues, went on to a film career in supporting roles, and ended up as sidekick and ad hoc archivist on Merv Griffin's television talk show (1962–1986). The theme of this show was show biz nostalgia. Griffin would often ask Treacher, with reference to one or another old star from music hall, variety, vaudeville, or burlesque whose name had come up in the conversation, "Do you remember him, Arthur?" It was the show's running gag.

107 Humphries, *More Please*, 268.

108 Leslie, *A Hard Act to Follow*, 163.

109 See *The Fashion Diary of a Victorian Housewife: Dame Edna's Wardrobe 1956–1983* (1983); Soumilas, *A Peep in Dame Edna's Closet* (1986); Wheelahan, *Dame Edna's Frock-a-Thon: A Journey from Cardigan to Couture* (1999).

110 Russell, "I'm Only a Faded Rose," on *Anna Russell's Guide to Concert Audiences*.

111 Solomon, *Re-Dressing the Canon*, 7.

112 See RuPaul, *Letting It All Hang Out*, 180–4; Ramet, "Gender Reversals and Gender Cultures," 6–8; Griggs, *S/He: Changing Sex and Changing Clothes*, 124; Ekins, *Male Femaling*, 43–4; Ackroyd, *Dressing Up, Transvestism and Drag*, 89–140.

113 Qtd. in Lahr, "Eddie Izzard," 174.

114 Coupland, *Generation X*, 17.

115 Everage [Humphries], *My Gorgeous Life*, 203.

116 Cixous and Clément, *The Newly Born Woman*, 22.

117 Maclean, *Narrative as Performance*, 38.

118 Qtd. in Lahr, *Dame Edna Everage and the Rise of Western Civilisation*, 73.

119 James, "Approximately in the Vicinity of Barry Humphries," 36.

120 Lahr, "Playing Possum," 58.

121 Humphries, "27th April 1978," 145.

122 Melzer, *Dada and Surrealist Performance*, 121.

123 Ibid., 135.

CHAPTER TWO

1 Barry Humphries' inscription in my copy of *Bizarre* reads: "For Paul / A youthful folly / (ALBEIT RARE!) / Best wishes / *Barry Humphries*." Humphries signed it 10 October 1998, after his evening performance at Theatre on the Square, San Francisco.

2 James, "Approximately in the Vicinity of Barry Humphries," 39.

3 Dunstan, *Ratbags*, 30.

4 Humphries, *More Please*, 253–4.

5 Humphries and Garland, *The Complete Barry McKenzie*, v. Because *The Wonderful World of Barry McKenzie* (1968) and *Bazza Pulls It Off* (1971) are unpaginated, and *Bazza Comes into His Own* (1979) is paginated sporadically, 1–4 and 58–83 (introduction and addenda), excluding the comic strip pages, I have cited page numbers from *The Complete Barry McKenzie* (1988) in most of my references to the comic strip.

6 Humphries and Garland, *The Complete Barry McKenzie*, 138.

7 Humphries, *Bizarre*, 146.

8 Humphries, booklet, *Dada Days: Moonee Ponds Muse, Vol. 2 (1951–1983)*, n.p.

9 Barry Humphries, *Neglected Poems*, typescript, in possession of Paul Matthew St Pierre. For a full description of the typescript, see Chapter 3. Barry Crocker performs the song on his LP *Barry McKenzie's Party Songs* (1972).

10 Humphries, *My Life as Me*, x.

11 Humphries, *Bizarre*. 7.

12 Jameson, *The Prison-House of Language*, 93–4.

13 Rutherford, "'Managers in a small way': The Professionalisation of Variety Artists 1960–1914," 116. See also Note 30, Chapter One.

14 See Leslie, *A Hard Act to Follow*, 22, 72–4; Wilmut, *Kindly Leave the Stage* (109–15); Kilgarriff, *Grace, Beauty and Banjos*, 185–93.

15 Humphries, *Bizarre*, 7.

16 Brissenden, Introduction to *A Nice Night's Entertainment*, by Barry Humphries, xvii. See also Lahr, "Edna Takes Manhattan," 6.

17 James, "Approximately in the Vicinity of Barry Humphries," 40.

18 Everage [Humphries], *My Gorgeous Life*, 239–40. See also *Dame Edna's Work Experience* (1996) and Dame Edna's other stage shows.

19 Clark, *Leonardo da Vinci*, 111.

20 Jameson, *The Prison-House of Language*, 112.

21 Coleman, *The Real Barry Humphries*, 69.

22 Humphries, *Bizarre*, 47–52. Humphries himself has even posed as the Mona Lisa (with hair and grooming by Helen Robertson and Carol Hayes) in a photograph by Terry O'Neal that is featured in John Hind, "Above Everage" (1992).

23 In November 1999 I wrote a letter to the editor of the *National Post* (Toronto) defending Barry Humphries and his neologism "face furniture." See Appendix 3 for copies of the article by columnist Shinan Govani and my letter in response to it.

24 Hind, "Above Everage," 118–23, 197.

25 Humphries, *Bizarre*, 53.

26 Machen, *Ornaments in Jade*, 55.

27 Humphries, introduction to *Ornaments in Jade*, by Arthur Machen, vii.

28 Tomkins, *Duchamp*, 395–7.

29 Brissenden, Introduction to *A Nice Night's Entertainment*, by Barry Humphries, xi.

30 King, *Wrestling with the Angel: A Life of Janet Frame*, 60–1.

31 Humphries, *More Please*, 158.

32 St Pierre's transcription. In his liner notes to "The Dada Tapes" section of *Dada Days*, Humphries refers to "The word Wubbo with its vague aboriginal resonance." Humphries, booklet, *Dada Days: Moonee Ponds Muse, Vol. 2, (1951–1983)*, n.p.

33 Melzer, *Dada and Surrealist Performance*, 108. See also Tomkins, *Duchamp*, 70–1; Legman, "Translator's Note," 184. M. Hébert, Jarry's math teacher at Lyceum Henri-iv, Rennes, is the object of his satire in *Ubu Roi*.

34 Melzer, *Dada and Surrealist Performance*, 112.

35 Lahr, *Dame Edna Everage and the Rise of Western Civilisation*, 103.

36 Jarry, *King Turd*, 11–12.

37 Humphries, *More Please*, 166–8.

38 *Paston's Melbourne Quarterly* (Spring 1958) is unpaginated.

39 Humphries, *More Please*, 167.

40 Duchamp, *The Writings of Marcel Duchamp*, 106–7.

41 Derrida, *Of Grammatology*, 35.

42 Plant, "Barry Humphries," 8.

43 Humphries, *More Please*, 121.

44 "Dadact" is my neologism for an act of Dada, any shocking and subversive act performed in person, art, or literature in the heterodox spirit of Dada; the word itself deconstructs *Dada* (a being) and *actus* (a doing).

45 Leslie, *A Hard Act to Follow*, 118–20.

46 Plant, "Barry Humphries," 8–9.

47 Moreau, "The Laws," n.p.

48 Cabanne, *Duchamp & Co.*, 187.

49 Maclean, *Narrative as Performance*, 25.

50 Conrad, "Barry Humphries," 276–89.

51 Humphries, *More Please*, 228–9; Humphries and Garland, *The Complete Barry McKenzie*, vii, ix.

52 Humphries and Garland, "Barry McKensie, Australian at large," cartoon, *Private Eye*, 10 July 1964, 12.

53 Jameson, *The Prison-House of Language*, 112.

54 Coleman, *The Real Barry Humphries*, 116–17.

55 Humphries, "Why Bazza Is a Virgin," 33.

56 Coleman, *The Real Barry Humphries*, 84.

57 Humphries, *More Please*, 229.

58 Humphries, *A Nice Night's Entertainment*, 179.

59 Coleman, *The Real Barry Humphries*, 85.

60 Alomes, *When London Calls*, 219.

61 Humphries, *More Please*, 230.

62 Wilmut, *From Fringe to Flying Circus*, 73.

63 Humphries and Garland, "Barry McKensie, Australian at large," cartoon, *Private Eye*, 10 July 1964, 12.

64 Humphries and Garland, cartoon, *Private Eye*, 24 July 1964, 10.

65 Humphries, with Beresford, *Barry McKenzie Holds His Own: An Original Photoplay*, n.p.

66 Humphries, "Why Bazza Is a Virgin," 33.

67 Leslie, *A Hard Act to Follow*, 36.

68 Humphries, "Why Bazza Is a Virgin," 32.

69 Ibid., 33.

70 Cirlot, *A Dictionary of Symbols*, 50.

71 Alomes, *When London Calls*, 102.

72 Humphries, *More Please*, 84 and 104, respectively.

73 Qtd. in Lahr, *Dame Edna and the Rise of Western Civilisation*, 111–12.

74 Humphries, *Women in the Background*, 100.

75 Patterson [Humphries], *The Traveller's Tool*, 28.

76 Humphries, "Why Bazza Is a Virgin," 34.

77 Humphries, *Neglected Poems*, 55.

78 Humphries and Garland, *The Complete Barry McKenzie*, 84.

79 Ibid., 26.

80 Humphries, *More Please*, 231.

81 Alomes, *When London Calls*, 83.

82 See Derrida, *The Ear of the Other, Otobiography, Transference, Translation*, 98–104.

83 Legman, "Translator's Note," 188.

84 Humphries, *Bazza Pulls It Off!* n.p.

85 Humphries and Garland, *The Complete Barry McKenzie*, v.

86 Britain, *Once an Australian*, 1–2.

87 Coleman, *The Real Barry Humphries*, 85–7.

88 James, "Approximately in the Vicinity of Barry Humphries," 42.

89 Brissenden, Introduction to *A Nice Night's Entertainment*, by Barry Humphries, xvii.

90 Humphries, *More Please*, 60.

91 See Humphries, *More Please*, 188; Humphries, *My Life as Me*, 77; Lahr, *Dame Edna Everage*, 64.

92 Humphries, *More Please*, 254.

93 Humphries and Garland, *The Complete Barry McKenzie*, 125.

94 Ibid., 42.

95 Ibid., 43.

96 Ibid., 125.

97 Ibid., 41 and 43, respectively.

98 *Wido* is a Salopeanism signifying a person of superior intelligence (i.e., someone with a "wide" knowledge).

99 Derrida, "Khora," 89.

## CHAPTER THREE

1 Alomes, *When London Calls*, 231.

2 Eliot, "Reflections on *vers libre*," 36.

3 Peter Coleman, et al., comps, *A Return to Poetry 2000* (2000); Les Murray, comp., *The New Oxford Book of Australian Verse*, 3rd ed. (1996); Peter Porter, ed., *The Oxford Book of Modern Australian Verse* (1996).

4 Everage [Humphries], *My Gorgeous Life*, 1.

5 Qtd. in *The Compact Edition of the Oxford English Dictionary* (1971).

6 Humphries, comp., *The Barry Humphries Book of Innocent Austral Verse*, 10.

7 Ibid.

8 Ibid., 86.

9 Humphries, *Moonee Ponds Muse*, Vol. 1 (1991).

10 Humphries, comp., *The Barry Humphries Book of Innocent Austral Verse*, 10.

11 See Green, perf., *The Tom Green Show: Early Exposure*, videocassette, VSC, 2001.

12 Zmuda, with Hansen, *Andy Kaufman Revealed!* 259–91.

13 de Lisle, "Dame Edna's Prop Tricks Sotheby's," 3.

14 For a list of these publications, see Appendix 6.

15 Suleiman, *Risking Who One Is*, 144. Humphries' position on "the death of the author" may also derive from Marcel Duchamp. See my discussion in Chapter 2, and Tomkins, *Duchamp: A Biography*, 395–7.

16 Alomes, *When London Calls*, 228.

17 Ibid., 224–9, 252.

18 Everage [Humphries], *My Gorgeous Life*, 194.

19 Alomes, *When London Calls*, 220 and 226, respectively.

20 *Artist of the Week*, BRAVO! 31 October 1999 (repeat broadcast).

21 Took, "Barry Humphries," 226.

22 Prince, *A Dictionary of Narratology*, 67.

23 I transcribed Dame Edna's comment from a notebook entry I made immediately after the performance I attended at the Booth Theatre, New York, Saturday, 11 March 2000.

24 Below, and in Chapter 6, I discuss Les as an animal.

25 Humphries, comp., *The Barry Humphries Book of Innocent Austral Verse*, 65.

26 Humphries, *Neglected Poems and Other Creatures*, 141.

27 Dunkling and Gosling, *Everyman's Dictionary of First Names*.

28 Humphries, *More Please*, 97–8.

29 Everage [Humphries], *My Gorgeous Life*, 204.

30 Frame, *Owls Do Cry*, 1.

31 Humphries, comp., *The Barry Humphries Book of Innocent Austral Verse*, 27.

32 Humphries, *More Please*, 22.

33 Humphries, *Neglected Poems and Other Creatures*, 128.

34 Alomes, *When London Calls*, 220.

35 Beaver, *The Spice of Life*, 96.

36 Humphries, comp., *The Barry Humphries Book of Innocent Austral Verse*, 82.

37 Humphries, *Neglected Poems and Other Creatures*, 120.

38 Jameson, *Postmodernism, or, The Cultural Logic of Late Capitalism*, 314.

39 Ibid., 314–15.

40 Aquinas, *The Summa Theologica*, vol. 1, 147. First Part, Question 25 ("The Power of God"), Article 4 ("Whether God Can Make the Past Not To Have Been?"): In refuting the proposition "It seems that God can make the past not to have been," Thomas Aquinas begins by quoting St Jerome: " 'Although God can do all things, He cannot make a thing that is corrupt not to have been corrupted.' Therefore, for the same reason, He cannot effect that anything else which is past should not have been."

41 Humphries, *Neglected Poems and Other Creatures*, 6.

42 Ibid.

43 Barry Humphries, *Neglected Poems*, transcript, in possession of Paul Matthew St Pierre.

44 Humphries, *Neglected Poems and Other Creatures*, 6.

45 Humphries, "The Confessions of Barry Humphries," in *The Bulletin Book*, 102.

46 Jahn, *Muntu*, 102, 151.

47 Ong, *Orality and Literacy*, 177.

48 Eliot, "The Love Song of J. Alfred Prufrock."

49 Lahr, "Edna Takes Manhattan," 6.

50 Humphries, *My Life as Me*, 215.

51 Duchamp, *The Writings of Marcel Duchamp*, 105.

52 Humphries, *Neglected Poems and Other Creatures*, 28–9.

53 Humphries, *More Please*, 13–23.

54 Ibid., 21.

55 Tzara, *Chanson Dada*, 46.

56 Though the poem does not appear in *The Barry Humphries Book of Innocent Austral Verse* (1968), the sleeve annotations on the LP *The Barry Humphries Record of Innocent Austral Verse* feature this disclaimer: "Many of the verses in this album were included in 'The Barry Humphries Book of Innocent Austral Verse.' "

57 Humphries, *Neglected Poems and Other Creatures*, 110.

58 Dame Edna coins this phrase in the television show *The Dame Edna Experience*, series 2.2 (1989). See Table 1.3.

59 Bernhardt, *My Double Life: The Memoirs of Sarah Bernhardt*, 303.

60 The audience would no doubt have first heard these cheers, respectively, in Humphries' songs "Great Big Fish" and "Wendy the One-Eyed Wombat," both from the LP *Barry Humphries' Savoury Dip* (1971).

61 Duchamp, *The Writings of Marcel Duchamp*, 171.

62 Humphries, *Neglected Poems and Other Creatures*, 174–87.

63 Frame, *Owls Do Cry*, 1.

64 Dutton, *Out in the Open*, 486–9.

65 Ibid., 487.

66 Humphries, *My Life as Me*, 107.

67 See Kilgarriff, *Grace, Beauty and Banjos*, 48–9.

68 Rose, *With a Twinkle in My Eye*, 221.

69 "Canto Two" features the lyrics "Who is it drinks at the billabong / Where the air is loud with the Emu's song / And the black snake watches what the Dingo does / And the possums dance and the blow flies buzz / What is lurking around each corner? Weird Australian flora and fauna." See Humphries and Davis, *The Last Night of the Poms* (1981).

70 Cixous, *Readings: The Poetics of Blanchot, Joyce, Kafka, Kleist, Lispector, and Tsvetayeva*, 60.

71 The transcriptions of "Wendy the One-Eyed Wombat" and "Great Big Fish" are my own, from the LP *Barry Humphries' Savoury Dip* (1971).

72 Everage [Humphries], *My Gorgeous Life*, 13.

73 Everage [Humphries], *Dame Edna's Coffee Table Book*, 80.

74 Lahr, *Notes on a Cowardly Lion: The Biography of Bert Lahr*, 198.

75 Humphries, *Neglected Poems and Other Creatures*, 120.

76 Humphries, *More Please*, 51 and 52 respectively.

77 Arthurs and Scott, "I Had to Be Cruel to Be Kind," in *Sheard's 29th Comic and Variety Annual*, 6–7.

78 *The Dame Edna Experience*, series 2.3 (1989).

79 Gammond, *Music Hall Song Book*, 118.

80 Ibid., 72.

81 Meadwell and Brawn, *The Novello Music Hall Songbook*, 61.

82 Speaight, *Bawdy Songs of the Early Music Hall*, 61, 59, 36, and 77, respectively.

83 Ibid., 9.

84 Qtd. in Lahr, "Frank Sinatra," 58.

85 Lahr, "Edna Takes Manhattan," 6.

86 Lahr, *Notes on a Cowardly Lion*, 203.

87 Humphries, Rowley, and Myers, *The Sound of Edna: Dame Edna's Family Songbook*, 54.

88 Ibid., 38.

89 Ibid., 68.

90 Everage [Humphries], *My Gorgeous Life*, 12.

91 Gammond, *Music Hall Song Book*, 7.

92 Meadwell and Brawn, *The Novello Music Hall Songbook*, 11.

93 Humphries, *The Life and Death of Sandy Stone*, 16.

94 Duchamp, *The Writings of Marcel Duchamp*, 22.

95 Qtd. in Peterson, *Tristan Tzara*, 35. "Next, carefully cut each of the words that form this article and put them in a bag. / Gently shake. / Then sort each cutting one after another. / Copy conscientiously / in the order in which they came out of the bag." (St Pierre's translation)

96 Mink, *Marcel Duchamp, 1887–1968*, 20.

97 Humphries, *More Please*, 177.

98 Duchamp, *The Writings of Marcel Duchamp*, 141.

99 Maclean, *Narrative as Performance*, 150.

100 Humphries, *More Please*, 147.

101 Schwitters, "Theo van Doesburg and Dada," 275.

102 Humphries, *A Nice Night's Entertainment*, 27.

103 Humphries, *More Please*, n.p.

104 Everage [Humphries], *My Gorgeous Life*, 122.

105 See Jahn, *Muntu*, 185–216.

106 Derrida, *Dissemination*, 330–9.

107 Caws, *The Art of Interference*, 64.

108 Derrida, *Acts of Literature*, 305.

109 See Bhabha, *The Location of Culture* (1994).

110 Humphries, *The Life and Death of Sandy Stone*, 17.

111 Ibid., 17–18.

112 Humphries, Rowley, and Myers, *The Sound of Edna: Dame Edna's Family Songbook*, 6 and 14, respectively.

113 See Chapter 4 for a full discussion of these monologues.

114 Cottom, "Ethnographia Mundi," 87.

115 Humphries, *More Please*, 195.

116 Huelsenbeck, "En Avant Dada," 24–5.

117 Jameson, *Postmodernism, or, The Cultural Logic of Late Capitalism*, 404.

118 Dessau, *Rowan Atkinson*, 118.

119 Humphries, *My Life as Me*, x.

## CHAPTER FOUR

1 Humphries, *The Life and Death of Sandy Stone*, 125.

2 Ibid., 49.

3 Ibid.

4 Humphries and Garland, *The Complete Barry McKenzie*, ix.

5 Lowry, *Under the Volcano*, 43.

6 Humphries, *A Nice Night's Entertainment*, 14.

7 White, Letter to Frederick Glover, 13 May 1960, 165.

8 Dutton, *Out in the Open*, 232.

9 Ibid.

10 Humphries, *The Life and Death of Sandy Stone*, 3.

11 Ibid., 5.

12 Ibid., 34.

13 Ibid., 30 and 82, respectively.

14 Ibid., 5.

15 See hooks, "Selling Hot Pussy."

16 Humphries, *The Life and Death of Sandy Stone*, 3, 5, 6, 6, and 7, respectively.

17 Ibid., 3, 4, 4, 6, 6, 6, 8, and 8, respectively.

18 Ibid., 4, 7, 7, 7, and 8, respectively.

19 Matthews, *Cockney Past and Present*, 140.

20 James, "Approximately in the Vicinity of Barry Humphries," 32.

21 Today, most people probably believe "dailies" to be not rushes in filmmaking but disposable contact lenses!

22 Humphries, *The Life and Death of Sandy Stone*, 9.

23 Ibid., 10.

24 Ibid., 10, 10, 10, 10, and 11, respectively.

25 Frame, *The Carpathaians*, 170.

26 Humphries, *The Life and Death of Sandy Stone*, 12, 11, 12, and 13, respectively.

27 Shlain, *The Alphabet Versus the Goddess*, 30.

28 Humphries, *The Life and Death of Sandy Stone*, 10.

29 Ibid., 20.

30 Ibid.

31 Coleman, *The Real Barry Humphries*, 48.

32 Prince, *A Dictionary of Narratology*, 67.

33 Humphries, *The Life and Death of Sandy Stone*, 24–5.

34 Compare the phallic Kenneth Grocock, the antagonist in Humphries' novel, *Women in the Background* (1995).

35 Ribemont-Dessaignes, "History of Dada," 101.

36 Humphries, *The Life and Death of Sandy Stone*, 31 and 32, respectively.

37 Ibid., 32–5.

38 Ibid., 28.

39 Ibid., 30.

40 Ibid., 34.

41 Ibid., 31.

42 Humphries, *More Please*, 103.

43 See Humphries, "Confessions of a Conder Fan" (1977).

44 Qtd. in Mink, *Marcel Duchamp, 1887–1968*, 14.

45 Coleman, *The Real Barry Humphries*, 97.

46 Humphries, "The Confessions of Barry Humphries," 20.

47 Huelsenbeck, "En Avant Dada," 24; Huelsenbeck, "Dada Lives!" 280.

48 Ribemont-Dessaignes, "History of Dada," 102.

49 *The Museum of Modern Art, New York: The History and the Collection*, 128.

50 Humphries, *The Life and Death of Sandy Stone*, 41, 42, and 43, respectively.
51 Ibid., 43 and 44, respectively.
52 Ibid., 46.
53 Ibid., 48 and 47, respectively.
54 Ibid., 42.
55 Ibid., 50.
56 Ibid., 49.
57 Ibid., 50. See also 92.
58 Humphries, *More Please*, xiv.
59 Humphries, *The Life and Death of Sandy Stone*, 54.
60 Ibid.
61 Ibid., 58.
62 Ibid., 61.
63 As miscellany, *A Load of Olde Stuffe* comprised as many as ten sketches, featuring Martin Agrippa, Neil Singleton, Wendy Toole, and Brian Graham as well as Sandy and Edna.
64 Humphries, *The Life and Death of Sandy Stone*, 68.
65 Ibid., 65.
66 Ibid., 63, 68, 71.
67 Ibid., 75.
68 Ibid.
69 Ibid., 67, 69–70, 72–3.
70 Buffet-Picabia, "Some Memories of Pre-Dada, Picabia and Duchamp," 263.
71 Alec Guinness revived this music hall phrase in his *A Positively Final Appearance: A Journal 1996–98* (1999).
72 Leacock, "The Awful Fate of Melpomenus Jones," 15.
73 Humphries, *The Life and Death of Sandy Stone*, 75.
74 Ibid., 78.
75 Ibid., 89.
76 Ibid., 88.
77 Ibid., 77.
78 I explain the "not-to-have-been" in Note 40, Chapter 3.
79 Humphries, *The Life and Death of Sandy Stone*, 80.
80 Ibid., 80, 81, 83, and 86, respectively.
81 Ibid., 88.
82 Ibid., 92.
83 Bakhtin, "The Problem of Speech Genres," 92.
84 Frame, *Owls Do Cry*, 1.
85 Humphries, *The Life and Death of Sandy Stone*, 92–3.
86 Barthes, *La Chambre claire*, 135.
87 Ball, "Dada Fragments (1916–1917)," 52.
88 Humphries, *The Life and Death of Sandy Stone*, 94.
89 Ibid., 96.

90 Sartre, *Huis Clos*, 91.

91 Ibid., 87.

92 Humphries, *The Life and Death of Sandy Stone*, 102.

93 Ibid., 104.

94 Ibid.

95 Naipaul, *The Enigma of Arrival*, 19.

96 Ibid., 20.

97 Ibid., 33.

98 Humphries, *The Life and Death of Sandy Stone*, 94.

99 Naipaul, *The Enigma of Arrival*, 318.

100 Ibid., 135.

101 Humphries, *The Life and Death of Sandy Stone*, 112.

102 Ibid., 107–8.

103 Ibid., 108.

104 Ibid., 186.

105 Ibid., 118–19.

106 Ibid., 120.

107 Ibid., 121.

108 Ibid., 122.

109 Barthes, *Le Chambre Claire*, 138.

110 Bal, *Double Exposures*, 151.

111 Humphries, *The Life and Death of Sandy Stone*, 151.

112 Ibid.

113 Ibid., 164.

114 Ibid.

115 Ibid., 153.

116 Ibid., 164.

117 Ibid., 154.

118 Sandy Stone also delivers his reminder on the audiocassette *Barry Humphries Self-Indulgently Presents "The Life and Death of Sandy Stone"* (1990).

119 Humphries, *The Life and Death of Sandy Stone*, 160.

120 Humphries, Ibid.

121 Humphries, Ibid., 54.

122 Kift, *The Victorian Music Hall*, 63.

123 Humphries, *More Please*, 151.

124 Cottom, "What Is a Joke?" 16.

125 Bhabha, *The Location of Culture*, 1.

126 Humphries, *The Life and Death of Sandy Stone*, 126.

127 Ibid., 82.

128 Ibid., 119.

129 Ibid., 30.

130 Humphries, "27th April 1978," 147.

131 Humphries, *A Nice Night's Entertainment*, 19.

132 Ibid., 21.

133 Humphries' first one-person recordings, *Wild Life in Suburbia* (1958) and *Wild Life in Suburbia, Volume Two* (1959), are 7" EP, 33 RPM discs. On *Oliver!* (1960), the original London cast LP of Lionel Bart's musical, Humphries, as Sowerberry, sings "That's Your Funeral."

134 Humphries, *A Nice Night's Entertainment*, 40.

135 Naumann, "Introduction: Appropriation and Replication in the Art of Marcel Duchamp," 19.

136 Wilmut, *From Fringe to Flying Circus*, 73.

137 Humphries, *A Nice Night's Entertainment*, 40.

138 "Everage" is my neologism for woman, in particular Australian woman, in that Dame Edna Everage is the primogenitor of women (and men), Australian or not.

139 Humphries, *A Nice Night's Entertainment*, 42.

140 Ibid.

141 In his recording of "Buster Thompson," on *Sandy Agonistes*, repeated on *Dada Days: Moonee Ponds Muse, Vol. 2 (1951–1983)*, Humphries omits the clause "and she went like a bird at eighty," perhaps because the simile's figurative play on words is less apparent orally than visually.

142 Humphries and Garland, *The Complete Barry McKenzie*, 127. Barry McKenzie also uses this portal sexual idiom outside his comic strip, as in his signature song "My Little One-Eyed Trouser Snake," from *Private Eye's Blue Record* (1965): "I met an arty sheila / I never met before, / And something kinda told me / That she banged like a shit house door."

143 Humphries, *More Please*, 143. See also 183.

144 Humphries, *A Nice Night's Entertainment*, 44, 44, and 45, respectively.

145 Ibid., 45, 47, 45, and 47, respectively.

146 Ibid., 44.

147 In Hebrew "Deborah" means "a bee," and the name is associated with eloquence and industry. See Dunkling and Gosling, *Everyman's Dictionary of First Names* (1991).

148 According to Dunkling and Gosling, the nickname "Buster" is "for a jovial active boy," as in Buster Keaton.

149 Humphries, *A Nice Night's Entertainment*, 37.

150 Coleman, *The Real Barry Humphries*, 146.

151 Qtd. in Lahr, *Dame Edna Everage*, 104.

152 Humphries, *A Nice Night's Entertainment*, 38, 38, and 39, respectively.

153 Ibid., 39.

154 The word "monologous" is my neologism. It means "analogous with [something] through the agency of a stage monologue." Thus "Sandy Agonistes" is monologous with Milton's dramatic poem "Samson Agonistes" (1671), Australian consumer culture, and mass-production images.

155 Suleiman, *Subversive Intent*, 146.
156 Ibid., 147.
157 See Stam, *Subversive Pleasures*.
158 Ibid., 119–20.
159 Jahn, *Muntu*, 103.
160 Tutuola, *The Palm-Wine Drinkard*, 45–6.
161 Jahn, *Muntu*, 139.
162 Lahr, *Notes on a Cowardly Lion*, 45.
163 Eliot, "The Love Song of J. Alfred Prufrock."
164 Tutuola, *The Palm-Wine Drinkard*, 21.
165 Qtd. in Naumann, *Marcel Duchamp*, 48.
166 The Outer Circle Critics awarded Humphries the 2000 Special Achievement Tony Award for *The Royal Tour* on Broadway for his accomplishment and because the show could not be categorized as either "play" or "musical." Similarly, Humphries' unconventional books may defy classification, both the generic classes of fiction, biography, essay, and cookbook, and even the disciplinary class of literature.

## CHAPTER FIVE

1 Frame, "Prizes," 19.
2 Sartre, *Huis Clos*, 91.
3 Humphries, *More Please*, xi.
4 Suleiman, *Rising Who One Is*, 214.
5 Humphries, *My Life as Me*, x.
6 Ibid., 360.
7 Humphries, *More Please*, 291.
8 Lahr, *Dame Edna Everage and Rise of Western Civilisation*, 2.
9 Humphries, *More Please*, xii.
10 The phrase "writing his autobiography" seems redundant. Could Barry Humphries write someone else's autobiography? Or could somebody else write his? Yes. Ghost writers write them all the time, but no one could ghost Humphries' story. Only Barry Humphries could flesh it out. Still, in *Memoirs of Many in One* (1986), Patrick White recounts Alex Xenophon Demirjian Gray's autobiography, and in *The Autobiography of My Mother* (1996), Jamaica Kincaid's narrator, Xuela Claudette Richardson, puts together her dead mother's herstory.
11 Suleiman, *Risking Who One Is*, 2–3.
12 Humphries, *My Life as Me*, x.
13 Humphries reveals that "My parents' habitual name for me, Sunny Sam, stayed with me until I was at least six or seven years of age." Humphries, *My Life as Me*, 7.
14 Joyce, *A Portrait of the Artist as a Young Man*, 8.

15 The imagery of this mutilation scene in *Un Chien andalou*, with its associations with castration, also references Barry McKenzie in his sexual fastidiousness. See Linda Williams, "Dream and Rhetoric and Film Rhetoric."

16 Humphries, *More Please*, xi.

17 Humphries, *More Please*, ii; *My Life as Me*, iv.

18 Humphries, *More Please*, x.

19 Ibid., 195.

20 Ibid., 88.

21 Ibid., 90.

22 Ibid.

23 Ibid., 114.

24 Everage [Humphries], *My Gorgeous Life*, 21.

25 Humphries, *More Please*, 143. See also Humphries, *My Life as Me*, 55–6, 214–15.

26 Humphries charts the genealogies of both Edna May Beazley and Alexander Horace Stone in the program of *Just a Show* (1968), though he spells the name "Beasley."

27 Everage [Humphries], *My Gorgeous Life*, 20.

28 Ibid., 211.

29 Ibid., 219.

30 Everage [Humphries], *Dame Edna's Bedside Companion*, 20 and 21, respectively.

31 Naumann, *Marcel Duchamp*, 100–3.

32 The idea of the self as self-reflexive is clear in Ricouer's original title, *Soi-même comme un autre* (1990).

33 Humphries, *My Life as Me*, x.

34 Ricoeur, *Oneself as Another*, 45–6.

35 Whether "Alzheimer Remembers" (the preface) or "Ghostly Golfers" (Chapter 1) is the beginning of *More Please*, Barry Humphries' first utterance is the word "I."

36 Morley, *Lewis Morley*, front cover, 66, 78, and 79, respectively.

37 Ricoeur, *Oneself as Another*, 3.

38 Humphries, *More Please*, xii.

39 *Hamlet* 1.2.187–8.

40 *The Compact Edition of the Oxford English Dictionary* (1971) cites the last recorded use of the word "quippy" in 1569. Its meaning is similar to that of "quip": a clever, often sarcastic, remark. I have used the obsolete form of the word to suggest the rarity of Dame Edna's wit.

41 For the complete lyrics of "Broadening My Horizons," see Appendix 5.

42 Humphries, *More Please*, xi and 291.

43 Lahr, *Dame Edna Everage and the Rise of Western Civilisation*, 11.

44 Humphries, *More Please*, 84.

45 Ibid., 87.

46 Ibid., 88.

47 Ibid., 91.

48 Ibid., 93.

49 Ibid., 94.

50 Ibid., 94–5.

51 Humphries' bob is his marque, but it is also the marquee under which spectators gather before his shows.

52 My free translation of the Dutch is "a fashion plate."

53 Humphries, *More Please*, 84.

54 Dunkling and Gosling, *Everyman's Dictionary of First Names*.

55 The Joan Littlewood productions in which Humphries acted were *The Bedsitting Room* (1963) by Spike Milligan and John Antrobus, *The Merry Rooster's Panto* (1963) by Peter Shaffer, *Maggie May* (1964) by Lionel Bart, and *A Kayf Up West* (1964) by Frank Norman. He appeared in these Littlewood productions in succession, between his act at Peter Cook's Establishment Club (1962) and his own show *Excuse I: Another Nice Night's Entertainment* (1965).

56 Humphries, *More Please*, 8.

57 Dutton, *Out in the Open*, 486–9.

58 Humphries, *More Please*, 140.

59 Ibid., xii.

60 Ibid., 121.

61 Humphries, *More Please*, 215; Humphries, *My Life as Me*, 305–7.

62 Ibid., 209.

63 Ibid., 241–3. See also Humphries, *My Life as Me*, 177–82.

64 Humphries, *More Please*, 197, 213–18, and 229–30. See also Humphries, *My Life as Me*, 170–7.

65 Humphries, *More Please*, 197, 213–18, 229–30, and 257.

66 Ibid., 187. Martin Boyd was just sixty-six at the time (the same age Humphries is as I write this note), and he lived thirteen years longer, until 1972. See also Humphries, *My Life as Me*, 245.

67 Humphries, *More Please*, 246.

68 Ibid., 13–23.

69 Ibid., 315–16.

70 Lahr, *Dame Edna Everage and the Rise of Western Civilisation*, 241.

71 Alomes, *When London Calls*, 226 and 220, respectively.

72 Coleman, *The Real Barry Humphries*, 78.

73 Humphries, *More Please*, 255.

74 Coleman, *The Real Barry Humphries*, 76.

75 Humphries, *More Please*, 253.

76 Lahr, *Dame Edna Everage and the Rise of Western Civilisation*, 194–6.

77 Everage [Humphries], *My Gorgeous Life*, 205.

78 Ibid., 218.

79 Breton, "Free Union," 1717.

80 Humphries, *More Please*, 300–10.

81 Everage [Humphries], *My Gorgeous Life*, 218.

82 Humphries' second volume of autobiography was published not with the title *Are We Nearly There Yet?* but with the title *My Life as Me: A Memoir* (2002). In it Humphries does not acknowledge the appearance of the third biography of him, Ian Britain's "The Camberwell Tales," in his *Once an Australian: Journeys with Barry Humphries, Clive James, Germaine Greer and Robert Hughes* (1997), 21–83. Britain focuses on Humphries' childhood in Melbourne and his career successes in England, and follows the eventual structure of *More Please* and the contact pattern of Lahr's *Dame Edna Everage and the Rise of Western Civilisation* (1992).

83 Humphries, *My Life as Me*, 225–6.

84 Ibid., 226.

85 Humphries, *More Please*, 309.

86 Lahr, *Dame Edna Everage and the Rise of Western Civilisation*, 104.

87 Ibid., 111.

88 Ibid., 56. See also Humphries' own account of his and Lahr's backstage interaction: "The interviews, however, seemed interminable and I began to think he proposed to expand one article into several closely printed volumes." Humphries, *My Life as Me*, 225.

89 Humphries, "A Fugitive Art," 149–68.

90 Lahr, *Dame Edna Everage and the Rise of Western Civilisation*, 136.

91 Humphries, *More Please*, 289.

92 Lahr, *Dame Edna Everage and the Rise of Western Civilisation*, 136.

93 Humphries, *More Please*, 289–90.

94 Lahr, *Dame Edna Everage and the Rise of Western Civilisation*, 136.

95 Humphries, *More Please*, 293.

96 Dunstan, "John Barry Humphries," 34.

97 Humphries, *More Please*, xii.

98 See Janet Frame, *The Envoy from Mirror City* (1985), which is the second volume of her autobiography.

99 Humphries, *More Please*, 60.

100 See Dewey, "What is Developmental Dyspraxia?" (1995).

101 Humphries, *More Please*, 108.

102 Humphries, *Women in the Background*, 119.

103 Humphries, *More Please*, 115–6.

104 Patterson [Humphries], *The Traveller's Tool*, 10 and 11, respectively.

105 Ibid., 12.

106 Ibid., 14.

107 Respectively, but disrespectfully: a puritan or teetotaller; a pompous ninny; a homosexual; a lesbian.

108 Patterson [Humphries], *The Traveller's Tool*, 14.

109 Humphries, *Barry Humphries' Treasury of Australian Kitsch*, 9.

110 *New Edna – The Spectacle*, theatre program, n.p.

111 *Homme-age* is my neologism. In a BBC television interview on 5 June 1968 – he died 2 October 1968 – Duchamp stated "Well, *hommage* doesn't mean a thing." Qtd. in Naumann, *Marcel Duchamp*, 306. I would add that *homme-age*, the age of man, or patriarchy, is also meaningless.

112 Naumann, *Marcel Duchamp: The Art of Making Art in the Age of Mechnical Reproduction*, 17.

113 Patterson [Humphries], *The Traveller's Tool*, 30.

114 Brissenden, Introduction to *A Nice Night's Entertainment*, by Barry Humphries, xvii.

115 Forster, *Aspects of the Novel*, 75–89.

116 Patterson [Humphries], *The Traveller's Tool*, 15.

117 Ibid.

118 Later, Les says of his current research assistant, "she's got her feet on the desk, affording me a ring-side view of the map of Tasmania. And if you don't know what that is, it's a thickly wooded triangular appendage in the southern hemisphere with a reputation for mouth-watering seafood. Are you with me?" Patterson [Humphries], *The Traveller's Tool*, 24. He draws this analogy twice in *Les Patterson's Australia* (1978).

119 Dunkling and Gosling, *Everyman's Dictionary of First Names*.

120 Cirlot, *A Dictionary of Symbols*, 281.

121 Patterson [Humphries], *The Traveller's Tool*, 24.

122 Ibid., 64.

123 Ibid., 64.

124 Ibid., 14.

125 Ibid., 21.

126 Ibid., 22.

127 Ibid., 24.

128 Dunkling and Gosling, *Everyman's Dictionary of First Names*.

129 Patterson [Humphries], *The Traveller's Tool*, 24.

130 Ibid., 20.

131 Ibid., 21.

132 Ibid.

133 Ibid., 14.

134 Ibid., 24.

135 Ibid., 27.

136 Ibid., 30.

137 Ibid., 31.

138 Ibid., 32.

139 Ibid., 32, 33, 34, 35, 36, and 36, respectively.

140 Ibid., 39.

141 Stam, *Subversive Pleasures*, 112.

142 Patterson [Humphries], *The Traveller's Tool*, 16.

143 Stam, *Subversive Pleasures*, 113.
144 Patterson [Humphries], *The Traveller's Tool*, 29.
145 Emecheta, *Kehinde*, 4–6.
146 Ibid., 5.
147 Patterson [Humphries], *The Traveller's Tool*, 43.
148 Ibid., respectively.
149 Ibid., 60.
150 Ibid., 16.
151 Ibid., *The Traveller's Tool*, 130–3.
152 Ibid. 95.
153 Ibid.
154 Ibid.
155 I have transcribed this quotation from the television program *Artist of the Week*, BRAVO! 31 October 1999 (repeat broadcast).
156 Everage [Humphries], *Dame Edna's Coffee Table Book*, 91.
157 Qtd. in Naumann, *Marcel Duchamp*, 269.
158 Patterson [Humphries], *The Traveller's Tool*, 147.
159 White, *Riders in the Chariot*, 198.
160 Patterson [Humphries], *The Traveller's Tool*, 84–5, 94–118, and 130–2, respectively.
161 Humphries, *My Life as Me*, 309.
162 Humphries, *More Please*, xii.
163 Derrida, *Acts of Literature*, 58.
164 Humphries, "Why Bazza Is a Virgin," 33.
165 Humphries, *More Please*, 308.
166 Patterson [Humphries], *The Traveller's Tool*, 143.
167 Humphries, "A Fugitive Art," 151.
168 Dunkling and Gosling, *Everyman's Dictionary of First Names*.
169 <http://www.abu.nb.ca/courses/NTIntro/InTest/1EnocTex.htm>
170 <http://www.abu.nb.ca/courses/NTIntro/InTest/1EnocTex.htm>
171 Everage [Humphries], *My Gorgeous Life*, 138.
172 Lahr, *Dame Edna Everage and the Rise of Western Civilisation*, 34.
173 Humphries, *More Please*, 291
174 Everage [Humphries], *My Gorgeous Life*, 146.
175 Ibid.
176 Humphries, Mitchell, and McDonald, *Barry Humphries' Flashbacks*, 167.
177 Humphries, *Neglected Poems and Other Creatures*, 185.
178 Wheelahan, *Dame Edna's Frock-a-thon*, n.p.
179 Everage [Humphries], *My Gorgeous Life*, 41.
180 Ibid., 97.
181 Ibid., 95.
182 Ibid., 98.
183 Ibid.

184 Ibid., 100.
185 Ibid., 101.
186 Ibid., 97.
187 Ibid., 101.
188 Ibid., 277.
189 Chaucer, "The Canon's Yeoman's Tale," 219.
190 See Guinness, *A Positively Final Appearance*.
191 Everage [Humphries], *My Gorgeous Life*, 193.
192 Ibid.
193 Ibid., 194.
194 Ibid., 203.
195 Ibid. 203.
196 In Dutch, "housewife." I have cited the word *huisvrouw* in tribute to Peter Cook, who in his telegram to Edna invokes the disclaimer "OR I'M A DUTCH-MAN," and in tribute to Barry Humphries, who, fluent in German, has Edna Everage call herself at one point "a very restless and frustrated *Hausfrau*." Everage [Humphries], *My Gorgeous Life*, 211 and 210, respectively.
197 Everage [Humphries], *My Gorgeous Life*, 209.
198 Ibid., 211.
199 Ibid.
200 Telegraphy is a prototype of electronic mail. "E-mail" is a homophone of the French *émail* ("enamel").
201 Everage [Humphries], *My Gorgeous Life*, 215.
202 Ibid., 222.
203 Ibid., 211.
204 The original series of *Not Only … But Also* ran on BBC-2, 1965–66, and 1970. Cook and Moore made two more episodes of the show for the ABC TV (Australia) in 1971.
205 Humphries, *My Life as Me*, 309.
206 Brathwaite, *The Arrivants*, 18.

## CHAPTER SIX

1 Qtd. in Lambert, "Barry Humphries Is a Dandy," 58.
2 Humphries, *Women in the Background*, n.p.
3 Recalling his childhood home, Humphries has made a similar proclamation: "it was *potentially* haunted, by spirits yet unbidden – one day, perhaps, by me!" Humphries, *My Life as Me*, 6.
4 Lambert, "Barry Humphries Is a Dandy," 54.
5 See Patrick White's short story "Clay," in his collection *The Burnt Ones* (1964). White, who dedicated "Clay" to Barry Humphries and Zoe Caldwell, based the title character on Humphries.
6 Humphries, *My Life as Me*, 319.

7 Humphries, *Women in the Background*, 269.

8 Ibid., 1.

9 Master Barry Humphries, as in his 33 rpm EP disk *Ulysses Rag* (1967), is also *petit*. He is *un petit-maître*, "a dandy."

10 Humphries, *Women in the Background*, 16.

11 Dunkling and Gosling, *Everyman's Dictionary of First Names*.

12 Prolepsis, from the Greek *prolambenein* ("to anticipate"), is the literary device by which a future event is represented as if it has already happened, or the representation of something as existing before its time. Analepsis, from the Greek *analambanein* ("to take up"), is the literary device by which a past event is represented as if it is happening now, or the representation of something as existing after its time. Prolepsis is a flash forward, analepsis a flash back. See also *Barry Humphries' Flashbacks* (1999).

13 Humphries, *Women in the Background*, 18.

14 In Italian, the word *focolare* denotes a "hearth" or "fireside" and connotes a place where the family gathers.

15 Humphries, *Women in the Background*, 26.

16 Ibid., 24.

17 Ibid., 37.

18 Ibid., 101–2.

19 Ibid., 110.

20 Ibid., 109.

21 Ibid., 111.

22 Ibid., 112.

23 Idle, *The Road to Mars*, 145–6. See also my Chapter 1.

24 Humphries, *Women in the Background*, 131.

25 Ibid., 170.

26 Ibid., 29.

27 Ibid., 311.

28 Ibid., 117.

29 Ibid., 29.

30 "The convention of beginning the action *in medias res* ties a knot in time, so to speak." Frye, *Anatomy of Criticism*, 318.

31 Beckett, *Watt*, 113.

32 Humphries, *Women in the Background*, 325.

33 Ibid., 326.

34 Ibid., 58–60.

35 Rushdie, *Midnight's Children*, 19.

36 Ibid., 23.

37 Humphries, *Women in the Background*, 118.

38 Ibid., 212.

39 Ibid., 114.

40 Ibid., 100.

41 Ibid., 118.

42 Dunkling and Gosling, *Everyman's Dictionary of First Names.*

43 Humphries, *Women in the Background,* 326.

44 Ibid., 327.

45 Alternatively, it could be argued that, during the period February to March 1995, Yvette wrote only the epilogue or only the italicized end-unstopped last words.

46 Humphries, *Women in the Background,* 327.

47 Ibid., 326.

48 Prince, *A Dictionary of Narratology,* 64.

49 Receivers can surmise that Karina, Derek Pettyfer's lover in Chapter 16, is Kenneth Grocock's sister, whom Polly mentions in Chapter 20. When Inge Pinkhill offers Polly a cigarette after her performance with Lionel, Polly replies, "I don't smoke. I'd hate to get hooked like Karina." Recall when "Derek, still groggy from lunch, got quickly under the shower while Karina loitered on his patio, smoking a cigarette." See Humphries, *Women in the Background,* 296 and 227, respectively.

50 In Chapter 3 I discuss this concept with reference to Humphries' editorial power over superseded Austral poets.

51 Prince, *A Dictionary of Narratology,* 64.

52 *Je m'excuse.* I realize "one true love" is a soap opera cliché.

53 Prince, *A Dictionary of Narratology,* 80.

54 Humphries, *Women in the Background,* 325.

55 Ibid., 326.

56 Ibid., 327.

57 Bakhtin, *The Dialogic Imagination,* 324.

58 Dunkling and Gosling note that the Greek *Timotheos* means "honoring God."

59 Humphries, *Women in the Background,* 59.

60 Ibid., 240.

61 Ibid., 325.

62 Ibid., 326.

63 Ibid.

64 Ibid., 325.

65 The geographic coordinates of Gstaad, Switzerland, at 47° N. and 7.30° E., make it the antipodean underworld of Derek Quick's birthplace, Adelaide, Australia, at 35° S. and 140° E.

66 Humphries, *Women in the Background,* 327.

67 Ibid., 326.

68 Ibid., 27.

69 Ibid.

70 In *Hamlet,* Marcellus reacts to the reappearance of the ghost of the murdered king: "Thou art a scholar; speak to it, Horatio" (1.1.42). He reminds Horatio that, being fluent in Latin, he knows the language of ghosts.

71 Humphries, *Women in the Background*, 94.

72 Ibid., 148–9.

73 Ibid., 149.

74 Ibid.

75 Humphries, *Women in the Background*, 272. A student of the mimicidal Plato, Aristotle might be seen as a "reprieved mimic."

76 Humphries, *Women in the Background*, 273.

77 Ibid., 291.

78 Ibid., 292.

79 Ibid., 295.

80 Ibid., 296.

81 Ibid., 300.

82 Ibid.

83 Ibid.

84 Ibid., 60.

85 Ibid., 61.

86 Ibid., 63.

87 Ibid., 65.

88 Shakespeare, *Othello*, 5.2.7.

89 Humphries, *Women in the Background*, 77.

90 Ibid. 77.

91 Ibid., 23.

92 See also Humphries, *My Life as Me*, 263.

93 Humphries, *Women in the Background*, 191.

94 Ibid., 193.

95 Ibid. The Internet has its own collection of Christmas sites (e.g., <www.christmas.com>).

96 Ibid., 192.

97 Ibid., 253.

98 Ibid., 260–1.

99 Ibid., 319.

100 Ibid., 306–7.

101 Humphries, Mitchell, and McDonald, *Barry Humphries' Flashbacks*, 71.

102 Cirlot, *A Dictionary of Symbols*, 332.

103 Qtd. in Dunstan, *Ratbags*, 30.

104 Cirlot, *A Dictionary of Symbols*, 332.

105 Humphries, *Women in the Background*, 177.

106 Ibid., 269.

107 Ibid., 296.

108 Ibid., 301–2.

109 On 22 July 2003 Melbourne University conferred an honorary Doctor of Laws degree on Barry Humphries.

110 Armstrong, *Star Palms*, n.p.

111 While researching this book I twice wrote to Humphries telling him about my project. Knowing his feelings, I have not insulted him by asking for his cooperation, other than in giving me permission to quote from his works. Even as a serious academic I have tried to maintain my lightheartedness throughout and to give my readers, including Humphries, a chuckle. I hope no one says, "You did give me a chuckle. I laughed once."

112 Humphries, *Women in the Background*, 325.

113 White, *Tropics of Discourse: Essays in Cultural Criticism*, 122.

114 Ibid.

115 See Aritha van Herk, *Places Far from Ellesmere, a Geografictione: Explorations on Site* (1990). Jorge Luis Borges, *Ficciones* (1962).

CHAPTER SEVEN

1 Ouzounian, "An Audience with … Dame Edna and Barry Humphries: Veteran Actor Talks," M8.

2 Humphries, *More Please*, 296.

3 Ibid., 291.

4 See my discussion of the modality Laugh in Chapter 5. In French, I would say to Humphries, "j'ai pensé mourir de rire, de la contagion de rire" ("I nearly died of laughter, from the infectiousness of laughter").

5 See my discussion of Humphries' political correctitude in Chapter 5.

6 Humphries, introduction to *The Penguin Leunig*, 5.

7 Ibid.

8 Ibid., 5–6.

9 Frame, *The Carpathians*, 163.

10 Ibid., 170.

11 Humphries, introduction to *The Penguin Leunig*, 6.

12 Humphries, introduction to *The Art of Dominic Ryan*, 3.

13 Ibid.

14 Ibid.

15 Humphries, introduction to *Ornaments in Jade*, 55.

16 Humphries, "Detrimental Blokes," foreword, in *Knockers*, xiii.

17 Ibid., xii.

18 Humphries, foreword to *Ratbags*, xii.

19 Excuse I, Barry. The word "gypsy" is a misnomer, suggesting the Romany people came from Egypt. "Romany" is the right originary word, connoting Indians of low caste.

20 Humphries, foreword to *Night Voices: Strange Stories*, 9.

21 Ibid., 9.

22 Humphries, introduction to *The Importance of Being Earnest*, viii.

23 Humphries, "Glenn A. Baker Is a Sydney Writer," v–vi.

24 *Around the Loop*, theatre program, 5 and 14, respectively.

25 Humphries, foreword to *Max Oldaker*, n.p.

26 Ibid. See also Humphries, *More Please*, 158; Humphries, *My Life as Me*, 145–6.

27 Humphries, "Dame Edna Everage," interview by Sue Lawley, 172–7, 184.

28 Humphries, "Glenn A. Baker Is a Sydney Writer, vi.

29 Humphries, foreword to *The Golden Age of the Argonauts*, xii.

30 Ibid.

31 Ibid. Humphries made his contribution to ABC *Weekly* under the pseudonym "Ithome 32." Johnson is as proud of it as is Humphries: he prints the pseudonym in the context of his discussion of Humphries. See Johnson, *The Golden Age of Argonauts*, 87–8, 222.

32 Dutton, *The Innovators*, 153, 199–201.

33 Dutton, *The Australian Bed-Side Book*, 19–23. Humphries seems to have used his letter to Dutton in drafting his chapter "Sinny" in *More Please* (155–71).

34 Dutton, *The Innovators*, vi.

35 Humphries, "Lost at Life," 17.

36 Ibid.

37 Francis Lymburner died in 1972. For my definition of *hommage*, see note 111, chapter 5.

38 Humphries, "A Note of Exclamation," 8.

39 Ibid. 8.

40 Ibid., 9.

41 Humphries, untitled article in *Spike Milligan, a Celebration*, 127.

42 Ibid.

43 Untitled article in *Spike Milligan: His Part in Our Lives*, 97.

44 Everage [Humphries], *Dame Edna's Coffee Table Book*, 20.

45 Ibid.

46 Hind, "Above Everage," 123.

47 Humphries, Mitchell, and McDonald, *Barry Humphries' Flashbacks*, 151.

48 Mertins, "Anything but Literal," 228.

49 Humphries, *Les Patterson's Australia*, n.p.

50 Humphries, *Les Patterson's Australia*, 38–9.

51 Humphries, *Barry Humphries' Treasury of Australian Kitsch*, 9.

52 Ibid., 38.

53 Ibid., 5.

54 Ibid., 18.

55 Ibid., 80.

56 Ibid., 61. Throughout the book, "A.D.R." is Humphries' acronym for "Australian Democratic Republic."

57 Humphries, *Barry Humphries' Treasury of Australian Kitsch*, 28.

58 Ibid., 81–3.

59 Ibid., 57.

60 Ibid., 58.

61 Ibid., 62–3.

62 Ibid., 14.

63 Ibid., 42–3.

64 Ibid., 30 (picture) and 31 (caption).

65 Ibid., 9.

66 Dutton, *The Innovators*, 226.

67 I also discuss Humphries and intellect in Chapter 5.

68 Said, *Representations of the Intellectual*, 43–4.

69 Humphries and Garland, *The Complete Barry McKenzie McKenzie*, v.

70 Cirlot, *A Dictionary of Symbols*, 140.

71 Everage [Humphries], *Dame Edna's Coffee Table Book*, 54–5.

72 Everage [Humphries], *Dame Edna's Bedside Companion*, 149.

73 The word "fedora" derives from Victorien Sardou's play *Fédora* (1883).

74 Dame Edna pronounced the death of her husband, Norman Stoddart Everage, on stage, in *Back with a Vengeance* (1987).

75 Humphries, *Barry Humphries' Treasury of Australian Kitsch*, 86.

76 Bell, "Return to Oz," 77.

77 Cirlot, *A Dictionary of Symbols*, 53.

78 Ibid., 105.

79 As a descendant of a wizard, one of my Salopean ancestors, I imagine myself a wizard not a Harry Potter clone.

80 Jerry Seinfeld, *SeinLanguage* (1993); Tim Allen, *Don't Stand Too Close to a Naked Man* (1994) and *I'm Not Really Here* (1996); Paul Resier, *Couplehood* (1994) and *Babyhood* (1997); Ellen DeGeneres, *My Point – and I Do Have One* (1995); Drew Carey, *Dirty Jokes and Beer: Stories of the Unrefined* (1997); Kelsey Grammer, *So Far* (1995); Ray Romano, *Everything and a Kite* (1998); Garry Shandling, with David Rensin, *Confessions of a Late Night Talk Show Host: The Autobiography of Larry Sanders* (1998); Jon Stewart, *Naked Pictures of Famous People* (1998); Steve Martin, *Pure Drivel* (1998); Janeane Garofalo and Ben Stiller, *Feel This Book: An Essential Guide to Self-Empowerment, Spiritual Supremacy, and Sexual Satisfaction* (1999).

81 As in *Four Films of Woody Allen*: Annie Hall, Interiors, Manhattan, Stardust Memories (1982); and *Three Films of Woody Allen*: Zelig, Broadway Danny Rose, The Purple Rose of Cairo (1987).

82 As in Martin's collections *Picasso at the Lapin Agile and Other Plays* (1996) and *Wasp and Other Plays* (1998).

83 In her lyrical commentary on normalcy and madness in *Roseanne: My Life as a Woman*, Barr brings to mind the great writer Janet Frame in *Faces in the Water* (1961) and in her autobiographies, *To the Is-Land* (1982), *An Angel at My Table* (1984) and *The Envoi from Mirror City* (1985).

84 Garofalo and Stiller, *Feel This Book*, ix.

85 Shandling, with Rensin, *Confessions of a Late Night Talk Show Host*, 9.

86 In Dutch, *het kindje*, means "the kid." In a playful Dada spirit, one could homophonize it into "It Kid."

87　Auslander, *Presence and Resistance*, 139–40.

88　This phrase is from the title-page of the two-volume *Compact Edition of the Oxford English Dictionary* (1971).

89　*Monty Python's Flying Circus*, series 1, episode 1, BBC-1, 5 October 1969.

90　Boyd, *The Cardboard Crown*, 74.

91　Auslander, *Presence and Resistance*, 136.

92　Claudel, "Art Poétique," 88.

93　See Humphries, *My Life as Me*, 22.

94　Humphries has floated this title in several interviews.

95　See Margaret Plant, *Irreverent Sculpture* (1985) [catalogue]; Ted Gott, *Barry Humphries, Dada Artist* (1993) [pamphlet].

96　Wicks, *Master of None*, 293.

97　The French words *bricoleur* and *bricoleuse* mean "handyman" and "handy-woman."

98　I have drawn this metaphor from my own reader's tickets to the Birminghman Public Library (Warwickshire) and Mitchell Library (State Library of New South Wales).

99　John R. Cash, perf., "I Walk the Line," by Cash, recorded 2 April 1956.

100　John R. Cash, perf., "A Boy Named Sue," by Shel Silverstein, recorded February 1969.

101　In Dutch, "*Het Kindje Heet Edna*" means "A Boy Named Edna" [or "It Kid Named Edna"] and "*Wanneer zij lachte, wij lachten*" means "whenever she laughs, we laugh."

102　Rushdie, *Midnight's Children*, 39.

103　Rushdie, *The Wizard of Oz*, 23.

104　Poovey, "Creative Criticism: Adaptation, Performative Writing, and the Problem of Objectivity," 123.

105　In *québécois*, *kétaine* means "kitsch," and connotes things *de mauvais goût, de goût discutable, et démodé* ("in bad taste, of questionable taste, and outmoded.")

106　I happen to have a friend, from Cameroon, named Hilarious Ambe.

## APPENDIX SEVEN

1　Humphries, *The Life and Death of Sandy Stone*, 10.

2　C. Allen, *Art in Australia*, 162. See also T. Allen, *Clifton Pugh*, 55–8.

## APPENDIX NINE

1　For Humphries' explanation of his dress code, see his "Sartorial Insights" in Lambert, "Barry Humphries Is a Dandy," 57.

2　Livingstone, "A Dictum of Fashion," C22.

3 Kift, *The Victorian Music Hall*, 50.
4 I discuss Humphries' effrontery-talent equation in the Preface and Chapter 6.
5 White, Letter to Geoffrey and Ninette Dutton, 371.
6 Humphries, *More Please*, 327–8.
7 Marr, *Patrick White Letters*, 638.
8 Dutton, *Out in the Open*, 394.
9 Ibid., 431.
10 Lowry, "Through the Panama," 86.

### APPENDIX TEN

1 Everage [Humphries], *My Gorgeous Life*, 267.
2 Ibid., 21.

### ADDENDUM

1 Everage [Humphries], *My Gorgeous Life*, 204–5.
2 See my discussion in Chapter 2.
3 Humphries has made contributions in 1981, 1982, 1983, 1984, 1985, 1986, 1987, 1988, 1989, 1990, 1991, 1992, 1993, and 1997. He made an initial donation (of theatre programs, correspondence, and Barry McKenzie greeting cards) to PAM in 1972.
4 Humphries' handwritten changes to the "June 30, 1986" version, made 16 July 1986, seem minimal, limited to struck-through excisions of scenes and speeches. Still, the *mise en scène* remains more scenic than cinematic.
5 Barry Humphries and Diane Millstead, *Les Patterson Saves the World*, typescript, in possession of the author. In assembling primary and secondary sources for this book, I have become an inveterate collector of Barry Humphries materials. I acquired my typescript of *Les Patterson Saves the World* from Nicholas Pounder, Bookseller, Double Bay, Sydney. Eventually – in the unlikely event of my death – I plan to donate the film typescript and my entire Barry Humphries collection to the goddess PAM.
6 Humphries may have been anticipating a shift in his personal as well as in his professional relationship with Diane Millstead: their marriage came to an end in 1988.
7 "For the first time in forty years, a local film was a major force at the box office." Adams, "A Cultural Revolution," 63.
8 Martin, "George Miller, *Les Patterson Saves the World*," 223.
9 Humphries and Millstead, *Les Patterson Saves the World*, typescript, 48–9.
10 While studying for my doctorate at the University of Sydney, I rented a cottage at Avalon Beach, where a possum that lived in the attic was my mark of Australian prestige.

11 Barry Humphries and David Smilow, "The Dame from Down Under – An American Docu Comedy," typescript, 1997.091.004, Performing Arts Museum, Victorian Arts Centre, Melbourne.
12 Humphries, *More Please*, xi.
13 Barthes, "The Death of the Author," in *The Rustle of Spring*, trans. Richard Howard, 55.
14 Barthes, "The Death of the Author," in *Image-Music-Text*, trans. Stephen Heath, 148.
15 Humphries, *More Please*, 167.

# Bibliography

ARCHIVAL SOURCES

*Barry Humphries Collection, Performing Arts Museum, Part One.* Melbourne: Performing Arts Museum, Victorian Arts Centre, 1998.
*Barry Humphries Collection, Performing Arts Museum, Part Two.* Melbourne: Performing Arts Museum, Victorian Arts Centre, 1998.
Humphries, Barry. "List." MS 1987.202.512, Barry Humphries Collection. Performing Arts Museum, Victorian Arts Centre, Melbourne.
– *Neglected Poems.* Typescript in possession of the author.
Humphries, Barry, and David Smilow. "The Dame from Down Under – An American Docu Comedy." TS 1997.091.004, Barry Humphries Collection. Performing Arts Museum, Victorian Arts Centre, Melbourne.
Humphries, Barry, and Diane Millstead. *Les Patterson Saves the World.* TS 30 June 1986, in possession of the author.

PRINTED AND MEDIA SOURCES

Ackroyd, Peter. *Dressing Up, Transvestism and Drag: The History of an Obsession.* New York: Simon and Schuster, 1979.
Adams, Phillip. "A Cultural Revolution." In *Australian Cinema,* ed. Scott Murray, 61–9. St Leonards: Allen and Unwin, 1994.
– "The Mystery of the Surgical Boot in the Edna-Barry Psyche." *Bulletin,* 3 August 1968, 69.
Adair, Gilbert. "La Dame aux Gladioli." In *Myths and Memories,* 96–9. London: Fontana, 1986.
Alighieri, Dante. *The Inferno of Dante,* trans. Robert Pinsky. New York: Farrar, Straus and Giroux, 1994.
Allen, Christopher. *Art in Australia: From Colonization to Postmodernism.* London: Thames and Hudson, 1997.

Allen, Dave. *Dave Allen at Large*. BBC-1, 1971–73, BBC-2 1975–76. Television
series.

Allen, Tim. *Don't Stand Too Close to a Naked Man*. New York: Hyperion, 1994.

– *I'm Not Really Here*. New York: Hyperion, 1996.

Allen, Traudi. *Clifton Pugh: Patterns of a Lifetime*. Melbourne: Nelson, 1981.

Allen, Woody. *Four Films of Woody Allen:* Annie Hall, Interiors, Manhattan, Stardust Memories. New York: Random House, 1982.

– *Getting Even*. New York: Random House, 1971.

– *Side Effects*. New York: Random House, 1980.

– *Three Films of Woody Allen:* Zelig, Broadway Danny Rose, The Purple Rose of
Cairo. New York: Random House, 1987.

– *Without Feathers*. New York: Random House, 1975.

Alomes, Stephen. *When London Calls: The Expatriation of Australian Artists to
Britain*. Cambridge: Cambridge University Press, 1999.

Apollinaire, Guillaume. *Les Mamelles de Tirésias*. Paris: Gallimard, 1924.

Aquinas, Thomas. *The Summa Theologica*. 2 vols. Trans. the Fathers of the English
Dominican Province and Daniel J. Sullivan. Chicago: Encyclopaedia Britannica,
1952.

Armstrong, Sue. "Barry Humphries." In *Star Palms*, n.p. London: Gollancz, 1988.

Arthurs, George, and Bennett Scott. "I Had to Be Cruel to Be Kind." In *Sheard's
29th Comic and Variety Annual*, 6–7. London: Sheard, 1905.

Auslander, Philip. *Presence and Resistance: Postmodernism and Cultural Politics in
Contemporary American Performance*. Ann Arbor: University of Michigan Press,
1992.

Bailey, Peter. "A Community of Friends: Business and Good Fellowship in London
Music Hall Management c. 1860–1885." In *Music Hall: The Business of Pleasure*,
ed. P. Bailey, 33–52. Milton Keynes and Philadelphia: Open University Press, 1986.

– "Introduction: Making Sense of Music Hall." In *Music Hall: The Business of
Pleasure*, ed. Peter Bailey, viii–xxiii. Milton Keynes and Philadelphia: Open University Press, 1986.

Baker, Sidney J. *The Australian Language*. Sydney: Currawong, 1978.

– *Australian Language: An Examination of the English Language and English
Speech as Used in Australia*. Sydney: Currawong, 1966.

Bakewell, Joan. "The Man within." *Sunday Times Magazine* (London), 16 May
1976, 36.

Bakhtin, M.M. "The Problem of Speech Genres." In *Speech Genres and Other Late
Essays*. Trans. Vern W. McGee, 60–102. Austin: University of Texas Press, 1986.

Bal, Mieke. *Double Exposures: The Subject of Cultural Analysis*. New York and
London: Routledge, 1996.

– *Narratologie: Essais sur la signification narrative dans quatre romans modernes*.
Paris: Klincksieck, 1977.

– *Narratology: Introduction to the Theory of Narrative*. Trans. Christine van
Boheemen. Toronto: University of Toronto Press, 1985.

Ball, Hugo. "Dada Fragments (1916–1917)." In *The Dada Painters and Poets: An Anthology*, 2nd ed., ed. Robert Motherwell, 51–4. Cambridge, MA, and London: Belknap, 1981.

Banks, Morwenna, and Amanda Swift. *The Jokes on Us: Women in Comedy from Music Hall to the Present Day*, 195–6. London: Pandora, 1987.

Barr, Roseanne. *Roseanne: My Life as a Woman*. New York: Harper and Row, 1989.

"Barry Humphries, 1996." *Australian Style* 25 (1998): 107.

Barthes, Roland. *La Chambre claire: Note sur la photographie*. Paris: Gallimard Seuil, 1980.

– "The Death of the Author." In *Image-Music-Text*. Trans. and comp. Stephen Heath, 142–8. New York: Hill and Wang, 1977.

– "The Death of the Author." In *The Rustle of Spring*. Trans. Richard Howard, 49–55. Berkeley and Los Angeles: University of California Press, 1989.

– *Le Plaisir du texte*. Paris: Éditions du Seuil, 1973.

Beaver, Patrick. *The Spice of Life: Pleasures of the Victorian Age*. London: Elm Tree, 1979.

Beck, Chris. "Barry Humphries, Humorist." In *On the Couch with Chris Beck*, 115–19. Sydney: HarperCollins, 1996.

Beckett, Samuel. *Watt*. London: Picador, 1988 [1953].

Bell, Max. "Return to Oz." *The Face* 66 (1985): 72–4, 77.

Beresford, Bruce. "Getting 'The Getting of Wisdom.'" *Quadrant* 21, 10 (October 1977): 25–6.

Bernhardt, Sarah. *My Double Life: The Memoirs of Sarah Bernhardt*. Trans. Victoria Tietze Larson. Albany: State University of New York Press, 1999.

Betjeman, John. *Letters, Volume Two: 1951 to 1984*, ed. Candida Lycett Green. London: Methuen 1995.

Bhabha, Homi. *The Location of Culture*. London and New York: Routledge, 1994.

bissett, bill. *Th influenza uv logic*. Vancouver: Talonbooks, 1995.

Blundell, Graeme, comp. *Australian Theatre: Backstage with Graeme Blundell*, ed. Katherine Steward. Melbourne: Oxford University Press, 1997.

Bonython, Kym. *Ladies' Legs and Lemonade*. Adelaide: Rigby, 1979.

Borges, Jorge Luis. *Ficciones*, ed. Anthony Kerrigan. New York: Grove, 1962 [1956].

Boyd, Martin. *The Cardboard Crown*. 1952. Melbourne: Lansdowne, 1971.

Boyd, Robin. *The Australian Ugliness*. Melbourne: Cheshire, 1961.

Brathwaite, Edward. *The Arrivants: A New World Trilogy*. Oxford: Oxford University Press, 1973.

Breton, André. "Free Union." In *The Norton Anthology of World Masterpieces: The Western Tradition*. Vol. 2, 2nd. ed. Sarah N. Lawall and Maynard Mack, 1717. New York and London: Norton, 1999.

Brisbane, Katharine. "Australian Drama." In *The Literature of Australia*, ed. Geoffrey Dutton, 268–9. Rev. ed. Harmondsworth: Penguin, 1976.

Brissenden, R.F. Introduction to *A Nice Night's Entertainment: Sketches and Monologues 1956–1981*, by Barry Humphries, xi–xix. Sydney: Currency, 1981.

Britain, Ian. *Once an Australian: Journeys with Barry Humphries, Clive James, Germaine Greer and Robert Hughes*. Oxford: Oxford University Press, 1997.

– "Bazzamatua." *24 Hours* (Sydney), August 1996, 36–41.

Bryars, Gavin. *A Man in a Room, Gambling*. Gavin Bryars, Juan Muñoz, and the Gavin Bryars Ensemble. Point 289 456 514–2, 1998. Compact sound disc.

Buffet-Picabia, Gabrielle. "Some Memories of Pre-Dada, Picabia and Duchamp." Trans. Ralph Manheim. In *The Dada Painters and Poets: An Anthology*, 2nd. ed., ed. Robert Motherwell, 253–67. Cambridge, MA, and London: Belknap, 1981.

Busby, Roy. *British Music Hall: An Illustrated Who's Who from 1850 to the Present Day*. London: Elek, 1976.

Burns, D.R. "An Everage Review." *Observer* (Sydney), 15 November 1958, 627.

Cabanne, Pierre. *Duchamp & Co*. Ed. Peter Snowdon. Paris: Terrail, 1997.

Callaghan, Morley. *A Time for Judas*. Scarborough: Avon, 1983.

Carey, Drew. *Dirty Jokes and Beer: Stories of the Unrefined*. New York: Hyperion, 1997.

Carpenter, Humphrey. *A Great, Silly Grin: The British Satire Boom of the 1960s*. New York: Public Affairs, 2000. Originally published as *That Was the Satire That Was*. London: Gollancz, 2000.

Carter, Graydon. "Editor's Letter: Advice and Consent." *Vanity Fair*, March 2001, 70.

Caws, Mary Ann. *The Art of Interference: Stressed Readings in Verbal and Visual Texts*. Princeton: Princeton University Press, 1989.

Chaucer, Geoffrey. "The Canon's Yeoman's Tale." In *The Works of Geoffrey Chaucer*, 2nd ed., ed. F.N. Robinson, 215–23. Boston: Houghton Mifflin, 1957.

Cheshire, D.F. *Music Hall in Britain: Illustrated Sources in History*. Newton Abbot: David and Charles, 1974.

Cirlot, J.E. *A Dictionary of Symbols*. 2nd ed. Trans. Jack Sage. London: Routledge and Kegan Paul, 1971.

Cixous, Hélène. *Readings: The Poetics of Blanchot, Joyce, Kafka, Kleist, Lispector, and Tsvetayeva*. Ed. and trans. Verena Andermatt Conley. Minneapolis: University of Minnesota Press, 1991.

Cixous, Hélène, and Catherine Clément. *The Newly Born Woman*. Trans. Betsy Wing. Minneapolis: University of Minnesota Press, 1986.

Clark, Al. *Making Priscilla*. Ringwood: Penguin, 1994.

Clark, Kenneth. *Leonardo da Vinci: An Account of His Development as an Artist*. Rev. ed. London: Penguin, 1959.

Claudel, Paul. "Art Poétique." In *Oeuvres completes*, vol. 5, ed. Robert Mallet, 8–127. Paris: Gallimard, 1953 [1913].

Cocteau, Jean. *Parade*. Paris: Rouart-Lerolle, 1919.

Coleman, Peter. *Bruce Beresford: Instincts of the Heart*. Pymble: Angus and Robertson, 1992.

– *Obscenity, Blasphemy, Sedition: The Rise and Fall of Literary Censorship in Australia*. 1962. Sydney: Duffy and Snellgrove, 2000.

– *The Real Barry Humphries*. London: Robson, 1990.

Coleman, Peter, Rosemary Dobson, Peter Goldsworthy, Janice Grant, Marion Halligan, Ashley Hay, David Malouf, Richard Tognetti, Robyn Williams, and Salvatore Zofrea, comps. *A Return to Poetry 2000*. Sydney: Duffy and Snellgrove, 2000.

Collin, Francesca. *The Arts and Entertainment in London, in Association with London Transport*. London: Ward Lock, 1997.

Conrad, Peter. "Barry Humphries on the Couch." In *Feasting with Panthers*, 276–89. London: Thames and Hudson, 1994.

– "Superstars and Others." In *Feasting with Panthers*, 7–16. London: Thames and Hudson, 1994.

Coombs, Anne. *Life and Death in the Sydney Push*. Ringwood: Penguin, 1994.

Cottom, Daniel. "What Is a Joke?" In *Text and Culture: The Politics of Interpretation*, 3–48. Minneapolis: University of Minnesota Press, 1989.

– "Ethnographia Mundi." In *Text and Culture: The Politics of Interpretation*, 19–102. Minneapolis: University of Minnesota Press, 1989.

Coupland, Douglas. *Generation X: Tales for an Accelerated Culture*. New York: St Martin's, 1991.

Coveney, Michael. *Maggie Smith: A Bright Particular Star*. London: Gollancz, 1992.

Cronin, Russell. "Sir Les Patterson: *Arena* Shares Dry-Cleaning Tips with the Antipodean Gastronome." *Arena* (Autumn-Winter, November-December 1988): 78–81.

Davidson, Jim. "Deepest Camberwell: The Antics of Mr Humphries." *Meanjin* 40, 3 (October 1981): 400–4.

Davies, Robertson. *Fifth Business*. Toronto: Macmillan, 1970.

– *Murther and Walking Spirits*. Toronto: McClelland and Stewart, 1991.

Davis, Anthony. *Laughtermakers: The Story of TV Comedy*. London: Boxtree, 1989.

Deasey, Denison. "Barry Humphries." *Australian Letters* 2, 1 (1959): 24–5.

DeGeneres, Ellen. *My Point – and I Do Have One*. New York: Bantam, 1995.

Delfont, Lord. *Curtain Up! The Story of the Royal Variety Performance*. London: Robson, 1989.

Derrida, Jacques. *Acts of Literature*, ed. Derek Attridge. New York and London: Routledge, 1992.

– *Dissemination*, ed. and trans. Barbara Johnson. Chicago: University of Chicago Press, 1981.

– *The Ear of the Other: Otobiography, Transference, Translation*, ed. Christie V. Mcdonald, trans. Avital Roneil and Peggy Kamuf. New York: Schocken, 1985.

– *Of Grammatology*, trans. Gayatri Chakravorty Spivak. Baltimore and London: Johns Hopkins University Press, 1976.

– "Khora," trans. Ian McLeod. In *On the Name*, trans. Ian McLeod, David Wood, and John Leavey, Jr., 89–127. Stanford: Stanford University Press, 1995.

Dessau, Bruce. *Rowan Atkinson*. London: Orion, 1999.

Dewey, D. "What Is Developmental Dyspraxia?" *Brain Cognition* 29, 3 (December 1995): 254–74.

Dickins, Barry. "Les Patterson Saves the World." Review of *Les Patterson Saves the World* (Humpstead movie). *Cinema Papers* 64 (July 1987): 46.

Duchamp, Marcel. *The Writings of Marcel Duchamp*. Ed. Michel Sanouillet and Elmer Peterson. New York: Da Capo, 1973.

Dunkling, Leslie, and William Gosling. *Everyman's Dictionary of First Names*. 3rd ed. London: Dent, 1991.

Dunstan, Keith. "John Barry Humphries." In *Ratbags*, 21–39. Sydney and Auckland: Golden, 1979.

– *Knockers*. Melbourne: Cassell Australia, 1972.

– *Wowsers, Being an Account of the Prudery Exhibited by Certain Outstanding Men and Women in Such Matters as Drinking, Smoking, Prostitution, Censorship, and Gambling*. Melbourne: Cassell Australia, 1968.

Dutton, Geoffrey, ed. *The Australian Bed-Side Book: A Selection of Writings from The Australian Literary Supplement*. Melbourne: Macmillan, 1987.

Dutton, Geoffrey. *The Innovators: The Sydney Alternatives in the Rise of Modern Art, Literature and Ideas*. Melbourne: Macmillan, 1986.

– *Out in the Open*. St Lucia: University of Queensland Press, 1994.

Ekins, Richard. *Male Femaling: A Grounded Theory Approach to Cross-Dressing and Sex-Changing*. London and New York: Routledge, 1997.

Eliot, T.S. "The Love Song of J. Alfred Prufrock." In *Collected Poems, 1909–1962*, 13–17. London: Faber, 1974.

– "Reflections on *vers libre*." In *Selected Prose of T.S. Eliot*, ed. Frank Kermode, 31–6. New York: Harcourt Brace Jovanovich, Farrar, Straus and Giroux, 1975.

Ellis, Bob. "The Monologue." *Meanjin* 45, 2 (June 1986): 169–73.

Emecheta, Buchi. *Kehinde*. Oxford: Heinemann, 1994.

Everage, Dame Edna [Barry Humphries]. "Ask Dame Edna." *Vanity Fair*, February 2003, 116.

– "Ask Dame Edna." *Vanity Fair*, October 2002, 296.

– "Dame Edna." Interview with Barry Humphries (as Dame Edna Everage). *Independent Times* (Vancouver) 13, 8 (October 2002): 5, 14–15.

– "Dame Edna Everage." Interview by Sue Lawley. In *Sue Lawley's Desert Island Discussions*, by Sue Lawley, 172–7, 184. London: Hodder and Stoughton, 1990.

– "Dame Edna Goes to Hollywood!" *Vanity Fair*, April 2002, 316.

– *Dame Edna's Bedside Companion*. London: Weidenfeld and Nicolson, 1982.

– *Dame Edna's Coffee Table Book: A Guide to Gracious Living and the Finer Things of Life by One of the First Ladies of World Theatre*. London: Harrap, 1976.

– "Dame Edna's Xmas Telex." In *The Pick of Punch*, comp. Miles Kingston. London: Folio Society, 1998, 36–9.

- "Dear Dame Edna ..." *Vanity Fair*, March 2001, 236–7.
- "Dear Dame Edna ..." *Vanity Fair*, May 2001, 118, 120.
- "Dear Dame Edna ..." *Vanity Fair*, July 2001, 90–1.
- "Dear Dame Edna ..." *Vanity Fair*, August 2001, 92, 98.
- "Edna Everage (alias Barry Humphries)." Interview by Russell Harty. In *Russell Harty Plus*, by Russell Harty, 172–7. London: Elm Tree 1974.
- "Edna, the Renaissance Woman." *Radio Times* (London), 3–9 December 1977, 4–5, 9.
- *My Gorgeous Life: An Adventure*. Melbourne and London: Macmillan, 1989. Also published as *My Gorgeous Life: The Life, the Loves, the Legend*. New York: Simon and Schuster, 1989.
- "A Letter from Edna Everage." In *"Punch" Down Under*, comp. Barry Humphries, ed. Susan Jeffreys, 114–16. London: Robson, 1984.
- "A Word from the Dame." *Cleo* 121 (November 1982): 152–4.
- Untitled Article in *The Court of King Rolf*, ed. Mark Walker, 41-2. London: Partridge, 2000.

*The Fashion Diary of a Victorian Housewife: Dame Edna's Wardrobe 1956–1983*. Melbourne: Performing Arts Museum, Victorian Arts Centre, 1983.

Fawcett, Brian. *Gender Wars: A Novel and Some Conversation about Sex and Gender*. Toronto: Somerville House, 1994.

Felstead, S. Theodore. *Stars Who Made the Halls: A Hundred Years of English Humour, Harmony and Hilarity*. London: Laurie, 1946.

Fielding, Henry. *The History of Tom Jones, a Foundling*. London: Millar, Dublin: Smith, 1749.

Fields, Gracie. "There's a Cabin in the Pines." On *Stars of Variety*. Music Collection, 1994. Compact sound disc.

Flanders, Michael, and Donald Swann. *The Bestiary*. Parlophone CDFSB 13, 1991. Compact sound disc.

Forster, E.M. *Aspects of the Novel*. 1927. Harmondsworth: Penguin, 1962.

Fowler, G.W., and Ernest Gowers. *A Dictionary of Modern English Usage*. 2nd ed. Oxford: Clarendon, 1965.

Frame, Janet. *The Adaptable Man*. New York: Braziller, 1965.
- *An Angel at My Table*. New York: Braziller, 1984.
- *The Carpathians*. Auckland: Hutchinson, 1988.
- *The Edge of the Alphabet*. New York: Braziller, 1962.
- *The Envoy from Mirror City*. New York: Braziller, 1985.
- *Faces in the Water*. Christchurch: Pegasus, 1961.
- *Owls Do Cry*. Christchurch: Pegasus, 1957.
- "Prizes." In *The Reservoir*, 19–26. New York: Braziller, 1963.
- *Scented Gardens for the Blind*. Christchurch: Pegasus, London: Allen, New York: Braziller, 1963.
- *To the Is-Land*. New York: Braziller, 1982.

Franklin, Miles. *My Brilliant Career*. Edinburgh: Blackwood, 1901.

Freberg, Stan. "Show Folk." On *Stan Freberg Presents The United States of America, Vol. 2: The Middle Years*. 1961. Rhino R2 72476, 1996. Compact sound disc.

Frye, Northrop. *Anatomy of Criticism: Four Essays*. Princeton: Princeton University Press, 1971 [1957].

Games, Alexander. *Pete and Dud: An Illustrated Biography*. London: Chameleon 1999.

Gammond, Peter, ed. *Music Hall Song Book: A Collection of 45 of the Best Songs from 1890–1920*. London: EMI Music, 1975.

Gänzel, Kurt. *The British Musical Theatre, Volume 2, 1915–1984*. London: Macmillan, 1986.

Garofalo, Janeane, and Ben Stiller. *Feel This Book: An Essential Guide to Self-Empowerment, Spiritual Supremacy, and Sexual Satisfaction*. New York: Ballantine, 1999.

Gifford, Denis. "Barry McKenzie (series)." In *The British Comic Catalogue, 1874–1974*, n.p. London: Mansell, 1975.

– *Entertainers in British Films: A Centenary of Showbiz in the Cinema*. Westport: Greenwood, 1998.

Godfrey, Dave. *Death Goes Better with Coca-Cola*. Erin: Press Porcépic, 1973 [1967].

Gott, Ted. *Barry Humphries, Dada Artist*. Canberra: National Gallery of Australia, 1993.

Govani, Shinan. "Me, Myself and Eye." *National Post* (Toronto), 26 October 1999, A18.

Grace, Patricia. *Baby No-Eyes*. Auckland: Penguin, Honolulu: University of Hawai'i Press, 2000.

– *Potiki*. Auckland: Viking, 1986.

– *Cousins*. Auckland and New York: Penguin, 1992.

Grammer, Kelsey. *So Far*. Toronto: Viking, 1995.

Green, Benny, ed. *The Last Empires: A Music Hall Companion*. London: Pavilion, 1986.

Green, Tom, perf. *The Tom Green Show: Early Exposure*. Prod. Ray Hagel, dir. Darcy De Toni. 65 min. VSC, 2001. Videocassette.

Griffin, Merv, and Arthur Treacher. *Merv Griffin and Arthur Treacher in London: 'Alf and 'Alf: Songs of the British Music Hall*. MGM SE-4381, 1966. Sound recording (LP).

Griggs, Claudine. *S/He: Changing Sex and Changing Clothes*. Oxford and New York: Berg, 1998.

– "Barry Humphries." In *Double Exposure, Take Four*, by Roddy McDowall, 225. New York: Morrow, 1993.

– *My Name Escapes Me: The Diary of a Retiring Actor*. Harmondsworth: Penguin, 1996.

Guinness, Alec. *A Positively Final Appearance: A Journal 1996–98*. London: Hamish Hamilton, 1999.

Harding, James. *George Robey and the Music-Hall*. Sevenoaks: Hodder and Stoughton, 1990.

Harty, Russell. *Russell Harty Plus*. London: Elm Tree, 1974.

Heide Park and Art Gallery. *Dame Edna Regrets She Is Unable to Attend: Humour and Satire in Contemporary Sculpture*. Buleen: Heide Park and Art Gallery, 1992.

Herd, Juliet. "Just a Suburban Boy." *Australian Weekend Magazine*, 16–17 October 1993, 16–17.

Van Herk, Aritha. *Places Far from Ellesmere, a Geografictione: Explorations on Site*. Red Deer: Red Deer College Press, 1990.

Hibberd, Jack. "Breakfast at the Windsor." *Meanjin* 40, 3 (October 1981): 395–9.

Hiebert, Paul. *Sarah Binks*. Toronto and London: Oxford University Press, 1947.

Hind, John. "Above Everage." *Gentlemen's Quarterly* 40 (October 1992): 118–23, 197.

– "Spunky: Barry Humphries Is Currently Touring the Country with His Latest Stage Show, *Back with a Vengeance*, which Features Two of Australia's Most Notorious Exports, Dame Edna Everage and Sir Les Patterson." *Blitz* 59 (November 1987): 64–8.

Hollander, Anne. *Sex and Suits: The Evolution of Modern Dress*. New York: Random House, 1994.

Honri, Peter. *Working the Halls: The Honris in One Hundred Years of British Music Hall*. Farnborough: Saxon House, 1973.

Howell, Georgina. "Barry's Secret Sorrow." *New Idea* (Melbourne) 13 January 1996: 20, 159–60.

hooks, bell. "Selling Hot Pussy: Representations of Black Female Sexuality in the Cultural Marketplace." In *Black Looks: Race and Representation*, 61–77. Toronto: Between the Lines, 1992.

Hooton, Joy. "Australian Autobiography and the Question of National Identity, Patrick White, Barry Humphries, and Manning Clark." *A-B, Auto-Biography Studies* 9, 1 (Spring 1994): 43–63.

Hopkins, Gerard Manley. "Pied Beauty." *Poems of Gerard Manley Hopkins*, ed. Robert Bridges. London: Milford, 1918.

Hornadge, Bill. "Bazza McKenzie." In *The Australian Slanguage: A Look at What We Say and How We Say It*, 190–2. 1980. Rev. ed. North Ryde: Methuen Australia, 1986.

Huelsenbeck, Richard. "Dada Lives!" In *The Dada Painters and Poets: An Anthology*, 2nd ed., ed. Robert Motherwell, 277–81. Cambridge, MA, and London: Belknap, 1981.

– "En Avant Dada: A History of Dadaism." 2nd ed. Trans. Ralph Manheim. In *The Dada Painters and Poets: An Anthology*, ed. Robert Motherwell, 21–47. Cambridge, MA, and London: Belknap, 1981.

Humphivitch, Beria [Barry Humphries]. "Reign of Terror for Australian Writers and Artists." *Broadside*, 18 September 1969, 5.

Humphries, Barry. "Acting," "America," and "Honours." In *The Great Australian Book of Humorous Quotes*, comp. Bill Wannan, 5, 11, 154–5. Melbourne: Currey O'Neill, 1988.

– *Around the Loop*. Phillip Street Theatre, Sydney, 1956. Program.

– *At Least You Can Say You've Seen It: A Tragi-Farce in Two Acts, for Those Too Drunk to Dance*. Elizabethan Theatre, Sydney, 1974. Program.

– "Australians Abroad." In *Hammond Innes Introduces Australia*, ed. Clive Turnbull, 179–87. Melbourne: Hill of Content, 1971.

– "Back in the Decadent Dump, or, How to Desert a Cultural Renaissance." In *"Punch" Down Under*, comp. Barry Humphries, ed. Susan Jeffreys, 51–3. London: Robson, 1984.

– *Back with a Vengeance*. Theatre Royal Drury Lane, London, 1987. Program.

– "Barry Humphries." Interview by Murray Bramwell. In *Wanted for Questioning: Interviews with Australian Comic Artists*, by Murray Bramwell and David Matthews, 33–44. North Sydney: Allen and Unwin, 1992.

– "Barry Humphries (alias Edna Everage)." Interview by Russell Harty. In *Russell Harty Plus*, by Russell Harty, 41–8. London: Elm Tree, 1974.

Humphries, Barry, comp. *The Barry Humphries Book of Innocent Austral Verse*. Melbourne: Sun, 1968.

Humphries, Barry. *Barry Humphries' Treasury of Australian Kitsch*. Melbourne: Macmillan, 1980.

– *Bizarre*. London: Elek, New York: Bell, 1965.

– Booklet to *Dada Days: Moonee Ponds Muse, Vol. 2 (1951–1983)*. Performed by Barry Humphries. Raven Records Australia RVCD-34. 1993. Compact sound disc.

– "But Why Didn't Rudy Drop By?" *New York Times*, 8 July 2000, A25.

– *A Chorale for Coral*. London: Privately printed, 1992.

– "*Cleo* Mate of the Month: Barry Humphries." *Cleo* 121 (November 1982): 105–13.

– "Collecting Porter." In *Paeans for Peter Porter: A Celebration for Peter Porter on His Seventieth Birthday by Twenty of His Friends, 16 February 1999*, ed. Anthony Thwaite, 38–9. London: Bridgewater, 1999.

– "The Confessions of a Conder Fan." *Quadrant* 21, 10 (October 1977): 39–47.

– "Confessions of a Victoria Gentleman." In *Victoria with Love: Some Personal Views of Life in Victoria, Australia*, ed. Gina O'Donahue, 28–43. Melbourne: Government of Victoria 1981.

– "The Confessions of Barry Humphries." *The Bulletin Book: A Selection from the 1960's*, ed. Peter Coleman, 101–3. Melbourne: Cheshire, 1966 (reprint). Originally published in *Bulletin*, 6 November 1965.

– "A Conscientious Chaperon." In *Australians on Arthur Boyd*, ed. Lisa Bowman, 4–5. Melbourne: Australia Post, 1998.

– "A Conversation with Barry Humphries on Patrick White." Interview by Jill Kitson. *Quadrant* 37, 4 (April 1993): 53–7.

– "Crone Zone." In *The Oxford Book of Australian Schooldays*, comp. Brenda Niall and Ian Britain, with Pamela Williams, ed. Cathryn Game, 239–41. Melbourne: Oxford University Press, 1998.

– "Detrimental Blokes." Foreword to *Knockers*, by Keith Dunstan, xi–xvi. Melbourne: Cassell Australia, 1972.

– *An Evening's Intercourse with the Widely Liked Barry Humphries*. Her Majesty's Theatre, Melbourne, 1981. Program.

– *Excuse I: Another Nice Night's Entertainment*. Theatre Royal, Sydney, 1965. Program.

– "Fibro-itis." Foreword to *The Fibro Frontier: A Different History of Australian Architecture*, by Charles Pickett, 4–5. Sydney: Powerhouse and Doubleday, 1997.

– "A Fillip for Phil Philby Films." *Quadrant* 26, (July 1981): 18.

– Foreword to *The Golden Age of the Argonauts*, by Rob Johnson, xii–xiii. Adelaide: Griffin, 1997.

– Foreword to *Max Oldaker: Last of the Matinée Idols*, by Charles Osborne, ix–xi. London: Michael O'Mara, 1988.

– Foreword to *Night Voices: Strange Stories*, by Robert Aickman, n.p. London: Gallancz, 1985.

– Foreword to *Patrick Hockey, His Life and Work*, by Sandra McGrath, 7. Sydney: Beagle, 1994.

– Foreword to *Ratbags*, by Keith Dunstan, xi–xii. Sydney and Auckland: Golden, 1979.

– Foreword to *Travelling Light: Punch Goes Abroad*, ed. Susan Jeffreys, 9–10. London: Grafton, 1988.

– "A Fugitive Art: An Interview with Barry Humphries." Interview by Jim Davidson. *Meanjin* 45, 2 (June 1986): 149–68.

– "Glenn A. Baker Is a Sydney Writer (the enigmatic footnote to one of Mr Baker's popular newspaper features)." Foreword to *Perpetual Motion: Travels with Glenn A. Baker*, by Glenn A. Baker, v–vi. St Leonards: Allen and Unwin, 1993.

– "Hats and Glads." In *Autographs: Contemporary Australian Autobiography*, ed. Gillian Whitlock, 3–9. St Lucia: University of Queensland Press, 1996.

– *Housewife! Superstar!!* Theatre Four, New York, 1977. Program.

– "Humorless Generation." In *Dear Australian: An Anthology Based on a Selection of the Most Memorable Letters to* The Australian *1964–1981*, comp. Phil Pearman, 52. Sydney: Lansdowne, 1982.

– *The Humour of Barry Humphries*, comp. John Allen. Sydney: Currency, 1984.

– "Hungarian Goulash." In *Travelling Light: Punch Goes Abroad*, ed. Susan Jeffreys, 23–5. London: Grafton, 1988.

– "In Search of Bohemia." In *The Australian Bed-Side Book: A Selection of Writings from* The Australian *Literary Supplement*, ed. Geoffrey Dutton, 19–23. Melbourne: Macmillan, 1987.

– Introduction to *The Art of Dominic Ryan 1979–81*, by Dominic Ryan, 3. Melbourne: Dodo Works, 1984.
– Introduction to *Dreamers and Academics*. London: Louise Whitford Gallery, 1981.
– Introduction to *Humping My Bluey*, by Graham McInnes, 5–7. London: Hogarth, 1986 [1966].
– Introduction to *The Importance of Being Earnest*, by Charles Osborne, vii–viii. London: O'Mara, 1999.
– Introduction to *Ornaments in Jade*, by Arthur Machen, vii–x. Oxford: Caermaen, 1997.
– Introduction to *The Penguin Leunig: Cartoons by Michael Leunig*, by Michael Leunig, 5–6. Harmondsworth: Penguin, 1974.
– Introduction to *"Punch" Down Under*, comp. Barry Humphries and ed. Susan Jeffreys, 6–8. London: Robson, 1984.
– Introduction to *A Sentimental Bloke*, by C.J. Dennis, 7–8. Sydney: HarperCollins, 1992 [1915].
– *Isn't It Pathetic at His Age*. Program. Comedy Theatre, Melbourne, 1978.
– *Just a Show*. Fortune Theatre, London, 1969. Program.
– *Just a Show*. Tivoli Theatre, Sydney, 1968. Program.
– "The Last Australian Hero: The Filming of 'The Adventures of Barry McKenzie.'" In *Pick of Punch*, ed. William Davis, 101–3. London: Hutchinson, 1974.
– "The Last Australian Hero: The Filming of *The Adventures of Barry McKenzie*." In *Punch at the Cinema*, ed. Dilys Powell, 76–8. London: Robson, 1981.
– *Les Patterson's Australia*. Melbourne: Sun, 1978.
– *Less Is More Please*. London: Penguin, 1996.
– *The Life and Death of Sandy Stone*. Ed. Collin O'Brien. Sydney: Pan Macmillan, 1990. (Rev. ed. London: Penguin, 1991.)
– *A Load of Olde Stuffe: A Divertissement in Two Acts, for Those Too Drunk to Dance*. Playbox Theatre, Sydney, 1971. Program.
– "Lost at Life: A Recollection of Francis Lymburner." In *Francis Lymburner 1916–1972*, by Hendrick Kolenberg and Barry Pearce, 17–18. Sydney: Art Gallery of New South Wales, 1992.
– *Moonee Ponds Muse, Vol. 1*. Performed by Barry Humphries. Raven Records Australia RVCD-17. 1991. Compact sound disc.
– *More Please*. London: Viking, 1992.
– "Mr Les Patterson's Historic Address to the British." *Quadrant* 21, 4 (April 1977): 10–11.
– *My Life as Me: A Memoir*. London/Camberwell: Michael Joseph/Viking, 2002.
– *Neglected Poems and Other Creatures*. Sydney: CollinsAngus and Robertson, 1991.
– *New Edna – The Spectacle*. Theatre Royal Haymarket, London, 1998. Program.
– *A Nice Night's Entertainment: Sketches and Monologues, 1956–1981*. Sydney: Currency, 1981.

– "A Note of Exclamation." In *Margaret Olley*, by Barry Pearce, 8–9. Sydney: Art Gallery of New South Wales, 1997.

– "A Novel Called Tid." *Paston's Melbourne Quarterly: A Journal of Literary Pleasantry for the Entertainment of the Public and the Edification of the Young* n.v. (Spring 1958): n.p.

– "Passionfruit Pavlova." In *The Old Boys' Cookbook*, comp. Peter Coleman, 102–4. Melbourne: Heinemann, 1996, 102–4.

– "Professor Patterson's Christmas Package for the Poms." In *Punch Lines: 150 Years of Humorous Writing in* Punch, ed. Amanda-Jane Doran, 179–81. London: HarperCollins, 1991.

– "Pseuds' Corner." *Quadrant* 19, no. 9 (December 1975): 89.

– "The Real Barry Humphries." Interview by Andrew Olle. In *On Interviewing*, by Andrew Olle, with Robert Pullan, 78–83. Sydney: ABC Books, 1992.

– "A Recollection." In *Something Like Fire: Peter Cook Remembered*, ed. Lin Cook, 61–5. London: Methuen 1996.

– *Remember You're Out, A New Barry Humphries Event*. Melbourne Princess Theatre, Melbourne, 1999. Program.

– "The Royal Australian Prostate Foundation." In *The Secret Policeman's Other Ball*, ed. Martin Lewis and Peter Walker, n.p. London: Eyre Methuen, 1982.

– "Rupert Murdoch." *Spitting Images*, by Barry Humphries and others, 50–1. London: Century Hutchinson, 1987.

– "Sandy Comes Home: The Ruminations of a Revenant." *Single Voices*, by Barry Humphries and others, 42–55. London: BBC Books, 1990.

– "Sartorial Insights." In "Barry Humphries Is a Dandy, a Bitch, a Brilliant Satirist, a Foppish Dresser and Now a Debut Novelist," by C. Lambert. *Australian Style* 16 (1996): 57.

– *Shades of Sandy Stone: The Reveries of a Returned Man*. Edinburgh: Tragara, 1989.

– "The Sins of Barry Humphries." *Quadrant* (January-February 1983): 36–7.

– "Sold Out." In *Great Southern Landings: An Anthology of Antipodean Travel*, ed. Jan Bassett, 292–3. Melbourne: Oxford University Press, 1995.

– "Taboo." In *Pick of Punch*, ed. William Davis, 33–4. London: Hutchinson, 1974.

– *Tears before Bedtime*. Australian tour, 1983. Program.

– "27th April 1978." In *The Power of Speech: Twenty-Five Years of the National Press Club*, ed. Tony Maniaty, 144–52. Sydney: Bantam, 1989.

– Untitled article in *My Favourite Betjeman: A Selection of His Poems by a Selection of Admirers*, comp. and ed. Anthony Kilmister and Donald Lenox, 26. London: Parkinson's Disease Society, 1985.

– Untitled article in *Spike Milligan, a Celebration: The Best of Milligan*, comp. Roger Sawyer, 127. London: Virgin, 1996.

– Untitled article in *Spike Milligan: His Part in Our Lives*, comp. Maxine Ventham, 92–7. London: Robson, 2002.

– "Up and Down Under Style." In *"Punch" Down Under*, comp. Barry Humphries and ed. Susan Jeffreys, 19–21. London: Robson, 1984.

– "Who Will Black Up?" In *Dear Australian: An Anthology Based on a Selection of the Most Memorable Letters to* The Australian *1964–1981*, comp. Phil Pearman, 52. Sydney: Lansdowne, 1982.

– *Women in the Background*. Melbourne: Mandarin, 1995 (London: Heinemann, 1996).

– "Why Bazza Is a Virgin." *Forum* 1, no. 1 (1973): 31–4.

Humphries, Barry, comp. *A Garland for Stephen Spender*. Edinburgh: Tragara, 1991.

– *"Punch" Down Under*. Ed. Susan Jeffreys. London: Robson, 1984.

Humphries, Barry, and Bruce Beresford. *The Adventures of Barry McKenzie*. Melbourne: Sun, 1973.

Humphries, Barry, and Nicholas Garland. "Barry McKensie, Australian at large." Cartoon. *Private Eye*, 10 July 1964, 12.

– "Barry McKenzie." Cartoon. *Private Eye*, 11 December 1964, 12.

– "Barry McKenzie's Naughty Night." Cartoon. *The Penguin Private Eye*. Harmondsworth: Penguin, 1965, n.p. (7 pp. )

– *Bazza Comes into His Own: The Final Fescennine Farrago of Barry McKenzie, Australia's First Working-Class Hero*. Melbourne: Sun, 1979.

– *Bazza Pulls It Off! More Adventures of Barry McKenzie*. Melbourne: Sun, 1971.

– Cartoon. *Private Eye*, 24 July 1964, 10.

– *The Complete Barry McKenzie*. London/Sydney: Methuen/Allen and Unwin/Haynes, 1988.

– *The Wonderful World of Barry McKenzie*. London: Private Eye/Deutsch, 1969 [1968].

Humphries, Barry, and Ross Fitzgerald. "Craig Steppenwolf: A Monologue for the Music Hall." *Quadrant* 19, 8 (November 1975): 47–50.

Humphries, Barry, David Mitchell, and Roger McDonald. *Barry Humphries' Flashbacks*. Sydney: HarperCollins, 1999.

Humphries, Barry, with Bruce Beresford. *Barry McKenzie Holds His Own: An Original Photoplay*. Melbourne: Sun, 1974.

Humphries, Barry, and others. *Single Voices*. London: BBC Books, 1990.

– *Spitting Images*. London: Century Hutchinson, 1987.

Humphries, Barry, Nick Rowley, and Stanley Myers. *The Sound of Edna: Dame Edna's Family Songbook*. London: Chappell Music, 1979.

Idle, Eric. "Penis Song (Not the Noël Coward Song)." On *Monty Python Sings*. Virgin, 1989. Compact sound disc.

– *The Road to Mars: A Post-Modem Novel*, 15–6. New York: Pantheon, 1999.

Ireland, David. *City of Women*. Ringwood: Penguin, 1981.

Jahn, Jahnheinz. *Muntu: An Outline of the New African Culture*, trans. Marjorie Grene. New York: Grove, 1961.

James, Clive. "Approximately in the Vicinity of Barry Humphries." In *Snake Charmers in Texas: Essays 1980–87*, 30–44. London: Cape, 1988. (Reprinted in *Reliable Essays: The Best of Clive James* [London: Picador, 2001, 2002].)

– *Falling Towards England*. London: Cape, 1985.
– *The Metropolitan Critic: Non-Fiction 1968–1973*. London: Picador, 1995 [1974].
– *The Remake*. London: Picador, 1988.
– "Up Here from Down There." Review of *When London Calls*, by Stephen Alomes. In *Reliable Essays: The Best of Clive James*, 284–5. London: Picador, 2002 [2001].
Jameson, Fredric. *Postmodernism, or, The Cultural Logic of Late Capitalism*. Duke: Duke University Press, 1991.
– *The Prison-House of Language: A Critical Account of Structuralism and Russian Formalism*. Princeton: Princeton University Press, 1972.
Jarry, Alfred. *Ubu Roi*. Paris: Éditions Mercure de France, 1896.
– *King Turd*, trans. Beverley Keith and G. Legman. New York: Boar's Head, 1953.
Jebb, Julian. Review of concert performance of *Housewife-Superstar!!* by and with Barry Humphries, Apollo Theatre, London. *Plays and Players* 23, 8 (May 1976): 33–4.
Johnson, Quendrith. "Who in Dame-Nation Is Barry Humphries? Dame Edna's Manager Shares the Lowdown on Why There Is Nothing Like a Dame." *Venice* 13, 8 (May 2001): 62–6.
Johnson, Rob. *The Golden Age of the Argonauts*. Adelaide: Griffin, 1997.
Jones, Margaret. *Thatcher's Kingdom*. Sydney: Collins, 1984.
Joyce, James. *A Portrait of the Artist as a Young Man*. Harmondsworth: Penguin, 1976 [1916].
Kahn, Madeleine. *Narrative Transvestism: Rhetoric and Gender in the Eighteenth-Century English Novel*. Ithaca and London: Cornell University Press, 1991.
Karpel, Bernard, comp. "Did Dada Die? A Critical Bibliography." In *The Dada Painters and Poets: An Anthology,* 2nd ed., ed. Robert Motherwell, 318–97. Cambridge, MA, and London: Belknap, 1981.
Kennedy, D.A. *The Art Works of Barry Humphries*. Melbourne, 1958. Catalogue.
Kift, Dagmar. *The Victorian Music Hall: Culture, Class and* Conflict. Trans. Roy Kift. Cambridge: Cambridge University Press, 1996.
Kilgarriff, Michael. *Grace, Beauty and Banjos*. London: Oberon, 1998.
– *It Gives Me Great Pleasure: Production Guide and Chairman's Handbook for Old Time Music Hall*. Rev. ed. London: French, 1986 [1972] (page citations are to the revised edition).
Kincaid, Jamaica. *The Autobiography of My Mother*. New York: Farrar, Straus and Giroux, 1996.
King, Michael. *Wrestling with the Angel: A Life of Janet Frame*. Washington: Counterpoint, 2000.
Kingsley, Madeleine. "Face to Face." *Radio Times*, 13–19 August 1977, 52–6.
Konigsberg, Eric. "The Fame of the Dame: Can a Rude, Clueless, Provincial Australian Woman Who's Actually a Man Conquer Broadway and Win a Place in the American Cultural Pantheon? Barry Humphries' Dame Edna Is on the Verge." *New York*, 29 November 1999, 118–20, 121, 122, 124.

Krum, Sharon. "Barry and Me: Not Your Everage Kind of Marriage." *The Austra-lian Women's Weekly*, July 2000, 34–8.

Lahr, John. "Barry Humphries: Playing Possum." In *Light Fantastic: Adventures in Theatre*, 46–100. New York: Delta, 1996.

– "Bob Hope, the CEO of Comedy." In *Show and Tell: New Yorker Profiles*, 198–226. Woodstock and New York: Overlook, 2000.

– "Dame Edna Everage." In *Automatic Vaudeville: Essays on Star Turns*, 57–62. New York: Knopf, 1984.

– *Dame Edna Everage and the Rise of Western Civilization: Backstage with Barry Humphries*. New York: Farrar, Straus and Giroux, 1992.

– "Eddie Izzard, the Izzard King." In *Show and Tell: New Yorker Profiles*, 171–82. Woodstock and New York: Overlook, 2000.

– "Edna Takes Manhattan." *Age* (Melbourne), 26 February 2000, Saturday extra.

– "Frank Sinatra: Sinatra's Song." In *Show and Tell: New Yorker Profiles*, 52–84. Woodstock and New York: Overlook, 2000.

Lahr, John. *Notes on a Cowardly Lion: The Biography of Bert Lahr*. 1969. Berke-ley: University of California Press, 2000.

– "Notes on Fame." In *Automatic Vaudeville: Essays on Star Turns*, 231–43. New York: Knopf, 1984.

– "Peter Cook, Bedazzled." In *Light Fantastic: Adventures in Theatre*, 107–18. New York: Delta, 1996.

– "Playing Possum." *New Yorker*, 1 July 1991, 38–9, 42, 46, 48–66.

Lahr, John, ed. *The Diaries of Kenneth Tynan*. London: Bloomsbury, 2001.

Lambert, C. "Barry Humphries Is a Dandy, a Bitch, a Brilliant Satirist, a Foppish Dresser and Now a Debut Novelist." *Australian Style* 16 (1996): 54–9.

LaWhore, Miss Cookie. "Cookie Does the Dame: Simply Aussie 'Housewife' Claims She Started the Women's Movement." *XTRA! West* (Vancouver), 17 Octo-ber 2002, 27.

Lawler, Ray. *The Summer of the Seventeenth Doll*. London: Angus and Robertson, 1957.

Lax, Eric. *Woody Allen: A Biography*. New York: Knopf, 1991.

Leacock, Stephen. "The Awful Fate of Melpomenus Jones." In *Literary Lapses*, 12–15. Toronto: McClelland and Stewart, 1957 [1910].

Legman, G. "Translator's Note." In *King Turd*, trans. Beverley Keith and G. Leg-man, 184–9. New York: Boar's Head, 1953.

Leighton, Harry. *We're Australians but Still Britannia's Sons*. London: Charles Sheard, 1897.

Leslie, Peter. *A Hard Act to Follow: A Music Hall Review*. New York and London: Paddington, 1978.

Lewisohn, Mark. "Barry Humphries." In *Radio Times Guide to TV Comedy*. Lon-don: BBC, 1998, 340–3.

de Lisle, Rosanna. "Dame Edna's Prop Tricks Sotheby's." *Independent*, 20 June 1999, 3.

Livingstone, David. "A Dictum of Fashion: Like It or Not, We Are What We Wear." *Globe and Mail* (Toronto), 1 October 1994, C22.

"Look What Happened to the Kid from Camberwell: From the Backyard Beginnings in Melbourne to a Glittering Career on Broadway, Barry Humphries Has Always Been a Bit of a Character (or Two)." *Arts Centre Preview* (July/August 2003): 4–5.

Lowry, Malcolm. *The Selected Letters of Malcolm Lowry*. Ed. Harvey Breit and Margerie Lowry. Philadelphia: Lippincott, 1965.

– "Through the Panama." In *Hear Us O Lord from Heaven Thy Dwelling Place*, 29–98. Philadelphia and New York: Lippincott, 1961.

– *Under the Volcano*. London: Cape, 1967 [1947].

Machen, Arthur. *The Hill of Dreams*. London: Richards, Boston: Estes, 1907.

– *Ornaments in Jade*. Oxford: Caermaen, 1997.

MacInnes, Colin. *Sweet Saturday Night: Pop Song 1840–1920*. London: Panther, 1969 [1967].

Maclean, Marie. *Narrative as Performance: The Beaudelairean Experiment*. London and New York: Routledge, 1988.

Malley, Ern [James McAuley and Harold Stewart]. *The Darkening Ecliptic*. Melbourne: Reed and Harris, 1944.

Mander, Raymond, and Joe Mitchenson. *British Music Hall: A Story in Pictures*. London: Studio Vista, 1965.

Marr, David. *Patrick White: A Life*. London: Cape, 1991.

Marshall, Anthony. *Trafficking in Old Books*. Melbourne: Lost Domain, 1998.

Martin, Adrian. "George Miller, *Les Patterson Saves the World*." In *Australian Film 1978–1994*, ed. Scott Murray, 223. Melbourne: Oxford University Press, 1995.

Martin, Steve. *Picasso at the Lapin Agile*. London: Samuel French, 1996.

– *Pure Drivel*. New York: Hyperion, 1998.

– *Shopgirl*. New York: Hyperion, 2000.

– *Wasp and Other Plays*. New York: Samuel French, 1998.

Matthews, William. *Cockney Past and Present: A Short History of the Dialect of London*. London: Routledge, 1938.

McCalman, Janet. "Suburbia from the Sandpit." Review of *Beasts of Suburbia: Reinterpreting Cultures in Australian Suburbs*, ed. Sarah Ferber, Chris Healy, and Chris McAuliffe. *Meanjin* 53, 3 (Spring 1994): 548–53.

McDowall, Roddy. *Double Exposure, Take Four*. New York: Morrow, 1993.

McInnes, Graham. *Humping My Bluey*. London: Hamish Hamilton, 1966.

McQueen, Humphrey. *Suburbs of the Sacred*. Ringwood: Penguin, 1988.

Meadwell, Robert, and Geoffrey Brawn, eds. *The Novello Music Hall Songbook*. London: Novello, 1997.

Melzer, Annabelle Henkin. *Dada and Surrealist Performance*. Baltimore and London: Johns Hopkins University Press, 1994 [1980].

Mertins, Detlef. "Anything but Literal: Sigfried Giedion and the Reception of Cubism in Germany." In *Architecture and Cubism*, ed. Eve Blau and Nancy J. Troy, 219–51. Cambridge, MA, and London: MIT Press, 1997.

Mink, Janis. *Marcel Duchamp, 1887–1968: Art as Anti-Art.* Köln: Taschen, 1995.

Minogue, Kenneth. "What's the Big Idea?" *National Post* (Toronto), 8 January 2000, B7.

Moreau, Jean Salomon. "The Laws." Unpublished essay. 1981.

Morgan, David. *Monty Python Speaks: John Cleese, Terry Gilliam, Eric Idle, Terry Jones and Michael Palin (and a Few of Their Friends and Collaborators) Recount an Amazing – and Silly – Thirty-Year Spree in Television and Film ... in Their Own Words, Squire!* New York: Avon, 1999.

Morley, Lewis. *Lewis Morley: Photography of the Sixties.* London: National Portrait Gallery, 1989.

Morris, Lucie. "Dama Edna's Drunken Son in B&B Rampage." *UK Mail*, 30 July 2002, 16.

Motherwell, Robert, ed. *The Dada Painters and Poets: An Anthology.* 2nd ed. Cambridge, MA, and London: Belknap, 1981.

Murray, Les, comp. *The New Oxford Book of Australian Verse.* 3rd ed. Melbourne: Oxford University Press, 1996.

Murray, Scott, ed. *Australian Cinema.* St Leonards: Allen and Unwin, 1994.

– *Australian Film 1978–1994.* Oxford: Oxford University Press, 1995.

*The Museum of Modern Art, New York: The History and the Collection.* New York: Abrams, and the Museum of Modern Art, 1984.

Naipaul, V.S. *The Enigma of Arrival: A Novel in Five Sections.* London: Viking, 1987.

– *A House for Mr Biswas.* London: Collins, 1961.

– *Miguel Street.* London: Deutsch, 1959.

Naumann, Francis. M. "Introduction: Appropriation and Replication in the Art of Marcel Duchamp." In *Marcel Duchamp: The Art of Making Art in the Age of Mechanical Reproduction*, 15–23. New York: Abrams, 1999.

– *Marcel Duchamp: The Art of Making Art in the Age of Mechnical Reproduction.* New York: Abrams, 1999.

Niall, Brenda. *The Boyds: A Family Biography.* Melbourne: Melbourne University Press, 2002.

– *Martin Boyd: A Life.* Melbourne: Melbourne University Press, 1988.

Van Nunen, Linda. "Gladly Edna." *ELLE* 1, 1 (March 1990): 78–80, 82.

O'Brien, Collin. "Sandy's Australia." In *The Life and Death of Sandy Stone*, ed. Collin O'Brien, xi–xxxii. Sydney: Macmillan, 1990.

O'Connor, Garry. *Alex Guinness, the Unknown: A Life.* London: Sidgwick and Jackson, 2002.

Ong, Walter J. *Orality and Literacy: The Technologizing of the Word.* London and New York: Routledge, 1982.

Ouzounian, Richard. "An Audience with ... Dame Edna and Barry Humphries: Acid-Tongued Star of Stage, Screen and TV Drops Pearls of Wisdom about Her Alter Ego and Everything Else." *Toronto Star*, 4 November 2000, M1, M9.

– "An Audience with … Dame Edna and Barry Humphries: Veteran Actor Talks Behind Mrs Everage's Back, and about His Own Long, Varied Career … Rough Spots and All." *Toronto Star*, 4 November 2000, M1, M8.

Palmer, Scott. *A Who's Who of Australian and New Zealand Film Actors: The Sound Era*. Metuchen, NJ, and London: Scarecrow, 1988.

Paskin, Barbra. *The Authorized Biography of Dudley Moore*. London: Sigdwick and Jackson, 1997.

Patterson, Sir Les [Barry Humphries]. *The Traveller's Tool*. London and Melbourne: Macmillan, 1985.

Peterson, Elmer. *Tristan Tzara: Dada and Surrational Theorist*. New Brunswick: Rutgers University Press, 1971.

Plant, Margaret. "Barry Humphries." In *Irreverent Sculpture*, 8–21. Melbourne: Monash University Gallery, Department of Visual Arts, 1985.

"Poetaster." *The Compact Edition of the Oxford English Dictionary*. Oxford: Oxford University Press, 1971.

Porter, Peter, ed. *The Oxford Book of Modern Australian Verse*. Melbourne: Oxford University Press, 1996.

Poovey, Mary. "Creative Criticism: Adaptation, Performative Writing, and the Problem of Objectivity." *Narrative* 8, 2 (May 2000): 109–33.

Powell, Anthony. *Journals 1990–1992*. London: Heinemann, 1997.

Prince, Gerald. *A Dictionary of Narratology*. Lincoln and London: University of Nebraska Press, 1987.

Ramet, Sabrina Petra. "Gender Reversals and Gender Cultures: An Introduction." In *Gender Reversals and Gender Cultures: Anthropological and Historical Perspectives*, ed. Ramet, 1–21. London and New York: Routledge, 1996.

Raymond, Jack. *Show Music on Record: The First 100 Years*. Rev. ed. Washington and London: Smithsonian Institution Press, 1992.

Reiser, Paul. *Babyhood*. New York: Bantam, 1997.

– *Couplehood*. New York: Bantam, 1994.

Ribemont-Dessaignes, Georges. "History of Dada." Trans. Ralph Manheim. In *The Dada Painters and Poets: An Anthology*, 2nd ed., ed. Robert Motherwell, 99–122. Cambridge, MA, and London: Belknap, 1981.

Ricoeur, Paul. *Fallible Man*. Rev. ed., trans. Charles A. Keebley. New York: Fordham University Press, 1986 [1965].

– *Oneself as Another*, trans. Kathleen Blamey. Chicago and London: University of Chicago Press, 1992.

Riemer, A.P. *Inside Outside: Life Between Two Worlds*. Pymble: Angus and Robertson, 1992.

Robinson, Fred Miller. "Tray Bong! *Godot* and Music Hall." In *Approaches to Teaching Beckett's* Waiting for Godot, ed. June Schlueter and Enoch Brater, 56–63. New York: Modern Language Association of America, 1991.

Romano, Ray. *Everything and a Kite*. New York: Bantam, 1998.

Roper, David. *Bart! The Unauthorized Life and Times, Ins and Outs, Ups and Downs of Lionel Bart.* London: Pavilion, 1994.

Rose, Clarkson. *Beside the Seaside.* London: Museum, 1960.

- *Red Plush and Greasepaint: A Memory of the Music-Hall and Life and Times from the Nineties to the Sixties.* London: Museum, 1964.

- *With a Twinkle in My Eye.* London: Museum, 1951.

Rudner, Rita. *Naked Beneath My Clothes: Tales of a Revealing Nature.* New York: Viking, 1992.

RuPaul. *Letting It All Hang Out: An Autobiography.* New York: Hyperion, 1995.

Rushdie, Salman. *Midnight's Children.* New York: Penguin, 1991 [1980].

- *The Wizard of Oz.* BFI Film Classics. London: BFI, 1992.

Ruskin, Pamela. "The Compleat Humphries." *Walkabout* 34, 12 (December 1968): 40–4.

Russell, Anna. "I'm Only a Faded Rose." On *Anna Russell's Guide to Concert Audiences.* Coronet KLP 524, 1954. Sound recording (LP).

Rutherford, Lois. "'Managers in a Small Way': The Professionalisation of Variety Artists 1960–1914." In *Music Hall: The Business of Pleasure.* Ed. Peter Bailey, 93–117. Milton Keynes and Philadelphia: Open University Press, 1986.

Said, Edward W. *Representations of the Intellectual: The 1993 Reith Lectures.* New York: Pantheon, 1994.

Saro-Wiwa, Ken. *Sozaboy: A Novel in Rotten English.* Port Harcourt: Saros, 1985.

Sartre, Jean-Paul. *Huis Clos.* Ed. Jacques Hardré and George B. Daniel. New York: Meredith, 1962. [1947].

Scott, Harold. *The Early Doors: Origins of the Music Hall.* London: Micholson and Watson, 1946.

Schwitters, Kurt. "Theo van Doesburg and Dada." 2nd ed. Trans. Ralph Manheim. In *The Dada Painters and Poets: An Anthology,* ed. Robert Motherwell, 273–6. Cambridge, MA, and London: Belknap, 1981.

Seinfeld, Jerry. *SeinLanguage.* New York: Bantam, 1993.

Shandling, Garry, with David Rensin. *Confessions of a Late Night Talk Show Host: The Autobiography of Larry Sanders.* New York: Simon and Schuster, 1998.

Shears, Richard. "'I Just Want to Forget Him': Barry Humphries' First Wife Reveals the Man Behind the Make-Up." *New Week,* 5 February 1996, 32–3.

Sher, Antony. *Characters: Paintings, Drawings and Sketches.* London: Nick Hern, 1989.

Shlain, Leonard. *The Alphabet Versus the Goddess: The Conflict Between Word and Image.* New York: Viking, 1998.

Shmith, Michael. "Edna the Eternal." *The Weekend Australian,* 30–31 May 1998, 17–18.

Snowdon. *Sittings 1979–1983.* London: Weidenfeld and Nicholson, 1983.

- *Snowdon on Stage, with a Personal View of the British Theatre, 1954–1996, by Simon Callow.* London: Pavilion, 1996.

Solomon, Aliisa. *Re-Dressing the Canon: Essays on Theater and Gender*. London and New York: Routledge, 1997.

Soumilas, Diane. *A Peep in Dame Edna's Closet*. Melbourne: Performing Arts Museum, Victorian Arts Centre, 1986.

Speaight, George, comp. *Bawdy Songs of the Early Music Hall*. Newton Abbot: David and Charles, 1975.

Stam, Robert. *Subversive Pleasures: Bakhtin, Cultural Criticism, and Film*. Baltimore and London: Johns Hopkins University Press, 1989.

Stanislavsky, Constantin. *My Life in Art*. Trans. J.J. Robbins. Boston: Little, Brown, 1938 [1924].

Stewart, Jon. *Naked Pictures of Famous People*. New York: Rob Weisbach, 1998.

St Pierre, Paul Matthew. Letter to the editor, 1 November 1999. *National Post* (Toronto): A19.

– Letter to the editor, 3 November 2002. *National Post* (Toronto): A19.

– *Song and Sketch Transcripts of British Music Hall Performers Elsie and Doris Waters*. Lewiston, NY; Lampeter, Wales; and Queenston, ON: Edwin Mellen, 2003.

Suleiman, Susan Rubin. *Risking Who One Is: Encounters with Contemporary Art and Literature*. Cambridge and London: Harvard University Press, 1994.

– *Subversive Intent: Gender, Politics, and the Avant-Garde*. Cambridge and London: Harvard University Press, 1990.

Taylor, Edward Durham. *The Great TV Book: 21 Years of LWT*. London: Sidgwick and Jackson, 1989.

Thompson, Harry. *Peter Cook: A Biography*. London: Hodder and Stoughton, 1997.

Thomson, Ken, ed. *Barry Humphries: Bepraisements on His Birthday*. London: Enitharmon, 1994.

Tinkerbelle [Andy Warhol]. "Barry Humphries/Dame Edna: The Two Faces of Everage." *Interview* 7, 12 (December 1977): 26–7.

Tomkins, Calvin. *Duchamp: A Biography*. New York: Henry Holt, 1996.

Took, Barry. "Barry Humphries." In *Comedy Greats: A Celebration of Comic Genius Past and Present*, 218–30. Wellingborough: Thorsons, 1989.

Tutuola, Amos. *My Life in the Bush of Ghosts*. London: Faber, 1954.

– *The Palm-Wine Drinkard and His Dead Palm-Wine Tapster in the Dead's Town*. London: Faber, 1952.

Tzara, Tristan. *Approximate Man, and Other Writings*, trans. Mary Ann Caws. Detroit: Wayne State University Press, 1973.

– *Chanson Dada: Selected Poems*, trans. Lee Harwood. Toronto: Underwhich/Coach House, 1987.

Vahimagi, Tise, comp. *British Television: An Illustrated Guide*. 2nd ed. Oxford: Oxford University Press, 1996.

Waters, Elsie, and Doris Waters. "Gert, Daisy, a Piano and How!" *World of Variety*. Elsie Waters, Doris Waters, Arthur Askey, Jack Warner, and Tessie O'Shea. Music Collection, 1996. Audiocassette.

Waters, Elsie, and Doris Waters, comps. *The Gert and Daisy Song Book.* Originally published in *Home Companion,* 30 January 1937.

Waugh, Evelyn. *The Loved-One: An Anglo-American Tragedy.* London: Chapman and Hall, Boston: Little, Brown, 1948.

Wheelahan, Libby. *Dame Edna's Frock-a-thon: A Journey from Cardigan to Couture,* ed. Kirsten Freeman. Melbourne: Performing Arts Museum, Victorian Arts Centre, 1999.

White, Hayden. *Tropics of Discourse: Essays in Cultural Criticism.* Baltimore and London: Johns Hopkins University Press, 1978.

White, Patrick. *The Aunt's Story.* London: Eyre and Spottiswoode, 1948.

– "Clay." In *The Burnt Ones.* London: Eyre and Spottiswoode, 1964.

– *Flaws in the Glass: A Self-Portrait.* London: Cape, 1981.

– "From Wigan to Wagga." In *Patrick White Speaks,* 145–8. Sydney: Primavera, 1989.

– *The Living and the Dead.* London: Routledge, 1941.

– *Memoirs of Many in One.* London: Cape, 1986.

– Letter to Barry Humphries. 7 October 1973. In *Patrick White Letters,* ed., David Marr. 419–21. London: Cape, 1994

– Letter to Barry Humphries. 24 August 1965. In *Patrick White Letters,* ed. David Marr. 282. London: Cape 1994.

– Letter to Frederick Glover. 13 May 1960. In *Patrick White Letters,* ed. David Marr. 165. London: Cape 1994.

– Letter to Geoffrey and Ninette Dutton. 27 July 1970. In *Patrick White Letters,* ed. David Marr. 370–2. London: Cape 1994.

– *Patrick White Letters,* ed. David Marr. London: Cape, 1994.

– *Riders in the Chariot.* 1961. Harmondsworth: Penguin, 1964.

– *The Twyborn Affair.* London: Jonathan Cape, 1979.

– *Voss.* London: Eyre and Spottiswoode, New York: Viking, 1957.

*Who's Who of Australian Writers.* Melbourne: Thorpe 1991.

Wicks, Ben. *Master of None: The Story of Me Life.* Toronto: McClelland and Stewart, 1995.

Williams, Haydn. "Hatterr and Bazza, Post-Colonial Picaros." *The Commonwealth Review* 2, 1–1 (1990–91): 204–11.

Williams, Linda. "Dream Rhetoric and Film Rhetoric: Metaphor and Metonymy in *Un Chien andalou.*" *Semiotica* 33, 1–2 (1981): 87–103.

Wilmut, Roger. *From Fringe to Flying Circus: Celebrating a Unique Generation of Comedy 1960–1980.* London: Eyre Methuen, 1980.

– *Kindly Leave the Stage! The Story of Variety 1919–1960.* London: Methuen, 1985.

Yeats, W.B. *Selected Poetry.* Ed. A. Norman Jeffares. London: Macmillan, 1962.

Zmuda, Bob, with Matthew Scott Hansen. *Andy Kaufman Revealed!* Boston: Little, Brown, 1999.

INTERNET SOURCES

*Dame-Edna.Com, the Official Website*, 18 June 2000 <www.dame-edna.com>
*Mona Lisa Images for the Modern World, or a Giocondophiliac's Delight, Re-sources and Web Links to Monalisiana and related subjects*, 18 September 2003
    <http: //www.studiolo.org/Mona/MONALIST.htm>
*The Book of Enoch*, 30 October 2003
    <http: //www.abu.nb.ca/courses/NTIntro/InTest/1EnocTex.htm>

# Index